CW00925396

THE KURDS

THE KURDS

Nationalism and Politics

Edited by

Faleh A. Jabar and Hosham Dawod

SAQI

London   San Francisco   Beirut

ISBN 10: 0-86356-825-4
ISBN 13: 978-0-86356-825-1

A full CIP record for this book is available from the British Library.
A full CIP record for this book is available from the Library of Congress.

Manufactured in Lebanon

SAQI
26 Westbourne Grove, London W2 5RH
825 Page Street, Suite 203, Berkeley, California 94710
Tabet Building, Mneimneh Street, Hamra, Beirut
www.saqibooks.com

Contents

Foreword

Ethnicity, Nationalism and the Unitary State in the Middle East: The Case of the Kurds

Faleh A. Jabar and Hosham Dawod

With the advent of the 21st century, ethnic relations are assuming the central role that nationalism occupied at the beginning of the 20th century, when the principle of self-determination was heralded by two contrasting leaders: the revolutionary Russian Vladimir Lenin and the liberal American Woodrow Wilson. Since more than 8000 languages dot the planet, and dozens of religions and races mix with them, these markers of ethnicities are trapped in fewer than 200 states, the very political units that may satisfy nationalist yearnings. Ethnicity may prove to be thornier and more problematic. The case of the Kurds is now to the fore. And Iraq, the focus of international politics, is its arena.

This volume approaches the ethnic question in a specific region, the Middle East, and on the basis of a specific case, the Kurds, focusing most attention on Iraq, where the first Kurdish federal polity is taking shape.

The book examines ethnicity from a wider theoretical perspective, scrutinizing the long-accepted underpinnings of what ethnicity is and is not. Most importantly, it develops, through a diversified critique of modernist, essentialist and historical schools, a more complex and fluid understanding of ethnicity. The role of language, material culture and religion is examined, together with the role of social organization – tribe, sect, Sufi lodges and city – in defining the ethnic self. Cases are drawn not only from Iraq but also from the modern or recent history of Iraq, Turkey and Iran.

The authors of this volume include, among others, Fred Halliday, Martin Van Bruinessen, Joyce Blau, Maria O'Shea, Sami Zubaida, Gareth Stansfield and Michael Gunter, each authors of works on the Kurds or the Middle East.

They hail from various disciplines that combine history, anthropology and sociology with politics, geography and linguistics, lending the debate a rich and intricate character.

PART ONE

Defining Kurdish Nationalism

Can We Write a Modernist History of Kurdish Nationalism?

Fred Halliday

Introduction: The Debate on Nationalism

The history of Kurdish nationalism presents a set of challenges: on the one hand, that of writing the history of Kurdish nationalism as it has developed in the modern Middle East, in several countries; on the other, that of relating the case of Kurdish nationalism to broader debates within the social sciences on nationalism. In recent years the first challenge has been taken up by many writers, Kurdish and from other Middle Eastern nationalities, as well as by Western writers. I have in recent years had occasion to read, for book reviews, two very rich studies of Kurdish nationalism, Gerard Chaliand's *The Kurdish Tragedy* (London: Zed Books, 1994) and Susan Meiselas's *Kurdistan in the Shadow of History* (New York: Random House, 1997). The purpose of this chapter is to explore the second dimension, how to relate Kurdish nationalism to the general, theoretical and comparative debate on nationalism in social science: to examine this topic may serve not only to cast light on the Kurdish case but also to probe the different theoretical approaches to nationalism present within contemporary social science. These particular arguments are ones I have sought to develop at greater length elsewhere.[1]

The Kurds are a case that no theory of nationalism can or should avoid. Now numbering over 25 millions, they are, according to the theory of self-determination, the largest people in the world not to have their own state. Their nationalist movement is strong in three core Middle Eastern states – Iran, Iraq and Turkey – and has, recurrently, been a factor in the domestic and international politics of these countries. Kurds have also been active in the politics of Syria, and there has, since the 1980s, been a large Kurdish diaspora in western Europe that has participated in funding, promoting and shaping the nationalist movements, a powerful example of what Ben Anderson has called 'long-distance nationalism'. In terms of human rights violations, the Kurds have suffered as much as any other people in the Middle East, facing massacre, poison gas, mass deportation, linguistic discrimination and a general refusal by all three states in which they are concentrated to grant them regional and cultural, let alone national, rights. Nor is this story over: despite some improvements in the 1990s, the situation of the Kurds remains precarious. National self-determination, in the sense of a state in all or part of Kurdistan, remains elusive. Neither conditions within these states nor the international conjuncture favours Kurdish self-determination. As of early 2006 the overall situation is at best complex: a slight easing in cultural and some political controls in Turkey, continued political denial of Kurdish rights in the name of Muslim identity in Iran and a political opening heavily hemmed in by Turkey in Iraq.

The conventional approach to nationalism, one espoused in most history, if only implicitly, and in nationalist narratives themselves, treats nations as historic entities. They have a clear, national, identity, based on language, custom and historic memory. They have a clear 'national' territory. They have, by dint of their 'nationhood', a right to an independent state. This is the claim made by all nationalist movements in the world, the Kurds included. It implies a history in which the self-awareness of an already existing nation develops, 'awakens', 'arises', has a 'revival' and so forth. The failure to achieve the desired and assumed goal, that of an independent state, is then ascribed to obstacles: an insufficiently determined or honest leadership, a lack of sufficient 'national' awareness on the part of the people themselves, the adoption of inappropriate ideological programmes, the oppressive, chauvinist character of the dominant state, the treachery, strategic opportunism or indifference of the major Western powers. The goal is assumed to be attainable, the failure to reach it then being explained in terms of such obstacles, setbacks or deviations. The actual history of ideology and political mobilization is measured against a national ideal, not the other way around.

Such historical and 'natural' accounts of nationalism have, however, increasingly been challenged from within the social sciences by what is broadly termed the 'modernist' approach, as elaborated by, among others, Ernest Gellner, Eric Hobsbawm, Ben Anderson and Umut Ozkirimli. This argues that, in simplified terms, nations are recent and contingent creations, the product of the development of modern economic, social and political conditions. Their historic character cannot be assumed, nor can it be assumed that any one set of characteristics, e.g. a common language or social character, pertains to them. Territory is something claimed, but not necessarily precise in its borders or justly belonging to one people rather than to others. There is no one or final outcome of the nationalist movement: national independence may be achieved, in the form of an independent state, but it may not. There are plenty of regional entities in the world that could, on 'historic' grounds, claim independence but do not: Bavaria, Crete, Gilan, California. All members of the community may be included in the state, but sometimes a part is left out, across the frontier. This modernist approach recognizes the relevance and ideological force of political claims – to territory, definitions of culture, independence – but does not assume that these are somehow naturally given. They are part of politics.

Modernism in its tougher form is not itself a conclusive answer. Those espousing a more historical, 'natural' approach to nations point to long-standing ethnic, linguistic and customary communities and to the continuities between contemporary nations and these earlier, pre-modern peoples and cultures. A middle position, between the historical and modernist approaches, is taken by writers such as Anthony Smith, whose emphasis on the pre-modern basis, or 'substratum', of nations allows for modernist change but on the basis of historic continuities.[2] Within modernism, there is also a wide range of different approaches: Gellner stresses industrialization and the shift from pre-modern village communities; Anderson emphasizes the growth of print culture and of peoples who are conscious of a common identity, 'imagined communities'; Marxist writers, such as Hobsbawm, examine the rise of national economies and social classes as the basis for nationalism.[3]

There are two major objections to the modernist approach. One is that it denies the relevance of historical continuity by locating the emergence of nations in a purely modern context, i.e. since the late 18th century only. The other is that modernism cannot explain the emergence of nationalism in relatively underdeveloped, pre-industrial contexts. The factors that modernists identity as shaping nationalism, be they industrialization, print capitalism or modern social classes, often do not apply. This would be true for nationalism in many colonial countries and in semi-colonial but non-industrial societies such as China and Iran. Both of these objections apply, with much force, to the case of the Kurds: a distinct Kurdish language and people have existed for millennia; on the other hand, 'Kurdistan' has been largely isolated from modern socio-economic change. Kurdish nationalism is, indeed, a challenge to modernism, in whichever variant it is formulated.

But, by the same token, modernism may be seen as a challenge to Kurdish nationalism, in its conventional forms. That this latter challenge, to the claims of nationalism, may not in fact be valid can only be made clearer by examining the implications of modernism for the Kurdish case, as for others. What follows is one attempt to sketch a framework for a modernist account of Kurdish nationalism, to examine how far such an approach can be applied and to suggest some implications for contemporary Kurdish politics.

The Modernist Context

The strict modernist argument, as advanced by a narrow reading of Gellner, that nationalism developed as a result of industrialization and of the impact on state and society of that process, finds little support in Kurdistan.[4] Here we have, indeed, one of the most striking political disjunctures within Kurdish nationalism: in several cases, Kurdish nationalism has been organized by parties proclaiming adherence to a socialist or Marxist conception of class and appealing to the 'working class' (e.g. Komala in Iran, the PKK in Turkey), but, as with so much else in nationalism, this has reflected a gap between political rhetoric and aspiration, on the one side, and reality, on the other. Kurdish nationalism has not been a nationalism of the working class, be it a single working class in all Kurdish areas or a working class within any one of the three main states or a working class uniting Kurds with other workers within their multi-ethnic states (i.e. Iranian, Arab, Turkish). In none of the three countries where Kurds have their main communities were the Kurdish areas focuses of industrialization, these lying elsewhere, in the Arab cities of Iraq (Basra, Baghdad), in the major cities of Iran (Tehran, Tabriz, Isfahan, Abadan) and in the western part of Turkey (Istanbul, Izmir). Kurds migrated to these cities, but we cannot say, on the basis of available evidence, that there was a large ethnically distinguishable Kurdish presence, organized in the form of a Kurdish national movement, within the working classes of any of these three states. Similarly, the migration of Kurdish workers to western Europe, especially Germany, from the 1960s was not a major causative factor in the growth of the Kurdish nationalist movement in Turkey and other Middle Eastern states, even if it provided financial and ideological support.

However, the modernist claim need not rest on a narrow, industrial-society model: rather, starting from the rise of modern industrial society in Europe and the USA, it seeks to show how the impact of this society was felt throughout the world, in economic change and industrialization certainly, but also in the political, social and ideological changes that accompanied the subjugation to this model of the world, in the two centuries 1800–2000 that are also the lifespan of modern nationalism. Here, in schematic form, four broad processes, associated with modernity, can be identified:

War and great power conflict

The rise of any nationalism has to be seen not only in terms of what nationalism itself emphasizes, namely the endogenous growth of a nationalist consciousness and organization, but in the exogenous context of the clash of states and the weakening or transformation of dominant states. The conflict of great powers, from the Napoleonic wars through to the end of the Cold War, played a major part in the rise of modern nationalism across the world. These conflicts weakened established states and empires, above all those such as the Ottoman Empire and the Chinese Empire, which were unable to compete. Japan, by contrast, did compete by both industrializing and becoming an expansionist and nationalistic state. The death knell of European colonialism was sounded by the two World Wars, even for those states such as Britain and France that won.

In the case of the Kurds of the Middle East, this international context was of great importance: World War I provided the context for the emergence of the first Kurdish nationalist movements in Turkey and Iraq. It was the weakening of the Ottoman Empire by World War I, and the spread of the idea of self-determination proclaimed by both the Bolshevik revolution (Lenin) and American liberalism (President Wilson) that led to the emergence of the first demands for Kurdish independence. In the case of Iran, it was World War II that played a similar role: the intervention of Soviet forces in the north, together with the British, in August 1941 enabled the autonomous republic of Mahabad to be established. Similarly, it was the re-establishment of collaboration between great powers after each war, in 1918 and 1945, that removed the room for manoeuvre of the Kurdish forces in each state. After the two World Wars came the Cold War: this too had a major influence on the Kurdish forces, that of Iraq after the revolution of 1958 seeking to develop alliances with both the USSR and the USA, while the PKK in Turkey saw itself as part of the worldwide socialist movement, until the collapse of the USSR in 1991. The KDP of Iran, for its part, was ideologically dominated by pro-Soviet ideas until it to some extent broke free of these in the 1970s under the influence of its secretary-general, Abdel-Rahman Qasemlu. Other forms of interstate conflict affected Kurdish nationalism in the 1980s and 1990s, specifically war between Middle Eastern states: the Iran–Iraq war of 1980–88, the Iraq–Kuwait war of 1990–91, the Arab–Turkish rivalry of the same years and the US invasion of Iraq in 2003. These world and regional events did not determine the character of Kurdish nationalism, but they did provide an essential part of the context in which it developed.

Nationalism and state-building

The development of Kurdish nationalism, from the late 19th century onwards, was in considerable degree a result of the rise of modernizing states and of nationalism among the majority peoples who dominated them: Turks, Iranians, Arabs. Western pressure on the Ottoman Empire from the 18th century onwards both weakened that state and led, by the end of the 19th century, through 1908 and then the rise of Kemalism, to the emergence after 1923 of a new Turkish state. The Pahlavi regime in Iran, a product of the military coup of 1921, was for its part a product of the crisis of that society during World War I: its project, modernizing state and society and promoting a form of Iranian nationalism, served to encourage the emergence of Kurdish nationalism in Iran. In Iraq, first the Hashemite monarchy from 1920 and then, after 1958, a succession of military regimes dominated by Arab nationalism also provided incentive and context for the rise of Kurdish nationalism.

The national state context for Kurdish nationalism is important in two other respects. First, it provides a focus on the real, as distinct from aspirational dimension of Kurdish nationalism. Kurdish nationalism proclaims a unified Kurdish people, aiming to create a single state. But the reality is that there is no single Kurdish nationalist movement, ideology or politics; the history of modern Kurdish nationalism is that of three distinct movements, corresponding to the different contexts of Iran, Turkey and Iraq, with different campaigns and different ideological characters. This difference has repeatedly taken the form of alliances with states against other Kurdish groups, e.g. the alliance of Iranian Kurds with Iraq or of Iraqi Kurds with Iran and Turkey. The three movements have to some degree inspired each other but have not found a united form, and they are located within three specific, modernizing states. Secondly, a focus on the modernizing state explains the changes in Kurdish politics, which have largely been a result of what has happened at the centres of power in each state: the major dates in the Kurdish movement in Iraq are determined by what happened in Baghdad, in

Iran by what happened in Tehran. If there is to be a fundamental change in the position of Kurds within Turkey, it will involve changes in the policy of the Turkish state, at the centre.

Ideological example

Ideas on their own do not determine political behaviour: this is the weakness of the approach, most famously espoused by Elie Kedourie in his *Nationalism*,[5] that sees the spread of nationalism as above all the product of ideology and its diffusion. Ideas most certainly do play a role in determining the character of nationalist and other political movements, and Kurdish nationalism is no exception. Nationalism provided an ideology – of communities termed 'nations', of the right to independence, of the right to revolt and resist – that has been adopted all over the world. Since the 1920s there have been several variants of Kurdish nationalism in each of the three core states, and in each case this has reflected external ideological forces: Marxism, liberalism and Islamism, to name but three. As Abbas Vali has shown in his work (*see* chapter three), the Kurds have, indeed, reflected the full range of ideological currents seen in the modern Middle East.

This ideological formation accounts for two striking features of Kurdish nationalism. One is the recurrent influence within it of Marxist ideas, even though, as already noted, Kurdish society has been relatively underdeveloped and the leadership has not been drawn from a proletarian social background. Marxism has served ideological functions, of opposition to dominant, pro-Western states (Pahlavi Iran, Kemalist Turkey, Hashemite Iraq) and of providing a basis, or at least aspiration, for uniting the struggle of the Kurdish people with that of other oppressed groups within that society. The PKK ideology, a rigid 'orthodox' Marxism similar to that of groups emerging in the 1980s in Ethiopia, was, as much as anything, a product of the militant left-wing culture of the Turkish student and urban guerrilla movement of the 1970s. The other striking feature is the place of Islamist ideas: these too have been used as occasion has required. Thus the revolt of Shaikh Said in Turkey in 1925 drew on his role as leader of a Sufi order. In Iran during the 1978–79 revolution, on the other hand, the predominantly Sunni Kurdish population was cautious about the Islamic upheaval taking place elsewhere in the society, and soon came to clash with it: the Kurdish areas remained opposed to the Islamic republic and to the Islamization programme introduced by the new regime. The very fact that in the name of Islamic unity Khomeini denied the political rights of ethnic minorities strengthened secular nationalism among the Kurds. In Iraq, there has been Islamist influence within the Kurdish autonomous areas in the 1990s, in part as a result of Iranian influence, in part because of Sunni fundamentalists pursuing their own agenda. In neither the case of Iran or of Turkey is there any fixed, permanent, ideological character to the movement, but rather a shifting set of ideological orientations, responding to circumstance. As common sense suggests, Kurdish forces have adopted whatever generally available ideological programme and vocabulary has suited them best at the time.

Socio-economic change

Once these three other formative influences have been taken into account, it becomes possible to look at those factors that the modernist sociological theory of nationalism particularly emphasizes, the transition from pre-industrial to industrial society and the emergence of modern classes. It is not possible to explain the rise of the three main components of Kurdish nationalism in terms either of a single Kurdish nation or of the class structure of one or three Kurdistans. But there has certainly been social change within each of the three Kurdish areas – one, perhaps the most important, has already been mentioned, the formation and consolidation of the modern state – but other elements of change would include education, urbanization, changes in agrarian relations, the shifting position of women, and migration, either to cities elsewhere within the country or abroad. A complete analysis of the development of Kurdish nationalism in each state would have to look at these, while avoiding an explanation that reduced the history of each movement to its social base. Two aspects of Kurdish society have been evidently important for the history of nationalism: on the one hand, traditional forms of power, be they of sheikh, aga or tribal leader, and the ways these have sought to respond to the rise of, and opportunities presented by nationalism; on the other hand, the emergence of new leading groups among the Kurds, merchants and businessmen and intellectuals, as a result of modern education and migration. How far Kurdish nationalism as a whole can be explained by the emergence of new popular classes must remain a relevant but open question: but it is a contingent question, to be answered by research, not by theoretical diktat.

Conclusion

The orthodox history of nationalism starts from where the ideology of nationalism ends: one people, one consciousness and culture, one territory, one movement. All else, and in particular the failure to reach independence within a single state or to form a united national movement across modern, 'artificial' boundaries, is then seen as a failure. A modernist approach in no way denies the legitimacy of peoples to self-determination or the importance of historical memory in shaping political culture. But it does leave open the question of which peoples do achieve independence, of whether and how nationalist movements emerge, and of the organizational and ideological forms nationalism takes. It is a programme to study not historical determination or final liberation but more open, contingent, historical processes. What the summary observations in this chapter suggest is that, despite the claims of nationalist historians, on the one hand, and of a narrow, industrializing conception of nationalism, on the other, it may be possible to write a modernist history of the Kurds. The hope must also be that the Kurdish movements will have a modernist outcome: the attainment of national and democratic rights within each state or, on a democratic basis, within an independent state. Modern history and the forms of modern state the Kurds confront have not yet allowed this. But modernity, in the form of generally accepted international norms and of precedent in international politics and, where pertinent, law, entails that the Kurds are, like all contemporary peoples, entitled to no less – if 'they', or some parts of 'them', so wish.

Notes

1. Fred Halliday, *Nation and Religion in the Middle East* (London: Saqi, 2000), Arabic translation Saqi, 2000. For an excellent survey of theories of nationalism see the work of the Turkish writer Dr Umut Ozkirimli, *Theories of Nationalism* (London: Macmillan, 2001). For a comparable argument, as to how in regard to Somalia and Eritrea international factors such as colonialism, boundary delimitation, post-colonial discrimination and war have formed contemporary nationalism, as opposed to either historical or modern industrial factors, see Dominique Jacquin-Berdal, *Nationalism and Ethnicity in the Horn of Africa: A Critique of the Ethnic Interpretation* (Edward Mellen Press, 2002).
2. Anthony Smith, *The Ethnic Origins of Nations* (Oxford: Blackwell, 1986); Smith, 'The Origins of Nations', *Ethnic and Racial Studies* 12 (1989), pp. 340–67; Smith, *National Identity* (London: Penguin Books, 1991).

3. Ernest Gellner, *Nations and Nationalism* (Oxford: Basil Blackwell, 1992); Benedict Anderson, *Imagined Communities* (London: Verso, 2nd edn, 1992); E. J. Hobsbawm, *Nations and Nationalism since 1780* (Cambridge: Cambridge University Press, 1990).
4. Gellner, *Nations and Nationalism*, Chapter 3, 'Industrial Society', and Chapter 6, 'Social Entropy and Equality in Industrial Society'.
5. Elie Kedourie, *Nationalism* (London: Hutchinson, 1960).

Kurdish Paths to Nation[1]

Martin van Bruinessen

In this chapter, I shall be using such terms as 'Kurdish society' and 'Kurdish culture' in a rather loose sense, and include in it groups and individuals who may not in all contexts identify themselves as Kurds. Kurdish society is highly heterogeneous. There are not only vast cultural differences between one region and another, but within any single region there are populations that differ in language, religion or way of life from the majority and that may consider themselves – or may be considered by the majority – as less Kurdish or not Kurdish at all. Christian and Jewish minorities have generally not been considered as Kurds, although culturally they may have much in common with their Muslim neighbours and although they may even have Kurdish as their mother tongue. Heterodox communities living among the Kurds, such as the Alevis, the Ahl-i Haqq or Kaka'is and the Yezidis, tend to have an ambivalent relation with Kurdish identity, especially when they also differ from their more orthodox Muslim neighbours in spoken language. Ethnicity is not the expression of objective cultural traits, however; it is produced in social interaction, and it is susceptible to change as a consequence of political action. The states between which Kurdistan was divided for the last three quarters of the 20th century all had policies designed to change the ethnic map, most clearly Turkey, which has attempted to deny the existence of the Kurds and to destroy Kurdish ethnicity. Iran and Iraq, though less radical, have also engaged in efforts at ethnocide, with various degrees of success.[2] On the other hand, the emergence of a mass-based Kurdish national movement since the 1960s has also had a great impact on people's self-identification. It has sought to foster a sense of shared destiny among all those who might loosely be called Kurds, including the religious and linguistic minorities as well as those who had effectively been assimilated to the dominant ethnic group associated with the state. The 1980s and 1990s were a period in which the ethnic identity of minority communities was intensely contested by Kurdish nationalists, thinkers identifying with the Turkish, Iranian or Iraqi state nations and propagandists for smaller ethnic entities. Separatist nationalist tendencies emerged among the speakers of Zaza (a language closely related to Kurdish proper), the Yezidis and the Kurdish Alevis, and narrow regional solidarities appeared to be strengthening at the expense of a more inclusive sense of ethnic identity. The latter phenomenon is most clearly visible in Iraqi Kurdistan, where the fierce rivalry between the two major political parties has reinforced the division of the region into two ecologically, socially and culturally different zones that are increasingly feeling distinct from one another.

Who Is a Kurd?

There are no reliable estimates of the number of Kurds in any of the countries where they live. This is for a number of reasons. One is a matter of government policy: in the interests of national integration, the governments concerned do not usually enumerate the various linguistic and religious groups within their borders separately, or when they do they are reluctant to publish the results. Another reason is that it may depend on the political and social context whether a person will identify himself or herself as a Kurd or not.

The 1965 census in Turkey was the last one that asked people for their native languages and other languages spoken. Almost four million, or 12.7 per cent of the population, then identified themselves as speakers of Kurdish; 7.1 per cent of the population spoke it as their first language.[3] This gives only a very rough indication of the number of people identifying themselves as Kurds. Those mentioning Kurdish as a second language must have included ethnic Turks, Arabs, Armenians and other Christian groups living in ethnically mixed regions where Kurdish was the lingua franca. Others may have been persons of mixed parentage or Kurds who were at least as fluent in Turkish as in Kurdish. Those who actually considered themselves Kurds would clearly have exceeded the 7.1 per cent figure. Many people must have been reluctant to stigmatize themselves by proclaiming Kurdish identity, and some of the enumerators may have 'corrected' their data in order to arrive at politically acceptable figures.[4]

Although we cannot really know how many people in Turkey considered themselves as Kurds in 1965, it is safe to say that the percentage of people who do so thirty years later has risen perceptibly. Only a small part of this increase is to be attributed to the higher birth rate of Turkey's eastern provinces as compared to the western part of the country. The rise is chiefly due to the fact that numerous people who thought of themselves as Turks in 1965 are currently defining themselves primarily as Kurds. This includes many young people whose parents or grandparents had assimilated to Turkish culture, voluntarily or under pressure. Partly overlapping with this group are the offspring of mixed marriages, whose ethnic identity is inherently ambiguous. Almost everyone in Turkey may find a distant Kurdish ancestor if he or she goes back far enough. Those with at least one Kurdish grandparent (whose numbers include the late presidents Ismet Inönü and Turgut Özal) constitute a vast reservoir of potential Kurds. *Mutatis mutandis*, the same is true of the Kurds in Iran and Iraq.

Put simply, among the Kurds (as among any ethnic group) we find a core whose ethnic identity is unambiguously Kurdish, surrounded by more peripheral groups whose identification with Kurdish ethnicity is more ambivalent and for whom Kurdish identity is only one of several options. This is, however, putting it too simply, for on closer inspection even the ethnic core appears not to be so unambiguously definable at all. Each member of the core has, just like the more peripheral 'potential Kurds', a number of overlapping identities, some of which may exert a stronger appeal to his or her loyalties than the Kurdish identity. He or she belongs to a village and perhaps to a notable family of some renown, to a tribe, to a region, to a dialect group and to a religious community. Within the core, moreover, we find so wide a range of cultural variety that it is impossible to define it by a number of common cultural traits.[5]

Nevertheless, there is considerable agreement among oriental authors, at least from the early 16th century on, as to whom to call Kurds. The Ottoman historians describing the incorporation of Kurdistan into the Ottoman Empire in the early 16th century; the late 16th-century ruler of Bitlis, Sharaf Khan, who wrote a detailed history of all Kurdistan's ruling families towards the end of that century; Evliya Çelebi, the Turkish traveller who spent years in various parts of Kurdistan in the mid-17th century – all of them used the name 'Kurd' in practically the same way and applied it to the same population. So did Ottoman and Persian administrators, down to the early 1930s, when mentioning Kurds became unacceptable in Turkey. Their Kurds consisted of those tribesmen of eastern Asia Minor and the Zagros, settled as well as nomadic, who were not Turkish, Arabic or Persian-speaking.[6] They included speakers of Kurdish proper as well as Zaza (in the north-west) or

Gurani (in the south-east, with more isolated pockets throughout present-day Iraqi Kurdistan), Sunni Muslims as well as Shi'is and the adherents of the various heterodox sects in the region. There was only some ambiguity about the Lor and Bakhtiari, living to the south-east of the Kurds proper, whom some authors called Kurds and others considered as separate groups. (The same ambiguity still persists in the self-definition of at least some of the Lor today.) It is important to note also whom they appeared *not* to include among the Kurds: the numerous non-tribal peasants and townsmen living in the same area, who included Muslims as well as Christians, and many of whom spoke Kurdish (or Gurani or Zaza) dialects as their first language. I shall return to the matter of these non-tribal groups below.

Unity and Variety among the Kurds

The great orientalist and expert on the Kurds, Vladimir Minorsky, once claimed that the various Kurdish dialects (from which he excluded Zaza and Gurani) showed, underneath their obvious differences, a remarkable unity, which was especially remarkable when compared with the great variety of very dissimilar Iranian languages spoken by the inhabitants of another mountainous area, the Pamirs. He concluded that this basic unity of the Kurdish language derived from a single language spoken by a large and important people, and suggested that these might have been the Medes (whom Kurdish nationalists in fact like to see as their ancestors).[7]

This view was criticised by the linguist D. N. MacKenzie, according to whom there are but few linguistic features that all Kurdish dialects have in common and that at the same time distinguish them from other Iranian languages. MacKenzie argued that Kurdish proper differs in a number of major aspects significantly from what is known about Median. Kurdish has a strong south-west Iranian element, whereas Median presumably was a north-west Iranian language. Both Zaza and Gurani, however, belong to the north-west Iranian group, and MacKenzie believed that many of the differences between the northern ('Kurmanji') and southern ('Sorani') dialects of Kurdish proper could be explained by the profound influence of Gurani on the latter.[8] MacKenzie's message, which he appeared to direct at Kurdish nationalist ideologues as much as at Minorsky, was that the Kurds had neither common origins nor basic cultural unity.

There is wide agreement in recent studies of ethnicity and national identity that cultural unity or diversity in themselves are not decisive factors – although appeals to an (alleged) common history and common culture are of course of tremendous importance in mobilizing ethnic or national sentiment. The first European nation–states in the age of nationalism were not at all culturally homogeneous. In 1789 only half of the Frenchmen spoke any French at all and only 12–13 per cent spoke it correctly; the others spoke only various *patois*. At the time of Italy's unification in 1860, only 2.5 per cent of its population used Italian for everyday purposes; even some of the leading nationalists were less than fluent in the 'national' language.[9] In the case of the Kurds, it is remarkable that long before the age of nationalism there already was a sense of common identity among tribes whose cultures were 'objectively' quite diverse.

It is not difficult to point out considerable cultural differences within what nationalists claim to be the Kurdish nation. The more extreme claims of some nationalists include the Lor and Bakhtiari, who speak closely related languages. These groups now do not generally consider themselves as Kurds, although this name was occasionally applied to them in the past. The speakers of Gurani and Zaza, on the other hand, have for centuries been considered as Kurds by themselves and by their Kurdish-speaking neighbours, as well as by such outsiders as Turkish and Arabic authors. This was in spite of the fact that their languages cannot be understood by native speakers of Kurdish proper (apart from the few who have expended considerable effort to learn them).[10]

Even Kurmanji and Sorani, the major dialect groups of Kurdish, are not mutually understandable either, although speakers of one may learn the other relatively easily. In fact, within these dialect groups too there is so much variation that people from different regions may prefer communicating in Turkish, Persian or Arabic because they only imperfectly understand each other's Kurdish. In each of the countries in which the Kurds live, moreover, the official language has had a considerable influence on the various Kurdish dialects, most clearly in vocabulary but also to some extent in syntax. Closely related dialects spoken on either side of an inter-state boundary have thus begun drifting apart.

Religion, the other central element of culture, also appears to divide rather than unite the Kurds. The majority are Sunni Muslims, adhering to the Shafi'i school (*madhhab*) in the details of their religious obligations, but large numbers in southern and south-eastern Kurdistan (in Iraq as well as Iran) are Twelve Shi'i Muslims like the majority of the populations of Iran and southern Iraq. These Shi'i Kurds should not be confused with the Alevi

Kurds of north-western Kurdistan. Although the Alevis also venerate Ali and the other eleven Imams of the Shi'a, they do not in general accept the canonical obligations of orthodox Islam and they have their own religious rituals, different from those of the Shi'is as well as those of the Sunnis. Alevi Kurds constitute only a minority among the Alevis of Turkey, and they often feel closer to their Turkish-speaking co-religionists than to the Sunni Kurds. A somewhat similar religion is that of the Ahl-i Haqq or, as they are called in Iraq, the Kaka'i. Many Ahl-i Haqq claim that their religion is an esoteric sect within Shi'i Islam, but some wish to place themselves outside Islam altogether. Even further removed from Islamic orthodoxy is the Yezidi religion, once widespread in central and north-western Kurdistan but now restricted to a few small areas in Iraq and the Armenian Republic and smaller pockets in Syria and Turkey.[11] The now dwindling Christian and Jewish communities of the region are not commonly considered as Kurds, although some of them have Kurdish as their first language.

Among the Sunni speakers of Kurdish proper we find groups with quite different material cultures. The sociologist Rudolph, noting that in a relatively small area in south-eastern Turkey there were communities that differed considerably in the degree of their dependence on agriculture or animal husbandry as well as in other aspects of material culture such as house type, ventured the hypothesis that these represented two originally quite distinct ethnic groups. The geographer Hütteroth, however, who did fieldwork in the same area, suggested that the differences in material culture were simply due to different ecological circumstances.[12] Hütteroth's explanation is basically the same as the one we find a few years later, further worked out theoretically, in an article by Fredrik Barth on Pathan tribesmen, among whom he had observed even wider cultural diversity. In spite of their cultural differences, these groups were acutely aware of their common Pathan identity.[13]

In the Kurdish case, however, some of the cultural differences correlate with a distinction between tribesmen and a non-tribal subordinated peasantry. In many parts of Kurdistan we find such groups existing beside each other. The tribesmen tend to consider themselves as the only 'real' Kurds, and the non-tribal peasants used to be designated by various ethnic or 'caste' terms (*ra'yat, guran, miskên, kelawspî, kurmanc*) distinguishing them from the tribes (*'ashiret, kurd*). The history of the region suggests that the *ra'yat* must be of quite heterogeneous origins and include descendants of various older populations as well as impoverished Kurdish tribesmen.[14]

The cultural differences mentioned above have been losing much of their importance owing to the massive migration and urbanization that have taken place during the past few decades. In the large cities it does not matter much whether one's grandparents were nomads or small peasants, or what language they spoke at home. For most public purposes one did not use the language of the village but the official language of the state – Turkish, Arabic or Persian. This fostered, on the one hand, an increasing awareness of common Kurdishness among people of different regional origins in the same country, but, on the other hand, caused a widening cultural gap between the Kurds of Turkey, Iraq and Iran. Compulsory education and military service, various forms of political mobilization (elections, mass demonstrations), economic development and the ensuing internal migration, and especially 'national' radio and television have integrated even the most distant villages into the 'national' life of their states. Separate histories, for at least the past seventy-five years, and different processes of socialisation have made the Kurds of each country rather different from those in the neighbouring states.

Nationalism, Nationhood and National Rights

Kurdish nationalists have always been apprehensive about these cultural divisions. Their aim has been self-determination in one form or another; and that aim obviously required unity. Kurdish nationalists have frequently suspected the Turkish, Iraqi and Iranian governments of deliberately reinforcing the existing intra-Kurdish differences – and not without justification. For instance, the governments of the Shah's Iran and Republican Iraq, both of which broadcast radio programmes in Kurdish, had parallel programmes in a number of different dialects, while their Persian- and Arabic-language programmes obviously used the standard language only. This was generally perceived as an attempt to keep the Kurds divided and prevent the emergence of a standard Kurdish.[15]

In the dominant political discourse of the 20th century, self-determination has been associated with *nations*: American President Woodrow Wilson's 'Fourteen Points' and other wartime speeches, Joseph Stalin's influential writings on the national question and the Charter of the United Nations all refer to the *right of self-determination of nations*. Kurdish nationalists have therefore often spent much effort to prove that the Kurds constitute a nation. Neither Wilson nor the United Nations provided a definition of what was meant by this term.[16] The Kurds might have qualified for Wilson, but by the end of World War I the Kurdish nationalists were too weak to press their claims effectively. The UN Charter (1948) implicitly referred to the colonized peoples of Asia and Africa only, or more precisely those peoples that were colonized by Western powers. Stalin, however, did provide a definition, which has had great importance to the Kurdish movement. Kurdish nationalists, claiming to represent a nation by this definition, have attempted to receive Soviet support for their cause. The definition also loomed large in the debates between Kurdish nationalists and the left movements of their countries; most of the left-wing parties denied the Kurds' status as a nation and told them to content themselves with that of a *national minority* (which in Stalinist theory does not have the right of self-determination and cannot establish its separate communist party).

Stalin defined the nation by five characteristic features: common history, language, territory, economic life and culture, expressing a common 'national character'. Only when all of these are present does a group of people constitute a nation in Stalin's sense (and, by implication, deserve socialist solidarity in its struggle for self-determination).[17] Kurdish nationalists could convincingly claim a common history and a large piece of territory associated with their people, but their opponents in the debates denied the existence of a common economic life. The unity of language and the unity of culture too were sensitive issues, although they were less frequently contested by the non-Kurdish left.

It was in debates within Turkey's Kurdish movement itself that the language question assumed grave importance: Zaza had to be declared a Kurdish *dialect*, not a related but different *language*, for the second alternative would by Stalin's definition exclude the Zaza-speakers from the Kurdish nation. Later some of the Zaza-speakers were to perceive in this attitude of the Kurdish movement towards Zaza a precise parallel to the way the Turkish authorities had declared Kurdish to be a Turkish dialect. The rigid insistence on linguistic unity as a criterion for nationhood in Stalin's definition thus indirectly became one of the factors contributing to the recent emergence of a separatist Zaza nationalism.

Although most Kurdish nationalists nurture the dream of a united and independent Kurdistan, the leaders of the Iranian and Iraqi Kurds have for pragmatic reasons usually restricted their demands to self-determination within the framework of the existing states, i.e. political autonomy and cultural rights. They refrained from openly embracing pan-Kurdish ideals.[18] When in Turkey the Kurdish movement re-emerged in the 1960s, initially as a part of the reborn left movement, its first demands were for recognition of the existence of Kurds, cultural rights and economic development. As Lenin and Stalin's thought gradually became more widely known in Turkey, the concept of self-determination came to dominate political discourse, and by the late 1970s it had become the professed aim of virtually all Kurdish parties and organizations in Turkey. The party that was most successful in waging a guerrilla war against the Turkish state and building up a mass following among Turkey's Kurds, the PKK, long proclaimed that the independence of all of Kurdistan was its ultimate objective. It made, in fact, efforts to draw Iraqi and Iranian Kurds into its orbit, becoming a significant factor in both the Iraqi and Iranian parts of Kurdistan and competing notably with the Iraqi KDP. By the early 1990s, however, it became clear that its leader, Abdullah Öcalan, had moderated his ambitions and was hoping for a negotiated settlement with the Turkish government alone. Many years before his ultimate capture and trial, it had become clear that he envisaged a solution within the framework of the Republic of Turkey.[19]

All significant Kurdish leaders thus appear to have reconciled themselves to the prospect that their people would remain a divided nation or, perhaps, constitute three closely related but separate nations.

Ethnic Boundaries and the Kurdish Ethnie

Since the anthropologist Fredrik Barth's influential work on ethnic boundaries, it has become widely accepted that ethnicity is not simply determined by objective cultural traits but that boundary maintenance is the major constituent factor.[20] The culture of an ethnic group may show quite wide internal variation owing to differing ecological circumstances and it may undergo considerable change over time, but neither of these factors affects its ethnic identity as long as the group remains capable of maintaining a clear boundary between itself and its environment. Ethnic groups, in this view, are primarily defined by the boundaries that mark them off from other ethnic groups. Effective boundary maintenance requires of course the use of clear boundary markers, symbols of group identity. It is often cultural traits that are used as boundary markers, but there is no a priori reason why certain traits become boundary markers and others not; moreover, traits that were once important may lose their significance and give way to others.

It may be helpful to apply this approach to the Kurdish case, and investigate which social boundaries were and are most carefully maintained among the Kurds and their neighbours. Before World War I, the most conspicuous of all boundaries was that between Muslims and Christians or Jews. Turkish and Arabic-speaking Sunni Muslims were much less alien to the Sunni Kurds, and the boundaries separating them were fuzzy. In the 15th century, Turkish and Kurdish nomadic tribesmen merged in a single large tribal confederacy, the Boz Ulus.[21] In later centuries, Ottoman documents contain references to tribes described as 'Turcoman Kurds' or 'Kurdish Turcomans', terms that are not well understood but that suggest a degree of cultural merger between Turkish and Kurdish elements and the absence of a clear ethnic boundary between them.[22] At least one Arabic-speaking tribe, the Mahallami (in the Tor Abdin, east of Mardin), considered itself as Kurdish and was considered as such by other Kurds.[23] Zaza-speaking tribesmen were never even mentioned as a distinct group but always considered as Kurds.

The Yezidis were in a different position. On the one hand, they were not considered as Muslims and they emphasized their distinct identity by various external signs; on the other hand, as tribespeople and Kurdish speakers they were much closer to the Muslim Kurds than most Christians were. There was a clear boundary between Sunni Kurds and Yezidis but its importance varied from time to time. By the beginning of the 20th century several tribes in the provinces of Urfa and Mardin, in present-day Turkey, appear to have had Yezidi as well as Muslim segments (which probably was due to gradual conversion of Yezidi tribes to Islam).[24] It is not entirely clear how sharply defined the boundary between Alevi and Sunni Kurds was. The difference between Alevism and Sunni Islam may not have mattered much among nomads, who have been notoriously lax in orthodox religious practice, but have gained significance among settled populations, which were more susceptible to orthodox teachings. Several nineteenth-century sources speak of the Kizilbash (Alevi) as if these constituted a distinct ethnic community besides Sunni Kurds and Ottoman Muslims. The fact that there were speakers of Turkish, Kurdish and Zaza among these Kizilbash does not appear to have been considered significant.[25]

Language, in other words, did not play an important part as a boundary marker, but religion did; and the boundaries separating Christians from Muslims were much more unambiguous than those between heterodox and orthodox.

Perhaps the most important boundary of all, however, was the aforementioned one between tribal and non-tribal populations. The Muslim–Christian boundary was especially sharp where it coincided with that separating tribesmen and non-tribal peasants or craftsmen. Where Christianskalp were tribally organized and militarily strong, as the Nestorians of Hakkari and the Jacobites of the Tor Abdin still were for most of the 19th century, Kurdish tribesmen treated them as equals. There were even Kurdish tribes that incorporated Christians as members.[26] The non-tribal populations of the region included speakers of Kurdish, Zaza and Gurani as well as Armenian, Aramaic, Arabic and perhaps Turkish, and there were Sunni and Alevi Muslims among them as well as Christians. The tribesmen made no sharp ethnic distinctions among these non-tribal groups, referring to them by the blanket term of *ra'yat* ('subjects'), by slightly more precise terms such as *feleh* (for Christian peasants, especially Armenians) and *kurmanc* (for Muslim peasants in northern Kurdistan), or by terms of local scope that differed from region to region. The tribesmen referred to themselves simply as *'ashiret* ('tribe') or as *kurd*.[27]

There was yet another significant boundary in the region: that between the representatives of Ottoman high culture – military-bureaucratic officials, higher religious functionaries, urban notables – and the various local populations. The former were a quite distinct group that kept a distance from the common people by their use of Ottoman Turkish and an elaborate etiquette. The urban populations of major cities in Kurdistan had a similar, Turkicized culture. The *shehri* (urbanites) constituted a distinct social category that was not associated with any of the vernacular rural groups – although some of the *shehri* in the region would become leading Turkish nationalists and others opt for Kurdish nationalism.

Given this complex of cross-cutting ethnic boundaries – some sharp, some fuzzy – one concludes that the Kurdish *ethnie* had a core consisting, by the early 20th century, of the Kurdish-speaking Muslim tribes. The Zaza- and Gurani-speaking tribes, or at least the Sunnis among them, who lived in similar ecological environments and shared a common history with their Kurdish-speaking neighbours, were in most senses also part of the core.[28] The Alevi, Yezidi, Shi'i and Ahl-i Haqq tribes were more peripheral; and the non-tribal peasantry, whatever their language or religion, were not considered, and did not consider themselves, as part of the *ethnie*. Christians and Jews were also excluded from it, but many individuals and even entire groups crossed the boundary by formally converting to Islam; they were accepted as Kurds.

The most ambivalent group were the *shehri*, the townspeople of Kurdistan. As one of them, Ziya Gökalp, wrote around 1915, '*shehrinin milliyeti yoktur*', 'the urbanite has no ethnic identity',[29] and soon there would be a debate in a Kurdish journal as to whether the *shehri* of towns like Bitlis, who were turcophone, were Kurds or Turks. Those urban notables who were related to tribes of the region understandably tended to identify themselves with the Kurds, but most of the *shehri* long remained ambivalent. The same is true of the non-tribal peasantry, who only after the 1960s gradually became accepted as Kurds.

This composition of the Kurdish *ethnie* was reflected in the membership of the first Kurdish nationalist associations, established in Istanbul between 1908 and 1920.[30] These were mostly educated members of the tribal or religious elite, and overwhelmingly Sunnis. Among them we find speakers of the northern and southern Kurdish dialects as well as a few Zaza speakers, but very few Alevis and no Yezidis.[31] Not surprisingly, there were no members of peasant or urban craftsman backgrounds, and in the Kurdish rebellions of the 1920s and 1930s these social strata remained aloof. One of the prominent *shehri* members of several Kurdish associations was the medical doctor Abdullah Cevdet, who had earlier been one of the founders of the Young Turk Committee of Union and Progress. Cevdet was the mentor of another famous *shehri*, Ziya Gökalp, who had a lifelong ambivalent relation with the Kurds, but who opted for Turkish ethnicity and became one of the chief ideologues of Turkish nationalism.[32]

Paths to Nationhood

The British sociologist Anthony D. Smith, who is one of the foremost scholars of nationalism, has made a distinction between two radically different roads to nationhood, which take their origins in two different ideal types of ethnic community or *ethnie*.[33] His discussion of these types and their evolution, although not immediately applicable, is useful to an understanding of the Kurdish situation. Smith uses the French term *ethnie* to indicate communities that not only share certain myths of origin and descent, the association with a certain territory and at least some common elements of culture, but also a sense of solidarity among (most of) their members. It is the awareness of belonging together that distinguishes the *ethnie* from the *ethnic category*, people with a common culture and common myths of origin but lacking solidarity and deliberate boundary maintenance mechanisms. The *nation* represents a higher degree of integration than the *ethnie*, being characterized by a mass, public culture and by a certain degree of economic and political integration.[34]

The first of Smith's ideal types is what he calls the 'lateral–aristocratic' *ethnie*, whose members constitute a military–aristocratic stratum, which has little social depth but may be widely extended in geographical space. The other is what he calls the 'vertical–demotic' type, in which different social strata share in (more or less) the same culture and are held together by a belief in common origins and a strong commitment to a common religion. Lateral–aristocratic *ethnies* may grow into nations if they succeed in culturally integrating the various communities that they dominate. Smith speaks of 'bureaucratic incorporation', for the state usually plays a key role in the process. This is the process by which such European nation-states as France, England and Spain were formed. Vertical–demotic *ethnies* may (but do not necessarily) develop into nations through a process of internal mobilization by a nationalist intelligentsia, which usually involves a reinvention of the ethnic past and the claim of sacred ties to a homeland. Such 'demotic' nations may emerge beside the earlier 'nation-states' but also inside and against them, among the subject populations of an aristocratic *ethnie*.

Spain constitutes an especially instructive example for comparison with the Kurdish case: the 'aristocratic–lateral' Castilians succeeded in incorporating most of the population of the Iberian peninsula (excluding Portugal) into the Spanish nation, but the Catalans, Basques and Galicians never entirely gave up their distinct ethnic identities, which later became the basis for 'demotic' nationalisms. The Spanish and Catalan identities are not mutually exclusive; even the most fervent Catalan nationalist is, at least in some ways, also a Spaniard. It is also important to notice that Catalan nationalism emerged well after the successful incorporation of the Catalans into the Spanish nation.

The case of the Kurds, however, is a little more complex. Until the beginnings of the present century, the Kurds and the other peoples of the region were the subjects of the Ottoman military and bureaucratic elite, who constituted a sort of aristocratic–lateral *ethnie* (united by the Ottoman language, the state variety of Sunni Islam, and a particular Ottoman *ethos*), although many of its members originated from various demotic *ethnies*. The Kemalist elite of Turkey was in most relevant respects the successor of this Ottoman elite; in spite of its Turkish nationalist and populist ideology, it remained just as distant from the tribes and the peasantry.[35] This elite fostered a reinvented Turkish culture, with which Turkish villagers, let alone the Kurds, initially had little affinity. Its deliberate efforts at nation-building, however, by means of the forced assimilation of especially the Kurds and the suppression of traditional religious styles, as well as by the more benign means of mass education, general conscription into the army and the use of modern mass media, were largely successful. The gentler methods of 'bureaucratic incorporation' practised in Iraq during the mandate and under Hashemite rule also resulted in a distinct Iraqi national identity, and the same was true, *mutatis mutandis*, of Iran under the Pahlavi shahs.[36]

By the beginning of the 20th century, as was shown in the preceding section, the Kurds too were rather like an aristocratic–lateral *ethnie*, consisting of (mostly Sunni Muslim) tribesmen dominating a peasantry and various other population groups considered as less or not at all Kurdish. Following the Armenian deportations and massacres of 1915 and the final expulsion of Armenians from north-eastern Turkey in the immediate post-war years, there remained very few Christians in eastern Turkey. The Muslim–Christian boundary thus became irrelevant. The Kemalist policy of secularization, from 1924 onwards, affected other ethnic boundaries as well. Common religion had united Kurds and Turks in the resistance against Armenian territorial claims, but the disestablishment of Islam and its replacement by Turkish nationalism as the state ideology inevitably loosened the bond between the Kurds and their Turkish neighbours. It decreased, on the other hand, the distance between Sunnis and Alevis. Social mobility and urbanization moreover began to blur the distinction between tribal and non-tribal people. By the 1960s, the Kurdish nationalist intelligentsia, although of elite backgrounds, had decided that the non-tribal peasantry were real Kurds and directed their nationalist propaganda at them. The subject peasantry were gradually incorporated into the dominant *ethnie*. (A similar incorporation of minorities had in fact begun earlier, with the conversion of Armenians and other Christians to Islam.[37])

Two processes of incorporation, involving the same peasant, lower-class urban and marginal tribal populations, thus have been at work simultaneously: incorporation into the emerging Turkish (or Iraqi, or Iranian) nation-state and incorporation into the Kurdish *ethnie*. The peasantry was late in actively opting for an identity, but among the Alevi tribes of Turkey there was in the 1920s a lively debate on which identity to choose, Kurdish or Turkish. Some of their chieftains threw in their lot with the Kurdish nationalists,[38] some opted for the secular state against their long-time hostile Sunni Kurdish neighbours and declared themselves to be 'real Turks',[39] and many others went on considering Alevism as their only relevant identity. The Yezidis, Kaka'is and other similar communities in Iraq, as well as the Christians of Kurdistan, faced analogous choices, although they were not subject to great pressure to declare themselves Arabs until the Ba'ath party came to power.[40]

For several decades, the process of nation-building in Turkey, Iraq and Iran continued quite successfully, without however being capable of preventing the gradual incorporation of peripheral groups into the Kurdish *ethnie*. Kurdish identity, however, especially in Turkey, remained subordinate to the state-based national identity until the late 1960s and 1970s, when we see the emergence of Kurdish nationalist mass movements. This resurgence of Kurdish nationalism resembled the 'ethnic revival' in Europe's nation-states; it had more than a few things in common with the Basque and Catalan movements in Spain (although the latter movements emerged in relatively privileged parts of Spain, whereas Kurdistan was a disadvantaged region). The new Kurdish movement, most clearly so in Turkey, was spawned by the twin processes of mass education and urbanization. It was born in the large cities, where Kurdish students and intellectuals and, later, labour migrants became more aware of being different from the dominant *ethnie* and of a certain discrimination against them.

The Kurdish movement of the 1960s and 1970s gives the impression that successful ethnic incorporation had taken place: among the leaders and the rank and file we find in Turkey Sunnis and Alevis, Kurdish and Zaza speakers as well as monolingual Turkish speakers of Kurdish descent. In the Iraqi Kurdish movement we find not only speakers of all Kurdish and various Gurani dialects, Yezidis and Shi'is as well as Sunni Muslims, but also Assyrians (sometimes called 'Kurdish Christians', a concept that would have been unthinkable a few decades earlier), and even some Arabic-speaking Faylis.[41] This does not mean that support for the movement or even for the idea of a Kurdish nation was general. In Iraq, the number of so-called *jash*, Kurds who could be mobilized by the central government to fight against the Kurdish movement, remained in the same order of magnitude as that of the *peshmerge*, the guerrilla fighters. Certain tribes became *jash* because their chieftains distrusted the Kurdish politicians, others because their long-time rivals had become *peshmerge*, and many others worked for the government out of fear or greed. However, the division between supporters and opponents of the Kurdish movement did not follow any of the aforementioned linguistic and religious dividing lines.

The Resurgence of Intra-Kurdish Ethnicity

In the course of the 1980s, as said before, the processes of incorporation into one large Kurdish *ethnie* began to be countered by the resurgence of less inclusive ethnic identities. Again a comparison with the emergence of Catalan nationalism in Spain may be enlightening, the difference being that the Kurdish *ethnie* this time around found itself in the position of the Spanish. The emergence of these centrifugal forces was to some extent due to the very successes of the Kurdish nationalist movement in fostering a national awareness and building up the infrastructure of a Kurdish nation. At least two different forms of this ethnic resurgence can be observed: regional–linguistic particularism ('Badinan' versus 'Soran') in Iraqi Kurdistan, and separatist tendencies among the minority language and religious communities (Zaza and Alevi) in Turkey.

An awareness of the vast social, economic and cultural differences between the Kurmanji-speaking northern part of Iraqi Kurdistan ('Badinan') and the Sorani-speaking south is in itself nothing new. It has been a major cause of frictions within the Iraqi Kurdish movement at least from the early 1960s on. Badinan used to be economically backward and strongly dominated by tribes; the southern districts long were more urbanized and scored much higher in education and economic development, which made the role of the tribes there less prominent. It was the Sorani Kurdish dialect that acquired official status in Iraq and was fostered as a literary language and a medium of education, while Kurmanji was neglected. The medium of instruction in schools in Badinan was not Kurmanji but Arabic or Sorani.

In the early 1960s, there was a fierce struggle for leadership of the Kurdish movement between Barzani and his tribal allies on the one hand and the urban, university-educated, Sorani-speaking members of the political bureau of the Kurdistan Democratic Party (KDP) on the other. These rivals represented not only different social strata, with sometimes conflicting class interests and contrasting views of the political struggle, but also the two major regions of Iraqi Kurdistan. Barzani won the struggle, first militarily, soon also politically. Co-opting some of his former rivals, along with other southern politicians, he succeeded in uniting Kurds from all districts under his leadership. By the end of the 1960s, linguistic and religious differences no longer divided the movement, which remained firmly united until its sudden collapse in March 1975.

The movement that re-emerged in the following years has been characterized by fierce rivalry between leaders with localized power bases. Chief among them were Jalal Talabani, who found his strongest support in the Sulaymaniya (Silemani) region, and Barzani's sons Idris and Mas'ud, whose primary power base, like their father's, consisted of the tribes of Badinan. Talabani, himself born in Koi Sanjaq, had been a member of the old KDP politburo and in 1975 founded the Patriotic Union of Kurdistan (PUK), whereas the Barzani brothers reconstituted their father's KDP. The other Kurdish leaders most of the time allied themselves with one or the other of these two, sometimes shifting their allegiances. Whatever else changed during the 1980s, the polarization of the movement between Talabani and the Barzanis remained a constant. This was in part precisely because these leaders, more than others, exemplified 'Soran' and 'Badinan' and the stereotyped conceptions that those regions had of themselves and of one another.[42]

Neither the repressive policies of Saddam Hussein, culminating in a genocidal offensive against Kurdish positions in 1988, nor the opportunities offered by the establishment of a safe haven under international protection in 1991 had the effect of persuading the Kurdish leaders to place common interests first. Their rivalries not only continued but were exacerbated by the economic and political conditions of the 1990s. Following relatively free elections, in which the PUK and KDP received almost equal numbers of votes, they formed a coalition government – without, however, giving it real power. Differential access to economic resources and foreign political patronage – the KDP, which controlled the Turkish border, earned vast sums from customs duties and fees besides engaging in smuggling on its own account, and simply refused to share this income with its coalition partner – was a cause of increasing tension. This culminated in a fratricidal war that broke out in 1994 and continued, with interruptions due to international intervention, until 1998. In 1996, the KDP called in the support of Saddam's troops to dislodge the PUK, which it accused of collusion with Iran, from the regional capital of Erbil. Since then, there have de facto been two regional governments, based in Erbil and Sulaymaniya.[43]

The conflict between the PUK and the KDP has deepened the gulf between 'Soran' and 'Badinan' (even though the KDP now controls more than just Badinan). On both sides a resurgence of primordialism and negative prejudices about the other has been noted – although it is difficult to gauge how widespread these responses are. Political leaders in the Sulaymaniya region are known to have agitated against the alleged danger of domination by the Badinanis (who in the present geopolitical constellation control the supply lines of the southern region). In Badinan, on the other hand, political resentment against Talabani and the PUK tends to be translated into a negative attitude towards all of Sulaymaniya or even 'the Soran' in general. There is a feeling among some people in Badinan – again, it is not clear how many share it – that the region had better take care of its own interests rather than make sacrifices for the whole Kurdish region.

The recently emerging Zaza and Alevi nationalisms in Turkey are part of a different dialectical relationship with the development of Kurdish nationalism. The same process of urbanization and migration that gave rise to a modern Kurdish awareness in the large cities also brought Alevi villagers (among them Turkish as well as Kurdish or Zaza speakers) to the Sunni towns of the region and into direct competition for scarce resources with their new Sunni neighbours. The political polarization of the 1970s aggravated Sunni–Alevi antagonism as radicals of the right and left chose these communities as their recruiting grounds and provoked mutual scapegoating ('fascist' Sunnis versus 'communist' Alevis). A series of bloody Sunni–Alevi clashes, perhaps better called anti-Alevi pogroms, did much to strengthen a common Alevi awareness.[44] In the region where these clashes took place, it did not matter much whether one was a Kurd or a Turk; one's primary identity was the religious one. There were Turks and Kurds on both sides of this divide – which gave rise to such surprising phenomena as Sunni Kurds supporting the pan-Turkish Nationalist Action Party and young Turkish-speaking Alevis declaring themselves to be Kurds.

In the 1980s Alevism underwent a remarkable cultural and religious revival, an indirect and unintended consequence of the repressive measures taken by the military in the wake of the coup of 1980. Political radicalism – Islamist as well as Marxist or Kurdish nationalist – was severely repressed, but instead of reverting to the strict laicism of the Kemalist period, the military fostered a mix of conservative Sunni Islam and Turkish nationalism, in the hope of pre-empting more radical Islamic currents and combating Marxist thought. Religious education became an obligatory subject in all schools; the state built mosques in villages where there was none. This imposition of Sunni Islam could only make the Alevis more aware of their distinctly non-Sunni identity. Whereas numerous young Alevis had in the 1970s become leftists and thought of Alevism as a political identity, the new situation obliged them to look at it as a cultural and religious movement.

The Turkish and Kurdish immigrant communities in western Europe played a major role in this reorientation. Activists of various political persuasions had tried in the 1960s and 1970s to organize these communities, but here too the 1980 coup was a watershed. Large numbers of highly politicized and experienced organizers came to western Europe as refugees. The most successful were radical Sunni Muslim groups and Kurdish nationalists, among whom the PKK gradually became dominant. The Turkish regime meanwhile attempted to regain control of the migrant communities by bringing the major mosque federations under the control of the *Diyanet* organization. It was in response to these increased Sunni activities in Turkey that Alevis also began organizing themselves, after long having kept a low profile or even hidden their religious affiliation. Alevi associations were established, attracting many young Alevis who previously had been prominent in various leftist or Kurdish organizations. A few of the smaller leftist organizations were entirely Alevi in membership; these too now tended to emphasize their Alevi identity in combination with their Marxism–Leninism, and to think of the Alevis as a sort of nation, to the extent of speaking of Alevistan as their homeland.[45]

These activities abroad stimulated an Alevi revival in Turkey too, where the gradual political liberalization of the late 1980s made the establishment of religious and social Alevi associations possible. This was supported by those elements in the government that were anxious about the progress of the Islamist Welfare Party and the increasing popularity of the PKK among the Kurds. Various conciliatory gestures were made towards the Alevis, in a transparent effort to neutralize the community's alienation from the state and to prevent the PKK from making further inroads among the Kurdish (and Zaza) Alevis.[46]

In fact, the one region where the PKK has had great difficulties in establishing itself, and, where it always has had to compete with other radical political movements, was the heartland of Kurdish Alevism, Dersim (which comprises the present province of Tunceli and its neighbouring districts). The population of Dersim is almost exclusively Alevi and largely Zaza-speaking. Since at least the 1960s, Dersim had always been more inclined towards the radical left than to Kurdish nationalism. The PKK, which had its origins in the Turkish left, was initially Marxist and militantly anti-religious but had in the late 1980s adopted a conciliatory attitude towards Sunni Islam, in a successful attempt to gain more grassroots support in the Sunni regions. This obviously did not help to make the party more popular among the Alevis, and it may even have strengthened Alevi particularism. A wave of purges in PKK ranks in the early 1990s, in which a popular Dersimi disappeared, further fed Alevi suspicions of the PKK's intentions (although most of those purged were not Alevis!).

In the perception of the PKK, on the other hand, the entire Alevi revival was directly engineered by the state in order to sow division among the Kurds, and its protagonists were all considered as government agents. By the mid-1990s, the PKK had established its own Alevi association and was successfully promoting the view that Kurdish Alevism was different from Turkish Alevism because it was rooted in old Iranian rather than old Turkish religion and because it had always been in opposition to the state. The Kurdish Alevis remain torn between various claims to their identity, by Turkish and Kurdish nationalists, Alevi particularists and spokesmen for even narrower loyalties.[47]

The strengthening of Alevi distinctness under the influence of political developments is perhaps not so surprising; after all, Alevi communities have long – at least for the past few centuries – maintained a strict boundary with their Sunni neighbours of whatever language or tribal affiliation. What is relatively new is the emergence of a wider Alevi identity transcending the various Alevi communities, the efforts to reconstruct Alevi belief and ritual at the supra-local level, and a discourse on Alevism as a type of ethnicity. The emergence of Zaza nationalism, however, is something entirely new, and it is still forcefully opposed by numerous Zaza-speakers who stick to their self-definition as Kurds. To understand why it emerged, I believe we have to look again at the migrant communities in western Europe rather than at the situation in Turkey (unless one subscribes to the popular conspiracy theory that blames it all on the Turkish intelligence services).

In Turkey, where all local languages besides Turkish were banned (until 1991), it did not appear to matter much whether one originally was a Kurmanji- or a Zaza-speaker. In Europe, however, one of the issues with which Kurdish activists attempted to mobilize Kurdish migrant workers was the demand for mother-tongue education, i.e. for official recognition of the fact that Turkish is not the native language of every immigrant from Turkey, and for the acceptance of Kurdish as one of the mother tongues taught to immigrants' children in school. This faced the Zaza-speakers with an awkward dilemma: should they also demand that their children in German schools be taught Kurmanji instead of Turkish as their 'mother tongue'? Some in fact did, just as generations before them had always learned Kurmanji as the lingua franca in their region, but a certain uneasiness remained. This was clearly an issue on which the interests of Zaza-speakers and Kurmanji-speakers were not identical.

A related issue that contained the seeds of conflict was the language to be used in Kurdish journals published in Turkey, especially in European exile. Several journals appeared during the 1960s and 1970s, and most of them were exclusively in Turkish, with at the most an occasional poem in Kurdish.[48] In the late 1970s, a few periodicals ventured to publish entirely or largely in Kurdish – which usually meant that each issue was confiscated and the editors prosecuted. One of these publications, the short-lived cultural magazine *Tirêj*, was also the first significant modern Kurdish journal to have a small section in Zaza.[49] After the 1980 military coup, Kurdish publishing activities were no longer possible in Turkey, but writers and journalists carried on in European exile, especially in Sweden. Various Kurdish cultural institutes were established and, from the mid-1980s on, there was a true revival of Kurdish literature in Europe.[50]

The first serious Kurdish literary journal in Europe, published by the Kurdish Institute in Paris, had sections in the major dialects Kurmanji and Sorani (written in Latin and Arabic script, respectively). The entire Kurdish intelligentsia recognized that there is not a single standard Kurdish dialect and that the geopolitical division of the Kurds could be overcome only by using both major dialects. The journal had, moreover, a third section in Zaza, which proved more controversial.[51] Certain influential Kurdish nationalists were fiercely critical of the effort to develop Zaza as a written language. The arguments they used – for the sake of unity and progress, and to prevent enemies from breaking up the nation – were not unlike those with which Turkey has opposed the use of Kurdish.

Such debates on the status of the Zaza language and the desirability of its development or demise had a strong impact in the small circle of Zaza intellectuals in exile and caused a parting of minds. Many continued perceiving themselves as Kurds but demanded recognition of their distinct identity within the wider Kurdish nation. Others distanced themselves from Kurdish nationalism altogether and gradually began speaking not only of Zaza as a different language but of the Zaza speakers as a distinct people. In the late 1980s, the first Zaza journal was published, and it was emphatically non-Kurdish. It carried articles in Zaza, Turkish and English but not in Kurdish, it spoke of the Zazas as a separate people, whose identity had too long been denied not only by the Turkish state but by the Kurds as well, and it coined the new name of Zazaistan for the ancient homeland of this nation.[52]

This journal appears to have had only a very small circle of readers initially, but precisely because it met with very angry Kurdish reactions, its thesis that the Zazas are a doubly oppressed people gained credibility, and gradually growing numbers of Zazas were won over to its views. There appears not to be an organized Zaza nationalist movement yet, but publishing activities, both political and scholarly, have gone on increasing.[53] More recently, however, the debate as to whether the Zazas are a distinct people or not has abated. There is now a vigorous literary production in Zaza, most of it published in Europe, which by and large simply avoids the question of Zaza versus Kurdish ethnicity. Several of the leading authors have maintained their affiliation with Kurdish political and cultural associations. The struggle for recognition of Zaza as a distinct subculture – or, rather, set of subcultures – appears to have been won.[54]

Conclusion

During the 20th century, Kurdish ethnicity has been affected by a variety of social, economic and political factors: nation-building policies of Turkey, Iran, Iraq and Syria, improved communications, mass education and mass literacy (at least in the language of the state), increased geographical and social mobility, four decades of political and military struggle by Kurdish nationalist parties, the destruction of much of traditional village life, and the emergence of a significant, highly educated and vocal Kurdish diaspora. Most of the Kurds have become more integrated socially and economically into the states in which they live, but this has not had the effect of weakening Kurdish ethnicity.

It is true that ethnicity became to some extent a matter of personal choice. Some early 20th-century personalities, such as Ziya Gökalp and Shükrü Sekban, were aware of this possibility of choosing one's ethnic identity and advocated opting for Turkish identity, which they believed offered greater possibilities for progress.[55] The government of Turkey and, to a lesser extent, those of Iraq and Iran later exerted various forms of pressure to persuade Kurds and other minority groups to align with the dominant ethnicity of the state. These efforts were partially successful; many Kurds were assimilated and the Kurds of Iraq, Iran and Turkey who did not assimilate are nevertheless more different from one another than their great-grandparents were.

It was precisely this process of integration into non-Kurdish states, however, that also strengthened an awareness of an overarching, common identity among Kurds from different regions, dialects and creeds – without, however, wiping out the boundaries between these subgroups. A significant 'vertical' integration into the Kurdish *ethnie* has taken place: non-tribal peasant communities that in the past were not considered as Kurds proper are now to all intents and purposes parts of the Kurdish *ethnie*, and even some formerly Christian communities have become assimilated. There is a large educated middle class and a public sphere that partly overlaps with the Turkish, Persian and Iraqi–Arabic public spheres. Kurdish intellectuals have produced the symbolic markers of Kurdish ethnicity: works of historiography, linguistics, folklore studies and, most of all, poetry and prose literature. Political movements have had the effect of sharpening the ethnic boundaries separating the Kurds from the dominant ethnic groups in their states.[56]

At the same time, however, internal divisions among the Kurds have not disappeared and some internal ethnic boundaries appear in fact to have become more significant during the past decades. Improved communications and increased contacts between Kurds from different regions and of different subcultures have certainly not led to a more homogeneous Kurdish culture. Not only have the Kurds in general become more aware of being Kurds, but the same is true of distinct subgroups among the Kurds, as well as those that have an even more ambivalent relationship with Kurdish ethnicity. The tolerance of pluralism in Kurdish society has increased, however, also among Kurdish nationalist politicians. Even so centralist and authoritarian a party as the PKK has never propagated a unified Kurdish culture but has, to the contrary, celebrated diversity, establishing separate daughter organizations for each significant subgroup or minority and giving all of them space in its print and electronic media. The awareness has grown that Kurdish society represents a mosaic, of which not all components identify equally strongly with the whole, and of which the outer boundaries may occasionally shift – but which will always remain a mosaic.

Notes

1. An earlier version of this chapter appeared in French as 'Nationalisme kurde et ethnicités intra-kurdes', *Peuples Méditerranéens*, no. 68–9 (1994), pp. 11–37.

2. Martin van Bruinessen, 'Genocide of Kurds', in Israel W. Charny (ed.), *The Widening Circle of Genocide* [= *Genocide: A Critical Bibliographic Review*, vol. 3] (New Brunswick, NY: Transaction Publishers, 1994), pp. 165–91.

3. 2,219,547 people mentioned Kurdish (Kurmanji) as their mother tongue, another 1,753,161 as their second language. The latter number may include many Zaza speakers: 150,644 gave Zaza as their first language, and 112,701 said they spoke it as a second language. For a sophisticated analysis of the ethnic data contained in the censuses from 1935 to 1965 and an extrapolation to 1990, see: Servet Mutlu, 'Ethnic Kurds in Turkey: A demographic study', *International Journal of Middle East Studies*, 28 (1996), pp. 517–41.

4. In the province of Tunceli (former Dersim), for instance, which is predominantly Zaza-speaking, the 1965 census registered only seven native Zaza speakers among a total population of over 150,000; around half said their mother tongue was Kurdish.

5. Martin van Bruinessen, 'Kurdish Society, Ethnicity, Nationalism and Refugee

Problems', in: Philip G. Kreyenbroek and Stefan Sperl (eds), *The Kurds: A contemporary overview* (London: Routledge, 1992), pp. 33–67.

6. We also find Kurdish tribes mentioned as far away from this region as western Anatolia, eastern and north-eastern Iran, but all of these tribes retained memories of their ancestors migrating there from the said region. A good overview of the tribes included among the Kurds a century ago is: Mark Sykes, 'The Kurdish Tribes of the Ottoman Empire', *Journal of the Royal Anthropological Institute*, 38 (1908), pp. 451–86.

7. V. Minorsky, 'Les Origines des Kurdes', *Actes du XXe congrès international des orientalistes* (Louvain, 1940), pp. 143–52.

8. D. N. MacKenzie, 'The Origins of Kurdish', *Transactions of the Philological Society*, 1961, pp. 68–86. MacKenzie is a trained linguist (Minorsky was not), but his conclusions are based on his determination of a small number of isoglosses, and it is not impossible that another selection of isoglosses might have yielded different results.

9. These examples are taken from E. J. Hobsbawm, *Nations and Nationalism since 1780* (Cambridge University Press, 1990), pp. 60–1.

10. It is sometimes claimed by speakers of Kurmanji that they understand Zaza without effort. They probably mean that they recognize single words, which is not surprising. Asking such persons to translate even a single line from an oral or written Zaza text usually results in great embarrassment.

11. On the various religions in Kurdistan see: Martin van Bruinessen, 'Religion in Kurdistan', *Kurdish Times* (Brooklyn, NY), vol. 4, no. 1–2, 1991, pp. 5–27 and 'Introduction: The Kurds and Islam', *Les Annales de l'autre islam*, no. 5 (1998), pp. 13–35, both reprinted in *Mollahs, Sufis and Heretics: The role of religion in Kurdish society. Collected articles* (Istanbul: The Isis Press, 2000); Philip G. Kreyenbroek, 'Religion and Religions in Kurdistan', in: Christine Allison and Philip G. Kreyenbroek (eds), *Kurdish Culture and Identity* (London: Zed Books, 1996), pp. 85–110; idem, 'On the Study of Some Heterodox Sects in Kurdistan', *Les Annales de l'autre Islam*, no. 5 (1998), pp. 163–84.

12. Wolfgang Rudolph, 'Einige hypothetische Ausführungen zur Kultur der Kurden', *Sociologus*, 9 (1959), pp. 150–162; Wolfgang Hütteroth, 'Beobachtungen zur Sozialstruktur kurdischer Stämme im östlichen Taurus', *Zeitschrift für Ethnologie*, 86 (1961), pp. 23–42.

13. Fredrik Barth, 'Pathan Identity and its Maintenance', in: Fredrik Barth (ed.), *Ethnic Groups and Boundaries* (Boston: Little, Brown & Co., 1969), pp. 117–34. Barth's view, based on these and similar observations, that the identities of ethnic groups are not determined by their cultures but by the boundaries separating them from others will be considered at greater length below.

14. See the discussion of these non-tribal groups in: Martin van Bruinessen, *Agha, Sheikh and State: The social and political structures of Kurdistan* (London: Zed Books, 1992), pp. 105–21.

15. See on this subject the excellent study by Amir Hassanpour, *Nationalism and Language in Kurdistan, 1918–1985* (San Francisco: Mellen Research University Press, 1989).

16. Interesting observations on President Wilson's reckless use of the concept of self-determination are made in Senator Daniel Patrick Moynihan's *Pandaemonium: Ethnicity in International Politics* (Oxford University Press, 1993), Chapter 2 ('On the "self-determination of peoples"').

17. In his first and best-known article on the subject ('Marxism and the National Question', written in 1912–13), Stalin defined the nation as '*a historically constituted, stable*

community of people, formed on the basis of a common language, territory, economic life, and psychological make-up manifested in a common culture'. In his later writings on the subject (collected in: Joseph Stalin, *Marxism and the National–Colonial Question*. San Francisco: Proletarian Publishers, 1975), he never endeavoured to formulate a more sophisticated definition.

18. In the 1960s and 1970s, however, Kurdish activists from neighbouring Iran, Turkey and Syria regularly visited or came to stay in the 'liberated areas' of Iraqi Kurdistan. In the 1970s, both the Barzanis and the Talabani group, moreover, established special relationships with Kurdish sister organizations in Turkey and Iran, thereby also exporting their rivalries. The aim of this cooperation was to support the struggle of the Iraqi Kurds, not to organize pan-Kurdish activities.

19. Martin van Bruinessen, 'Turkey, Europe and the Kurds after the Capture of Abdullah Öcalan', in: van Bruinessen, *Kurdish Ethno-nationalism versus Nation-building States. Collected articles* (Istanbul: The Isis Press, 2000), pp. 277–88.

20. Fredrik Barth, 'Introduction', in: Barth (ed.), *Ethnic Groups and Boundaries* (Boston: Little, Brown & Co., 1969), pp. 9–38.

21. Faruk Demirtas, 'Bozulus hakkinda', *Ankara Üniversitesi Dil ve Tarih-Cografya Fakültesi Dergisi*, 7 (1949), pp. 29–60; Tufan Gündüz, *Anadolu'da Türkmen asiretleri: Bozulus Türkmenleri (1540–1640)*. Ankara: Bilge Yayinlari, 1997.

22. Numerous tribes referred to as 'Türkman Ekradi' or 'Ekrad Yörükani' are listed in: Cevdet Türkay, *Basbakanlik arsivi belgeleri'ne göre Osmanli Imparatorlugu'nda oymak, asiret ve cemaatlar* (Istanbul: Tercüman, 1979).

23. Mark Sykes, 'The Kurdish Tribes of the Ottoman Empire', *Journal of the Royal Anthropological Institute*, 38 (1908), p. 473. The situation has changed, however: most Mahallami still living in the region consider themselves as Arabs rather than Kurds, but many of those who migrated to Lebanon in the mid-20th century still tend to identify themselves as Kurds vis-à-vis their Arab neighbours.

24. See e.g., Sykes, 'The Kurdish tribes', pp. 469, 473–4.

25. Thus the population statistics for the province of Ma'muret el-'Aziz (which included Dersim, Harput and Malatya), compiled from Ottoman yearbooks (*salname*) by Cuinet, list 'Muslims', 'Kizilbash' and 'Kurds' as the major categories, besides various Christian denominations. The 'Muslims' probably include non-tribal peasants as well as most of the urban population, irrespective of language. See: Vital Cuinet, *La Turquie d'Asie. Géographie administrative*, tome II (Paris: Leroux, 1892), pp. 322ff.

26. For examples see my *Agha, Shaikh and State*, pp. 107, 117–8.

27. The name *kurd* in fact may originally have referred to nomadic tribalism rather than a linguistically defined 'ethnic' identity. Medieval Arabic authors occasionally apply such labels as 'Arab Kurds' to nomadic groups that appear to have no relation to the present, ethnically defined Kurds.

28. It is significant that Ziya Gökalp, in his study of Kurdish tribes (written between 1920 and his death in 1924, but not published until 1975), includes the Zaza speakers among the Kurds. Ziya Gökalp, *Kürt asiretleri hakkinda sosyalojik tetkikler* (Istanbul: Sosyal Yayinlar, 1992).

29. Ziya Gökalp, *Türklesmek, Islamlasmak, Mu'asirlasmak* ('Turkicization, Islamization, Modernization'). This text was published as a book in 1918 but it contains materials first published in the journal *Türk Yurdu* from 1913 on.

30. Martin van Bruinessen, *Agha, Shaikh and State*, pp. 275–81; Ismail Göldas, *Kürdistan Teali Cemiyeti* (Istanbul: Doz, 1991); Janet Klein, *Claiming the Nation: The Origins and Nature of Kurdish Nationalist Discourse: A study of the Kurdish press in the Ottoman Empire* (MA thesis, Near Eastern Studies, Princeton University, 1996);

Hakan Özoglu, "'Nationalism' and Kurdish Notables in the Late Ottoman–Early Republican Era", *International Journal of Middle East Studies*, 33 (2001), pp. 383–409.

31. Later, in the 1930s, the Kurdish nationalist association in exile, Khoybun, idealized Yezidism as the one truly Kurdish religion, but it did not have prominent Yezidi members either. (Some of my informants claim that Haco, the chieftain of the Hevêrkan tribe and a Khoybun member, was a Yezidi, but he was not openly so, and his descendants vehemently deny it).

32. Kurdish nationalists have always claimed that Gökalp was really a Kurd. More recently it has been claimed that he was a Zaza. See: Zilfi Selcan, *Zaza milli meselesi hakkinda* (Ankara: Zaza Kültürü Yayinlari, 1994), p. 3. Both claims are based on the fact that Gökalp's family originated from the district of Çermük. For Gökalp's ambivalent relation with his possible Kurdish roots, see: Rohat, *Ziya Gökalp'in büyük çilesi Kürtler* (Istanbul: Firat Yayinlari, 1992).

33. Anthony D. Smith, *The Ethnic Origins of Nations* (Oxford: Blackwell, 1986); idem, 'The Origins of Nations', *Ethnic and Racial Studies*, 12 (1989), pp. 340–367; idem, *National Identity* (London: Penguin Books, 1991). These works are clearly indebted to the seminal work by Ernest Gellner, *Nations and Nationalism*, but much richer in concrete historical description.

34. In his *National Identity* (p. 14), Smith gives the following definition of the nation: *'a named human population sharing an historic territory, common myths and historical memories, a mass, public culture, a common economy and common legal rights and duties for all members'.*

35. There are insightful observations on this subject in: Serif Mardin, 'Center–periphery Relations: A key to Turkish politics?', *Daedalus,* 102 (1973), pp. 169–90.

36. Abbas Kelidar (ed.), *The Integration of Modern Iraq* (London: Croom Helm, 1979); Philip C. Salzman, 'National Integration of the Tribes in Modern Iran', *Middle East Journal*, 25 (1971), 325–336.

37. In various parts of Kurdistan there are communities that retain a memory of having been Armenian or Nestorian. Some of these already converted before the 1915 massacres, others converted thereafter, apparently in order to save themselves from genocide or expulsion. These communities speak Kurdish, and some may have had Kurdish as their mother tongue even before conversion.

38. Thus some chieftains of the large Alevi tribe Koçgiri of western Dersim (presently the Zara district of Sivas province) in 1920 and 1921 wrote letters to the Kemalist National Assembly demanding autonomy on the ground that they were Kurds. This led to the first Kurdish rebellion against the Kemalist movement. See: M. Nuri Dersimi, *Kürdistan tarihinde Dersim* (Halep: Ani Matbaasi, 1952), p. 129; Hans-Lukas Kieser, 'Les Kurdes alévis et la question identitaire: le soulèvement du Koçgiri-Dersim (1919–21)', *Les Annales de l'autre Islam*, 5 (1998), pp. 279–316, especially 299–303.

39. This was the option apparently chosen by the Alevi tribes Khormek and Lolan of the Varto district, which actively fought against Shaikh Sa'id's Kurdish (and Sunni Muslim) rebellion in 1925. The Khormek chieftains' view of the events, with their assertion of having real Turkish origins, are given in: M. Serif Firat, *Dogu illeri ve Varto tarihi* (Ankara, 1945 and numerous reprints). The self-view of the Lolan elite as 'real Turks' is expressed in: Burhan Kocadag, *Lolan oymagi ve yakin çevre tarihi* (Yalova, privately published, 1987).

40. The Iraqi Constitution recognizes two nationalities, Kurds and Arabs, as well as unspecified minorities. In practice, however, the government considers all minorities

as Arabs. In 1987, on the eve of the genocidal *Anfal* campaign, the Iraqi Ba'ath regime carried out a national census in which everyone had to indicate whether he/she was a Kurd or an Arab, the only two self-definitions permitted. The Yezidis and many Assyrian Christians chose to be Kurds; Middle East Watch believes that this 'betrayal of the Arab nation' was the reason for the mass extermination of Yezidis and Assyrians who gave themselves up to the Iraqi army in the aftermath of the *Anfal* campaign. See: Middle East Watch, *Genocide in Iraq: The Anfal campaign against the Kurds* (New York: Human Rights Watch, 1994), pp. 312–7.

41. The Faylis were until the 1970s a large and prosperous Shi'i community of west Iranian descent, most of whom lived in Baghdad and other large cities in eastern central Iraq. There is a Fayli dialect, related to southern Kurdish and Lori, but many Faylis speak only Arabic. Most Faylis had no Iraqi citizenship, although they had lived in Iraq for generations. In the 1970s and 1980s, over 100,000 Faylis were expelled to Iran. See: Monir Morad, 'Kurdish Ethnic Identity in Iraq', in: Turaj Atabaki and Margreet Dorleijn (eds), *Kurdistan in Search of Ethnic Identity* (Utrecht: Houtsma Foundation, 1990), pp. 70–8; and Ali Babakhan, *Les Kurdes d'Irak: leur histoire et leur déportation par le régime de Saddam Hussein* (Paris: privately published, 1994). In the mid-1970s, several Faylis held leading positions in the Iraqi Kurdish movement and rich Faylis made significant contributions to financing the movement.

42. This does not mean that these leaders enjoyed the support of the entire population, or even a majority, in their respective regions. The Sulaymania region, from which most PUK leaders hail and where this party has its strongest support, is but a part of the Sorani-speaking zone. Even in this region, support for the KDP is not negligible. The region of Erbil, which also is Sorani-speaking, long constituted a buffer zone between Sulaymania and Badinan, where both parties had influence but which neither could control. Since 1996, Erbil has been incorporated into the KDP territory.

43. Michiel Leezenberg, 'Irakisch-Kurdistan seit dem zweiten Golfkrieg', in: Carsten Borck et al. (eds), *Ethnizität, Nationalismus, Religion und Politik in Kurdistan* (Münster: Lit, 1997), pp. 45–78; David McDowall, *A Modern History of the Kurds*, revised ed. (London: I. B. Tauris, 2000), pp. 387–91.

44. On the clashes, see: Ömer Laçiner, 'Der Konflikt zwischen Sunniten und Aleviten in der Türkei', in: Jochen Blaschke and Martin van Bruinessen (eds), *Islam und Politik in der Türkei* (Berlin: Parabolis, 1989), pp. 233–254.

45. I first encountered the name Alevistan in the Turkish newspaper *Hürriyet* in 1976, in a report on subversive activities in Germany. Maoist enemies of the state allegedly conspired to divide Turkey into Kurdistan in the east, Alevistan in the centre, and a Sunni Turkish remnant in the west. In the 1980s there was an ephemeral ultra-left organization in Germany, *Kizil Yol*, which similarly proclaimed its intention to liberate Alevistan. Many Kurdish nationalists and leftists of other persuasions suspected that these were machinations by the Turkish intelligence services, designed to provoke a Sunni and Turkish nationalist reaction.

46. Martin van Bruinessen, 'Kurds, Turks and the Alevi revival in Turkey', *Middle East Report*, 200 (1996), 7–10 (reprinted in *Kurdish Ethno-nationalism versus Nation-building States*, pp. 31–42).

47. Martin van Bruinessen, "Aslini inkar eden haramzadedir!': The debate on the ethnic identity of the Kurdish Alevis', in: Krisztina Kehl-Bodrogi, et al. (ed.), *Syncretistic Religious Communities in the Near East* (Leiden: Brill, 1997), pp. 1–23.

48. The most complete survey of periodicals published by and for Kurds in Turkey is: Malmîsanij & Mahmûd Lewendî, *Li Kurdistana Bakûr û li Tirkiyê rojnamegeriya Kurdî (1908–1992)* (Ankara: Öz-Ge, 1992). It lists 65 periodicals published

between 1960 and 1980, many of them appearing semi-legally or illegally.

49. Only three issues of *Tirêj* could appear in Turkey in 1979 and 1980. The fourth and final issue was published in Sweden. There was in fact one earlier journal that published a few brief pieces – a song text, a folktale and a word-list – in Zaza. This was the short-lived *Roja Newé*, the first and only issue of which appeared in Istanbul in 1963 (see Malmîsanij & Lewendî, *Rojnamegeriya Kurdî*, pp. 159–61).

50. Discussed more extensively in: Martin van Bruinessen, 'Transnational Aspects of the Kurdish Question' (working paper, Robert Schuman Centre for Advanced Studies, European University Institute, Florence, 2000).

51. This magazine, *Hêvî/Hiwa*, began publication in 1983. Its Zaza section appeared under the responsibility of Malmîsanij, who had also written the Zaza contributions in *Tirêj*, and was later also to contribute Zaza material to various other journals. While continuing his efforts to preserve Zaza oral tradition and to win more respect for Zaza culture, Malmisanij was to firmly oppose Zaza separatism when this emerged.

52. The Zaza journal *Ayre* and its successor *Piya* were published monthly in Sweden from 1986 to 1991 by Ebubekir Pamukçu. The editor's own most substantial contribution to the journal was an analysis of the Dersim rebellion from a Zaza nationalist point of view, which later appeared as a book in Turkey: *Dersim Zaza ayaklanmasinin tarihsel kökenleri* (Istanbul: Yön, 1992).

53. The most substantial of these booklets is Zilfi Selcan, *Zaza milli meselesi hakkinda* (Ankara: Zaza Kültürü Yayinlari, 1994). The same author also wrote a PhD thesis on Zaza grammar: 'Grammatik der Zaza-Sprache. Nord-Dialekt (Dersim-Dialekt)' (Berlin: Wissenschaft & Technik Verlag, 1998). The most important Zaza nationalist journals of the 1990s are *Desmala Sure* and *Ware* (both published in Germany, and both no longer appearing).

54. There are now several cultural journals in Zaza, the leading one being *Vate* (published in Sweden and Germany since 1997), which has contributions from the three major Zaza subcultures of Dersim (Alevi), Palu and Siverek (both Sunni). Other publications are primarily associated with one of them. Several scholarly grammars and good dictionaries (of Dersim, Palu and Siverek Zaza) have been published, and there is now a modest book production in Zaza.

55. Gökalp developed this idea in a series of articles published in the journal *Küçük Mecmu'a* in 1922, which were reprinted as an appendix to his *Kürt asiretleri hakkinda sosyolojik tetkikler* (Istanbul: Sosyal Yayinlar, 1992). Sekban had been a Kurdish nationalist before publishing his call for assimilation. See: Dr. Chukru Mehmed Sekban, *La Question kurde: des problèmes des minorités* (Paris: Presses Universitaires de France, 1933). Turkish translations of this brochure, which were published for obvious political reasons, are not faithful to the original but constitute interesting material on a history of attempts to claim the Kurds as a Turkic people.

56. In an interesting paper, Daniele Conversi has attempted to show how ethno-national movements have deliberately used political violence as a boundary mechanism. He argues that recourse to violence is more likely where few cultural boundary markers such as language are available, and he presents the PKK, in which many leading activists did not speak Kurdish well, as an example: Daniele Conversi, 'Violence as an Ethnic Border. The consequences of a lack of distinctive elements in Croatian, Kurdish and Basque nationalism', in: Justo G. Beramendi et al. (eds), *Nationalism in Europe Past and Present* (Santiago de Compostela: Universidade de Santiago de Compostela, 1994), pp. 167–98.

The Kurds and Their 'Others':
Fragmented Identity and Fragmented Politics

Abbas Vali

Introduction

The Kurds constitute the largest stateless nation in the contemporary world. Some 30 million Kurds live in Kurdistan under the national jurisdiction of the four sovereign states of Turkey, Iran, Iraq and Syria, which in various ways deny Kurdish national identity and suppress its political and cultural manifestations by the force of arms. The division of Kurdistan after World War I and the consequent structural diversity of Kurdish societies, administered by different political and economic regimes, have deprived the Kurds of political unity and cultural cohesion. Kurdish political organizations and movements, proliferating in the divided Kurdistan since 1918, have assumed different forms and pursued different objectives, but opposition to the denial of Kurdish identity and resistance to the imposed 'national' identities remain the fundamental cause of Kurdish rebellions. This dialectic of denial and resistance defines the political form and character of Kurdish nationalism.[1]

Kurdish nationalism is the politics of the affirmation of Kurdish national identity. Kurdish national identity is a product of modernity, albeit a specific form of it, associated in a close and specific way with the institution of the modern nation-state.[2] It has its roots in the political and cultural processes and practices of the construction of the modern nation-state and national identity in the multi-ethnic and multi-cultural societies of Turkey, Iran, Iraq and Syria in the inter-war period. The denial of Kurdish ethnicity and ethnic and national identities was the necessary condition of these processes in these societies. But the emergent national states in these countries and the official nationalist discourses that were constructed to legitimize their authoritarian rule and hegemonist political culture varied substantially in form and character. Their structural dynamics charted diverse paths of modernization and development, with diverse effects on the general political and cultural processes of denial and exclusion of Kurdish identity in their respective national territories.[3] Kurdish national identity has borne the mark of this political and cultural diversity of the 'other'; it has been deeply fragmented since its inception.

This diversity of the 'other', however, defines not only the fragmentation of Kurdish national identity but also its specifically transnational character. The dialectic of denial and resistance assigns a specifically transnational character to Kurdish nationalism, which, given favourable regional conditions, may surpass the political and cultural fragmentation of Kurdish identity. But this has never been more than a theoretical possibility. For the transnational ethos of Kurdish nationalism, too, has its structural limitations in the internal conditions and diverse development of Kurdish societies. These conditions, most significantly the underdeveloped social structure and the weakness of the bourgeoisie in urban areas, coupled with the entrenched power of landlordism and tribalism in the countryside, have seriously debased the transnational character of Kurdish nationalism, effectively undermining its centripetal tendencies. Kurdish nationalism, too, remains deeply fragmented. Deprived of its structural, political and cultural unity, it is reduced to local autonomist movements ridden with parochial interests and clientelist relations.

Nationalism, Modernity, Identity and Reason

The persistent failure of Kurdish nationalism to transcend the structural limits of this political and cultural fragmentation, and its undignified metamorphosis into abortive regional autonomist movements, is rooted in the chronic weakness of civil society in Kurdistan, which is perpetuated by the violence of the 'other'. This weakness defines, more acutely than any other factor, the abyss separating nationalism from regional autonomy and 'ethnic collectivism', and is a poignant reminder of the bitter lesson of modern European politics, that there is a necessary link between civil society and nationalism: a thriving and active civil society is the 'condition of possibility' of the concept of popular sovereignty in modern society, ensuring its articulation in the democratic political process in the face of the centralizing tendencies of the modern state.[4] The practical logic of this originally western European lesson perhaps applies to the divided Kurdistan more clearly than anywhere else in the contemporary world, with the notable exception of the troubled lands of the post-communist Balkans, where civil society had been no less systematically undermined. Now, more than ever before in its history, Kurdish nationalism needs to be grounded in an active and growing civil society, not just because it has to overcome the centrifugal tendencies of a deeply fragmented politics but also, and more importantly, because it has to create a nationalist political culture to enable it to withstand the crushing force of four violently aggressive official nationalisms.

The autonomist movements that currently dominate the Kurdish political scene are neither willing nor able to create such a culture; on the contrary, they thrive on the persistent weakness of civil society in Kurdistan. Characteristically parochial in ethos, they only affirm the fragmented nature of Kurdish national identity; they cannot overcome it. In fact, when they are patronized, maintained and used in cross-border politics by neighbouring sovereign states against their own fragmented self, as is often the case in the region, the autonomist movements seriously obscure the political and cultural boundaries separating ethnic and national identities. They characteristically have an ambiguous identity, vacillating between nationalism and ethnicism, often changing form and direction in pursuit of parochial interests and 'immediate' political objectives. This ambiguity defines the discourse and practice of the autonomist movements, as evidenced by their farcical politics and tragic history. The ambiguous relationship of the autonomist movements to their respective 'others', on the one hand, and their conflict of interest with and opposition to the Kurds and Kurdish movements across the national borders, on the other, cannot but exacerbate the fragmentation and diversity of the Kurdish national identity.

Foreign patronage and internal clientelism, the two fundamental elements of Kurdish autonomist movements, are both opposed to Kurdish national identity. They feed on and bolster ethnic relations and ethnic identities in Kurdistan, perpetuating the structural weakness and cultural backwardness of Kurdish nationalism. The periodic rise and demise of the autonomist movements in parts of Kurdistan testifies to this political truth. But beyond the retarding effects of the autonomist movements on the structural development and cultural formation of Kurdish nationalism, their persistence as the dominant mode of expression of Kurdish identity seems to point to a more grim conclusion; it looks as if modernity has bypassed Kurdish politics altogether.

This conclusion derives from the internal logic of the stagnant politics pursued by the autonomist movements in contemporary Kurdistan. These movements are essentially 'reactive' rather than proactive, and, like all reactive politics, their dynamics are characteristically 'external'; they are located outside their geopolitical boundaries, in the power and capacity of the central governments to establish and exercise territorial centralism in Kurdistan. Hence they always rise and fall in inverse ratio to the power and capacity of their respective central governments. The specific internal logic and dynamics of autonomist politics are by no means new in Kurdish history; they have a long and well-established pre-modern ancestry. They are strictly in line with the 'reactive' nature and 'external' dynamics of the 'centre–periphery' politics that defined the relationship between the Kurdish principalities and their Persian and Ottoman overlords. In this sense, therefore, the fundamental ethos and characteristic features of Kurdish politics have hardly changed for nearly two centuries. This ominous historical continuity is not just in spite of modernity but in the face of it. It signifies the historical stagnation of Kurdish politics.[5]

Politics of difference

It would, however, be a grave theoretical oversight, as well as a political folly, to attribute the political specificity of Kurdish nationalism solely to the internal conditions of Kurdish societies. True, the power and persistence of pre-modern and anti-modern political and cultural forces and relations in the existing Kurdish societies account for the fragmentary character of Kurdish national identity, but only in part. A rapid survey of recent theoretical writing on the politics of identity reminds us that identity, national or otherwise, always presupposes difference and is inconceivable without it. Identity is a relationship of the self and the other in difference; it always entails the trace of the other, and is ever haunted by it. Never fixed or stable, it changes in response to the difference(s) that define(s) the identity of the 'other'.[6] Moreover, identities change according to the change in the system of difference(s) that defines this relationship. They are always relational.

The implication of this point for our argument is clear: the political specificity of Kurdish nationalism is also defined in part by the changing relationship of Kurdish identity to its 'others'. This relationship, which is already implicit in the dialectic of denial and resistance, is one of violence, of political exclusion and suppression of 'difference'. The perpetual suppression of Kurdish identity is the condition of the Kurds' 'otherness' in these societies, their position as strangers in their own homes. That the Kurds remain unrepresentable is the fundamental cause of their obsession with their identity. This dialectics of violence defines not only the ethos of Kurdish national identity, but also the modality of its relationship with its others. It assigns a specific character to Kurdish nationalism, setting it apart from classical nationalism in western Europe. For while classical nationalism in Europe was inaugurated by modernity and accompanied by the birth of civil society and democratic citizenship, Kurdish nationalism, precipitated by the denial of Kurdish identity, rests by contrast on the suppression of civil society and democratic citizenship in Kurdistan. It is modern politics that thrives on the suppression of the conditions of modernity in Kurdistan: a paradox characteristic of the politics of forced assimilation systematically practised by its others.

Nationalism and modernity

This paradox accounts for the ambiguous relationship between Kurdish nationalism and modernity, an ambiguity that clearly lies at the root of its political weakness. True, the structural conditions of Kurdish nationalism have not allowed it to appreciate the political and cultural achievements of modernity. This was so in the formative period of Kurdish nationalism and it holds true for today. The Kurdish nationalists' enthusiasm for and appreciation of modernity has seldom surpassed the limits of a positivist belief in modern science and technology, which, characteristically encapsulated in modernist propositions for social 'progress', easily overlooks the most radical function of 'reason' in modernity, that is, the critique of tradition, and in particular of traditional authority, political and religious. Hence the by now common, though still largely mute, ambivalence of the nationalist intelligentsia towards tradition and traditional authority, voiced, if at all, in the banal language of self-justification in the wake of the political–military defeats repeatedly suffered by the autonomist movements. This ambivalence is the logical corollary of the ambiguous relationship of the nationalist intelligentsia to modernity. They presuppose each other, running in tandem through the very core of nationalist discourse and undermining its internal cohesion.

Although the ambivalence of the nationalist intelligentsia towards traditional authority effectively emasculates 'political reason', it is by no means the only cause of the chronic weakness of modernity in Kurdish nationalist politics and culture. The violence of the 'other' and the suppression of difference and of civil society in Kurdistan also effectively undermines the political and cultural conditions of modernity. So the story is more complex than it seems: modernity did not bypass Kurdish nationalism; rather, it created it without affirming it in discourse or in practice. The paradoxical outcome of this historical process is still with us; we have Kurdish nationalists without Kurdish nationalism – a historical anomaly that is nevertheless true.[7]

Politics of denial

Here we are not, however, dealing with this historical anomaly but with the specific political and cultural process that created it, namely, the construction of the nation-state in Turkey, Iran, Iraq and Syria, which began soon after the second division of Kurdistan. This process assumed a different form in each one of these four cases, but its strategic objective everywhere remained the same: to construct states whose identity was defined by the collective identity of their populations. This was deemed essential for the legality and legitimacy of political power. Theoretically, political authority in the new states was constitutional and democratic; it was derived from the collective will of the people, not from the whim of the reigning despot. Constitutionally, the democratic doctrine of 'popular sovereignty' provided the juridical ground for the making of this modern identity, but the ensuing political and cultural processes were very different.

The identity of the new states, their assumed unity with their respective nations, was forged by military power and new 'official/national' ideologies. The process of territorial centralism that followed the formation of these states ensured that the popular will embodied in the executive and legislative authority was exercised throughout their designated territories uniformly and without regional and local opposition or insubordination. But the new states soon found out that the realization of their modern claims to authority and legitimacy required more than an effective control over their recognized 'national' territories. Modernity had shifted the traditional locus of political power.[8] Thus the exercise of effective control over territory became increasingly tied to the exercise of effective control over its population, the 'subjects/citizens' of the new state. In fact, the population became the strategic objective of political power, which sought to affirm that the state and the nation were not only coterminous but also indivisible. This assumed 'organic' unity of the nation and the state was simultaneously reiterated by official nationalisms, which became the ideological component of the processes of the construction of the nation-state in these entities. The official discourse held that the nation and the state were the same, that they had the same identity; they were both sovereign and indivisible. The will of the state and its capacity to rule signified the will and power of the nation, the conditions of its independent existence.

The processes of state formation in these countries were modern, as were their intended and unintended outcomes. It is the democratic identity of the state and the nation, the ruler and the ruled, that changes the strategic objective of political power. The modern state defines the identity of its citizens by targeting and suppressing 'difference', that is, ethnic and cultural difference, thus bringing them in line with the identity of the sovereign, the national identity. Modern national identity is usually, though not always, the ethnic identity of the majority writ large by politics. In this sense, therefore, the nation-state and statelessness are both products of modernity. They are the dialectical opposites of the same historical process.

Although the institution of nation-state and its associated political and cultural processes and practices are widely hailed as the most impressive achievement of modernity, statelessness and its consequences are seldom accorded the same privileged position in modern philosophical and political discourse. The stateless person is seen as a relic of the past fighting against modernity, or merely as an accident of modernity fighting against history; either way, the result is the same: the stateless and his/her claims cannot be represented in or by the political and philosophical discourse of modernity, at least not as politics.[9] In the political discourse of modernity, statelessness is conceived as a humanitarian issue, evoking compassion and mercy, on a par with famine, hunger and homelessness. This is because a consideration of statelessness as politics and the stateless as a 'political subject' immediately invokes the thorny issue of rights, which, in the political discourse of modernity, is intrinsically linked with the institution of the nation-state and national sovereignty. Little wonder, therefore, that the stateless have no modern political identity. The identity and the claims of the stateless are denied by the modern nation-state, which turns the stateless into the historical other of modernity. This leads us back to the plight of the Kurds and their fragmented identity.

The sovereign states that suppressed Kurdish identity claimed popular-democratic legitimacy, and their claim, like all universal claims of modernity, was rooted in the Enlightenment and capitalist production. But liberal culture and the capitalist relations of production were still fairly rudimentary when the violent processes of state formation started in these countries. This meant that the uniform identity of the nation and the state, presumed and asserted in their constitutions, had to be forged by the force of arms. In practice, therefore, the process was reversed. It was the emergent states that defined the identity of their respective nations – both the outer boundary and the inner core of their national identities – in uneven historical processes in which cultural relations almost invariably lagged behind political relations. Hence the ideological weakness of official nationalisms in Turkey, Iran and (later on) Iraq, which had to be bolstered by intensifying the use of political violence in the processes of construction of uniform sovereign nations and national identities in these countries.

This reversal of process, however, was by no means a unique feature of nationalism in these societies. On the contrary, the pivotal role of the modern state in the construction of the nation and national identity, much noted in contemporary scholarship, is the hallmark of nationalism worldwide. The nation is the 'political form' of modernity, but almost everywhere in the modern world it was beaten into shape by the state that also gave it its history and identity.[10] This universal truth of nationalism also means that the political form of modernity is universal, but only in its particularity; that is, the modern states that make modern nations and define their identities vary in form and character, and these variations are historically constituted by the articulation of pre-modern forces and relations in modern political and cultural processes and practices. The strategic use of the past is intrinsic to the political and cultural processes and practices of the construction of the nation and national identity, but it is never without a cost. The cost is particularly high when nationalism is obsessed with the past and mobilizes it in order to create a modern future. For this obsession with the past undermines the relationship of the nation to modernity. Ethnicity replaces political reason as the main, if not the sole, principle defining the boundaries of an integrated national space in which the business of government is conducted. This displacement of political reason by ethnicity is a perversion of modernity which, against a background of chronic economic backwardness, engenders monsters.

Perverted modernity

The sovereign nations that were thus constructed by the modern states in Turkey, Iran (and later on) Iraq and Syria were the political forms of this perverted modernity. Their relationship with modernity had been interrupted by authoritarian states that embodied reason. But reason driven by sovereign ethnicity could hardly create the necessary conditions for rationalization in their multi-ethnic and multi-cultural societies. No wonder, therefore, that their violent drive for secularization led to armed opposition by the Kurds, who quickly turned against their authoritarian strategies of modernization. The perversion of modernity had seriously undermined the socio-cultural space that mediates between modernization and secularization in society. It was this disarticulation of the strategies of modernization and secularization in the new 'national' political field that drove 'official reason' into a war against religion and tradition. The 'official reason' embodied in the new states was a pillar of their authoritarian rule. It was mobilized to legitimize their strategies of modernization and secularization, but in 'national' political fields defined by sovereign ethnicities. The result was the marginalization of non-sovereign/subordinate ethnicities, whose opposition to the new states was heavily coloured by religion and tradition. The early Kurdish rebellions in Turkey and Iran were precisely reactions against this marginalization. The modern states had constituted national political fields in which they were unrepresented and unrepresentable.

Nor was the crucial incongruity between politics and culture just a historical accident belonging to the infancy of these nation-states; it was, rather, a permanent feature of their political processes, having its corollary in the constitutional definition of citizenship in the emergent nation-states. The doctrine of popular sovereignty, which defined the nature of authority and legitimacy in the constitutions of these states, was seriously undermined by notions of citizenship, which bore the identity of their dominant ethnicity. Those who did not qualify as ethnic Turks, Persians or Arabs were also excluded from citizenship of the emergent national states unless they renounced/denied their own ethnic and cultural identities. Those who failed to do so were forced to comply, and comply they eventually did, though often after initial acts of resistance, insubordination and revolt. For them membership of the new states was far from being free or voluntary; it was sanctioned by political compulsion. In fact, there was, and still is, in the constitutions of these states an essential incongruity between the conditions of sovereignty and the conditions of citizenship. This gap between popular sovereignty and 'ethnic' citizenship is bridged by political coercion, the main regulator of the relationship between the sovereign and the Kurds in these four national states.

This last point is particularly instructive. It suggests that political coercion and violence will persist in Kurdistan insofar as the conditions defining the relationship between the Kurdish and the sovereign identities remain unchanged. The most important issue in this respect is the modern conception of political sovereignty enshrined in the constitutions of these states. This conception has defined the boundaries of the Kurdish and sovereign identities, informing the conduct of these states vis-à-vis their Kurdish communities. It entails a trans-historical view of political power, beyond the realm of concrete politics as 'management of conduct' in the 'relations of force' in society. The notion of politics informed by the sovereign conception of political power remains outside the shifting boundaries of the existing relations among the actual political forces; and hence remains insusceptible to their dynamics and change. It is detrimental to the conduct of good government. The conduct of these states, their government of the Kurdish communities, should therefore be effectively detached from the issue of sovereignty. The administration of the Kurdish communities should instead be treated as a political process, belonging to the general realm of power and administration of the citizens.

Sovereignty and citizenship

A few words of explanation are in order. The modern conception of sovereignty defines the identity and legitimacy of political power while remaining external to the conduct of the state. It entails a juridical–political principle for the codification of political power which presupposes no reference to civil society. The modern concept of sovereignty as such signifies a unified 'national political field' inhabited by individuals as 'unified subjects' whose identity is defined by the identity of political power, which is always uniform, fixed and ethnic. In principle, therefore, it recognizes no difference, and the existing political, economic and cultural differences and interests in civil society are either excluded from the 'national political field' or subsumed in the totalizing reason of the state. In both cases, however, the result is the same: the exclusion or suppression of identities that do not conform with the uniform ethnic identity of political power codified in the constitution, and hence the designation of their expressions in the national political field as unconstitutional and illegitimate. The conduct of political power geared to sovereignty leads to the '*etatization*' of civil society, inhibiting its growth and development.

Crucial in this respect is the concept of citizenship, which regulates the relationship of the individuals, groups and communities within civil society to political power.[11] The concept of citizenship associated with sovereignty always bears the ethnic identity of political power. It is the primary locus of the unifying functions of the state within the juridical framework of sovereignty, and hence the primary means of the exclusion of non-sovereign political and cultural identities from the political process, even if they express their demands for the recognition of their 'rights' in peaceful and constitutional ways. Insofar as sovereignty remains the fundamental principle of the conduct of politics in the modern state, the concept of citizenship cannot provide a basis for the articulation of the democratic rights and interests of the non-sovereign identities – individuals, groups and communities – in the 'national' political process. These identities, rights and interests, it was argued, have their roots in modernity, but no concept of modern politics that is derived from or associated with sovereignty can understand or explain the 'lived experience' of the non-sovereign in the juridical–political framework of the modern state. The paradox calls for an understanding, if not a solution.

Sovereignty, Governance and Civil Society: The Argument

The first step in this direction, this explanation suggests, is the implementation of radical constitutional reforms, whereby the prevailing 'ethnic' conceptions of citizenship are replaced by democratic notions of citizenship that exclude all ethnic, racial and religious or cultural qualification for membership of state and society. But this proposition is not effective in isolation; in fact, it will subvert its own theoretical premises if the proposed constitutional reforms do not at the same time include a radical redefinition of the uniform ethnic identity of political power in these states: that is to say, a redefinition of the relationship between government and the legal unity of the state, which in effect involves a redefinition of the objectives, methods and tasks of political power in these societies. This is imperative for the proposed constitutional reform to succeed. But the critique of the juridical unity of the concept of sovereignty points to another, more important condition, which lies at the root of the radical redefinition of the conduct of the state. This condition concerns the relationship between political power and civil society: the redefinition of the conduct of the state requires a new juridical framework for the codification of political power, which necessarily involves a reference to civil society. It must take into account its ethnic, racial and cultural diversity, ensuring effective representation for all groups in the juridical codification of political power.

A consideration of the specificity of civil society is of vital importance in the attempt to redefine the identity of political power and the conduct of the government in the modern state. It is, in this sense, the correlative of the conduct of modern government; an essential prerequisite of a radical departure from the increasing '*etatization* of society', perpetually reinforced by the discourse and practice of sovereignty, and the transition to the 'governmentalization of the state', which could ensure a genuine democratization of the political process in the modern state. For a redefinition of the identity and conduct of political power in terms of the political 'technology of government' requires a civil society capable of representing forms of ethnic subjectivity and difference as invariables of a democratic political process in which governmental tasks and objectives are the sole principle of political struggle and contestation.[12]

The above argument refers to the unique position civil society occupies in the definition of the functional limits and boundaries of political (sovereign) power in the modern state. This is because civil society signifies an entity that is located in the unifying framework of the legal regulations of the state but is inaccessible to its centralizing functions.[13] It is in this sense both 'internal' and 'external' to the modern state, a 'transactional' domain at the frontier of political power.[14] As such, the boundaries of civil society define the limits of the centralizing functions of political power, the range of their efficacy in the modern state, hence creating the crucial space for the government to deploy appropriate techniques for its conduct in pursuit of national security. The point, however, is that when the techniques of government involve a reference to civil society, they also involve a redefinition of the relationship between the subject and political power – that is, a redefinition of the rights and liberties usually associated with the concept of citizenship – which means that the freedom of the subject-population vis-à-vis the state becomes a central component of the predominant rationality of government, an essential condition of its conduct in society.[15] In this sense, therefore, civil society enables the government to address political problems without requiring forms of legitimacy that are derived from a prior obligation on the part of its subjects-citizens to obey its authority. In other words, the conduct of the government no longer requires sources of legitimacy outside its own functional efficacy.[16]

The argument for separating the Kurdish question from political sovereignty is, in effect, a quest to redefine the character of this question in the 'national' politics of these states. The transformation of the Kurdish question from a question of national security to a practical political issue in the daily conduct of the government, we have seen, above all requires a corresponding change in the identity of political power in these states, a proposition that is effectively inconceivable without reference to civil society and its pivotal role in the restructuration/reconstruction of the political process. The order of reasoning thus points to the political 'objectification' of civil society as both the means and the condition of the requisite transition from sovereignty to governmentality in these states.[17] The political objectification of civil society, in a manner discussed above, can ensure the autonomous rationality of government, in which the central question of how to govern, that is, of finding the appropriate techniques for dealing with problems of state-national security, can be posed and answered without invoking notions of authority and legitimacy associated with the concept of sovereignty.[18]

Civil society and Kurdish identity in Turkey and Iran

But what of the actual state of civil society in Turkey and Iran?[19] Is it mature enough to ensure such a transformation in the identity of political power? Debate on the nature and boundaries of civil society in Iran and Turkey indicates a wide range of opinion. The current arguments largely bear the mark of the political and cultural conditions that precipitated them, that is, the struggles for the democratization of the political process, which clearly involve redefinitions of the limits of political power and hence of the boundaries of civil society. In this sense, therefore, the arguments for civil society in Turkey and Iran are inseparable from the popular quest for the democratization of the political process: civil society is conceived as a means of delimiting the boundaries of political power, enhancing popular participation in the political process and ensuring democratic accountability. This relationship with democratization defines the political and theoretical contours of the debate on civil society. The competing conceptions of civil society and the attempts to define its character and boundaries are closely related to the strategies of democratization and mobilization and the forms of struggle that they involve.

The point is of particular importance in this context. For it means that the character and boundaries of civil society and its development and maturity would clearly depend on the outcome of the prevailing forms of struggle for democratization of the political process, which are contingent upon the changing balance of forces in the political field in Turkey and Iran. In other words, the politics of democratization that defines the contours and shifting boundaries of both political power and civil society is not only inseparable from the quest to redefine the identity of political power but identical with it. They constitute the two sides of the same process.

The strategic question in this respect is, therefore, how democratic are the quests for democratization of the political process in Turkey and Iran?

Or, in other words, how democratic are the arguments for civil society in Turkey and Iran? The answer to this question involves a swift survey of the conceptual formations of the current debates in Turkey and Iran. In view of the subject matter of this essay, the survey will be concerned particularly with the issues of ethnicity and ethnic and national difference in the democratic process. Whereas in Turkey ethnicity and the ethnic issue in non-official and semi-official discourse in the academy and the media are veiled references to the Kurdish question, in Iran the issue is more complex.

The case of Turkey

Arguments for civil society in Turkey vary widely in form and character. Nonetheless, they share common theoretical presuppositions. It is assumed that civil society and democratic order are interdependent; they are the conditions of the existence of each other – a mature democracy presupposes a mature civil society, and vice versa. This mutual interdependence is required to delimit the boundaries of political power and ensure public accountability, a condition necessary for the survival and development of both civil society and democratic order.

It is commonly agreed that there exists in Turkey a limited though quite vibrant civil society alongside a weak but functional democratic political process. A strong interventionist state and an aggressive nationalist ideology are held responsible for this mutual weakness of civil society and democratic process in Turkey, especially in view of a steady rise in the executive power of the state at the expense of the legislative and judiciary, precipitated by three successive military coups and the growing power of the military in national politics since 1960. The accent of the argument here is on the autonomy of civil society, perceived as an institutional field outside the juridical domain of state power, but increasingly violated by the expanding range and increasing efficacy of its centralizing functions within the Turkish society at large. The arguments for civil society, then, are arguments for the expansion and consolidation of the democratic process but within the juridical–political framework of Turkish sovereignty as codified in the 1980 constitution.[20]

The arguments for civil society in Turkey seldom exceed the confines of this framework, which, as we have seen, is the intersection of sovereignty and official Kemalist ideology. In fact, they mostly involve conceptions of political power, authority and legitimacy, which are intrinsic to Turkish sovereignty, and notions of political agency and practice, which are defined by the principles of Kemalist discourse. The commitment to secularism, the

Turkish nation-state and Turkish civilization required by the Kemalist and demanded by its civil and military guardians within and outside the state apparatuses in effect delineates the boundaries of the contemporary discourse on democratization and civil society. Kurdish and Islamic identities are thus by definition outside the domain of constitutional politics. They exist, if at all, as 'extra-political' issues requiring extra-political means of expression and solution. There is therefore a closure, a silence, in the discourses of democratization and civil society on the questions of Kurdish and Islamic identity, amounting to the denial/exclusion of these identities from such discourse and practice and justified within the normative framework of the constitution, which sanctions violence against the non-sovereign others. The persistence of this anti-democratic closure/silence and the legitimating of the denial of the difference and violence against the other confirm, above all, the practical truth of our theoretical argument: the development of civil society is inconceivable without changing the identity of political power. They are the two sides of the same process; they presuppose each other. A mature civil society implies democratization of the political process through which the change in the identity of political power in Turkey can be thought.

This general overview is by no means an exhaustive survey of the contemporary debate on civil society in Turkey. There are also a few, more radical contributions, which manage to break out of this normative framework, though only partially. For they go only as far as recognizing the necessity of including the Kurdish and Islamic identities in the discourse of civil society and democracy in Turkey, without taking into account the implications for either Kemalist ideology or the identity of political power in the Turkish polity. Hence recognition of the cultural identity of the Kurds and the associated cultural rights and liberties also forms the basis of their prescribed solution to the Kurdish question in Turkey. According to these arguments, political decentralization and a redefinition of the limits of political power thus suffice to ensure the democratic development of civil society. They are never extended to include the question of sovereignty and the identity of political power. Notwithstanding the radicalism of these arguments in the Turkish political scene, this shortcoming must significantly reduce their political import.[21]

There are different reasons for this shortcoming, both political and theoretical. There can be little doubt that political prudence and the fear of state persecution are major considerations in this regard, as is commitment to specific essentialist theoretical discourses, which remain oblivious to the relationship between civil society and the identity of political power.

The main reason, however, is the political ambivalence of the democratic intelligentsia towards Kemalism and its commitment not only to modernity but also to secularism and the rational organization of the state and society. This ambivalence, which is nurtured by the commitment of the democratic intelligentsia to modernity and the supremacy of reason, looms large in the contemporary democratic evaluation of Kemalism. It is no exaggeration to say that Kemalism continues to define the limits of democratic argument in Turkey, especially with respect to the Kurdish identity and rights.

Iran

Iran is composed of many non-sovereign ethnic communities; numerically the Azeri community is by far the largest of them, followed by the Kurdish community. In political terms, however, the Kurds continue to occupy the forefront of opposition to the sovereign identity, and the suppression of Kurdish identity has played a more important role in the construction and definition of the uniform Iranian national identity, at least since the collapse of the Azerbaijan republic in 1947, when Azeri nationalism lost its political cohesion and direction. It is thus justified, in political terms, to say that in contemporary Iran the discourse and practice of ethnic and national difference refers primarily to the Kurds and Kurdish identity.

In Iran the current debate on civil society has a different political context, conceptual framework and strategic objective. It is an important aspect of political factionalism and power struggle within the Islamic regime since the presidential elections in 1997, and a means of discussing the contending positions on the character of political authority, government and legitimacy in the Islamic Republic. The political specificity of the debate gives it an immediacy that is lacking in the Turkish equivalent. But as in Turkey, in Iran too the boundaries of the civil society debate are defined by the sovereign discourse, that is, political Islam, and more specifically radical political Shi'ism identified with the person of Khomeini and the revolutionary leadership.

The centrality of Islam and Islamic institutions and identity to the debate assigns a strategic character to it. This is mainly because political Islam defines not only the ethos of the regime but also the identity of political power in the Islamic Republic. But Islam and Islamic identity feature on two different levels in the current civil society debate in Iran: a general historical level and a specific political level. Although these two levels are not fully delineated, conceptually or politically, and mostly complement one another in the argument, they are nevertheless distinct in that they entail different notions of political power, authority and legitimacy, and hence deploying and privileging different definitions of the concept of civil society in the discourse.

On the general level the argument is historical and comparative. It is concerned mainly with the compatibility of Islamic juridical–political and cultural processes and practices with modern secular political and cultural processes and practices historically associated with the rise of civil society in the West. The underlying assumption, therefore, is that civil society is an aspect of modernity presupposing determinate discursive and non-discursive processes and practices, which are given to the histories of the modern Western societies. This assumption defines the historicist character and comparative perspective of the debate. Most arguments against the presence or the possibility of the development of civil society in Iran are informed by essentialist conceptions of Islam and modernity. These are perceived as incompatible if not mutually exclusive: Iranian society is essentially Islamic, and the uniform Islamic essence that defines the course and direction of its history cannot provide for the development of civil society, which is essentially a Western and hence alien institution. These essentialist arguments entail a very ambiguous notion of civil society, which is hardly explained, let alone conceptualized, in either Iranian or Western historical and political contexts.

But the essentialist Shi'i opposition to the concept of civil society is seldom confined to this argument alone. The comparative historical argument is more often than not compounded with another, strictly political, which derives its authority from Khomeini's doctrine of *Wilayat al-Faqih*, i.e. 'Governance of the Muslim Jurist', and the conceptions of government, power and sovereignty entailed in it. These conceptions are repeatedly invoked to oppose and reject the notions of political power, sovereignty and legitimacy historically and conceptually associated with the rise and development of civil society in the West. What actually warrants the essentialist rejection of civil society as non-Islamic and alien, however, is not so much its Western historical ancestry as its association with democracy and democratic governance, especially in the current phase of power struggle in the Islamic Republic. In the particular context of the Islamic Republic, the discourse of civil society questions the identity of political power; it is democratic. It is, above all, democracy and democratic rule that are at stake in the power struggle and in the political orientation of the contending forces within the regime and the society at large. This point is particularly noteworthy, for it testifies both to the strategic character of the concept of civil society and to its instrumentality in the current political conjuncture in Iran.

The arguments for civil society and the need to develop and expand its domain in the Islamic Republic, on the other hand, find it compatible with Islam. The advocates of civil society do not form a homogeneous bloc politically or ideologically; Islamists and secularists are grouped together in a broad reformist alliance, which is sustained by their common opposition to the hard-line Islamists identified with Khomeini's doctrine of *Wilayat al-Faqih*, and especially its insistence on the indivisible unity of the religious political authorities in the sphere of government and the unassailable supremacy of the Shari'a in the social and political organizations of the Islamic community.[22]

The secular intelligentsia almost invariably deploy the comparative historical framework, but their point of reference is mostly Iranian history rather than Islam. The latter, though remaining central to the argument, is taken to form only an aspect of the complex process of the historical development of Iranian society. Broadly speaking, in the secular argument civil society is variously conceived as an autonomous institutional ensemble outside the domain of political power but capable of delimiting its boundaries. The autonomy of civil society and its role in delimiting the boundaries of political power both presuppose a democratic political process, which is the essential condition of existence of civil society in the secular argument. The secular argument for civil society, in its various forms, is an argument for the democratization of the political process, but within a normative framework, which by definition excludes non-sovereign identities and rights. The secular critique of the Islamic political sovereignty, implicit or explicit, is an argument in favour of national Iranian sovereignty in which the ethnic, i.e. the Persian, identity of the sovereign is never questioned. The secular democratic discourse on civil society hardly includes any reference to ethnic difference and identity. It clearly affirms the Persian identity of political power, and its imposition on non-Persian identities in Iranian society is seen as unproblematic, not violating the democratic character of the proposed secular alternative.[23]

The Islamist protagonists of civil society in Iran adopt a different approach, which further confirms the strategic position of this concept in their reformist discourse. The Islamic reformists, both within and outside the government, use the concept of civil society to refer to the 'rule of law', which, from their point of view, is coterminous with democracy.[24] They also emphasize the autonomy of the civil institutions from the state and their role in delimiting the boundaries of political power, but they do not define the conceptual contours of the reformist discourse, which are heavily coloured by the notions of 'legality' and 'responsibility' of power. The Islamic reformist preoccupation with these notions is an indication of the nature of political struggle and the hegemony of hardliners in the state apparatuses in the Islamic Republic. For the reformist quest for 'legal and responsible government' is but a thinly disguised attack on the doctrine of *Wilayat al-Faqih*, the supreme principle for the organization of the state and politics advocated by their conservative adversaries. But despite its pivotal position in the debate, the concept of law remains rather ambiguous and little defined in the Islamic reformist discourse, especially with regard to the role of religion and religious authority in the process of legislation. The reformist argument for the 'rule of law' is couched in the most general terms, leaving its content almost entirely unspecified. Hence the ambiguous status of religious authority in the reformist conception of civil society.

Nonetheless, the reformist emphasis on the legality and accountability of political power, and especially its identification of the rule of law and responsible government with democratic order and constitutional government respectively, may help throw some light on the issue. The expositions of the institutional form and juridical–political processes of the rule of law, often attempted in the context of Western historical development, indicate that the concept of law in the Islamic reformist discourse is secular, predicated on the sovereignty of reason. It is also secular law that defines the character of political authority and the boundaries of political power in the reformist discourse. The protagonists of the reformist discourse invoke the constitutional law to refer, though in quite different ways, to the source and limits of political power. Although in a normative political framework this could be taken to account for the democratic character of the reformist discourse, in the Iranian context it is quite different. This is due mainly to the specificity of the constitution of the Islamic Republic.

The constitution of the Islamic Republic contains two different and diametrically opposed conceptions of political sovereignty and authority, each entailing different notions of the source and boundaries of political power: the divine and the popular–democratic.[25] This conceptual diversity not only undermines the political coherence of the Iranian constitution but also turns it into a highly strategic area for political contestation in the civil society debate. The divine conception of sovereignty, which underpins the doctrine of the *Wilayat al-Faqih*, essentially recognizes no limits to political power other than that which is prescribed by the Shari'a. Nor does it allow for the expression of difference – national, ethnic or socio-economic. Muslims are subsumed into the general category of the Umma, denoting a uniform community defined by faith. The divine conception of sovereignty therefore entails a conception of polity that is coterminous with society; it leaves no room for any conception of civil society.

The popular–democratic conception of sovereignty, on the other hand, entails a conception of political authority and power whose boundaries are defined by law, which is also the basic principle of the legitimacy of the state. It does therefore clearly provide for the existence of civil society, legally delineating its boundaries and protecting it against the centralizing functions of political power, but without being able to recognize or respect national or ethnic difference in society at large. This grave anomaly in the popular–democratic conception of sovereignty has been discussed in some detail in the preceding section of this essay and need not be repeated here. It suffices to say that the ethnic character of political power defines the boundaries of the democratic political process, thus marginalizing or excluding all non-sovereign national and ethnic differences from it. The non-sovereign nationalities and ethnicities are by the same token excluded from the juridical–political conditions of citizenship and hence from the democratic political process.

True, unlike the Turkish constitution, the constitution of the Islamic Republic recognizes ethnic difference; Iran is perceived as a multi-ethnic and multi-cultural society, and this perception unambiguously informs the relevant parts of the constitutional law. This amounts to the recognition of non-sovereign ethnic minorities in the Islamic Republic. But the notion of ethnic minority in the Iranian constitution is strictly cultural, designating a community of language, custom and tradition bound together by a common history. The ethnic community and its history are 'local'; they lack political and discursive autonomy, which, in the constitution, is accorded only to the sovereign, the Persian ethnicity. Thus, although ethnic identities are constitutionally recognized, they remain strictly local, and juridical–political relations play no role in defining their boundaries. They have no political rights vis-à-vis the sovereign, which define the means and conditions of their access to and participation in the constitutional political process. In the constitution of the Islamic Republic, the identity of political power is uniform and ethnic; Persian ethnicity defines the identity of the sovereign, the conditions of citizenship and hence the boundaries of the state and civil society.

The uniform ethnic identity of the sovereign and the citizen in the constitutions of the Kemalist Turkey and the Islamic Iran, though conceptualized differently and involving different discursive and political processes and practices, has important implications for the democratic ethos of the current debate on civil society. It indicates, above all, that the sovereign Turkish and Persian ethnicities that define the conditions of citizenship and political and cultural participation also specify the ethnic boundaries of civil society in these states. In so doing, they function as ethnic bars on civil processes and practices, excluding non-sovereign ethnic differences from the juridical–political boundaries of civil society. The existence of non-sovereign ethnic communities and identities in civil society is either completely denied, as is the case in Turkey, or recognized solely in cultural terms, as in Iran. In both cases, however, they have a non-civil existence, remaining outside the juridical–political boundaries of civil society in an extra-constitutional political space inhabited by force.

This excursion into the current debates on civil society in Turkey and Iran clearly illustrates the simple truth of the earlier theoretical argument regarding the retarding effects of the concept of sovereignty on the democratization of the political process in the modern state. The exclusion of non-sovereign identities and the associated political and cultural rights from consideration is a clear indication of the domination of these debates by the discourse of sovereignty – the hegemonic political discourse in Turkey and Iran since the formation of the modern state, perpetuated by the active consent of both the reformist and the conservative participants, who refuse to question the ethnic identity of political power in these societies. This consensus, which amounts at best to silence and at worst to denial of non-sovereign identities and their civil and democratic rights, is anti-democratic. It seriously undermines the radical thrust and democratic ethos of the civil society debates in Turkey and Iran. The civil and democratic political forces in Turkey and Iran must redefine the juridical–political boundaries of the debate; they must abandon their modern obsession with the pre-modern discourse of sovereignty.

Conclusion

This discussion suggests that the discourses of civil society and democratization in Turkey and Iran must be predicated on a democratic quest for changing the ethnic identity of political power, to ensure the representation of non-sovereign identities and rights in political, social and cultural processes. This is essential if civil society is to be representative of difference and dissent, capable of bolstering the democratic process and ensuring popular participation and accountability. But the quest to change the identity of political power is also the central plank of the proposed solution to the Kurdish question in Turkey and Iran. In both cases the theoretical proposition results from a radical critique of the concept of sovereignty, and hence the demand for a radical constitutional reform involving the de-ethnification of the conditions of citizenship. This common theoretical foundation inextricably ties the Kurdish question to the development of civil society and the democratization of political process in Turkey and Iran. It thus points to a common political direction which should be recognized and appreciated.

In the present circumstances in Kurdistan, in the aftermath of the repeated failure of the autonomy plans, there are many who would readily recognize this common direction and appreciate its political import, but only a few would wish to support it publicly. To many who are genuinely interested in the proposed political solution, the underlying theoretical proposition is sound but highly impractical. The reasoning is sad but convincing: it seems highly unlikely that the four sovereign states ruling the divided Kurdistan would ever want or dare to detach Kurdish identity from the conditions of political sovereignty, at least not insofar as their prevailing official nationalist/statist discourses and the requisite 'national' institutions remain in force. This is because Kemalism, Khomeinism and Ba'athism, despite their fundamental differences, all insist on the denial of Kurdish national identity as a prerequisite of their national sovereignty. This view is intrinsic to their self-perceptions as sovereign and independent states. It is manifest in the distrust, fear and paranoia that have thus far endorsed political violence against the Kurds and rejected their demand for a political solution. But the current alternative to the recognition of the Kurdish national identity, in so far as it is an alternative at all, is no less utopian. The military solution variously practised by these states is irrational and unsafe. It is less likely to ensure their 'national sovereignty', especially when democratic process and civil society in their sovereign domains are still weak and underdeveloped.

Notes

1. Before 1514 the bulk of the territory known as Kurdistan was administered by the successive regimes ruling Iran. This had been the case at least since Buyid times in the 10th century AD, when the territory was referred to by its current name and its geographical limits within the shifting boundaries of the state were delineated. In 1514 the newly founded Safavid state lost the greater part of its Kurdish territory to

its powerful neighbour, the Ottoman state, and this division, which was ratified in the Zahab treaty of 1639, remained in force until the dissolution of the Ottoman Empire in 1918. During this period, the Ottoman Kurdish territory was ruled indirectly from Istanbul through a tributary structure involving the semi-autonomous Kurdish principalities; these eventually fell victim to the process and practice of territorial centralism that followed the advent of state-managed modernization, culminating in the Tanzimat reforms of 1837. By the late 1870s the last Kurdish principality had fallen to Ottoman centralism and the Ottoman state was in full control of its Kurdish territory. In Iran, too, the semi-autonomous Kurdish principalities, which had sustained the military and fiscal structures of an uneasy tributary relationship with the state for nearly four centuries, succumbed to the combined force of internal decay and the growing external pressures from the declining Qajar state in need of revenue. The destruction of the Kurdish principalities by the Ottoman and the Qajar states seems to have had the same effect on the political and administrative structures in Kurdistan before 1918: in both cases the power of the princes was replaced by the authority of the religious leaders, who were closely associated with the Sufi orders, the tribal lineage and landed property, and who played a decisive role in the organizational structure of the Kurdish movements for the decades to come (notably Sheikh Ubaydallah's movement in 1880–82). Sheikhs and aghas continued to dominate the leadership of the Kurdish movements after 1918, when the eastern possessions of the Ottoman Empire were partitioned by Britain and France, and parts of the Kurdish territory were attached to the newly created states of Iraq and Syria. Uprisings led by Sheikh Said (1925) and Sheikh Reza (1937) against the Kemalist state in Turkey, the rebellions of Sheikh Mahmoud (1920s) and Mullah Mustafa Barzani (1940s, 1960s, 1970s) against the Iraqi state, and Semko's rebellion (1920s) and the movement culminating in the Mahabad republic (1947) in Iran all show this specific, though quite uneven articulation of religion, tribal lineage and landownership in the leadership of the Kurdish movements before recent times. This structural specificity of Kurdish movements has changed significantly in Turkey and Iran since the 1970s, largely owing to growing urbanization, the development of commodity production and the modern middle class, and the influence of secular ideologies, especially Marxism–Leninism: the emergence of the Kurdistan Workers' Party (PKK), the Socialist Party of Kurdistan and the People's Democractic Labour Party (HADEP) in Turkey, as well as of a socialist leadership in the Kurdistan Democratic Party of Iran (KDPI) and the formation of the Revolutionary Association of the Toilers of Kurdistan (KSRKI, now CPI) in Iranian Kurdistan, all testify to this shift. In Iraqi Kurdistan, by contrast, the formation of the predominantly urban, socialist-oriented Patriotic Union of Kurdistan (PUK) in the 1960s has not been able to dislodge Barzani's Kurdish Democratic Party (KDP) or to undermine its power in its traditional constituencies of support, where tribal lineage and religious affiliation have proved remarkably resistant to external influence and change. General histories of the Kurds and Kurdistan are scarce, both in European and Middle Eastern languages. For informed but highly descriptive modern political histories see: W. Jwaideh, 'The Kurdish Nationalist Movement: Its origins and development' (PhD dissertation, Syracuse University, 1960), D. McDowall, *A Modern History of the Kurds* (London: I. B. Tauris, 1996).

2. Modernity is an elusive concept, remaining ambiguous despite its wide currency in contemporary post-Marxist and post-liberal discourse. This ambiguity is largely due to the association of the concept with the philosophical foundations of post-structuralism and post-modernism, which are diverse and heterogeneous. They

assume or propound different conceptions of modernity informed by their critical evaluation of the conditions of the construction of the 'subject' and 'subjectivity' in Western political and philosophical discourse since the Renaissance. These conditions vary widely but are defined, in various ways, by the triumph of 'reason' and its intrinsic relationship to 'freedom'. The relationship between reason and freedom has been a central theoretical presupposition of the discourse of modernity, especially since the Enlightenment, when it was inextricably linked with the idea of 'progress'. Thus the current concepts of modernity, despite their variations, share a common trait: they signify the 'sovereignty of reason' in discourse and practice, emphasizing its intrinsic link with freedom and progress in the domains of history, politics and culture. Hence the critical association of modernity with modernism as both the ideology and strategy of an 'endogenous' modernization, ensuring freedom and progress. The contemporary critique of modernity rejects this central theoretical presupposition. Reason, it is variously argued, has failed to ensure freedom; nor has it been the real locus or agent of modernization, which was for the most part carried out by political and economic agencies with scant regard for human freedom and happiness. The history of the development of Western societies since the Enlightenment is thus held to demonstrate this failure. Although this argument clearly refers to a fundamental inconsistency in the conceptual structure of the political and philosophical discourse of modernity, its critical value should not be exaggerated; it raises more theoretical problems than it proposes to solve. The case in point here is the conceptualization of the relationship between the discourse and practice of modernity in post-modern discourse, which almost invariably leads to the conflation of modernity with the historical experience of modernization in the West. This assumed identity of the 'concept' with the 'real' is firmly grounded in essentialism; it is underpinned by the assumption that the modern West is not just the locus of reason and rationalist discourse and practice but identical with it, albeit in the context of a failed historical experience. Hence the failure of the West is the failure of reason. The implications of this essentialist assumption for Eastern/ Oriental societies are clear: they fall outside the domain of reason experiencing a problematic relationship with an exogenous modernity. This essentialist assumption has an uneasy co-existence with the anti-essentialist argument that informs the post-modern critique and rejection of the universal claims of modernity. The concept of modernity informing this essay is different. It signifies a 'discursive formation' in the Foucauldian sense, that is, a specific discourse and its non-discursive conditions of the existence; in this case, the discourse of 'reason' and its economic, political and cultural conditions of possibility. The relationship between the discursive and non-discursive, that is, the possibility of modernity, is defined by strategies of power, which are also constitutive of the 'subject' in modern society. It is in this sense that the conditions of modernity and the conditions of the constitution of the 'subject' in modern society coincide: they both presuppose the articulation and dominance of reason in societal processes and practices engendered and sustained by strategies of power in society. This means, therefore, that reason/power has no specific locus or agency, nor can any general or uniform conception of modernization, endogenous or otherwise, be deduced from the conditions of its articulation in society. The relationship between reason and freedom, too, remains contingent upon the conditions of the constitution of the subject defined by the prevailing strategies of power and modes of 'resistance' to them. Modernity so defined cannot be identified with any specific traits of modern society – be it of capitalist economic form, rationalization or the nation-state – in a historicist manner, whether Marxist or Weberian. Nor can it identified with the historical experience of 'modernization' in any specific society. This is because the strategies of power and the forms and conditions of their operation vary widely from one society to another. For example, the idea of modernity and the discourse of reason, science and technology, secular education and the rule of law were introduced to the Ottoman and Iranian societies by a modernist intelligentsia in the early to mid-19th century. But the institutional processes and practices of modernity were created by modern constitutional states almost a century later. The modern state in Turkey and Iran – and later on in Iraq and Syria – became both the institutional representation of reason and the agent of modernization. Although there was little new in this transformation, it produced some specific effects defining the characteristic features of modernity in these societies, which will be explained in the course of this essay. Two interesting but quite different accounts of modernity are found in C. Taylor, *Sources of the Self: The making of the modern identity* (Cambridge: Cambridge University Press, 1992), and A. Touraine, *Critique of Modernity* (Oxford: Blackwell, 1997).

3. The new states, which emerged out of the ruins of the old in Turkey and Iran, and those founded by colonial powers in Iraq and Syria were fundamentally different formations. Their structural developments were diverse, having different consequences for the economic, political and cultural developments of Kurdish territories in their jurisdictions. This crucial diversity can be illustrated by the contrasting political development and conduct of the Kurdish landowning class in Turkey and Iran. In Turkey, the Kemalist policy of total denial of the Kurd and Kurdish identity and the brutal suppression of Kurdish movements led not only to the suppression of Kurdish language and culture but also to the political and cultural decline of the Kurdish landowning class, both tribal and non-tribal, which was thus expelled from the ethnically defined spheres of political rights and representation. The introduction in 1948 of the multi-party system, confined to the ethnically defined political process, though it still denied Kurdish representation, turned Kurdistan into a market in which Turkish parties competed for Kurdish votes by dispensing political and economic favours. This led to the political revival of the Kurdish landowning class, albeit in the framework of a new clientelism, which formed the mainstay of Turkish parliamentary politics in Kurdistan before it was undermined by the appearance of the PKK in the political scene. In Iran, by contrast, the politics of territorial centralism pursued by Reza Shah involved detribalization, which significantly weakened the political organization of the Kurdish tribes in the 1930s. The sudden (though temporary) revival of tribal political power in 1941 contributed both to the rise of the Kurdish republic and to its swift demise in 1947. In the following decade, the Kurdish landowning class, especially the tribal leadership, was largely co-opted into the precarious power structure in Iran, which, owing to the overcentralization of power and the absence of a genuine pluralist political process, failed to generate an effective clientelist structure in Kurdistan. The implementation of land reforms in the early 1960s undermined not only the economic foundation of the Kurdish landowning class but also their political power base in the countryside. In the upsurge of nationalist politics that followed the 1979 revolution, the landowning class was largely absent; with few notable exceptions, it played little role either in nationalist politics or in opposition to it. For discussions of aspects of diverse structural developments of Kurdish societies in Turkey and Iran see: Martin van Bruinessen, *Agha, Sheikh and State: The social and political structures of Kurdistan* (London: Zed Press, 1992); R. Olson (ed.), *The Kurdish Nationalist Movement in Turkey in the 1990's* (Lexington: Kentucky University Press, 1996); H. J. Barkey and G. Fuller, *Turkey's Kurdish Question* (New York: Rowman & Littlefield, 1998);

A. Vali, 'The Making of Kurdish Identity in Iran', *Critique*, vol. 3, no. 7, Fall 1995; A. Vali, 'Kurdish Nationalism in Iran: The formative period, 1942–47', *The Journal of Kurdish Studies*, vol. II, no. 2, 1997; D. McDowall, *A Modern History of the Kurds*. For a detailed discussion of diverse state linguistic and cultural policies in Kurdistan see: A. Hassanpour, *Nationalism and Language in Kurdistan* (San Francisco: Mellon University Press, 1994).

4. This point is explained by, among others, Calhoun and McCrone, both drawing on modern European history. See: G. Calhoun, 'Nationalism and Civil Society' in: Calhoun (ed.), *Social Theory and Identity* (Oxford: Blackwell, 1994); and D. McCrone, *The Sociology of Nationalism* (London: Macmillan, 1998).

5. Kurdish principalities were semi-autonomous juridico-political entities within the boundaries of the Ottoman and the Iranian states. Little is known about their conditions before the early 16th century, when the military conflict between the Ottoman and the Safavid states and the subsequent partition of the Kurdish territory gave them an unprecedented prominence in regional politics. It seems that the Kurdish principalities officially recognized and submitted to the supreme authority of their Ottoman and Iranian overlords in Friday Khotbas, [Religious Sermons delivered in mosques on Fridays] which were read in the names of the reigning monarchs. In practice, their relationships with their respective authority were regulated in a tributary structure, which at times closely resembled feudal vassalage. The mutation in the form of this tributary relationship depended largely on the political and military powers of the Ottoman and Iranian states and the effective range of their centralizing functions, which defined, though in an inverse manner, the actual boundaries of political and administrative power in the Kurdish principalities. Hence the 'reactive' nature of their politics vis-à-vis the two states, which quickly degenerated into armed conflict when the balance of power was disturbed in periods of acute centralization or decentralization of state power. For explanations of the structures and organizations of the Kurdish principalities in different periods of their development see: van Bruinessen, 'Kurdish Society, Ethnicity, Nationalism and Refugee Problems'; Amir Hassanpour, *Nationalism and Language in Kurdistan*; C. J. Rich, *Narrative of a Residence in Koordistan*, 2 vols (London: Cape, 1836).

6. Recent years have witnessed an explosion in discourse on identity, largely as a result of the growing academic interest in the works of the post-structuralist philosophers, especially Jacques Derrida, and the post-modernist appropriations of them. But despite the academic fashion, serious theoretical writing on the subject is rather scarce. See: J. Derrida, *Of Grammatology* (Baltimore: Johns Hopkins University Press, 1970) and *Writing and Difference* (London: Routledge, 1978); E. Laclau (ed.), *The Making of Modern Political Identities* (London: Verso, 1994) and *Emancipations* (London: Verso, 1997); W. E. Connolly, *Identity and Difference: Democratic negotiation of a political paradox* (Ithaca, NY: Cornell University Press, 1991); and G. Bennington, *Negotiations* (London: Verso, 1995).

7. A discrepancy between discourse and practice is a common feature of modern political movements. In the case of Kurdish nationalism the issue is more complex. It is not so much a discrepancy as a total absence of nationalist political practice; the nationalist discourse enjoys popular appeal but lacks popular political existence, that is, the means and conditions to translate it into political practice. It is a popular political idea rather than a mass political ideology. But this crucial difference cannot be reduced only to the absence of an effective mobilizing force in Kurdistan; it amounts to the fundamental difference that exists between sovereignty and autonomy, so deeply rooted in the structural conditions of Kurdish nationalism. The

formation and development of the PKK bear witness to the truth of this argument. It is the only significant modern Kurdish political organization, which started its campaign with a clear nationalist strategy demanding independence for Kurdistan; but in March 1993, after barely a decade of active nationalist politics, it changed its strategic objective, asking for the creation of a federal political system in Turkey; this demand was further modified to autonomy in November 1998, when its leader came to Europe in search of a political solution to the armed conflict with Turkey. However, the radical change in the strategic objective of the PKK does not seem to have affected its nationalist discourse, which appears side by side with arguments for a political solution in the framework of Turkish sovereignty. This paradox testifies not only to an ambiguous political identity but also to the curious case of nationalists without nationalism, which characterized the discourse and practice of the Mahabad republic five decades earlier. For the political development of the PKK see: R. Olson (ed.): *The Kurdish Nationalist Movement in Turkey in the 1990s* (Lexington: University Press of Kentucky, 1996); and H. J. Barkey and G. Fuller, *Turkey's Kurdish Question* (New York: Rowman & Littlefield, 1998). For the discourse and practice of the Republic see: A. Vali, 'Kurdish Nationalism in Iran: The formative period, 1942–47', *The Journal of Kurdish Studies*, vol. II, no. 2, 1997.

8. This point invokes Foucault's argument in his much-quoted essay on governmentality. Foucault, however, does not explore the full implications of his own argument for the conceptualization of modern politics and governmentality, largely because of his problematic approach to and treatment of some of the fundamental philosophical premises of liberal political theory. This point has been noted by some recent critics of his writings on power and governmentality. Foucault's essay on governmentality appears in G. Burchell et al. (eds), *The Foucault Effect* (London: Harvester Wheatsheaf, 1991). For critical analysis and commentary on Foucault's essay, see: B. Hindess, *Discourses of Power from Hobbes to Foucault* (Oxford: Blackwell, 1996), and 'Politics and Governmentality', *Economy and Society*, vol. 26, no. 2, 1997; C. Gordon, 'Governmental Rationality', and G. Burchell, 'Peculiar Interests: Civil society and governing the system of natural liberty', both in: Burchell et al., 1991; A. Barry et al (eds): *Foucault and Political Reason: Liberalism, Neo-Liberalism and Rationalities of Government* (London: University College London Press, 1996).

9. The changing ethnic and racial composition of west European societies and the associated problems of social and political marginalization and exclusion have led to a revival of scholarly interest in the concept of citizenship. Social and political theorists have rightly pointed out the shortcomings of the normative concept of citizenship in the increasingly multi-ethnic and multi-cultural societies of western Europe and North America, and the failure of these societies to ensure democratic representation of the ethnic and racial groupings. They have thus argued for a redefinition of the conditions of citizenship and political participation in democratic societies, to ensure the representation of the 'marginal' and 'excluded' in political and cultural processes. The recent 'revisionist' works on citizenship and ethnicity clearly pose important questions regarding the nature of democracy and democratic process in the contemporary West, but fail to provide appropriate answers to them. The often-quoted work of Will Kymlicka, *Multicultural Citizenship* (Oxford: Oxford University Press, 1997), is a prime example: for him the inability of the democratic process to represent ethnic and cultural difference is rooted in the inadequacies of the concept of citizenship, that is, the rights and conditions of its realization in society. But in so doing he fails to relate it to political sovereignty and its restrictive effects on the democratic political process, thus arguing for a change in the conditions of

citizenship without a change in the 'ethnic' identity of the sovereign, the identity of political power. The discourse of rights within which Kymlicka poses and answers his questions is defined by the discourse of sovereignty, which leaves no room for non-sovereign identities; the marginal, the excluded or the stateless remain unrepresented and unrepresentable. Political theory must break out of the narrow ethnic confines of the discourse of sovereignty if it is to represent the unrepresented.

10. This idea is hardly new; it has been around since Renan's seminal essay 'What Is the Nation?', a new English translation of which appeared in H. Bhabha (ed.), *Nations and Narrations* (London: Routledge, 1988). In recent years it has informed an increasingly influential body of literature, which entertains 'constructionist' conceptions of the nation and nationalism, exemplified best by the works of Ernest Gellner (*Nations and Nationalism*, Cambridge: Cambridge University Press, 1988), and Benedict Anderson (*Imagined Communities*, London: Verso, 1983). For a critical discussion of the idea and a theoretical evaluation of the constructionist conceptions of the nation and nationalism, its political and methodological significance and theoretical limitations and wrongs, see: my essay 'Nationalism and Kurdish Historical Writing', in: *New Perspectives on Turkey*, no. 14, spring 1996.

11. It is widely held that the concept of citizenship regulates the boundaries of the state and civil society in the democratic order. This is clearly argued by David Held and Bhikhu Parekh in their contributions to a collection edited by Geoffrey Andrews: *Citizenship* (London: Lawrence and Whishart, 1991). The truth of the argument notwithstanding, it largely exaggerates the autonomy of the regulatory function of citizenship in the democratic process by overlooking the limitations that the ethnic identity of political power imposes in the development of civil society. This issue will be discussed in the following section of this essay. See also: B. S. Turner (ed.), *Citizenship and Social Theory* (London: Sage, 1993), especially contributions by Hindess, Kalberg and Turner.

12. On this point see: Graham Burchell's discussion and development of Foucault's concept of govermentality in his essay in G. Burchell et al., *The Foucault Effect*.

13. Civil society always functions within the unifying framework of the legal regulations of the state, which clearly dispels the myth of its autonomy widely held by its contemporary enthusiasts. This point is forcefully put by Althusser in his brief but incisive critique of Gramsci's concept of civil society. Althusser's conception of social totality structured by the dominance of the economic level leads him to the other extreme, arguing for the total dependence of civil society on dominant class relations, and hence subjected to their centralizing functions through the medium of the state. See: L. Althusser, *Reading Capital* (London: New Left Books, 1970), p.168; also his 'Ideology and Ideological State Apparatuses', in: L. Althusser, *Lenin and Philosophy* (London: New Left Books, 1971).

14. The concept of 'transactional domain' is borrowed from Graham Burchell; see: Burchell et al., *The Foucault Effect*.

15. This argument is developed by Barry Hindess in his discussion and critique of Foucault's concept of governmentality and political reason; Hindess, *Discourses of Power* and 'Politics and Governmentality'.

16. See: Hindess, 'Politics and Governmentality'.

17. On this point see: G. Burchell, *The Foucault Effect*.

18. Ibid.

19. The discussion of civil society and democratic process in the remaining part of this essay will be confined to Turkey and Iran, excluding Iraq and Syria. Syria is excluded because of the absence of democratic process and the dearth of information on the

state of civil society, especially with regard to ethnicity and ethnic difference; while the social, political and cultural conditions of Iraq after the Gulf War of 1991, and the complete concentration of political power in the coercive and security apparatuses of the state, render absurd any discussion of civil society. As far as civil society and democratic process are concerned, the current situation in Iraq is only a culmination of the process that started under Ba'ath rule, which by definition implied the closure of civil society.

20. There is a growing body of literature on civil society and democratic process in Turkey, which mostly remains within the normative framework of constitutional politics, thus excluding consideration of non-constitutional issues such as Kurdish and Islamic identities. Only a few writers break out of this narrow political and methodological framework. See for example: B. Toprak, 'Civil Society in Turkey', and N. Gole, 'Authoritarian Secularism and Islamic Participation: The case of Turkey', both in: A. R. Norton (ed.), *Civil Society in the Middle East*, 2 vols. (Leiden: E. J. Brill, 1994, 1995); E. Ozbudun, 'Civil Society and Democratic Consolidation in Turkey', and L. Koker, 'National Identity and State Legitimacy: Contradictions of Turkey's democratic experience', both in: E. Ozdalga and S. Perrson (eds), *Civil Society and Democracy in the Muslim World* (Istanbul: Swedish Research Institute, 1997), vol. 7.

21. Toprak ('Civil Society in Turkey') and Gole ('Authoritarian Secularism and Islamic Participation) are examples of the partial recognition, but the crucial break with the normative constitutional framework is not carried to its logical conclusion. Koker ('National Identity and State Legitimacy') provides a more radical analysis, clearly departing from the normative premises of the constitutional framework. His radical approach to Kurdish identity is premised on his rejection of the Kemalist contours of the discourse of civil society and democratization in contemporary Turkey.

22. The volume *Jame-eyeh Madani va Iran-e Emrooz* (Civil Society and Present-day Iran; Tehran 1377/1997) contains a collection of articles by religious and secular writers who put forward different arguments in defence of civil society. See especially: Abdul Karim Soroush, 'Din va Jame-eh' (Religion and Society); see also: *Iran-e Farda*, special issues on civil society (Tehran, 1997), and *Iran Nameh* (A Persian Journal of Iranian Studies), special issue on civil society in Iran, vol. XIII, no. 4, Fall 1995, and vol. XIV, no. 1, Fall 1996.

23. Civil society (*Jame-yeh Madani*) was the battle cry of Khatami in the presidential elections of 1997. The concept was used to mean the rule of law, which was identified with democratic order. As such it became the central plank in the reformist platform attracting the active support of both religious and secular sections of the population. The reformist platform was opposed by the consevative hardliners in the regime who rejected the discoure of civil society in the name of the *Wilayat i Faqih* which, they argued, represented the revolutionary legitimacy and the ethos of the Islamic repubic. The debate on civil society and democratic order has continued more rigiorously since Khatami's victory, signifying the persistence of political struggle between the reformists and the conservative hardliners which is now clearly centered on state power. This struggle, and in fact the debate on civil society, is still is fought in terms of the competing definitions of Islam and their associated notions of political authority and legitimacy in which Khomeini and his concept of Wilatat i Faqih remain the point of reference. For the Islamic reformist argument for civil society and the rule of law during and since the presidential elections see the isses of the Tehran daily *Salam*, *Jame-eh*, *Toos*, *Keeyan*, *Neshat*. The conservative opposition to the reformist platform see the issues of the Tehran daily *Resalat* since Jan.1997.

24. See for example: Soroush ('Din va Jame-eh') and various speeches by Khatami before

and since the presidential elections in June 1997 printed in issues of *Salam* and the brief but rather interesting contribution of Hashemi Nejad in *Jame-eyeh Madani va Iran-e Emrooz*.

25. For a detailed and informed study of the politics of the preparation and ratification of the constitution of the Islamic Republic of Iran and its democratic and authoritarian contents, see the recent work of Asghar Schirazi: *The Constitution of Iran: Politics and the state in the Islamic Republic* (London: I. B. Tauris, 1997).

Ethnicity and Power:
Some Reflections on Ethnic Definitions and Boundaries

Hosham Dawod

This is an attempt to set down a number of ideas on the heated ethnic concerns that characterize the Middle East in general and Iraq in particular, where millions of Kurds aspire to autonomy. Ethnic, linguistic and religious pluralism has forcefully re-emerged in recent years at a time when the political orders seem unprepared for the resurgence of these social phenomena. Far from having withered away from the effects of 'integration' and 'assimilation', sub-state particularisms have survived and indeed flourished.

Of course, neither Iraq nor the Middle East has a monopoly here, undeniable regional differences notwithstanding. Several continents with various structures of society have sustained occasional outbursts of ethnic conflict: from the Indian sub-continent to Africa, from central and eastern Europe (especially in former Yugoslavia and the former USSR) to Ireland, from Canada to Algeria, from the United States to Spain and France. Even in Switzerland, only twenty-five years ago, six French-speaking provinces were allowed by referendum to secede from the German-speaking canton of Berne and form their own canton of Jura.

It sometimes happens in the social sciences that a concept creeps into general use without ever having been clearly defined, thereby causing considerable difficulties. The term 'ethnicity', used in the title in this book, is of this kind.

There are two major competing analyses on the nature of ethnicity. The first involves an essentialist emphasis on the inherent, primordial quality of belonging to an ethnic group and on the importance of the early socialization of the individual by way of his/her integration into a primary group. This concept tends to regard specific linguistic, religious and 'racial' traits as deriving directly from or producing a certain form of ethnic consciousness. Those who give precedence to primordial determinations also see a connection between ethnicity and kinship; and, by reason of the powerful emotional bonds existing among individuals, are convinced that they have ancestors in common and, in some cases, a special cosmic destiny. Emphasizing the importance of a shared lineage, Max Weber defines the ethnic group in these terms:

> We shall call 'ethnic group' those human groups that entertain a subjective belief in their common descent ... this belief must be important for the propagation of group formation; conversely, it does not matter whether or not an objective blood relationship exists. Ethnic membership (*Gemeinsankeit*) differs from the kinship group precisely by being a presumed identity ...'[1]

Weber makes a clear distinction between ethnic groups and nations as follows :

> The idea of the nation is apt to include the notions of common descent of an essential though frequently indefinite homogeneity. The 'nation' has these notions in common with the sentiment of solidarity of ethnic communities, which is also nourished from various sources, as we have seen before (ch. V, 4). But the sentiment of ethnic solidarity does not by itself make a 'nation'.[2]

The British sociologist Anthony D. Smith partly shares this concept of ethnicity:

> Human beings have always felt themselves bounded by multiple identities. Even in prehistoric societies, the family, clan and settlement vied for their allegiances. By the time we meet historical societies with written records, to the familial and residential circles of identity must be added those of the city state, social stratum and what I shall call the 'ethnic community' or *ethnie*. The *ethnie* can be defined as a human group whose members share common myths of origin and descent, historical memories, cultural patterns and values, association with a particular territory, and a sense of solidarity, at least among the elites.[3]

Smith's contribution is important, because he considerably enlarges the somewhat rigid 'primordialist' and substantivist perspective; we shall return to this question.

From another perspective, instrumentalist or situationist, some scholars see the frontiers between ethnic groupings as flexible and permeable, and claim that ethnicity may be adopted or rejected at will. Situationists place conflicts of interest at the centre of all ethnically expressed political rivalries; they believe a person may possess two or more identities according to his/her role in a given situation. Membership in an ethnic group may depend more on rituals of social acceptance and subjective identification than on any irreversible criteria imposed at birth.[4]

Some situationist writers offer a more dynamic, interactional approach, showing the *ethnie* to be a category whose continuity is also a matter of cultural differences between neighbouring groups. This more recent approach, developed on the basis of instrumentalist logic, leads to a displacement of the mechanisms of self-definition and ethno-genesis and towards a process of ethnification, and grants an important role to history. In this view, the *ethnie* is an open entity, in perpetual construction/deconstruction, to be defined from both the inside and the outside. It is a historical product, deeper than the roots of the groups that compose it, because it is a result of dialectical relationships between various units. There is no such thing as a 'pure *ethnie*'; and rather than speak of the origins of this or that *ethnie*, one should speak of the origins of a population.[5] However, none of these explications is satisfying on its own. First of all, the culture of this or that group is never fixed and given; neither is it a simple 'construct'. By 'culture' we mean a whole set of representations and principles that consciously organize the various aspects of social life, a set of norms, positive and negative, and the values attached to these ways of acting and thinking.[6] In addition, ethnic movements do not arise mechanically out of conflicts of interest.[7] And lastly, the process of political mobilization of ethnic resources is not simply a matter of manipulating the symbolic codes.[8] Indeed, irrespective of the 'symbolic interactions' argument, the question remains: why do people feel they have to belong to some *ethnie*?One of the most important contributions to the development of a theory of ethnicity was undoubtedly the work of the Norwegian anthropologist Fredrik Barth, who studied a Kurdish tribal group in northern Iraq during the 1950s. He undertook to deconstruct the current notion that 'culture' is an *aggregate*, formed unconsciously by individuals pursuing different goals: 'ethnic groups are categories of ascription and identification by the actors themselves.'[9] Through transactional encounters, these individuals were purported to reach minimal agreement on a set of values. Later, Barth took up his theory again.

Pursuing his critique, he postulated that an *ethnie* was above all a category of 'ascription', whose continuity depends upon the preservation of a fluid, unstable boundary, which the group strives to maintain in order to build, negotiate and reproduce its self-identity. Ethnicity thus results from the constantly renewed codification of cultural differences between neighbouring groups.

In this definition, ethnic groups or 'cultures' form relatively distinct fields of value integration, the discontinuities between them constituting 'ethnic boundaries'. Thus, cultures are not entities but aggregates with which each individual may have closer or looser ties at his/her convenience. This is why the ethnic sense of belonging must be consciously nurtured with intense symbolic activity.

Even though Barth later made substantial changes to his theory (especially as regards the historical dimension),[10] he remained convinced that the inscription of ethnic identity is a matter of choice. In accepting the fundamentally voluntary nature of ethnic identity, however, Barth raised a paradox which he did not solve: how can one conceptualize the elaboration of such quasi-objective entities on the grounds of individual choice? If, for example, we incorporate such a notion of choice into the constitution of ethnic identities in the Middle East, what do we do with notions such as the 'sacred' tie between land and people? Take, for example, the dispute that arose after the death of Yasser Arafat (November 2004). The Palestinian Authority's demand to bury the historic leader in Jerusalem had to do with the consecration of Al Quds as the permanent centre of Palestinian national identity, without which it might disintegrate. Faced with the Israeli refusal and painfully aware of the disproportion of forces, the Palestinians got around the problem with a cleverly symbolic move: they buried the historic leader, *Rayis*, in Ramallah, but in soil brought specially from Jerusalem. The Israelis saw Arafat's burial as a political and symbolic matter and therefore subject to negotiation. For the Palestinians, it was much more a sacred matter; the heart of their identity was at stake and that could not be negotiated – only, in extreme circumstances, displaced.[11]

Though starting from different premises, Dale Eickelman and Lawrence Rosen[12] both maintain, with regard to ethnicity in the Middle East and North Africa, that *no single trait of social identity is central in all situations*. Personal obligations are prescribed neither by kinship nor by ethnic or religious affiliation, nor by one's occupation, but rather by each of these identity components in turn, accordingly as they are activated by circumstances. What really matter are the personal networks of affiliation constructed by the individual, ethnicity being only one of several factors.[13] This point of view is paradoxical and indeed untenable with regard to ethno-religious groups.[14]

The specificity of the Muslim countries of the Middle East is that, depending on circumstances, ethnic identity may overlay and combine with the sense of belonging to a single religious community. The population statistics for these countries are largely based on religious criteria. Groups that do not subscribe to Islam are classified as national 'minorities'. Thus, in Iran, not only are the Armenians, Jews and Assyrians so categorized, but also the Zoroastrians, though they are ethnically Persian. Similarly, in certain Arab countries, it is customary to classify all non-Muslims as ethnic minorities, but also the followers of Islamic denominations that are not dominant in the country in question (Shi'is, Yezidis, Alevis).

Hence religious differences are likely to prove an important element in ethnic differentiation. This is the case with the Yezidis, the Shabak,[15] the Ahli-Haqq and the Alevis who occupy, as religious groups, a place apart among the Kurds, or with the Druze among the Arabs of Syria and Lebanon, or with the Copts among the Egyptians.

It follows that, in order to identify an ethnic group, we need to take into account the parameters characterizing it as a given group of individuals and consider, at the same time, the ties that bind this group to other ethnic communities. Indeed, the ethnic composition of a region's population can be established only with reference to a wide variety of criteria. The theories of ethnicity we have reviewed thus far turn out to be relatively simplistic since they offer single-case relations between certain variables. However, specialists are less and less satisfied with these hasty generalizations and increasingly recognize the complexity of the dependent variables and correlative factors: the relative power of each group, reflected in its numbers, organization and access to resources; the role of elite groups; boundary maintenance and the part played by foreign and domestic wars in developing group cohesion; linguistic belongingness; population patterns; cultural contacts with other ethnic groups; levels of technological, economic, political and social development among the ethnic populations under consideration and in the countries where they are established, etc.

Let us take the case of the Kurds. Frequent attempts are made in historico-political journals to classify and situate the ethnic Kurds among the other Middle East groupings in terms of linguistic proximity and the sense of belonging. Actually, language alone does not always make possible necessary distinctions between peoples; hence other indices must be used. However, such discrepancies would be just as unavoidable using any other system of classification, which is why, even today, this is the system that prevails in the social sciences, under the rubric of ethno-linguistics. In order to classify *ethnies* in relation to each other, the system draws upon the genealogical study of languages, which allows them to be arranged in families according to indices of lexical or grammatical kinship. These families are divided into groups and some of these into sub-groups. For example, modern Kurdish, with all its dialects, is classified as an Indo-European tongue of the Aryan branch, i.e. Indo-Iranian, and is located in the north-west group of that family, which includes several modern languages. Ossete, Persian, Baluch, Pashtu, Tajik and Kurdish have many traits in common, but they also exhibit as many differences as exist between the various languages of other families – Slavic, Germanic or Latin. Hence there are several *ethnies* of linguistically Iranian origin, which today speak different languages and occupy different territories.[16]

Of course, the geographic boundaries of linguistic families or groups in the Middle East have changed continually throughout their history; and these changes have been clearly perceptible even over relatively short periods of time. Arabic, which the population of the Arabian peninsula were practically alone in speaking until the 7th century AD, is today spoken across a vast territory ranging from south-west Asia to North Africa, totalling nearly 10 per cent of the world's dry land. The area covered by the Turkish language group, which ranges today from the Balkan peninsula to north-eastern Siberia, has also grown considerably over the centuries.

The ethno-linguistic classification system, however, is far from perfect. No method has been elaborated to date that can account for such matters as the bilingual practices of certain *ethnies* or the gradual shift from one language to another. In trying to distinguish between other *ethnies* in Afghanistan and certain republics of Central Asia, Olivier Roy encountered the problem raised by linguistic criteria:

> In the area which concerns us, townspeople were generally bilingual (Turkish/Persian in Mazar-i Sharif, Tabriz, Bukhara and Samarkand, etc. [...]; Pashtu/Persian in Kabul and Qandahar), which was also true in certain parts of the countryside. However, even for those who regard language as the determinant trait of ethnicity, it remains to be determined exactly what we mean by a language: for example, the Persian domain has been arbitrarily divided between 'Farsi' (Iran), 'Dari' (Afghanistan) and 'Tajiki' (USSR). But are we talking about real divisions or merely political ones? In other words, is the distinction based on purely linguistic

criteria or is it because State strategies prefer to distinguish three different ethnies?[17]

The wider our selection of case studies, the more it would appear that, except where language affinity can be established with certainty, we need to depart from principles of linguistic classification wherever cultural and historical proximity occurs between ethnic groups and wherever a stable identity-consciousness survives despite linguistic changes. For a long time census figures (regularly kept in certain countries since the 17th century) were confined to keeping track of languages. It was not until 1920 that a direct question concerning ethnic affinity ('nationality') was introduced into the first census of the Soviet population. In the Middle East, only a few countries added it to their questionnaire (Lebanon and, paradoxically, Saddam's Iraq before 2003, as well as regimes which took religious diversity into account politically).

Sometimes the statistical questionnaire used in other countries in the region collect information on tribal or religious affiliation, country of origin or birth. These details help evaluate or justify (or manipulate) the chief ethnic determinants (for want of questions on nationality or language). Governments and various scientific and social bodies carry out these evaluations, by which the dimensions of many ethnic groups can be determined. But we might add that in all the countries of the Middle East, census figures, like other statistics, are often tendentious, because ruling groups will seek to hide the existence of ethnic and ethno-religious groups and national minorities, as well as the problems associated with them.

Under such conditions, and largely on account of forcible assimilation policies, it has been extremely difficult to identify objectively the size and number of ethnic and ethno-religious communities in countries such as Turkey, Iran, Saddam's Iraq and Syria, where the various *ethnies* do not enjoy equal rights. To which we must unfortunately add that there are specialists today who, because they know next to nothing of these peoples' historical development and of the ethnic processes at work, either support the policies of the ruling elite or else divide up the *ethnies* on a completely artificial basis. Some of these writers, moreover, blame anthropologists and others in the social sciences for having supposedly 'legitimated and ratified' an ethnic reality which in the last analysis is merely a 'colonial creation';[18] or for having helped the existing power structure control the populations and cultures they studied. Other anthropologists parry with a simple question: what is at stake here? Is it whether or not cultural and ethnic identities (there are other identities such as class, gender, etc.) have an objective content that the ethnologist can grasp empirically? If so, the answer is an emphatic 'yes'. Such content does exist. To deny this self-evident fact, obvious to one and all, on the pretext that human societies cannot be itemized and analysed, would be about as useless and absurd as to deny, in the name of anti-racism, the anthropo-biological differences among the human species.[19]

The awareness of ethnic identity – not to be confused with the politicization of ethnicity, though the one may lead to the other – constitutes, when there is no obstacle to its 'normal' development, the most important ethnic determinant of all. As this awareness takes shape over a long time, it becomes in fact an expression of the many elements entering into the formation of any ethnic community, although this awareness ultimately acquires a certain degree of autonomy. Thus it may subsist after the group in question has left the territory of the main ethnic core. Consciousness of national identity may in turn have an effect upon the factors that once generated it, notably through the emergence of movements for the revival and promotion of national languages. Such promotions, however, are not actual rediscoveries but intentional constructions or inventions, as we have been reminded by Eric Hobsbawn (*The Invention of Tradition*)[20] and Benedict Anderson, on nations as *Imagined Communities*.[21] Both have emphasized the fact that any claim to a historical identity contains imagined and imaginary elements, objects of dream and desire, always easily manipulated as the historical context evolves. The role of the intellectual elite in the creation of these movements is essential: they are the ones who first seek out specific markers or *differentia specifica* in the culture and history of their group. Or they may simply conjure up a history, as did a handful of Kurdish intellectuals in their fight against Turkish nationalism in decline, tracing the origins of their *ethnie* back to Zoroastrian culture. Only thereafter did they start demanding political autonomy.

'Ethnicizing intellectuals' are, according to Anthony Smith, 'ideologues' preparing to organize and lead political campaigns or guerrilla warfare.[22] For him, the notion of double legitimization is fundamental. Legitimization necessitates authoritative resources: these may be found either within the traditional communities or within the scientific state apparatus, with its technocratic structure and ideology of *progress*. The contrast between the *traditional world* and the *modern world*, between ethnic community and state, is inherent in the nature of these two types of institution. When the 'reformist' and 'assimilationist' institutions cannot solve this tension, then ethno-nationalism provides a solution, because in the last analysis it is at once traditionalist and modernist.[23] We must add that while Smith acknowledges that the existence of *ethnies* predates the industrial era, he nevertheless sees the recent resurgence of ethnicities as the basis for political and cultural movements within the context of modernization. He also rejects the idea that ethnic nationalism is doomed to wither away as the 'rational universalist' norms of achievement supplant 'traditional', 'particularist' and attributive norms as the basis of social order. His typology of nationalist movements leaves room for hybrid interaction between them and he acknowledges that the level of economic development in the countries under consideration also exerts an influence here.[24]

Let me, by way of conclusion, return to my original question: what is an *ethnie*? In the course of my empirical fieldwork in the Middle East and particularly in post-Saddam Iraq, I have observed that an *ethnie* is a set of local groups (tribes, village communities, urban populations) that lay claim to a common origin, lifestyles and social principles of organization and mindsets, which, although not necessarily similar, demonstrate through their very differences that they belong to a common tradition. And yet the notion of *ethnie* represents two very different modes of entity, according to whether or not they are subordinate to a nation-state. In the 19th-century Ottoman Empire's in-depth reforms (*Tanzimat*), designed, among other things, to achieve centralization for greater control over the various populations, *ethnies* corresponded to socio-cultural entities such as towns, village communities and tribes, all claiming a common origin but also demanding relative territorial autonomy. To recognize a common ethnic identity for individuals belonging to different tribes meant being aware of speaking the languages of the same family and following similar customs and principles. And yet this acknowledgement of a common ethnic identity in no way prevents wars, since ethnicity as such provides no guarantee to territorial access or material wealth, nor the possibility of concluding certain preferred kinds of marriage (parental and marital ties are essential to the tribal system). It is the individual's membership in a local solidarity group, tribe, clan or household (*Bin Mal* in Kurdish, *Bayt* in Arabic) that will, up to a point, ensure that s/he has access to these three advantages. Thus, in certain parts of Kurdistan, the basic conditions of existence of a social group were ensured by tribal organization (which combined political authority and the appropriation of a territory) and not by membership of a common *ethnie* or religious community.

However, ethnic grouping did not necessarily have the same meaning for *ethnies* and tribes belonging to the same state and subjected to its sovereignty.

Most often (as was the case in pre-2003 Iraq), state power was in the hands of a dominant *ethnie* and/or religious denomination, or even a single tribe from that dominant *ethnie*. Consequently, to be a member of a common *ethnie* no longer meant merely to belong to a cultural totality. It also meant that individuals and groups were being ranked, by dint of their ethnicity and tribal membership, in higher or lower positions in the bureaucratic hierarchy of the state. After the fall of Saddam Hussein, certain *ethnies* (and particularly the Kurds) demanded a measure of sovereignty over their territory, agitating for the creation of a federal state, with international recognition for its members.

Now as before, the reality of ethnicity lies on the Iraqi political horizon. Certain subjugated *ethnies* are driven to stress their identity in order to enforce demands of power sharing on the ruling ethnic group. This also holds true when smaller ethnic groups are dominated by a third, sharing the same territory, as is clearly seen with ethno-religious communities such as the Assyrians, Chaldeans or Turkmen, whose relations with both Kurds and Arabs are often strained. But if there is one thing that has proven difficult to reconstruct in post-Saddam Iraq (as elsewhere in the Middle East), it is power sharing.

Notes

1. Max Weber, *Economy and Society*, vol. 1, edited by Gunther Roth and Claus Wittich (New York: Bedminster Press, 1968), p. 389.
2. Max Weber, *Economy and Society*, p. 923; W. W. Isaju, 'Definition of Ethnicity', in: *Ethnicity*, vol. 1, no. 1, 1970.
3. Anthony Smith, 'The Politics of Culture: Ethnicity and nationalism', in: Tim Ingold (ed.), *Companion Encyclopaedia of Anthropology* (London: Routledge, 1994), pp. 706–733 ; 'LSE Centennial Lecture: The resurgence of nationalism? Myth and memory in the renewal of nations', *British Journal of Sociology*, vol. 47, issue no. 4, December 1996, pp. 575–598.
4. For a much fuller exposition of these arguments, see: Thomas Hylland Eriksen, *Ethnicity and Nationalism: Anthropological perspectives* (London, Pluto Press, 1993); M. Martinello, *L'Ethnicité dans les sciences socials contemporaines* (Paris, Presses Universitaires de France, Coll. Que sais-je ?, 1995).
5. André Bourgeot, 'Idéologie et appellations ethniques: l'exemple twareg', *Cahiers d'études africaines*, 48, 1972.
6. Maurice Godelier, *Métamorphoses de la parenté* (Paris, Fayard, 1994).
7. Anthony D. Smith, *Ethnic Revival in the Modern World* (Cambridge: Cambridge University Press, 1981).
8. Ernest Gellner, *Nations and Nationalism* (Oxford: Blackwell, 1983).
9. Fredrik Barth (ed.), *Ethnic Groups and Boundaries: The social organisation of culture difference* (Boston, 1969), pp. 13–14.

10. Fredrik Barth, 'Problem in Conceptualizing Cultural Pluralism, with illustrations from Sohar, Oman', in: D. Maybury (eds), 'The Prospects for Plural Societies', *Proceedings*, American Ethnological Society, 1984.

11. In the same way, Iraqi Kurds and Turkmen struggle over the control of oil-rich Kirkuk province, each seeking to legitimize their action with reference to 'history', to the mythological and the sacred, sole concepts capable of mobilizing the energies of the population.

12. Lawrence Rosen, *Bargaining for Reality: The construction for social relations in a Muslim country* (Chicago, Chicago University Press, 1984).

13. Dale F. Eickelman, *The Middle East: An anthropological approach* (Englewood Cliffs: Prentice Hall, 1981).

14. Cf. Lucette Valensi, 'La Tour de Babel: groupes et relations ethniques au Moyen-Orient et en Afrique du Nord', *Les Anales ESC*, 1986, pp. 817–838.

15. Amal Vinogradov, 'Ethnicity, Cultural Discontinuity and Power Brokering in Northern Iraq: The case of the Shabak', *American Ethnologist*, vol. 1, no. 2, 1974, pp. 207–217.

16. Cf. Emile Benveniste, *Indo-European Language and Society*, translated by Elizabeth Palmer (Coral Gables, FL, University of Miami Press, 1973).

17. Olivier Roy, 'Ethnies et politique en Asie Centrale', *Revue du monde Musulman et de la Méditerranée*, no. 59–60, 1991, pp. 17–36.

18. In France this thesis, pretty well discredited today, was prominently defended by Jean-Loup Amselle and Elikia M'Bokolo. Since then, anthropologists, historians and archaeologists have brought to light enough material to supersede that Manichaean vision. Cf. the volume edited by Jean-Loup Amselle and Elikia M'Bokolo, *Au Cœur de l'ethnie. Ethnie, tribalisme et etat en Afrique* (Paris, La découverte, 1985).

19. Cf. Jean-Pierre Digard (ed.), *Le Fait ethnique en Iran et en Afghanistan* (Paris: Editions du CNRS, 1988), pp. 10–11.

20. Eric Hobsbawm and T. Ranger (eds), *The Invention of Tradition* (Cambridge: Cambridge University Press and Canto Edition, 1992).

21. Benedict Anderson, *Imagined Communities: Reflections on the opinion and spread of nationalism* (London: Verso, New Left Books, 1983).

22. Anthony D. Smith, *Ethnic Revival in the Modern World*, p. 108.

23. Anthony D. Smith, *Theories of Nationalism* (London: Duckworth, 1971), p. 256.

24. Anthony D. Smith, 'Towards a Theory of Ethnic Nationalism', *Ethnic and Racial Studies*, vol. 2, no. 1, pp. 21–37.

PART TWO

Society, Language, Culture and History

Religion and Ethnicity as Politicized Boundaries

Sami Zubaida

Kurdistan, being a mountainous region, has, over the years, included a wide array of dissident religions and ethnic boundaries. The remoteness and isolation of mountains, whether in Europe or the Middle East, have always protected 'heretics' and dissidents from the reach of religious orthodoxy and the sword of its dynastic upholders. The majority of Kurds have emerged into modern times as Sunni Muslims, but with strong Sufi affiliations. There are also many Kurdish Shi'ite communities, some with distinct ethnic identities and dialects. Examples are the Fayli Kurds of the Khanaqin region in Iraq, the Zaza Kurds of southern Iranian Kurdistan, and the Zaza Alevis of Anatolya.

Christian sects that remained distinct from the main churches continued to exist in these mountains, preserving ancient rites and languages. The Nestorian rite flourished in the ancient world, primarily under the Persian Empire, and reached as far as India and China, but succumbed to the assaults of Byzantine orthodoxy. It survived in small pockets, including the Kurdish mountains. It was the powerful reach of the Catholic Church, under French protection, that eventually converted a section of this community, now designated Kildani (Chaldeans), to Roman allegiance, though keeping its own 'Eastern rite' and liturgical language. The remaining Nestorians were later designated Athuri (Assyrians). These Christians, together with the Kurdish–Jewish communities, spoke dialects of Aramaic, though many also knew Kurdish.

In addition to Muslims, Jews and Christians, exotic religions and sects, from Islamic and more ancient roots, persisted in the region. Syncretistic combinations of Muslim elements with pre-Islamic Persian and Shamanic religions include Yezidis, Ahli-Haq and Alevis. Each religion constituted a closed community with its own authorities and laws, mostly speaking dialects of Kurdish. According to Sunni authority, these sects were 'heretics', while

Christians and Jews were tolerated infidels.

Historically, these religious communities co-existed, mostly peacefully, with traditionally established relations of hierarchy, service and protections, such as the relation between Sunni chieftains and Christian peasants or the place of the Jews in the urban division of labour. Conflicts erupted at intervals, often related to wider alignments and wars, such as the Sunni/Shi'i conflicts generated by Ottoman/Persian rivalry. These conflicts, however, intensified and multiplied from the 19th century with the emergence of modern politics, nationalism and nation-states, and separatist movements.

Religious divisions and sentiments played a very important part in these conflicts and struggles. With the escalating decadence and diminution of the Ottoman Empire in the late 19th century, Sultan Abdul-Hamid played the Islamic card, attempting to rally the Muslims of the world in a holy struggle for his 'caliphate'. Many Sunni Kurds were recruited in this campaign, notably the irregular military force of the Hamidiyya, who then engaged in attacks on Armenians and other Christians, and played an important part in the early Armenian massacres. Subsequently, Sunnis and Yezidis played a part in the attack on the Assyrians by the Iraqi army in 1933.

In the Turkish war of independence following the defeat of the Ottomans in World War I and the occupation of the country by the Allies and the Greeks, the Kurds identified with that struggle as Muslims against Christian invaders. Once the Kemalist republic was established, however, its drive for Turkish nationalism and secularism, notably the suppression of Sufi orders, led to much discontent among the Kurds, and the notable rebellions, such as that of Sheikh Said in 1925, had definite religious motives. Said, a Naqshbandi Sheikh, and his followers aimed for an independent Kurdish state based on Islam, apart from the now secular Turkish Republic, which had abolished the caliphate the previous year.

Ideas and movements of Kurdish nationalism arose in the age of nationalism, with the collapse of the old empires and the emergence of nation-states. The European colonial empires drew lines on the map, dividing territories as nation-states with ethnic designations. The European regions of the Ottoman Empire were the first to establish states, such as the Greek or the Serb, on the basis of common ethnicity and religion. In the Middle East, states were designated 'Arab', 'Turkish' and 'Persian', and eventually 'Jewish'. The Kurds were left out, a fact that aroused a sense of injustice and anger leading to many rebellions. Crucially, however, it sharpened the sense of a Kurdish nationality and the quest for a Kurdish state, or at least recognition of separate identity. Nevertheless, these nationalist ideas and movements co-existed or were superimposed upon constructions and reconstructions of previous forms of identity, of tribe, region and religion. The religious boundaries that matter in more recent times are those within Islam. The Jews are gone, and the Christians are much reduced in number and of little political importance. The most important of the religious divisions in political terms is that between Sunnis and Alevis in Turkey, especially after the Sunni Islamic revival in that country and its politicization. In Iraqi Kurdistan, Islamic movements are divided between Iranian and Saudi allegiance, though they are all Sunnis. The stamp of different Sufi adherence (though not practice) still plays a part in the division of the nationalist leadership in that country. And the Sunni allegiance of most Iranian Kurds is a factor in their relations to the Shi'ite Islamic Republic.

To come back to the general Middle Eastern scene, religious differences and boundaries were politicized in different ways and directions as modern politics evolved in the region. Despite the expectations and aspirations of liberals, secularists and reformers, religious divisions continue to play various important roles in modern politics and conflicts in the region. These are often not in continuity with the past, but are reconstructions of religious sentiments and boundaries in relation to modern situations. What follows is an elaboration of these themes with respect to modern examples.

Religion, Communalism and Nationalism

Religious 'communalism' was, and remains, an important force of solidarity and allegiance in many parts of the world. It is not necessarily based on religious belief or practice, but on communal identification with a religion. Religion acts, in this instance, as an 'ethnic marker'. Northern Ireland presents us with the most prominent example in modern Europe, in which communal solidarity and conflict are based on Catholic/Protestant boundaries, but one in which most members of each community are not religiously observant. This kind of communalist organization and sentiment were and often still are the most important form of allegiance and solidarity in our region. Modern nationalism interacted with these communalist sentiments. An important component of nationalist support, especially at the popular level, was an extension of the communalist principle. European colonial powers were seen as Christians (and later, on the establishment of Israel, as Jews), an extension of a universal Christendom that included local Christian communities. The

European favour and protection for local Christians reinforced this view. European support for Greek, then other Balkan nationalist and separatist movements from the Ottoman Empire added further evidence. Ahmad Lutfi al-Sayyid, an Egyptian liberal nationalist in the early decades of the 20th century, describes this sentiment very well:

> ... whenever Egyptians see European statesmen acting in concert against Egyptian interests or sentiments and agreeing on measures which postpone the day of their independence, they tend to contrast their fortune with that of the Balkan domains of the Ottoman Empire. They conclude that these dependencies have won their independence through European intervention, because their inhabitants are Christians. The impression is thereby gained that there is a certain type of unity among the Christians in Europe, and consequently they wish for unity among Muslims capable of protecting their interests. As Christian unity saved the Balkan countries from the yoke of the Muslim Ottomans, Muslim unity would save Egyptians from European hegemony. This, we believe, is a naïve idea engendered by a faulty understanding of European politics in the East. (Quoted in J. M. Ahmad, *The Intellectual Origins of Egyptian Nationalism* [London: Oxford University Press, 1960], p. 61.)

World politics is then seen as a confrontation between Islam and Christendom, a view that is forcefully revived by some modern Islamists (and more covertly by many nationalists), referring to the West as 'Crusaders', evoking the historical assault on the lands of Islam, as well as drawing on Quranic verses against the Jews and the classics of European anti-Semitic literature to indict all Jews as enemies bent on world domination.

While most nationalist leaders and politicians in every country have proclaimed universal citizenship and equality of members of all religions before the law and in public life, the sentiments underlying nationalism in practice are imbued with these notions of religious solidarity and conflict. The discrimination against non-Muslims in many public spheres, notably in education and employment, as well as conflicts and hostilities at the popular level, are partly fed by these ideas and sentiments. Nationalism in its classic forms, whether liberal or totalitarian, has pitched its ideological thrust against communalism of all sorts – tribal, religious or ethnic – in favour of a homogenous and united nation. Yet, in practice, communalist sentiments, especially the religious ones, feed into its very fabric.

Religious 'Minorities' in the Nation-State

During the periods of European colonial rule, direct or indirect, in many Middle Eastern countries (British occupation, then dominance in Egypt, Mandates in Iraq and Syria), the prevailing sentiment of most non-Muslims (and many of the Muslim bourgeoisie) was favourable to European rule. They had a sense of security of life and property and the rule of law, all favourable to trade and commerce. Some degree of freedom of communication and expression also assured a limited scope for participation in public life. This situation was in marked contrast to the chaotic and repressive regimes that prevailed in the closing decades of Ottoman rule and during the depredations of World War I. At the same time, many non-Muslim intellectuals and professionals were prominently involved in the nationalist struggles and welcomed independence.

The independent states proclaimed equal citizenship regardless of religion or ethnicity. The colonial powers and the League of Nations were particularly sensitive and watchful with regard to the religious 'minorities', and Western press and public opinion was ever receptive to stories of discrimination or persecution of Christians or Jews. The independence movement in Egypt, led by Sa'ad Zaghloul, then the Wafd party he founded, was ever proclaiming the partnership between Muslims and Copts, with the slogan *al-dinu lil-lah wal-watan lil-jami'* (religion [is directed] to God, and the homeland to all [its children]). Only Lebanon emerged from colonial Mandate with a constitution recognizing communal boundaries and making explicit provisions for power-sharing between them. Turkey, Egypt, Syria, Iraq and Iran, followed by the Maghreb countries, proclaimed universal and equal citizenship.

This universalism, however, was qualified by rules and practices that continued aspects of the Ottoman *millet* arrangements. Non-Muslim communities, for instance, were designated as separate electoral constituencies for parliamentary representation in Iraq and Iran. In practically all successor states (not Turkey), personal status law was entrusted to religious authorities ruling in accordance with their own doctrines. Muslim personal status codes were derived from the Shari'a, and some instances entrusted to specialist Shari'a courts, while Christian and Jewish communities constituted their own religious courts, part of a wider corporate organization of the religious community. In most countries, Islam was proclaimed as the religion of the state, with a requirement that the head of state should be Muslim. More

Islamic elements were added in an ad hoc manner to the constitution following political exigencies, notably by Anwar Sadat in Egypt in 1971, then 1980, when he wrote into the Constitution that the Shari'a is the principal source of all legislation in Egypt.

It is widely perceived, quite correctly, that universal citizenship is a fiction and that non-Muslims continued to have distinctive political and social statuses in practice. In any case, for the most part 'citizenship' in the legal and political senses is an elusive concept in most Middle Eastern states, where the rule of law is tenuous and administrative practice capricious. This was particularly clear with regard to Jewish communities, which, at the inception of Israel and the successive wars it entailed, were subject to varying levels of persecution, by authorities and populace, throughout the region, culminating in mass migrations to Israel and elsewhere. Apart from small pockets here and there, ancient Jewish communities in Kurdistan, Iraq, Morocco, Yemen and elsewhere have been displaced. The situation with regard to Christians has varied over time and place.

Egypt is the country where Muslim–Coptic partnership in the nation has been the ideological cornerstone of the modern state. Even the suggestion that Copts are a 'minority' is greeted with howls of indignation from both sides. Copts see themselves, and are seen by liberal nationalists, as the original inhabitants of the country, maintaining a cultural and almost mystical continuity with the Pharaonic past. By the same token they arouse the antipathy of communalist and some religious Muslims. Political and communal leaders have on many occasions resorted to these sentiments as a political manoeuvre to acquire cheap legitimacy. The prominence of Coptic personalities in the Constitutional movement and the Wafd party in the first half of the 20th century made communalist agitation or innuendo a resort for their opponents, including at one point King Fuad in the 1920s, who played the Islamic card in a bid for the then recently vacant Caliphate against Wafd-dominated parliament. His son, Faruq, renewed the manoeuvring for the Caliphate and against the constitutional Wafd, at his accession in 1937. On that occasion the Palace, with the aid of the rector of al-Azhar, orchestrated a campaign against Copts as the agents of the Constitutionalist rejection of the Caliphate, and as such enemies of Islam. More recently, Islamist sentiments and actions have been directed against the Copts. While respectable leaders of the Muslim Brotherhood and Islamic intellectuals continue to proclaim the partnership nationalist slogans, many of their more radical followers and ordinary Muslims have followed different notions of communal separation and subordination. Radical Islamic groups continue to wage campaigns of violence, pillage and assassination against Copts in Upper Egypt. Partly as a result of these insecurities and the readiness of all Egyptians to seek opportunities elsewhere, Copts have been migrating in large numbers to North America, Australia and Europe. This is a tendency notable in all Middle Eastern Christian communities.

Patterns of Non-Muslim Inclusion in Modern Nation-States

The particular history of population composition and movement in each state has determined the mode of inclusion and exclusion of non-Muslims. We may discern two distinct patterns:

I. Egypt/Iraq/Lebanon/Syria. Christians and Jews were native, largely Arabic-speaking communities, sharing in the basic cultural patterns of the country, following class and region (e.g. rural–urban difference). Intellectuals and notables from these communities participated in the public life of the country, including nationalist/liberationist politics and the independence struggles. In modern states and societies, non-Muslims became largely integrated into the economic life and institutions. For the reasons enumerated above, however, their differences from Muslims continued to be marked. At the elite level we find many kinds of subtle discriminations in education and public employment. Intermarriage between communities, no longer rare among the educated, is almost always on the condition of conversion to Islam of the non-Muslim partner, especially if it is the man. At the popular level, communities of different religions may co-exist as good neighbours for generations, but face communalist hostilities arising from political or social changes altering the conditions of co-existence and harmony. Jewish communities suffered in this way at the inception of Israel, as we have seen. Copts in Upper Egypt and elsewhere are subject to communalist hostility since the rise of the Islamist current in 1970s, and politicians are not above playing on these sentiments when it suits them. In Iraq, many rich and educated Christians have benefited, on balance, from the Ba'ath regime, but their poorer co-religionists, especially in the north of the country, have suffered persecution and violence.

II. Turkey and the Maghreb. Here non-Muslims were mostly of different
ethnicity and language. In Turkey, the Christians were predominantly
Greek and Armenian (the most prominent communities in Istanbul,
as well as in many regions), as well as Assyrian, Syriac and Arab.
Jews were for the most part Sephardim, who were Ladino speakers
until recent times when they switched to Levantine French. Many,
especially the urban communities, also spoke Turkish, and in the case
of some of their elites, identified themselves as Ottomans. The modern
Turkish Republic, however, emerged from a war of independence
which pitched nationalists under Mustapha Kemal in a war against
the Greeks, leading to the exchange of populations between Greece
and Turkey. It is interesting to note that in this exchange the definition
of who was Greek and who a Turk was entirely in terms of religion.
Greek-speaking Muslims in Crete were classified as Turks, and Turkish-
speaking Christians as Greeks. Armenian nationalism and separatist
aspirations had already resulted in the famous massacres in the 1910s
and the depletion of their numbers. The Republic, though secular
by constitution, emerged in practice as a Muslim country: Sunni
Islam (of the Hanafi doctrine) became the implicit criterion of 'true'
Turkish citizenship. This did not only exclude Christians and Jews
(mostly nominally Turkish) but also the Alevis of the south-east, with
their esoteric religion and suspect allegiance. The Donme community,
Jews converted to Islam in the 18th century after a failed messianic
movement, remained distinct. Though sectors of this community
became ardent Kemalists and Turkish patriots, the community
continued to be viewed with suspicion and was subject to attacks and
provocation by nationalists and Islamists. Paradoxically, Sunni Kurds
(though of Shafi'i doctrine) could integrate into Turkish citizenship
much more easily than Turkish non-Muslims or Alevis. Middle-class
Kurdish families who settled in the major cities intermarried with the
Turkish bourgeoisie and became largely assimilated. In this respect,
religion continued to be the most important 'communal marker',
more so than ethnicity. The class factor is very important here, because
poor Kurds from peasant backgrounds continue to have distinct
identities and residential quarters in the main cities. This is also the
case with Alevi Kurds, who, nevertheless, remain distinct from their
Sunni compatriots. Islamist agitation, entirely Sunni, has often been
successful in recruiting and mobilizing Sunni Kurds against Alevis
and even conducting extensive massacres of Alevis in recent decades

in the eastern cities of Savas and Marash.

The countries of the Maghreb included indigenous Jewish communities, originally Arabic-speaking and sharing local cultural patterns. Under colonial rule, many Jews, especially of the elite classes, increasingly identified with the French in language, lifestyle and politics. This process went furthest in Algeria, where the colonial rulers offered full enfranchisement to the Jews as French nationals. The modern nationalist movements for independence in these countries sported much greater Islamic identification and more slogans than those of the Mashriq, which, as we saw, included many Christian elements.

The main religious division in Iran is between the Shi'i majority and the Sunnis. The Sunnis are predominantly ethnic Kurds, as well as Baluchis and some Turkmen. The Azeri, a numerically large ethnic and linguistic minority, are at the same time Shi'is, as are some Kurds. The lines of ethnic conflicts and struggles coincide largely with religious divisions. The Shi'i Azeris have a strong sense of ethnic identity and territorial belonging, yet also see themselves as a prominent part of Iran as a nation-state. Separatist sentiments among Azeris are negligible. This is partly explicable in terms of the historical background of Turkish dynasties ruling Iran and the prominent position occupied by Azeris in public life and in business, as well as in religious institutions. But in all these fields, religious affiliation plays an important integrative part not afforded to the Sunni ethnicities. Interestingly, with the liberalization of the political field in recent years, Kurdish voices are being heard speaking in terms of Sunni identity. Leading Kurds in the Islamic Republic are calling not only for Kurdish cultural rights but also for Sunni rights and liberties.

Middle Eastern Regimes and the Revival of Communalism

Politicians and ruling cliques are ever ready to exploit and further communalist sentiments. Indeed, the regimes of Iraq and Syria feature ruling cliques transparently based on kinship, tribal and religious affiliations, while Yemen has an openly tribal-based political system. Important elements of communal affiliations feature in all the countries in the region. These are not persistent features of Arab or Muslim societies, but elements that are actively fostered, often recreated, by the regimes and their political process. Tribalism, for instance, was openly revived by the government in Iraq in the 1990s, placing tribal members, even in the cities, under the authority and legal jurisdiction of their chiefs. Regime clientelism is a common process reinforcing communalism deals with different sectors of the population, granting them protection and material benefits in return for loyalty, cooperation and, where appropriate, business partnership. Or leading members of such groups assume positions within the ruling party, which is no more than a vehicle of loyalty to the leader, and use these positions to favour their affiliates. This encourages sectarian and communalist networks forming around patrons and notables of their community, doing deals with functionaries and parties on behalf of their members. Tribes, families, ethnic and regional groups, as well as religious communities can benefit from such arrangements. These practices tend to reinforce or reconstitute primary solidarities and antipathies between groups at the expense of common citizenship and ideological affiliations. The suppression or active hindrance of all other forms of social or political autonomies in most countries in the region enhances this particularistic solidarity. Conflicts and antipathies, then, are conceived in terms of particularistic membership, notably those of religious community.

Refinement and Oppression of Kurdish Language

Joyce Blau

We know from the work of Arab and Arab-language historians and biographers that the Kurds, from their entry into history in the 7th century with the Muslim conquest, were integrated into the region by their participation in both the expansion of Islam and the development of the Arabic language. This was noted by Prince Sharaf Khan ibn Shams al-din Bidlisi (1543–1604) in his work *Sharafnama*[1] and by the 17th-century traveller Evliya Çelebi.

Throughout their history, the Kurds showed true religious zeal. In the 10th century, the princes of small independent or semi-independent dynasties constructed many religious buildings. In the 12th century, Saladin, Salah al-Din al-Ayyubi, who defeated the Crusaders and conquered much of the Arab world in the name of Sunni Islam, left an impact on Egypt and Syria.[2] The Kurds produced many theologians and jurists, often highly distinguished. In various regions on which they also left a mark, many Kurds have held the position of Sheikh al-Islam up to the present and they have held chairs at al-Azhar University in Cairo. Martin van Bruinessen has found traces of Kurdish influence as far off as Indonesia: 'Kurds have made an impact on Indonesian Islam at least comparable to that of other reputed islamicizers.'[3]

The Kurdish elite wrote in the languages of their overlords. For example, 'Izz al-din Abu Hasan 'Ali ibn al-Athir, the historian, biographer and author of *al-Kamil* (d. 630/1233), ibn Khalikan (d. 681/1282) and Abul-Fida (d.732/1331) all wrote in Arabic. The high-ranking Ottoman dignitary Idris Hakim Bidlisi (d. 1520) wrote the *Hasht Bahasht* ('The Eight Paradises'), recounting the lives of the first eight Ottoman sultans, in Persian.

Creative poets were the first to use Kurdish, their mother tongue, in their work. The first known literary masterpieces that made the Kurdish language a symbol of collective identity, a marker of the identity of the Kurdish people, appeared in the 16th and 17th centuries, when the Ottoman and Persian Empires were consolidating and Kurdistan was then the focal point of the greed of its powerful neighbours, who fought over it relentlessly, leaving behind a trail of destruction. At the end of the 17th century, the poet and philosopher Ahmed Khani formulated the idea that the Kurds were a distinct people, in his *Mam u Zin*. This long '*mathnawi*' of 2,655 distichs, rich in poetic imagery and lyrical scenes, has immortalized Khani for the Kurds, as Firdawsi was immortalized by the Persians, and Homer by the Greeks. The sad romance of the two heroes, Mam and Zin, is replete with national symbolism, and patriotic declarations of faith abound. The poet wrote his romance as a reaction to the growing nationalism of the Ottoman and Safavid.

He says:[4]

(238) Safi shemirand vexwar durdi
       manendi deri lisane kurdi

(239) Inaye nizam u intizami
       keshaye cefa ji boy 'ami

(240) Da xelqi nebejitin ku Akrad
       be me'rifetin be asl u binyad

[Khani] has refined Kurdish speech, filtered the dregs
as had been done for Dari
Forging it into an ordered pattern
suffering the pains of labour for his people
So that no one could declare that the Kurds
are ignorant, lacking roots or high descent.

    He further adds defensively:[5]

(342) Ev miwe eger ne abdar e
       kurmanci ye ew qeder li kar e

(343) Ev tifle eger ne nazenin e
       nubar e qewi bi min shirin e

(344) Ev miwe eger ne pir leziz e
       ev tifle bi min qewi 'eziz e

(345) Mehbub u libas u gushwar e
       Milked min in ne miste'ar e

What if this fruit's not juicy?
It's Kermanji, that's its value.
What if this child's not charming?
It's the first-born, dearest to me.
Even if this fruit is not delicious,
This child is most precious to me
My beloved, her garments, her jewels
Are all mine and nothing is borrowed.

Whatever deficiencies the Kurdish language may have, it is still superior to other tongues, says Khani, who endeavours to extol the beauty and naturalness of his language as a marker of his ethnicity. Khani was a pioneer who instinctively knew that language and literature are bound to culture and 'nation' as well as being signs of ethnicity.

This attitude towards Kurdish was published throughout the 19th and 20th centuries. The poet Hajji Qadir Koyi (born around 1816, died in 1894)[6] wrote:

p. 9.   Millet be kiteb u be nusin
        Gheyri Kurdan niye le ruy zemin

Only the Kurds, of all the people of the world,
remain without books or literature.

p. 24.   Melen fesaheti kurdi be farisi naga
         Belagheteki heye hiç zimani naygate
         Le be te'esubi Kurdane be rewac u beha

Do not say the Kurdish language has not attained the purity of Persian
It possesses an eloquence that reaches unequalled heights
But lack of solidarity among Kurds has debased its value and price

p. 38.   Kiteb u defter u tarikh u kaghez
         Be kurdi ger bi nusraye zimani
         Mela w pir u sheikh u padshaman
         Heta mehshir dema nam u nishani

Had manuscripts and books, history and correspondence
all been written in Kurdish,

Then our Mullahs and Sheikhs and Kings and Princes
would have been recognized until the Day of Resurrection.

Hajji
If you take all Kurdish scholars, both great and small,
they have never read so much as two words in Kurdish.

The first Kurdish newspaper, called significantly *Kurdistan*, was published in 1898 as a bilingual Kurdish–Ottoman paper, not in Kurdistan itself but in Cairo, reflecting the difficulties facing the Kurdish cultural elite. In its first issue, published on 22 April 1898, Miqdad Midhat Badr Khan wrote: 'Today whatever happens in the world is reported in newspapers from which we learn a great deal. Unfortunately, the Kurds, brave and intelligent though they are, live without knowing what is going on on our planet. I am publishing this paper to inform you of the development of events in the world and to encourage you to read and write Kurdish.'

The outbreak of World War I and its aftermath altered the Kurds' situation. Then, following upon earlier division of Kurdistan between the Ottoman and Persian Empires, came the division of the Kurdish territory among the five states of Turkey, Persia/Iran, Iraq, Syria and Armenia. From then on, the fate of the Kurds and the development of their language and literature depended on the degree of freedom granted by those states, in which power was in the hands of ethnic groups more or less hostile to the Kurds.

In Soviet Armenia, the Kurdish community was considered a 'nationality' from the early 1920s, with full recognition of their language. They benefited from the support of the Armenian state and had their own schools, press, publishing house and radio broadcasts. Illiteracy among the Kurds, mostly Yezidis (and therefore illiterate), was soon overcome, and an intellectual elite began to flourish. Kurdish poets and prose writers published their works first in a modified Armenian alphabet, then in a Latin alphabet, and then, from 1946 on, in a modified Cyrillic alphabet. Kurdish studies developed in Leningrad as well as in Moscow, Yerevan and Baku, where several scholarship students from Iraq and Syria came from the early 1960s to complete their graduate studies and defend their doctoral theses. But after the collapse of the Soviet Union, the power takeover by the nationalist regime led by the Dashnak Party in Armenia has completely transformed the lives of the Kurds. More than 20,000 Kurds, who until then had lived peacefully beside their neighbours, were expelled and forced to seek asylum in Russian cities.

When after World War I the British annexed the Kurdish Vilayet of Mosul to the new Arab state of Iraq, their first act was to dismiss Turkish officials and replace them with Kurds 'assisted' by British advisers. In 1919, the British introduced Kurdish in place of Turkish for official matters and Persian for personal correspondence. The development of the Kurdish press in the town of Sulaimaniya – by Major E. B. Soane – facilitated the spread of Sorani Kurdish, which writers and poets renewed and perfected. Kurdish poets used the Arabic–Persian alphabet, which is however inadequate for transcribing Kurdish. This inspired Kurdish intellectuals and specialists to call for the adoption of a Latin alphabet. In Baghdad in 1933, Tawfiq Wahby, then governor of Sulaimaniya, published a booklet titled *Xondewariy Baw* ('Traditional Literacy'), proposing a Latin alphabet of 28 letters. The same year, Vladimir Minorsky wrote: 'Latin script comes into question when a new form of phonetic script is under consideration for a language just acquiring a literary importance. For the success of reform in Kurdish, it is essential that the Latin alphabet should be utilized in its most simple form with as few additions of conventional signs as possible.'[7] C. J. Edmonds was of the same opinion,[8] but the Kurds came up against social-political opposition: they were citizens of Iraq, an Arab state, where the knowledge and use of Arabic as well as a shared intellectual life were imposed on them. And the Iraqi government intensified its opposition to all attempts to Latinize the Kurdish alphabet. Further, it required Kurdish schools to teach only one language, and thus the language of Sulaimaniya was chosen and imposed on schools in all Kurdish provinces, including Bahdinan, where the dominant language belongs to the northern group of Kurdish dialects. The children in Zakho, 'Amadiya, 'Aqra and Dohuk felt that they were learning a foreign language, and left school, until finally the Bahdinan school system decided to teach in Arabic. It was only in the 1990s, with the establishment of the Kurdish Autonomous Region where the Kurds are finally masters of their own region, that the Bahdinan schools began to teach in Kurdish.

This era of freedom and especially of contact with the West (translations of Byron, Shelley, Lamartine, Pushkin, etc.) transformed poetic diction. The strait-jacket of classical and traditional poetry came off. New genres were adopted and enabled the Kurdish struggle to be rendered in a more dramatic and lively manner. Kurdish poets, writers and creative artists came out of their long isolation and Iraqi Kurdistan became the centre of Kurdish cultural life, where literary creation was to progress and develop.

On the other slope of the northern mountain range, the Turkish Republic was carrying out an assimilationist policy towards its Kurdish subjects. In the name of national unity, the Kemalist government denied the identity of the several million Kurds. Language being more than a mere instrument of communication, the Kemalist government ordered the Kurdish language, described as archaic and backward, to disappear. On 3 March 1924, the very day that the Caliphate was abolished, Mustapha Kemal decreed the prohibition of all Kurdish schools, associations and publications. Teaching and publishing in Kurdish were forbidden on pain of severe sanction. The ban was extended to speaking Kurdish in government offices and in public places. Physical separation from the family was another method used by Turkish authorities to prevent a child from speaking Kurdish. Use of the words 'Kurdish' or 'Kurdistan' was made a legal offence. Since then, the Turkish government has pursued a policy of forced assimilation of the Kurds.

Kurdish intellectuals went into exile to Syria and Lebanon under the French Mandate. A petition addressed to the Mandate authorities in June 1928 requested the right to use the Kurdish language and to teach in Kurdish in the Kurdish regions of Syria. The Mandate authorities refused. A number of intellectuals then gathered around Prince Jeladet Bedir Khan, who was under town arrest in Damascus after the defeat of the Mount Ararat insurrection. They became the architects of a Kermanji Kurdish revival. The Kurdish alphabet they developed, close to the new Turkish alphabet, was adopted and soon became the working tool of all Kurdish literature published by the northern group. Use of the alphabet was spread by the review *Hawar* ('The Call') in 1932. In the first issue, Prince Jeladet laid down the 'purpose and nature of the review' (p. 7). To comply with the requirements of the French mandatory authorities, which had just permitted publication, the editors wrote:[9] 'We have founded our review, *Hawar*, exclusively for scientific and literary aims. It will fulfil an important need for the Kurdish nation. On no account will it be concerned with politics. It will deal only with academic subjects of interest both to Kurds and to foreigners who wish to improve their acquaintance with the languages and nations of the East ... Here are the basic points of our programme: 1. Expansion of the use of the Kurdish alphabet by Kurds. Classification of Kurdish grammar and publication of grammar books in Kurdish and later on in French.' The other paragraphs of the programme dealt with Kurdish folklore, written literature, music, dance and customs.

But after World War II, the newly independent Syria prohibited all Kurdish publications, and Kurdish nationalists were prosecuted and thrown in prison.

Like the Turkish government, the government of Persia – and then of Iran – also carried out an assimilationist policy towards the Kurdish population. The first Persian constitution, adopted in 1906, made Persian the sole official language of the multilingual Persian Empire. After the 1921 coup d'etat, which brought Reza Khan to power, a circular issued in 1923 by the General Directorate of Education prohibited the use of Kurdish in schools. Kurdish schools were forbidden, Kurdish publications closed – the simple fact of owning a book written in Kurdish could cost the owner seven years' imprisonment. Kurds were arrested, humiliated and tortured on charges of speaking Kurdish. The ban was then extended to cultural traditions, dress, music and dance.

In the first programme of the Democratic Party of Kurdistan of Iran, founded on 16 August 1945, we read: 'The Kurdish people in Iran should have the right to study in their mother tongue. The official administrative language in the Kurdish territory should be Kurdish' (Article 2). In fact, the major period of development of Kurdish language and literature in Iran took place during the short-lived Kurdish Republic of 1946, when Kurdish became the official language of the administration, the press and the school. But all efforts to develop Kurdish language and literature were brutally stopped by the repression that followed the overthrow of the Republic in December 1946. The leaders were hanged and the intellectuals forced into exile. Again, the government imposed Persian as the sole official language of Iranian Kurdistan. And even today, opening a Kurdish school, even a private one, is against the law in Iran.

At the beginning of the 1980s the Islamic regime lifted the ban on Kurdish publications – subject, however, to severe censorship – but the teaching of Kurdish in schools remains prohibited. The monthly review *Sirwe* (named after a light breeze), founded in Urumiya by the poet Haymin (today put out by Ahmed Qadi), has played a major role in the development of Kurdish language and literature in Iran.[10] Other magazines came out, such as *Awene* ('The Mirror', Tehran, no. 1, 1986), edited by Sayyid Mohammad Mosavi, *Awiyer/Abider* (the name of a mountain), published in Sine in 1375/1996 and edited by Behram Weledbegi.

The 1970 truce between the Iraqi government and the Kurds provided the opportunity for significant development of Kurdish language and literature in Iraq. Poets and writers published their works in 29 new periodicals, of which two were published in Kirkuk, six in Hawler/Arbil and four in Sulaimaniya. Baghdad became the major Kurdish cultural centre. A Kurdish Academy of

Science was created in 1970, in Baghdad, and a University in Sulaimaniya the following year. An interesting phenomenon developed, which was to be repeated elsewhere. Kurdish intellectuals from various parts of Iraq, who until then had been fairly well integrated into Arab intellectual life, started to become 'Kurdicized'. Journalists, historians, linguists, scientists, engineers and others started to write in Kurdish. But this emergent literary creativity suffered the repercussions of the breakdown in negotiations between the Kurds and Saddam Hussein, who had come to power in Iraq, and then from the two Gulf wars.

During the same period, persecuted writers sought refuge in Europe, where they joined the hundreds of thousands of Kurdish immigrant workers. Sweden, which carries out an exemplary policy for integrating immigrants, takes into account the role of the mother tongue as the foundation on which bilingualism is built. If any part of a linguistic or cultural identity goes unrecognized, it ends up weakening the basis for continued language development in the minority language. Sweden has been the only country that grants Kurdish immigrant communities their identity as Kurds, and encourages their integration by developing this cultural identity. There has been a remarkable renaissance of Kermanji Kurdish, which, for lack of freedom, was fading away in Turkey and Syria. It called for a great deal of courage and perseverance for the young intellectuals to 'Kurdicize' their writing, when previously they had written only in Turkish or Arabic.

In the spring of 1991, after more than half a century of negation of Kurdish identity, Turgut Özal recognized the existence of the Kurdish language in Turkey. Kurdish poets and writers published their works in Kurdish and Kurdish–Turkish reviews and magazines put out by Kurdish publishing houses in Istanbul, Ankara and Diyarbakir. To do this they braved tremendous difficulties, not only the terrible war that was being waged in Turkish Kurdistan but also death threats, often carried out: over 4,500 Kurdish intellectuals have been assassinated in Turkey. In December 1991, *Rojname* ('The Journal'), the first magazine to be authorized, was published in Istanbul in Kurdish and Zaza by Ahmet Okçuoglu, with a circulation of 45,000. *Govend* ('The Round Dance'), edited by the poet Mazhar Kara, appeared at the same time in Diyarbakir. But the publications were often banned and their editors arrested, prosecuted and often even assassinated. These publications would then reappear shortly thereafter with a new name and another editor.

In Iraq, within the security zone created in 1992 to protect three Kurdish provinces, Kurdish literature flourished, and writers and poets, enjoying a hitherto unknown freedom, adapted readily to democracy. As early as 1992, 77 newspapers and magazines appeared, 38 in Hawler/Arbil, 25 in Sulaimaniya, 12 in Duhok and one in Kirkuk.

In 1996, US mediation resulted in a truce between the Kurdistan Democratic Party and the Patriotic Union of Kurdistan, and the establishment in the Kurdistan Region of two Kurdish zones. They soon began competing with one another in the area of publication. The universities of Sulaimaniya, Hawler/Arbil and Duhok developed their teaching, and opened their doors to several thousand students, who study under Kurdish professors and also well-known Arab professors from Baghdad universities. Today, in the two zones of Iraqi Kurdistan there are altogether about a hundred specialized Kurdish reviews, magazines and periodicals, devoted to all branches of learning, e.g. literature, women's literature, theatre, cinema, archeology, strategic research, etc.

Of interest are attempts to Latinize the Kurdish script, which are under way both in Arbil/Hawler and in Duhok. In Arbil/Hawler, magazines such as *Dicle* and *Golani Latini* have come out in the Kurdish–Latin alphabet, commonly known as the 'Hawar' alphabet. In Duhok, magazines and journals, such as *Peyv* ('The Word'), *Gazi* ('The Call'), *Metin* (the name of a mountain) and *Lalish* (a Yezidi newspaper), are published in both Latin and Arabic alphabets. The aims of this cultural revolution are, on the one hand, to create closer bonds with fellow Kurds across the border in Turkey and Syria and in the diaspora, and, on the other, to make the literature of Iraqi Kurdistan better known abroad and to benefit from literary advances in other parts of Kurdistan.

These efforts represent an important step in the Kurds' struggle to realize their dream of unifying the Kurdish language and, one day, Kurdistan. Today, most, perhaps even all Kurdish men and women of letters feel that Kurdish is a genuine medium of expression of their ethnic identity and an important criterion distinguishing them ethnically and nationally from their neighbours.

Notes

1. To date, the *Sharafnama*, or *The History of the Various Kurdish Princes and Dynasties*, written in Persian, is the source of our knowledge of medieval history.
2. The Ayyubids, who transformed the Syrian–Egyptian region into a stronghold of Sunnism and established states modelled on the semi-feudal family federation of Anatolian, Iranian and Kurdish tradition, also left their mark on the urban landscape

of Fustat. The city wall of Cairo was rebuilt with ramparts made up of mighty towers like those found in Diyarbakir. The rooms of the rich Cairene dwellings were separated by an *iwan* like those found in northern Mesopotamia. In size, Shafi'i's tomb, ample enough to receive the large numbers of Sunnites who came to pray at the master's tomb, no longer resembled the small Fatimid funerary monument.

3. Martin van Bruinessen, 'Kurdish 'Ulama and their Indonesian Students', in: *De Turcicis aliisque rebus. Commentarii, Henry Hofman dedicati* (Utrecht, 1991), p. 206.

4. Ahmed Khani, *Mam u Zin*, text annotated, translated, introduced and indexed by M. B. Rudenko (Moscow, Progress Publishers 1962).

5. Ibid., pp. 43–44.

6. In: Sa'id, *Komele Shi'ri Hajji Qadir Koyi* (Baghdad and Sulaimaniya: Dar al-Salam Publishing), 1925.

7. Vladimir Minorsky, 'Remarks on the Romanized Kurdish Alphabet', *Journal of the Royal Asiatic Society*, 190, 1933, pp. 643–650.

8. C. J. Edmonds, 'Some Developments in the Use of Latin Characters for the Writing of Kurdish, *Journal of the Royal Asiatic Society*, July 1933, pp. 629–642.

9. *Hawar*, year 1, Sunday 15 May 1932.

10. Salah al-Din Ayubbi publishers, P.O. Box 717, Urumiya.

Tying Down the Territory:
Conceptions and Misconceptions
of Early Kurdish History

Maria O'Shea

Introduction

For a variety of reasons, the history of both the Kurds and Kurdistan is poorly represented in conventional historical accounts of the Middle East, and it is easy to see why Kurds have come to feel that they are deliberately excluded from such accounts. As far as ancient history is concerned, we appear to know a great deal more about those civilizations that no longer exist, possibly because they now represent no possible threat to the present ruling powers. The Kurdish nationalist movement seems to have now reached such a level of consciousness that a more complete history is sought to complete the 'imagining' of the Kurdish nation.

The Kurdish nationalist discourse on Kurdish history has traditionally devoted most efforts to the examination of certain defining moments in Kurdistan's history, and the speculative ancient history of the Kurds was, until recently, usually accorded only brief coverage. This, until the last decade, usually consisted of noting the references of Greek historians and geographers to peoples whose names bore some etymological similarity to the Kurds, and an examination of the origins of the word 'Kurd', after Driver et al.[1] Writers on the Kurds, both Kurds and non-Kurds, were happy to reiterate that the Kurds were probably the descendants of the Medes or, less commonly, the Gutis, without feeling the need either to create a complete ancient history or to ensure an overlap between the history of the ethnos and that of Kurdistan itself. The imperative to establish an ancient territorial claim was subordinate to that of claiming a distinct ethnic identity to their neighbours and their descendants. The questions surrounding Kurdish origins, their ancient history and indeed that of their present territory, Kurdistan, were largely left unanswered, even in nationalist tracts.

However, the early attempts to establish an ancient separate identity for the Kurds fused with the desire to establish a continuity of habitation, identical to the extent of present territorial claims. The work of certain Kurdish writers has identified the history of the Kurds with that of the territory of Kurdistan, and this is best illustrated by an examination of the work of Mehrdad Izady of Harvard University, whose writing illustrates both the logical culmination of this fusion and the speed with which certain ideas can become part of the Kurdish nationalist discourse.

The difficulties inherent in attempting to clarify the ancient history of the Kurds and Kurdistan illuminate the ease with which one persuasively argued account can enter the pantheon of Kurdish nationalist myths.

Some Historical and Geographical Dilemmas

It has been claimed that geographical as well as historical accounts of a region or state 'tell it from the victor's angle'.[2] This arises from two tendencies. The first is that of generalizing about core doctrines, values and political orientations of nationalist movements, and thus losing the historical accuracy and dynamism inherent in conflicts. Secondly, there is a tendency to accept the dominance of state-centred core–periphery perspective and the assumptions arising out of that viewpoint. The sub-state actors are neglected and the stateless minority may be perceived as victims, rather than as creative and dynamic. Historians and geographers tend to read materials written in the languages of the dominant state, rather than the minority languages; thus the minorities' ideas are poorly represented in scholarly literature.[3]

It should be borne in mind that the history of Kurdistan and the history of the Kurds are in fact two distinct fields, and it is this obvious but fundamental axiom that fails to inform and flaws most attempts to establish and elaborate a history of both. A similar dilemma presented itself to the founders of modern Turkey. The Turks originated in Central Asia, and by the time they arrived in Anatolia many of the great Anatolian civilizations were already long past or in terminal decline, like the Byzantines. Apart from a school of nationalist thought in the 1930s, the Turks do not usually claim to be the descendants of these peoples, such as the Hittites, but use them to illustrate the ancient and illustrious history of Anatolia, or the present geographical expression of Turkey. Of the Turks themselves, nothing is really known before the 6th century AD. Following a period at the start of the Republic, during which Anatolian history was emphasized rather than pan-Turkism, investigation of the Central Asian origins of Turkic peoples continues. Until the end of the 19th century, Turkish history was considered to be that of the Ottoman Empire or of Islam, and, while emphasizing the newer, modernizing achievements of the Turkish Republic, the achievements of the past have been included in the nationalist myth. Thus, in less than eighty years, the breadth of Turkish history has dramatically widened, incorporating three very different pasts into the service of the national myth.[4] Of course, as in many other nationalist histories, the role and even existence of the non-ancestral other national groups, such as the Armenians, Greeks and Kurds, has been ignored or excised.

Nationalist Historical Constructs and the Building of a Myth

Pitifully little is really known of the early history of the Eastern Anatolia/ Zagros inhabitants. Accounts exist largely courtesy of the surrounding plains cultures. This has not prevented some Kurds from conflating a historical myth of continuous inhabitancy of the region with a clearly identifiable Kurdish ethnos, commencing at least as early as the time of the Medes, and even much earlier. Much of this mythology is based on etymological supposition. This makes accounts of the pre-Islamic period very confusing, especially when they refer to (usually unsourced) contemporaneous inscriptions and accounts. Moreover, as Izady correctly points out, 'Middle Eastern history has all too often been written by its hegemons'.[5]

Few issues have recently gripped Kurdish academics and even Kurdish sympathizers as much as the question of the origins of the Kurds, which they seem to feel must be decisively clarified and recorded. In historically autonomous states, continuity is expressed through the legal and political institutions, but people like the Kurds, with no state apparatus, need to exploit different resources to create a cultural continuity and a collective memory. As Anthony Smith described it, 'creating nations is a recurrent activity which has to be renewed periodically'.[6] The insistence on creating a myth of early origins appears to be part of this process.

Although they lack the dominant common ancestor folk-myth that exists in several tribally organized societies in the Middle East, many Kurds choose to believe that they are the descendants of the Medes, despite the absence of evidence that the Medes remained intact during successive waves of both invasion and migration from other tribes into this area.[7] This is also the starting point for most brief accounts of Kurds and Kurdistan, as well as the accepted lore of most 19th- and early 20th-century travellers and writers.[8] This innocuous supposition is persuasive, but the main territorial premise underlying it spawned further attempts to establish an older pedigree based on extending the same logic.

There is no reason to believe that the Medes or, indeed, any other group should have preserved their racial integrity, even in their mountain fastness, when the other defunct regional empires' inhabitants were absorbed into new ruling groups. It is of course more realistic to see the Kurds as an amalgam of the many groups that made their home in the Anatolia/Zagros axis and of those who passed through on their way to elsewhere. Indeed, Qassemlou confidently asserted that, 'it has been scientifically proved that Kurds are the descendants of the Zagros area, ancient residents of the Zagros area, and of the Indo-European tribes that entered this territory during the second millennium BC'.[9] He then goes on to establish credentials for the Gutis tribes. But on the same page he notes that the Kurds are generally regarded as the descendants of the Medes, and that their history begins with the conquest of Niniveh in 612 BC. He also discusses the etymology of the word 'Kurd', applying all common theories with equal enthusiasm.[10] An early exponent of this Medes ancestry theory was Hussein Al-Hussnni Mukriani, native of Rawanduz, possibly the possessor of the first printing press in Kurdistan, who wrote an account of Kurdish history, replete with Aryan motifs, in 1925. This work is little known and rarely referred to, as it stressed the Kurdish links with their Aryan homeland.[11]

The Gutis, who were established in the area to the north-west of the Kassites and north of the Akkadian Empire, also feature regularly in attempts to establish the origins of the Kurds. This is attractive, as considerably more is known about the Gutis, from Assyrian as well as Sumerian records. Their warrior history and temporary conquest of Akkadia and Sumer render them ideal candidates to be Kurdish ancestors. Waheed, in a 1955 Pakistani work on the Kurds, gives innumerable etymological suggestions for the origins of the Kurds, based on Assyrian inscriptions, and also suggests the Gutis as the Kurds' ancestors. Waheed writes that local tales have the boundaries of the 24th-century BC Gutian kingdom the same as those of present-day Kurdistan, until the absorption of most of it into the Assyrian Empire, and affirm that Kurds widely accepted the Guti as their ancestors.[12] His account of Gutian history continues as if they were the direct ancestors of the Kurds. This conclusion was also reached by Safrastian in 1945, who also discounted entirely the 'Medes were Kurds' theory in favour of the survival of the Guti under other names,[13] and Zaki Amin in 1931.[14] More recently, a United States Congressman told the US Congress that the Kurdish Guti kings ruled Persia and Mesopotamia for over 4,000 years.[15]

The culmination of attempts to establish an unbroken chain of Kurdish historical presence in Kurdistan, as well as a glorious history, is reached in one of the most outstanding, as well as astonishing attempts to create a complete Kurdish history by using a combination of remembered, recovered, invented and borrowed history,[16] that of Mehrdad Izady, a Kurdish scholar from the Department of Near Eastern Languages and Civilizations at Harvard University.[17] He traces the existence of Kurdish culture back more than 50,000 years, to include the Neanderthal findings in the Shanidar caves. His thesis is the astounding claim that, 'I treat as Kurdish every community that has ever inhabited the territory of Kurdistan and has not acquired a separate identity to this day, or been unequivocally connected with another identifiable nation, the bulk of which is or was living outside the territories of Kurdistan. This is consistent with what is accepted by consensus for the identification of the ancient Egyptians or Greeks, and the relationship they have to modern Egyptians and Greeks.'[18] Using this thesis, as well as judicious extension of the boundaries of Kurdistan, Kurds can claim credit for the Neolithic revolution;[19] the invention of agriculture (prior to Mesopotamia); the domestication of animals; the invention of material technologies, such as pottery, metalwork and textiles; cuneiform writing; and urban communities, until Kurdistan was overshadowed by Mesopotamia. According to Izady, although this claim is unsourced and elsewhere not mentioned, in the third millennium BC the Qutils established a unified kingdom and were the only Zagros group to conquer part of Mesopotamia, namely Akkadia and Sumer, which they ruled for 170 years.[20]

Izady elaborates on the existence of city-states and kingdoms before the Median Empire's hegemony. Rather than being absorbed or dispersed by invading groups, Izady posits that the indigenous peoples absorbed whichever of the new arrivals might contribute something. Contrarily, new arrivals were never allowed to establish a different ethnic dominance in the region, only to add cultural traits. Thus the Hurrians established a new identity for the existing peoples by unifying them, rather than displacing them. Political pluralism and liberal culture is also considered to have been a feature of 'all ruling houses with their roots in Kurdistan'.[21] The logical fate of the population of a weakened area beset by successive waves of Median and Scythian invaders escapes Izady, who then sees the Kurds, having been Aryanized, as the rulers of the new Median Empire. Although admitting to 1,500 years of Assyrian hegemony in the region and the integration of Aryan groups, the Medes and pre-Aryans, Izady appears to assume that the inhabitants of Kurdistan can form a continuous culture, despite such transformations as he describes. He claims that, 'Kurdish political hegemony stretched from Greece ... to the Straits of Hormuz' in the first century BC, having thrown off Achaemenian and Seleucid rule. Presumably he means that the Parthian Empire was Kurdish, thanks to its Median element.[22]

Even during the classical period, for which there are more sources, Izady continues his flawed axioms. A fundamental problem in Izady's reasoning is that he confuses the Kurds with Kurdistan. Although a history of a non-state area would be an admirable project, giving a broad scope to aid understanding, his desperate desire to associate the modern Kurds with the extent of their current territory informs and obfuscates all his work.

Although Izady's thesis is so fundamentally flawed, the overall theme is likely to become an inherent part of the Kurdish mythology. Indeed, many articles and works now refer to Izady as an authority on Kurdish history. The comprehensiveness of his work, as well as the assurance with which it is presented, imply a widely accepted version of events. The striking and novel use of maps makes the ideas presented both easily grasped and reproduced. Since the publication of this work, several of his themes have become explicit in other works, certainly in what might be loosely termed 'propaganda literature', in the way that the works of European and other travellers were cited. Citing Izady's work offers an alternative to charges of orientalism, lends a pseudo-academic tone to writings and can be used to justify almost any Kurdish nationalist myths. This also illustrates the difficulties inherent in working with secondary sources, especially for the ancient history of the region.

The burgeoning electronic media allow Kurds to disseminate ideas rapidly throughout Kurdish communities in the diaspora and also to other interested parties. The recent rapid growth in 'Kurdish' websites has meant that the work of Izady has received a much wider audience than could have previously been imagined. In perusing many of these sites, it is apparent that information on certain topics, especially on ancient history, has been lifted wholesale from Izady's writing.

Izady's work is the logical culmination of years of writing, both by Kurds and non-Kurds, on these themes. The writer of a 1990 article claims that, 'We are in possession of ancient historical records which establish beyond a doubt that the Kurds have been living continuously in the Kurdistan highlands since the beginning of history in 3000 BC.' The 'beginning of history' is defined as the time of the first written historical records in Sumer.[23] This confusing account continues to tell us that the Kurds are recorded in Sumerian records in reference to the Land of Karda, near to Lake Van and connected (how is not elaborated) to the Kur-ti-e, who lived to the west of the lake, with whom Tiglath Pileser I fought. Tiglath Pileser I also defeated the Gutis, so it is hard to see the tangent connecting the Guti with the Kur-ti-e,[24] who would then appear to be contemporary with them. The history of the Gutis then expanded, as well as their destruction at the hands of the Assyrians, who then 'waged war against ancient Kurds and their ethnic relations ... for 700 years'.[25] The Kashshu, the Guti, the Lulu and the Shubaru are all then considered to be Kurdish.

The same article refers to the 'Zagros nation', those many groups of Zagros peoples referred to in historical records. Thus there is a shift away from the purely philological argument to the territorial argument, whereby, as for Izady, any past inhabitant of present-day Greater Kurdistan was Kurdish. Indeed, al-Karadaghi claims that the Zagros tribes were homogeneous in speech and ethnically related. Among these groups the most prominent were the Elamites and the Kurds, who lived to their north. The Kurds are then claimed as of the Elamite group and as belonging to an ancient Caucasian race. Bizarrely, the Kurds are considered to belong to this ancient Caucasian race, and yet all the other Zagros groups were 'branches of the same ancient Kurds who appeared on the scene at historical times and in different parts of the Zagros highlands'.[26] The article concludes that, 'the kingdoms of Lullu, Guti, Nari, Urartu, and the new empires of Kassite and Hurri-Mittani were founded by the same group of people who were ethnically and linguistically related'.[27] The Kurds are then presumed to have 'coalesced with the Medes, when they changed their Caucasian language to the Median dialect'.[28] At the downfall of the Median Empire, the Medians did not migrate, but the ruling Median elite was absorbed by the Kurdish, non-Median subjects, who were already speaking Median.[29] To some extent this is logical, but ignores the effects of further invasions.

The art and material culture of the Medes is poorly recorded; indeed, the British Museum notes the elusive nature of Median artefacts,[30] yet there exists a plethora of attempts to draw connections between Median and Kurdish culture. The al-Karadaghi article is one of many attempts to compare Kurdish physical types, dress, music and war customs with those of the Medes.[31] Further attempts were made at an exhibition in New York in 1995 to link modern Kurdish head-dresses with archaeological remains of 1,800 to 2,900 years ago.[32]

Jwadieh, in his classic, much cited 1960 dissertation on the origins of Kurdish nationalism, devotes only 26 pages to the pre-Islamic history of the Kurds and does not refer to the existence of a Kurdish entity in that period. He notes that the Kurds never established a great empire of their own, but that, 'The Empire of the Medes, one of the reputed ancestors of the Kurdish people, was the only great national state which may be said to have been established by the Kurds.'[33] In his chapter on the history and origins of the Kurds, Jwadieh uses the same variety of philological and historiographic source material that still informs later writings on the topic, yet concludes, after Minorsky, that the 'Medes and the Parthians played a very important role in shaping the character and the composition of the Kurdish race and language,'[34] rather than reaching any firm conclusions on Kurdish origins. The ambivalent approach that Jwadieh adopts seems to imply that the ancient history of the Kurds and also their connection with the spatial expression of Kurdistan was a less important component of the nationalist movement at that time.

Kurdistan and the Kurds in Academic History

General texts on the history of the Middle East, both academic and popular, tend not to dwell on the Kurds, perhaps appropriately to their marginal locations in the empires and states that are seen as the main historical actors in the region. As discussed, the ancient history of the region is that of the successful empires, and to a large extent, the modern history is also that of the hegemons. The Kurds are marginalized in all their host cultures; thus their version of or role in history is not really covered by mainstream historians. Their historiographic materials are scattered and varied, and there are no central archives for Kurdish history.

However, on occasion, the coverage of the role of the Kurds in history or in the modern Middle East is so neglected, distorted or one-dimensionally portrayed that it is easy to see how the Kurds may see an academic complicity in a conspiracy to deny them or Kurdistan an existence. Certainly, it would appear that academics tend to approach their subjects from the direction in which they are most comfortable, and that is usually the history or political culture of one of the region's major powers. Thus approaches are informed by the absorbed prejudices of that culture.

Wallerstein sees recounting the past as a social act of the present; accordingly, all history is transitory knowledge and the truth changes as society does. There is no such thing as an uncommitted historian or social scientist; all assertions of truth are based on assumptions involving the metaphysics of values. He also notes that objective knowledge can be produced only when all major groups in the world system are represented.[35] It is certainly true that neither Kurds nor Kurdistan are well represented in mainstream Middle Eastern studies. There is generally a wide gulf in academic style and credibility between studies of Kurdistan and those of states, empires and the wider region.

In *The Shaping of the Modern Middle East*, Bernard Lewis notes that the Kurds are the one remaining linguistic and ethnic minority of any importance surviving in the central lands of the Middle East, and that there is evidence that they have been there since remote antiquity.[36] Other than that, they are mentioned only briefly as a complication to Arabism in Iraq.[37]

In *The Making of the Modern Near East*, Yapp accords the history of the Kurds a greater prominence, including the Ottoman attempts to destroy the remaining Kurdish emirates at the end of the 18th century, the increased conflict between the Armenians and the Kurds, the role of the Hamidiyya cavalry and the problems associated with dealing with the Kurds after World War I.[38]

Yet in the seminal *The Near East since the First World War*, Yapp allocates only a few scattered paragraphs to the Kurds. Although the various Kurdish insurrections are referred to, their underlying causes are not examined. The six wars between the Iraqi Kurds and the government are dealt with summarily; he covers the fifth war by saying only that, '[the government] resumed struggle against armed guerrillas in Kurdistan'.[39] The 1979 Iranian Kurdish uprising is mentioned, but its course and outcome is not, other than, '... it continued for several years'.[40]

In the updated section of the newest edition of the work, covering the period 1989–95, the increase in Kurdish nationalism since 1960 is noted for the first time. Despite a lack of detail on the nationalist violence in Turkey from the 1970s, there is room to establish that the violence was only on the part of the Kurds, and that it was financed by forced loans and the proceeds of crime.[41] Although establishing that 15,000 lives were lost between 1992 and 1995, as a result of the conflict in Turkish Kurdistan, and that 200,000 Turkish soldiers are based in eastern Turkey, Yapp asserts that the Turkish government made 'extensive concessions' to the Kurds in 1991, and that 'some degree of autonomy' was granted in 1993.[42]

In the same text, Yapp states that the Kurds of the Syrian Jezireh, 50 per cent of the population, are opposed to integration in Syria.[43] In fact, this area was the object of plans for an Arab cordon, not fully instituted, in the 1960s. And between 1965 and 1975, some 30,000 Kurds were forced to leave this area for Lebanon or major cities, as a result of official harassment and the implantation of 7,000 armed Arab settlers, displaced by the Tabqa Dam.[44] The ways in which the 1990 Gulf war affected the Kurds of Iraq is not mentioned, nor is the attempted genocide of the Kurds in Iraq.

A more balanced account of the recent history of the Middle East is that of Cleveland, who refers to the Kurds at several key junctures from 1920 onwards and up to their role in the 1990 Gulf war and the establishment of the 'safe havens' in May 1991. The activities of the Kurds or critical location of Kurdistan before 1920 are not discussed, but coverage of that period is necessarily brief.[45]

There have been several doctoral theses concerning aspects of Kurdish history[46] and several works on specific periods, notably the pioneering works of Robert Olson.[47] The work of Professor Ahmad, especially concerning Russian primary sources and the early 20th century is also unique,[48] and many non-historians have contributed to the oeuvre.[49] The majority of writing on Kurdish history appears in journal articles. Probably the broadest and bravest attempt at a history of the Kurds is McDowall's landmark *A Modern History of the Kurds*.[50] Even here, the coverage of the spatial frame is limited to after the Arab invasion, the Kurds of Syria and Russia are ignored (for reasons of space) and certain periods are dealt with very sketchily. Nevertheless, this work, aimed at the general reader, is the only substantial attempt at both presentation and analysis of the broad modern history of the Kurds. Before this work, the classic texts on Kurdistan generally followed a similar structure of dealing with Kurdistan according to its host states, with no reference to primary historiographic sources. They also tended to be edited works, with widely varying content and style from chapter to chapter, covering considerably more aspects of Kurdistan than the historical.

Kurdistan Before Islam

The Anatolia/Zagros axis has formed a natural barrier to empire expansion since Sargon I (2371–2316 BC) and his successors created the first Mesopotamian Empire. Sargon's Acadian Empire collapsed partly as a result of repeated raids by mountain dwellers from the central Zagros. The successive empires of Ur, Assyria and Babylon also failed to totally breach the Zagros divide. The Zagros region was home to many small kingdoms and city-states, mostly known of only through the records of the contiguous plains cultures. From 1244 to 650 BC much of western Kurdistan lay within the new powerful Assyrian Empire. Tiglath Piliser I waged war on a people called Kur-ti-e in the mountains of Azu, identified by Driver as the modern Hazo (Sasun) range to the west of Lake Van,[51] which is often offered as proof of the existence of ancestors of the Kurds.[52] For 700 years the Assyrians fought with many Zagros inhabitants such as the Gutis and the Kassites.

The constant friction between the plains and mountain dwellers so weakened the Zagros tribes that the Medes and other Aryan invaders found little resistance. The Median Empire, established by the Zagros tribes with help from the Persians to the east, was based in the heart of the Zagros range – for the first time an empire straddled this area, and for the last time the mountain dwellers were able to dominate the plains dwellers. Although technically the region was under Persian Achaemenian control by the sixth century BC, there is little evidence that the central government was able to exert any control over these mountains, nor indeed that they had any great interest in this inaccessible, poorly explored area.

At the start of the period of Persian/Greek rivalry within the Middle East, Xenophon noted in 401 BC that the Karduchoi, who inhabited the mountains to the east and south of the Botan River, were fully independent and paid no homage to the Persian ruler.[53] That the Karduchoi could have any connection with the Kurds is vehemently denied on philological grounds by MacKenzie.[54] The Greek historian Diodorus putatively noted that the inhabitants of these mountains were so much trouble to the empires and foreign armies that efforts were directed solely at dissuading them from raiding the plains.[55] Herodotus, the sole but by no means wholly reliable source for this period, does not mention any name that seems to relate to Kurds, but mentions a satrap of the Achaemenid Empire, which may be Bohtan.[56] Driver asserts that, 'the territory occupied by the Kurdish race in historic times seems to have been the district called by the Greeks Karduchia,

and by the Greeks and Romans Corduene or Gordiaea, by Syriac writers
Qaru, whence the earliest Arabic authorities derived the name Qarda, the
country bounded roughly on the north by Armenia, on the west by the river
Euphrates, on the south by the Arabian desert, and on the east by the ancient
kingdom of Media.[57] The extent of this district was small, in the hills between
Diyarbakir, Nusaybin and Zakho. The same article refers to an account by
the Greek geographer Strabo concerning the Kyrtii,[58] nomads and brigands,
who were spread over Armenia and the Zagros mountains in the second
century BC, although this does not tally with the small area assigned to these
proto-Kurds by other writers. The Syriac writers identified Qardu in terms of
mythical happenings, such as the beaching of Noah's ark on Ararat. Driver
also notes that a Babylonian Talmudic writer referred to Abraham's seven-
year sojourn among the Qardu. Qardu is also noted by Syriac historians as
a Nestorian diocese.[59] In the first century BC, Corduene was conquered by
the Armenian Tigranes II, and its king was executed. By 115 AD Corduene
again had a king, having only been superficially Armenicized.[60] We have no
way of knowing the ethnic composition of the inhabitants of Corduene,
nor of any of the peoples described who possibly were the ancestors of the
present Kurds. The *Encyclopaedia of Islam* compares the names of various
historic groups in the area, including the Khaldi (Assyrian: Urartu) who
were established around Lake Van in the ninth century BC, but who were
driven out by the Armenians from the seventh century BC. Whatever their
origins, the article concludes that the Kardu/Qardu or Karduchoi were
identical with the Kurds, and that this view was considered axiomatic at the
beginning of the 20th century.[61]

Around the time of the decline of the Hellenistic Empire, most of
the Zagros rulers either joined the Parthian federation or were absorbed
by it. During the four centuries of the Parthian era (247 BC–226 AD)
there were seven semi- or fully independent principalities around the area
that would later be known as Kurdistan. These included: Mada (Media);
Elymais (Luristan); Kerm (Kermanshah); Mukriyan (Mahabad); Shahrezur
(Sulaimaniya); Barchan (Barzan); and Sanak (Sahna).[62] Even the following
Sassanian Empire was unable to exert direct control over this region, the
eastern half of Kurdistan falling within its boundaries, and was forced to
resort to the use of vassal kings under the strong centralization drive of
Ardeshir II.

In the north of present-day Kurdistan, the Hittite Kingdom gave way to
the Uratian Empire based on the city of Van from about 1000 to 600 BC.
The inhabitants of this empire were absorbed or driven out by the invading

Scythians, Medes and Hayasa. This northern area became known as Armenia by the Greeks and Persians from around 500 BC and was absorbed into the Alexandrian Empire and thoroughly Hellenized. Armenia later became a province of the Roman Empire in 114 AD, as did Assyria. So at this time, Kurdistan was divided between rival empires, and the provinces of Armenia and Assyria were buffers against the Parthians. The Armenian and Assyrian provinces were converted to Roman Christianity very early, before 600 AD. Armenia was later divided between the Romans and the Persians in 387 AD. The Byzantines suppressed and attempted to disperse the Armenians. There was a brief resurgence of the monarchy in the ninth and tenth centuries in Lesser Armenia, and from the 11th to the 14th century there was an important Armenian kingdom around Cilicia, north of the Gulf of Alexandretta.

The presence of Armenians was to continue in this region, later bordering the area inhabited by the Kurds, until the end of the early part of the 20th century. The overlapping territorial claims of the Armenians and the Kurds and the ensuing conflict of interest continued to be an issue until the 1920s. It is clear, however, that the Kurds gradually expanded northwards, and that this process was to be much accelerated by the vicissitudes of the Armenians, their migrations, deportations and finally their annihilation within that region in the early 20th century.

By the time of the Arab invasion, a single ethnic term 'Kurd' (Arabic plural Akr(d)) was applied to an amalgamation of Iranian or Iranicized tribes. Of the latter, some were autochthonous (like the Kardu), some Semitic (hence Kurdish genealogies) and some Armenian.[63] The existence of Iranian non-Kurdish elements has been clearly established, in that the Gurani and Zaza languages are clearly not Kurdish, but probably remnants of the pre-Kurdish inhabitants of the region.[64]

Conclusion

As largely sub-state actors, Kurds are often denied a role in official regional histories, and suffer from the state-centred core–periphery perspective that informs much of even academic history. Divided between several states, and also retaining the legacy of long-standing internal divisions, the Kurds lack the state machinery necessary to generate an alternative history, which would award them a greater role.

As history is written by the hegemons, and Kurdistan lay at the margins of or within several early empires, our knowledge of even the Kurds' ancient history comes largely from the accounts of their neighbouring cultures or subjugators. Even so, sources are scant, ambiguous and occasionally contradictory. It is impossible with the information available to achieve a reasonable understanding of either the precise origins of the Kurds, when they coalesced into such an identifiable group, or their early history, much before the Arab/Islamic invasion. The available historiographic materials are not easily accessible and are often fairly impenetrable. Given the state of the knowledge, it is possible to write many contradictory historical accounts, and much of any such attempts will be extrapolation.

Even in modern European academic historical writing, the Kurds are either poorly represented or actually *mis*represented. Accounts of their history are error-strewn and tend to show the clear state biases of their authors. It is therefore not surprising that Kurdish nationalists are sceptical about conventional historical accounts, and seek to create their own versions, with themselves as the central actors.

Although it appears that the search for the ancient origins of the Kurds occupied the minds of European academics and writers more than those of the Kurds themselves, recently the matter has been devoted greater attention within the Kurdish nationalist discourse. The early and, to some extent, logical claim that the Kurds were the descendants of the Medes established the premise of territorial occupation within Kurdistan. Further attempts, using tortuous logic, have been made to mesh the territory of Kurdistan with the history of the Kurdish ethnos and provide twin myths of ancient Kurdish history and territorial rights. These attempts have culminated in a definitive account, which, in some ways persuasively, confuses the history of Kurdistan and in fact a region even wider in temporal scope with the history of its present dominant ethnic group, the Kurds.

For several reasons, practical and ideological, this version of history has become explicit in successive writing on the Kurds, and appears to have gained credibility by repetition. The dubiousness of the axiomatic approach taken in the first instance is concealed with repeated citation, until it enters the living Kurdish mythology.

Notes

1. G. R. Driver, 'Dispersion of the Kurds in Ancient Times', *Journal of the Royal Asiatic Society*, October 1921.

2. Colin Williams, 'Minority Nationalist Historiography', in: R. J. Johnston et al, *Nationalism, Self-Determination and Political Geography* (London: Croom Helm, 1988), p. 203.
3. Williams, 'Minority Nationalist Historiography', p. 204.
4. Mehrdad Izady, *The Kurds: A concise handbook* (London: Taylor and Francis, 1992), p. 23.
5. In the few instances when the Kurds have established an administration, e.g. Mahabad in 1946–47 or Free Kurdistan 1991–present, the existing chaos and short-term nature of the structure have not allowed such an expression of continuity.
6. Anthony Smith, *The Ethnic Origins of Nation*, p. 206.
7. For example, many Baluchis claim that their ancestors migrated from Aleppo in Syria in the ninth century (*The Baluchis and the Pathans*, Minority Rights Group, London no. 48, 1987). Kurds do have folk myths about their origins, notably stemming from Firdowsi's epic *Shahnameh*; also a myth concerning forty djinn expelled by King Solomon.
8. Abdul Rahman Ghassemlou, *Kurdistan and the Kurds* (London: Collets, 1965), p. 34.
9. His main source for this section is also cited in *Encyclopaedia Britannica*, namely Rashid Yasimi, *The Kurd and His Land, Race and History* (Tehran: no publisher available,1940, 1956), in Persian.
10. Personal communication from Sami Shooresh, Kurdish journalist.
11. Seyid Hussain Mukriani Al-Hussnni, *Gunchay Bahristan* (Aleppo: 1925).
12. Captain Sheikh Waheed, *The Kurds and Their Country* (Lahore: Evergreen Press, 1955), pp. 42–57.
13. Arshak Safrastian, *Kurds and Kurdistan* (London: The Harvill Press, 1948), pp. 16–31.
14. Mohammad Amin Zaki, *A Summary of the History of Kurdistan and the Kurds* (Cairo: al-Saadeh, 1936), in Kurdish, p. 61.
15. Bob Filmer, Democrat Congressman for San Diego on the floor of the US Congress 1 May 1997, pleading for recognition of Kurdish self-determination.
16. See: Bernard Lewis: *History*, pp. 11–38.
17. Mehrad Izady, *The Kurds*, pp. xiii–xiv, 23–72. Much of the rest of Dr Izady's book is well written, dealing exhaustively with many hitherto unexplored aspects of the Kurds and Kurdistan. However, certain sections, such as that on ancient history, are subject to seriously flawed reasoning, and the lack of citation ensures that his own conclusions are presented as factual evidence. However, its wide range of coverage and accessible tone, combined with its affordability and accessibility ensured that it rapidly became a 'bible' for both Kurds and Kurdophiles.
18. Izady, pp. xiii–xiv.
19. A claim advanced in the US Congress, see note 15 above.
20. Izady, pp. 30–31.
21. Izady, p. 31.
22. Izady, p. 35.
23. Mustafa al-Karadaghi, 'Summary of Kurdish History', *Kurdistan Times*, Winter 1990, p. 8.
24. Intriguingly, this dilemma was addressed by Safrastian, who noted that Henry Rawlinson erred in his deciphering of Assyrian cuneiform inscriptions, and that the land of Kurtie around Lake Van was in fact Khab-khi. Kurds could thus be associated with the Guti only in this period. The Kurtie or Qurtie were a 'red herring', yet obviously an attractive one to Kurdish historians. One aspect of Safrastian's thesis also

at least provides a justification for so much of the 'territorial habitation' argument, as he denies the possibility of intercontinental migration, claiming the Kurds, Arabs, Assyrians and Armenians as autochthonous races, living in their native habitats!

25. Al-Karadaghi, 'Summary', 1990, p. 16.

26. Al-Karadaghi, 'Summary', 1990, p. 20.

27. Al-Karadaghi, 'Summary', 1990, p. 50.

28. Ibid.

29. Al-Karadaghi, 'Summary of Kurdish History', *Kurdish Times*, 1992, p. 66.

30. Vesta Sarkhosh Curtis, *Persian Myths* (London: British Museum, 1989).

31. Al-Karadaghi, 'Summary', 1992, pp. 62–64.

32. *Kurdish Headdress: A matter of historic continuity* (New York, The Kurdish Museum, 1995).

33. Wadie Jwadieh, 'The Kurdish Nationalist Movement: Its origins and development' (PhD thesis, Syracuse University, 1960), p. iii.

34. Jwadieh, 'Kurdish Nationalist Movement', p. 27.

35. Peter Taylor, 'The Modern World System', in: R. J. Johnston and P. J. Taylor, *A World in Crisis: Geographical perspectives* (Oxford: Blackwell, 1989), pp. 272–273.

36. Bernard Lewis, *The Shaping of the Modern Middle East* (Oxford: Oxford University Press, 1994), p. 19.

37. Lewis, *The Shaping of the Modern Middle East*, pp. 94–95.

38. Malcolm Yapp, *The Making of the Modern Near East 1792–1923* (London: Longman, 1987).

39. Malcolm Yapp, *The Near East Since the First World War* (London: Longman, 1996), p. 325.

40. Yapp, *The Near East*, p. 348.

41. Yapp, *The Near East*, p. 482.

42. Yapp, *The Near East*, pp. 482–483.

43. Yapp, *The Near East*, p. 95.

44. Mustafa Nazdar, 'The Kurds in Syria', in: Gerard Chaliand, *People Without a Country* (London: Zed Press, 1993), p. 200.

45. Cleveland, 1994.

46. For example, Neulida Foccaro, 'Aspects of the Social and Political History of the Yezidi Enclave of Jabal Sinjar (Iraq) Under the British Mandate 1919–1932 (PhD thesis, University of Durham, 1994).

47. For example, Robert Olson, *The Emergence of Kurdish Nationalism and the Sheikh Said Rebellion, 1880-1925* (Texas: University of Texas Press, 1989).

48. For example, Mazhar Kemal Ahmad, *Kurdistan During the First World War* (London: Saqi Books, 1994), 'The Kurds of Sulaimanya and Baghdad Between the Two World Wars (paper given at the Sorbonne University, Paris, 1996), plus many works in Kurdish and Arabic.

49. Such as Mirella Galletti in Bologna, author of a doctoral thesis on Kurdistan ('Political Structure and Cultural Development in Kurdish Society', University of Bologna, 1974), and the first book in Italian on Kurdish history for a hundred years (*I Curdi nella Storia*, Chieti: Vecchio Faggio, 1990). Also, for example, Hamit Bozarslan and Professors Blau and Van Bruinessen.

50. David McDowall, *The Modern History of the Kurds* (London: I. B. Tauris, 1996).

51. Thomas Bois, 'Kurds', 'Kurdistan', in: *Encyclopaedia of Islam*, 1986, p. 447.

52. See p. 8, footnote 2.

53. Xenophon, *The Persian Expedition* (Harmondsworth: Penguin, 1984), pp. 11–28.

54. D. MacKenzie, 'The Role of the Kurdish Language in Ethnicity', in: F. D. Andrews,

The Lost Peoples of the Middle East (Salisbury, NC: Documentary Publications, 1989), p. 541.

55. In an illustration of how speculative all suppositions are concerning this early period, Sinclair adds that the Carduchians were skilled stone masons and possessed a king and a palace; 'without wanting to make assumptions about the history of the Kurds, none of this sounds like them.' T. A. Sinclair, *Eastern Turkey: An Architectural and Archaeological Survey* (London: Pindar Press, 1989), Vol. III, p. 360.

56. Izady, *The Kurds*, p. 35.

57. Bois, *Encyclopaedia of Islam*, p. 447.

58. Driver, 'Dispersion of the Kurds', p. 563.

59. MacKenzie ('The Role of the Kurdish Language') believes this and other accounts in Livy and Polybius were the first mentions of the Kurds. He regards them as a tribe, living to the north-west of the Persians, possibly neighbours of the Medes.

60. Driver, 'Dispersion of the Kurds', pp. 564–566.

61. Bois, *Encyclopaedia of Islam*, p. 448.

62. Ibid. Minorsky's article in the first edition of the encyclopaedia (*Encyclopaedia of Islam*, 1st edn, 1913–1936) on Kurds appears identical, so this view has not been really examined since the 1930s.

63. Izady, *The Kurds*, p. 35.

64. Bois, *Encyclopaedia of Islam*, p. 449. Although it is practical to assume Semitic elements in the Kurdish tribes, the popular genealogies are likely to have been invented to create a claim to Islamic status.

Tribal *Asabiyya* and Kurdish Politics:
A Socio-Historical Perspective

Hamit Bozarslan

For almost two centuries, tribes have been an important element of Kurdish society.[1] They are also the focal point of many tensions among the Kurds themselves. Since the 1920s, the urban intellectual elite has reprehended them as backward, factionalist, reactionary and even feudal entities. The Kurdish political parties have repeatedly accused them of being one of the main obstacles preventing the Kurds from achieving statehood. Indeed, many tribes have overtly collaborated with the central powers against the Kurdish nationalist movements. Yet no Kurdish political party could afford to ignore them. Even the most radical of them, such as the PUK and the PKK, have had to take them into account and accept some kind of *modus vivendi* with the 'patriotic' ones.[2]

As Ernest Gellner put it, tribes exist in a 'cultural continuum,'[3] covering large parts of North Africa, the Middle East and Central Asia. They are far from being an exclusively Kurdish phenomenon. The peculiar conditions of the Kurdish issue have, however, contributed to reshape the features of the tribal question in Kurdistan. Large-scale violence surrounding the Kurdish issue has certainly given rise to some specific constraints that the tribes have to face, and to specific opportunities from which the tribes can extract benefits. But as a general rule, Kurdish tribes act like others in the Middle East. They have a great ability to adapt themselves to changing situations and they behave according to their own interests and rules.[4] My assumption is that the Khaldounian concept of *asabiyya partly* explains their ability to transform themselves into components of an urban and modern environment.

In this chapter, I first suggest that the concept *asabiyya*, although widely criticized, may allow us to understand the survival and functions of tribal phenomena in a modern world. Second, I will analyse the relations between

Kurdish society and Kurdish nationalism, on the one hand, and, on the other hand, the tribal issue. Finally, by using some brief information on the Bucaks, I suggest that tribal *asabiyya* has multiple layers and functions, which together allow tribes to reproduce their internal cohesion and authority and become important players in a massively urbanized and modern environment.

Tribalism, Asabiyya *and Their Opponents*

Asabiyya, a key concept used by Ibn Khaldun, means blood solidarity, at the base of group cohesion in a tribal world. It has often been used by anthropologists who embraced segmentary lineage theory. Ernest Gellner undoubtedly employed the concept with great brilliance in an original theoretical construction.[5] But political scientists have also utilized it in order to understand the power relations in the Middle East and some other parts of the Muslim world as far as Central Asia.[6]

For many years, however, both the concept of *asabiyya* and the approaches highlighting the place of tribal relations in the Middle East have been severely criticized. Gellner's model, in particular, has become a target of sharp attacks. Critics of his model proposed a political, not a regulatory and institutionalized, reading of the social groups – and not only tribes – in the Middle East. According to them, Gellner invented an imaginary 'Muslim society', without taking into account the specific historicities of each Middle Eastern and other Muslim society. Moreover, his model of tribe–tribe and tribe–power relations was an almost systemic one, leaving no room for a history yet to be unfolded. By laying emphasis on the conflict-regulatory function of the tribes, Gellner's model read Middle Eastern history as an infra-political web of ahistorical conflicts.[7]

One should agree, in fact, that Gellner's model was too systemic; the culturally codified and unified 'Muslim society' that it suggested did not in fact exist (Gellner himself was aware that reality was much more complex).[8] Gellner's vision of the Muslim world can be read as a set of constant, institutionalized oppositions between unchanging, ahistorical, anthropological and institutional constraints. One can also suggest that a quasi-egalitarian tribal society, as it was presented by the segmentary lineage theory, never existed.[9] On the contrary, the tribal structures offered a framework of conflict for power in the Middle East. This framework was far from egalitarian. It was constantly reshaped by power relations both within and among tribes, or between the tribes and the outside world. Moreover, the tribal framework was far from being the sole conflict-ridden framework. The urban history of the Middle East shows that the cities were the main centres of power relations and conflicts and, compared to the countryside, they possessed an overwhelming supremacy. Tribes were thus only one component of a complex web of social and power relations, possessing rather limited scope for manoeuvre.

This basic concept obviously weakens any anthropological approach that overemphasizes the role of tribes and tribalism in the Middle East, as well as weakening the Gellnerian model. This concept also invites scholars to take particular care when using the concept *asabiyya*. Still, I would argue that one should not nip the flower in the bud, i.e. end the discussion for good, and that the debate on tribalism and *asabiyya* should continue since it involves hidden aspects that will unfold before scholars of the Middle East. For instance, in anthropology (which is not my own field) the concept *asabiyya* can be used in a non-segmentary, dynamic model, explaining the reproduction of tribes or the re-tribalization and the phenomenon of widespread violence in some Middle Eastern societies.[10] In political sociology (which is my field), this concept can be successfully used to understand the construction of some group solidarities.[11] As a concept 'borrowed' from anthropology, it can elucidate, to some extent at least, the emergence of political systems and some mechanisms of political domination in the Middle East. It can also be of some use in understanding the enigmatic durability of some political powers or the establishment of new republican dynasties as in Syria and Iraq under Saddam Hussein.

This does of course not mean that the Middle East is reducible to a pre-modern, tribal phenomenon, in which *asabiyya* would constitute the hidden essence or agenda of social and political actors. On the contrary, the modern history of the Middle East is that of political constructions, more or less successful state-building experiences, official state nationalisms and minority nationalisms, as well as that of more or less durable social mobilizations. Still, one should admit that not only did tribes survive but, in many cases, they also fully participated in these experiences. In many instances, they were among the winners.

This persistence of the tribal factor seems to suggest that, as elsewhere in the world, in the Middle East no society can be analysed solely within the framework of a universal temporal sequence of social evolution, including only state-building or nation-building processes or social mobilizations. Quite the opposite: societies are the frameworks of simultaneously co-existing modes of social organization. The minorities[12] can act in between these different modalities, playing distinct, sometimes contradictory, social and political roles. As a social organization, a tribe can have a 'tribal temporality', allowing it to manage its existence and its power relations with the outside world, but at the same time, it can act as a national or a trans-border regional actor. A tribal chief can find in his tribe the resources that allow him to become an actor in a national or a supra-national sphere. For instance, thanks to his position as a tribal leader, he can become a deputy in Turkey or a player in the Middle Eastern economic field. He can transcend the tribal world and be a part of a complex, non-tribal web of relations. But he can also use his position in these spheres to reinforce his power as chief or arbiter within his own tribal framework. What an outside observer might describe as an 'anachronistic' social organization, with a rigid, vertical hierarchy or blood solidarity, can in fact become an appearance of the 'multiple modernities', or at least, multiple webs of relations, allowing a group to play a few roles at the same time.

This also means that scholars should abandon clear-cut oppositions between tradition and modernity, or between the rural, which supposedly contains tradition, and the urban, which is supposedly the site of modernity. 'Modernity', not in the sense of a set of values and norms,[13] but as the action of societies or social groups to transform their material conditions,[14] is probably not synonymous with the 'passing of tradition'.[15] Therefore, examining tribes and *asabiyya* as group solidarity, does not mean analysing the Middle East as a traditional, rural world. Quite on the contrary, throughout the nineteenth and twentieth centuries, tribes themselves were transformed into modern and urban entities, using the resources of traditional repertoires in a modern world, and, in turn, using those of modernity within a traditional register in order to survive as cohesive groups in a competitive environment.

Tribes are certainly not the only entities to master such a complex game, combining traditional and modern repertoires and temporalities. The so-called revival of religious brotherhoods offers a similar case.[16] Minorities from the non-Western countries in Europe act also in a similar way. The more they cease to be "immigrant groups" and become a part of the European societies, the more they reactivate what one could call "traditional" repertoires. For instance, in spite of many linear expectations, the marriage based kinship relations have increased among them, particularly with the second generation.[17] This of course does not mean that these families evolve in a "traditional" fashion alone. On the contrary, their traditional repertoires offer them the necessary resources to become part of a modern world, while the resources of modernity are re-deployed within the traditional, enabling them to survive in a very competitive, and to some extent disintegrated modern environment.

In the case of tribes, access to modernity and to its material and, in some cases, symbolic resources is possible through the reactivation of traditional repertoires; but, in turn, these traditional repertoires themselves have to be 'updated' and modernized. A tribe has to invent its mechanisms of legitimization by modernity and by a universal (nationalist, Islamist, Marxist, etc.) discourse. It is true that often the patterns of traditional repertoires offer a solid framework for accessing power. To give an example, kinship groups around the Arab world were able, throughout the 20th century, to invade seats of power at the national level, and, without ceasing to serve their own interests, become the banner-bearers of Arab nationalism.

The Kurdish political space bears many similarities to other cases in the Middle East. Tribes constitute a permanent – although constantly reshaped – component of the Kurdish political space. The conflictual nature of the Kurdish issue, involving large-scale state coercion and violent Kurdish resistance, has engendered a set of constraints on tribes, but also offered many opportunities. The phenomenon of *asabiyya*, which must be debated, redefined and contexualized, explains the permanence of tribes and their role in the very contemporary Kurdish society and politics.[18]

Kurdish Society and Tribes

Paradoxically, Kurdish tribes, as probably elsewhere in the Middle East, have been reactivated as political actors in the wake of the modernization reforms of the 19th century. A closer examination may well conclude that the tribal phenomenon has not been the determining feature of Kurdish society during, or even centuries after what the historians call the classical age of the Ottoman Empire. Obviously, the tribes were there, but until the second half of the 19th century, they seemed rather to have a subordinate position in power relations.

Up to the 19th century, Kurdish emirates, which were officially recognized as autonomous entities by the Ottomans, or had obtained a de facto autonomy,[19] were strong enough to control towns and, to a large extent, impose their domination over the countryside. The Ottoman policy of centralization, initiated by the *Nizam-i Cedid*[20] and intensified later on in the wake of the *Tanzimat* reforms (1839), was intended explicitly to unify the Ottoman administrative system by putting an end to the derogatory forms of government in different parts of the empire. In the Kurdish regions, this policy succeeded in achieving its immediate aim, which was the destruction of the autonomous or semi-autonomous Kurdish principalities. With few exceptions, no autonomous Kurdish entity remained by the 1880s. But the Ottoman policy failed, in the sense that the new administration was incapable of governing with efficiency comparable to that of the emirates, not least because it was rejected by local Kurdish dignitaries. The new administration replaced the autonomous Kurdish entities, which were coercive but allocated resources; this administration was highly corrupt and exacerbated rather than combated problems linked to insecurity. The power vacuum provoked by the destruction of the Kurdish autonomous entities thus gave birth to a period of unprecedented insecurity.[21]

Tribes were the only organized forces that could face up to these challenges and thus, become 'new spaces of resistance to the centralization of administration and politics'.[22] Moreover, they were almost the natural frameworks to bring both security and resource-allocation to their members and their clientelized groups. It is no wonder that many of them won in strength by integration of peripheral groups under their protection. Thus, the policy of centralization led precisely to what it was intended to prevent: an unprecedented decentralization of the Kurdish region. According to the French traveller Ubicini, some '1,000 independent entities'[23] replaced the few dozens of former autonomous or semi-autonomous Kurdish entities.

Already by the end of the nineteenth century, many of these tribal entities had also a presence in towns and constituted real counter-powers challenging the weak Ottoman bureaucracy.[24] Many of them, such as the Jelalis, were spread over three imperial frontiers: Ottoman, Persian and Russian.[25] They could find in their division between these states, important resources and shelter to protect themselves from the military campaigns conducted against them by any one of those states.

The central government was able to establish its authority in a large part of Kurdistan only by the 1890s, and then only at the heavy cost of officially recognizing the autonomy of some of the Kurdish tribes, enrolled in the so-called Hamidiyya Cavalries.[26] As with the Cossacks in Russia, the centralization of the Empire required the integration of violent centrifugal dynamics within the official power structures. The Hamidiyya Cavalries marked in fact the end of the classical, Memluk-type, Ottoman administration, which, as Gellner rightly put it, could previously manage to get rid of the *asabiyya* dynamics.[27] In fact, by recognizing the legitimacy of some tribes and integrating them in the state's coercive structures, the Ottoman Empire constituted a kind of Kurdish *makhzen*. Like the Moroccan one, this *makhzen* too had no delineated frontiers; it was the geographically changing domain of obedience, compared to *siba*, territory of contest.

The Hamidiyya Cavalries also constituted a pattern for the state–tribe relations in Kurdistan in the 20th century. The modern Middle Eastern states, including Turkey, the most 'Jacobean' one among them, whose official credo was – and still is – the non-division of national sovereignty, had to take the tribal dynamics into account, and integrate some of the tribes as tribal militias within its agencies of violence. By so doing, modern states also adopted a policy of 'positive discrimination' in allocating economic and military resources towards them.

Kurdish Nationalism and Tribes

Kurdish nationalism, like the other Middle Eastern nationalisms, is a modern phenomenon.[28] In its origin, it was the doctrine of non-tribal or detribalized intellectual elites. These elites wanted to eradicate tribalism and religious brotherhoods[29] in order to allow the Kurds to enter into the world of 'civilization' and statehood. During the first half of the 20th century, however, many tribes and religious brotherhoods found in Kurdish nationalism a universal code which legitimized their rebellions against the central states, thus giving birth to complex relations between nationalism as a discourse and rural contest.[30]

In the second half of the 20th century, however, Kurdish nationalism became the dominant discourse of urban mobilization in Kurdistan. Still, tribes remained one of the main components of the Kurdish social and political spaces. Kurdish nationalist movements had, ever since, to face the tribal question both on the micro and macro levels. They had, and still have, to take tribes into consideration either as allies or as enemies.

The possibility of contracting alliances with some tribes – and religious brotherhoods – appeared already during the 1920s, a period when the nascent Kurdish nationalist intelligentsia was aware of its social and political weakness. It was weakly confined to urban centres and could not give birth there to 'the rise of a mass national movement'.[31] Suffering from such social marginalization, the Kurdish nationalist urban elite had no choice but to integrate tribes and religious brotherhoods, which were its 'social enemies', into its own contest. Indeed, these tribal and religious actors enjoyed the very human and military resources that the urban elite badly lacked. Moreover, they composed the only force that could effectively challenge the central power.[32] In turn, the nationalist discourse offered to the tribes and religious brotherhoods a political language that could give meaning to their rebellion. Later on, some of these tribes became the reservoirs of the Kurdish nationalist movements. Certain tribes, which joined the 1930 rebellion in Turkey, for instance, supported the PKK's guerrilla warfare many decades later. Other tribes supported the Kurdish legal initiatives, which formed Kurdish nationalist lists during elections or voted massively for them.[33] As late as the 1990s, the success of the Kurdish movement in Iraqi Kurdistan was due in part to the participation of the Kurdish tribes in the nationalist uprising. I believe that a micro-analysis will offer more cases of the impact of the tribal heritage of resistance in current Kurdish political life.

It goes almost without saying that the Kurdish nationalist movement has faced tribes as enemies as well. As Martin van Bruinessen suggests, the survival of tribes depends narrowly on the existence of a conflictual environment.[34] As is observed in some parts of the Middle East, broadly speaking, conflicts or even widespread violence, as in Iraq and Kurdistan of Turkey, are also the *sine qua non* of retribalization. Tribes are not only a potential ally for the movements challenging states, they are also a potential ally for these states against contesting movements. Their large numbers and the ability of the central authority to reactivate the disintegrating tribes by the injection of material and military resources offer the state the possibility of making allies in almost every locality where the *siba* (contest) has not established its own discursive, political and military hegemony.

Already in 1920s the Kemalist government, which theoretically rejected any kind of division of national sovereignty, established tribal 'militia' forces. Although no research is available on this subject,[35] one can suggest that, like the previous Hamidiyya militias, the new ones contributed widely to the militarization of tribal dynamics. They played a decisive role in the crushing of the Kurdish rebellions, namely that of Sheikh Said (1925), Ararat (1930) and Dersim (1936–1938).[36] As is attested by the negotiations between the Kemalist power and Simko in Iranian Kurdistan, tribal alliances were also instrumental in regional power relations.[37] The case of the pejoratively called *jash* militia[38] in Iraqi Kurdistan is also significant. Before joining the 1991 uprising, these militias, officially dubbed *Fursan Salah al-Din*, had an effective role in the coercive policies of the Ba'ath regime, including the Anfal operations in 1988.[39] In Turkish Kurdistan, some 75,000 'village guards' have been recruited during the last two decades.[40] Of course, not all these militiamen were of tribal origin. Moreover, the state forced some of them to take arms against the PKK. Nevertheless, the volunteering tribes constituted the main body of the guards. The leaders of these tribes obtained the obedience of their tribesmen, redistributing among them the financial and military resources allocated by the state. These resources strengthened the position of many tribes in the countryside or in urban areas; they allowed also some of the declining tribes to 'revive'. But, for some tribes, receiving military and financial resources and the approval of the state gave them the green light to become involved in drug-trafficking, an activity that brings much greater financial rewards than cooperating with the village guards.[41] Finally, thanks to their link with the state, some of the tribes, such as the Tatars in Sirnak or some tribes in Yuksekova and the Bucaks in Siverek, could transform themselves into urban entities, thus becoming the main political actors in small cities.

The Case of Bucaks: or How the Tribes Reproduce and Successfully Use Their Asabiyya

The integration of some tribes into urban life and their involvement in the informal or illegal – but nevertheless highly modern – economy during periods of widespread violence invites us to redefine the tribal question. My hypothesis is the following: in the second part of the 20th century, many tribes ceased to be rural entities but without abandoning traditional mechanisms of internal cohesion. On the contrary, it has been their ability to preserve their *asabiyya* and constantly to adapt it to the new conditions that has allowed them to become part of modern urban life. This ability consists in mastering simultaneously local and universal temporalities. The tribe remains mainly a kinship structure but, at the same time, it might play complex national or even regional political and economic roles. The resources and authority capitalized at any of these levels are channelled to the other levels.

In this regard, the case of the Bucaks is highly significant, although it has some unique features.[42] The Bucaks is a tribe that numbers today some 20,000 members; it emerged some two centuries ago, not as a tribe, but as a small family in the Siverek region (the current Urfa province). The family grew throughout the 19th century thanks to its ability to survive several conflicts. It contracted alliances with other groups, which were integrated into the family or were largely marginalized. The growing tribe filled the power vacuum resulting from the centralization drive by the Ottomans during the 19th century, and managed to accumulate both military and political resources. By the end of the century, the Bucaks were part of the Hamidiyya cavalries, their leader obtaining the title of pasha and having an official representative in Istanbul. They also occupied the seat of deputy after 1908, when the Ottoman parliament was reintroduced. For years, the chief of the tribe, Sedat, a close ally of Süleyman Demirel and Tansu Çiller,[43] was not only a deputy in the Great National Assembly but also the number one economic figure in Urfa province. He commanded a private army of 10,000 men (as the tribe has only some 20,000 members, many of its 'soldiers' are patently recruited from among clientelized groups). Moreover, as the government considered only a small section of this private army as 'village guards', the majority of the 'soldiers' were paid directly by Sedat from his own purse. Since its conflict with the PKK at the end of 1970s, the Bucaks have never been engaged in any large conflict. This private army, which, therefore, has no military function as such, remains a symbol of the tribe's political and economical power. It is naturally a tangible emblem of the immunity that Sedat Bucak obtained from the state.

Many other tribal leaders have small economic emporia and military forces. But the Bucaks are an exceptional case, not least because very few tribes have a permanent deputy in the Assembly and none of them commands such an imposing military force. Such a success is of course the result of opportunism and pragmatism, which have always been the leading principles of the Bucaks and, obviously, that has paid off.[44] Further, the Bucaks' success story can also be explained by their remarkable ability to use their tribal *asabiyya* and a traditional repertoire of mobilization in an urban environment.

For almost two centuries, the Bucaks' political centre has not been in rural areas, but in Siverek, a small and therefore controllable city. Since the power vacuum created by the Ottoman reforms in the 19th century, many tribes had a permanent presence in towns and some of them even moved their decision-making centres there. Some tribes, including the Bucaks, used the countryside base as a resource-producing area, those resources being imported into the city and placed at the disposal of their urban power centre. This link with the town allowed the tribes to negotiate with the appointed bureaucrats and often to clientelize them. In a couple of decades, they also became familiar with urban culture. These processes led to the formation of an educated social stratum, mainly in medicine, sciences and the law. As Lale Yalçin-Heckman observes, the 'existence' or even the survival of the tribe in a highly competitive environment requires, in fact, people skilled in many different fields, particularly the political and economic ones.[45]

The formation of this elite, though probably not a calculated long-term strategy, has allowed some tribes, including the Bucaks, to be prepared to face different scenarios. Accordingly, the Bucaks could confront the agrarian crisis of the second part of the 20th century and the consequent rural exodus not as a calamity but rather as an opportunity. They could regenerate the rural *asabiyya* in the urban centre, thus giving rise to what Michel Seurat calls the 'urban *asabiyya*',[46] and control sufficient resources to face the coming conflicts. They did not of course abandon the countryside, but they modernized (and rationalized) their agrarian activities, by extending them to hemp production.[47] Agriculture, however, became of secondary economic importance, as the Bucaks vigorously invested, for many decades, in much more dynamic activities such as construction or oil distribution. By becoming the number one economic force in the Urfa province, they could also claim to have a place in Turkey. In short, the Bucaks were far from living in the miserable situation of some other tribes, as portrayed remarkably on the silver screen by Yilmaz Güney in his film *Sürü* ('The Herd', 1978).

It should be added that during these transformations, the tribe suffered very heavy internal conflicts, but could constantly reproduce *asabiyya* around the leading family. This *asabiyya* in no way signifies an internal egalitarianism. It is rather an organized, even codified form of internal domination. Rather than being a simple blood solidarity, it can be defined as the ability to exert internal coercion against dissident families and individuals. It means also the ability to adopt a resource-allocation policy to loyal members. And, last but not least, it depends on success in reproducing patron–client relations with neighbouring tribes through intermarriage (as Sedat is married to a Kejan, his tribe has to build kinship alliances with the Kirvars, Isolis and Karakeçilis). Internal conflicts, pitching the leading family against dissident branches, and external conflicts, pitching the tribe against other tribes or families (such as the Söylemez[48]), were always the peak moments when members were asked to renew their loyalty to the chief.

In the regulation of these conflicts, the Bucaks completely changed the classical patterns of proximity and internal alliances in the tribal world. As is well known, the theoretical traditional pattern of internal tribal alliances presupposes conflicts among brothers, coalitions of brothers against cousins, of brothers and cousins against second cousins, and the whole family against outsiders. A brief account of the tribe's history, in which an anthropologist might find interesting elements, shows that in the case of Bucaks something else has happened:[49] the cousins were chosen as allies against brothers, and external elements – sometimes simple hired killers – were recruited against dissident cousins. The frontier between 'us' and 'others' certainly did not disappear during such transactions. With some exceptions, the 'foreigners' remained allies and did not become genuine members of the group. The tribe's success depended thus on its ability to maintain initial solidarity, negotiating such transactions and establishing a complex web of patron–client relations with the 'others'.

That was obviously the case during the internal vendetta that cost the lives of twenty-four tribal dignitaries in the 1960s. It was also the case during the 1990s, a period when the dissident branch was already marginalized, but it was threatening the leading branch by their engagement in the Kurdish nationalist movements. During the 1960s, and particularly during the 1990s, the external 'allies' could cover a wide range of far-right militants and security agents. Obviously, throughout its history some external elements were adopted by the tribe as 'inner clients'; consequently their descendants became legitimate members a generation on. But the high-ranking positions of the external elements – governors, high-ranking security officers – who were employed during the 1990s, could not and cannot allow such integration. The tribe had and still has to manage these new relations within the framework of patron–client–patron relations. The tribe itself is certainly a client, because its access to resources can be possible only if it accepts state protection. But the state agents – conducting a series of covert actions, including torture and murder – also badly need information on Kurdish nationalist activities, and in some cases they need tribal protection. During the 1990s, they often used the tribe's 'chateau' as a centre of torture of kidnapped Kurdish intellectuals or Mafia figures. No wonder that some of them called Sedat, the tribe's chieftain, by the affectionate and grateful term 'Sedat Abi'.[50]

These external elements were used as outside support in internal regulation and conflict resolution. With their help, the main dissident branch was completely crushed. Within a few decades, it became 'detribalized', some of its members joining the Kurdish nationalist opposition. The internal conflicts also served as an instrument of empowerment vis-à-vis the clientelized tribes, such as the Kejans or Kirvars, or the non-tribal populations. Throughout these external elements, which will never become its members, the tribe could transform itself into a decisive power bloc both in the Urfa region and in Turkey. Some other tribes or large families such as the Söylemez, which established an *asabiyya* based on 'predatory solidarity'[51] worked according to a similar pattern. By reactivating their internal *asabiyya*, and by switching from a patron–client pattern to a patron–client–patron pattern of relations, they could build a flexible, nationwide framework. The tribe and/or extended family always remained the core structure, but it could work only if it could incorporate militias, security agencies and politicians.

The last element to be examined is the capacity of the tribe to build symbolic kinship relations with its external collaborators. In fact, the material field in which tribes and other solidarity groups act does not allow them to secure their alliances by matrimonial strategies. Moreover, the matrimonial domain remains sensitive and, for obvious reasons, highly protected. Thus, the solidarity groups have to invent new, non-blood-based, symbolic kinship relations. Sedat Bucak, like many others, seems to have largely used the *kirve* institution[52] or witnessing in a wedding as means of building such relations. The status of 'Abi' ('grand brother') that he enjoys among the middle- or high-ranking death squads can also be read as a symbolic kinship, implying respect and mutual protection. The advantage of those symbolic kinship relations is that they do not threaten the group *asabiyya* nor its decision-making processes or its hierarchical structures, which allow coercion against and resource allocation to the members of the tribe.

All these points, which can probably also be observed elsewhere beyond Kurdistan, show how the tribe can survive in a highly competitive, even conflictual, largely urbanized environment. The capacity of reproducing the *asabiyya* becomes thus synonymous with the capacity of breeding social patron–client-based relations and acting in larger spheres than those of the initial tribal framework.

Scholars crucially lack extensive monographs as well as an overall map of the tribal phenomena in today's Kurdistan. It would, however, not be wrong to say that, in spite of the rapid urbanization and emergence of new, urban forms of action, tribes will remain, at least in the foreseeable future, important actors in the Kurdish political space.

In fact, in a largely 'retribalized' Iraq, the attitude of Kurdish tribes could be a decisive factor. Some of these tribes might well be able to support the central government in exchange for a status of 'most favoured lords' and a rewarding resources allocation policy. In another scenario, if the ongoing Kurdish experience of autonomy continues, the Barzani family, which has become a de facto tribe, might transform itself into a leading dynasty, mastering multiple repertoires and temporalities (as the leading Kurdish nationalist family becoming part of the state, while remaining, at the same time, a tribe or at least an extended family). In Turkish Kurdistan, too, tribes that are strong enough to threaten the state to change sides if they are abandoned[53] will remain an important element in the political space. They could contribute heavily to the emergence or at least the evolution of a new conflict.

Conclusion

Tribes can become a part of a conflictual situation and profit from it. The reason for this should certainly not be sought in its egalitarian structures or in its internal cohesion. On the contrary, *asabiyya*, group solidarity, requires authority and obedience. These can not be obtained without a constant mobilization. Mobilization, in turn, means not only resources allocation but also a syntax of hegemony (involving a set of values, duties and rights rather than a religious or secular *da'wa*), internal coercion and vertical authority structures. Throughout conflict, the group members are constantly constrained to renew their loyalty to the leading figure. Similarly, the *asabiyya*, instrument of internal clientelism and patronage, in no way prevents other relations with outside groups and power structures. On the contrary, the vertical tribal authority can use the *senses* and *mechanisms* of an initial *asabiyya* to build a solidarity network of a very different kind, including new, nationwide networks and symbolic forms of kinship.

Notes

1. Cf. M. van Bruinessen, *Agha, Sheikh and State: The social and political structures of Kurdistan* (London: Zed Press, 1992), and M. van Bruinessen, *Kurdish Ethnonationalism* (Istanbul: ISIS, 2000).
2. Even the PKK, which at the beginning adopted a very anti-tribal discourse, later on welcomed the 'dynamism and national characteristics' of some tribes and their 'self-esteem and self-confidence'. *Serxwebun*, quoted by L. Yalçin-Heckmann, 'Kurdish Tribal Organization and Local Political Process', in: A. Finkel and N. Sirman, *Turkish State, Turkish Society* (London: Routledge, 1989), p. 291.
3. E. Gellner, 'The Tribal Society and its Enemies', in: R. Tapper, *The Conflict of Tribe and State in Iran and Afghanistan* (London: Croom Helm, 1983), p. 437.
4. Still, some of them can become the sociological reservoirs or even banner bearers of a religious or a secular *da'wa*, such as nationalism or even 'Marxism'.

5. Cf., among others, E. Gellner, _Muslim Society_ (Cambridge, London and New York: Cambridge University Press, 1983); 'The Tribal Society and its Enemies', in: R. Tapper (ed.), _The Conflict of Tribe and State in Iran and Afghanistan_ (London: Croom Helm, 1983); E. Gellner and C. Micaud, _Arabs and Berbers: From tribe to nation in North Africa_ (London: Duckworth, 1972).

6. Cf., among others, A. Dawisha (ed.), _Beyond Coercion: The durability of the Arab state_ (London, New York and Sydney: Croom Helm, 1988), and O. Roy, 'Clientélisme et groupes de solidarité: survivance ou recomposition?', in: Gh. Salamé, _Démocraties sans démocrates: politiques d'ouverture dans le monde arabe et islamique_ (Paris: Fayard, 1994, pp. 397–411).

7. Cf., among others, A. Hammoudi, 'Segmentarity, Social Stratification, Political Power and Sainthood: Reflections on Gellner's theses', _Poznan Studies in the Philosophy of the Sciences and the Humanities_, 1996, vol. 48, pp. 265–289, and A. Mahé, 'Guerre et paix dans la théorie de la segmentarité. Lecture philosophique d'une théorie anthropologique', in: J. Hannoyer (ed.), _Guerres civiles. Economies de la violence, dimensions de la civilité_ (Paris: Karthala-Cermoc, 1999), pp. 47–67.

8. Cf. S. Zubaida, _Islam, the People and the State: Political ideas and movements in the Middle East_ (London: I. B. Tauris, 1993), and E. Gellner, _Nationalism_ (New York: New York University Press, 1997).

9. As D. F. Eickelman makes clear: '... segmentary groups simply do not occur in a balanced opposition to each other ... When groups combine, they do not do so in terms of the combinations anticipated through an application of segmentary lineage theory ... [and] there is considerable disparity in the political resources enjoyed by various groups, as opposed to the rough equality of people and resources presumed by segmentary lineage theory'; _The Middle East: An anthropological approach_ (Englewood Cliffs: Prentice-Hall, 1981), pp. 102–103.

10. Cf., for the Iraqi case, H. Dawod, 'Etatiser les tribus et tribaliser l'etat', _Esprit_, no. 2, 2001, pp. 21–40; F. A. Jabar, 'Shaykhs and Ideologues: Detribalization and retribalization in Iraq, 1968–1998', _Middle East Report_, no. 215, pp. 28–31.

11. One should, however, also be aware that tribes are not the only solidarity groups acting in Middle Eastern societies. Ethnicity and primary relations are the other sources that have led to construction of solidarity groups.

12. M. Rodinson, _L'Islam: Politique et croyance_ (Paris: Fayard, 1993), p. 132.

13. Cf. J. Habermas, _Le Discourse philosophique de la modernité_ (Paris: NRF), 1988.

14. One may prefer, with Thomas Nipperdey, the concept of modernization to that of philosophically determined 'modernity'. According to Nipperdey, the concept 'modernization' can be used as an analytical tool, which gives a common sense to the experiences of different societies throughout the two last centuries. T. Nipperdey, _Réflexions sur l'histoire allemande_ (Paris: NRF), 1992, p. 61. It is obvious that in the Middle East, as in many other parts of the world, access to 'modernization', in the sense of transformation of material conditions, has taken place at the cost of the political modernity as Habermas understands it.

15. D. Lerner, _The Passing of Traditional Society: Modernizing the Middle East_ (New York: Free Press, 1958).

16. Cf. E. Ödalga (ed.), _Naqshbandis in Western and Central Asia_ (Istanbul: Swedish Research Institute, 1999).

17. Cf. A. Gökalp, _Le Prix de la tradition: les mariages turcs et les prestations matrimoniales_ (Paris: CNRS, n.d.).

18. One should, however, add that the authoritarian and nationalist nature of the states, which criminalized any kind of identity formation, both offered an important

manoeuvre field to tribes and constituted an important factor leading to an 'unachieved modernity' that we observe in the later stages of the Kurdish nationalism. See: A. Vali, 'The Fragmentation of Identity and Politics in Kurdish Nationalism', *Comparative Studies of South Asia, Africa and the Middle East*, vol. XVIII, no. 2, 1998, pp. 82–95, and P. White, *Primitive Rebels or Revolutionary Modernizers? The Kurdish national movement in Turkey* (London: Zed Press, 2000).

19. It would be very hard to suggest an ideal type of these officially recognized autonomous entities and the entities that had a de facto autonomous status. M. van Bruinessen and H Boeschoten, *Evliya Çelebi in Diyarbekir* (Leiden and New York: E. J. Brill, 1988), Cheref Han, *Serefname. Kürd Tarihi*, trans. by M. E. Bozarslan (Istanbul: Deng Yayinlari, 1998); Nejat Göyünç and Wolf-Dieter Hütteroth, *Land an der Grenze. Osmanische Verwaltung im heutigen türkisch-syrisch-irakischen Grenzgebiet im 16. Jahrhundert* (Istanbul: Eren Yayincilik, 1997). Cf. also M. van Bruinessen, *Agha, Sheikh and State;* I. M. Kunt, *The Sultan's Servants. The transformation of Ottoman provincial government 1550–1650* (New York: Columbia University Press, 1993), N. Sevgen, *Dogu ve Güneydogu Anadaolu'da Türk Beylikleri-Osmanli Belgeleri ile Kürt Türkleri Tarihi* (Ankara: TKEA, 1982).

20. 'New Era' proclamed in 1793 by Selim III.

21. Celile Celil, trans. by M. Demir, *XIX. Yüzyil Osmanli Imparatorlugu'nda Kürtler* (Ankara: Öz-Ge, 1992). In this article I will leave aside Persian Kurdistan. Suffice to note that, although more centralized than the Ottoman one, it presents quite similar features and evolution. As H. Batatu puts it: 'The legacy of the Turks was that [...] the military confederations and principalities were destroyed. In their place arose a multitude of antagonistic tribes and tribal sections. In Baghdad Wilayat alone – one of the three wilayats of which Iraq was constituted – there were in 1918 at least 110 independent tribes, made up of 1186 sections'; H. Batatu, *The Old Social Classes and the Revolutionary Movements in Iraq. A study of Iraq's old landes and commercial classes and of its communists, Ba'athists, and free officers* (Princeton: Princeton University Press, 1978), p. 77. Batatu also notes that 'colonization' accelerated this process: 'the process of tribal disintegration was reversed [...]'. In Kurdistan, in the words of British political officer of Sulaimaniya, 'every man who could be labelled as a tribesman was placed under a tribal leader ... , petty village headmen were unearthed and discovered as leaders of long dead tribes: disintegrated sedentary clans [...] were told to reunite and remember that they had once been tribesmen'; ibid, p. 94.

22. M. Yegen, 'The Turkish State Discourse and the Exclusion of Kurdish identity', in: Sylvia Kedouri (ed.), *Turkey: Identity, democracy, politics* (London: Frank Cass, 1996).

23. Ubicini, quoted in C. Celîl, *XIX. Yüzyil Osmanli,* cf. also S. Longrigg, *Iraq, 1900 to 1950: A political, social and economic history* (Oxford: Oxford University Press, 1953).

24. H. Bozarslan, 'Remarques sur l'histoire des relations kurdo-arméniennes', *The Journal of Kurdish Studies*, no. 1, 1995, pp. 55–76.

25. C.Celîl, *XIX. Yüzyil Osmanli.*

26. B. Kodaman, *Sultan II. Abdülhamid Devri Dogu Anadolu Politikasi* {Ankara: TKAE, 1987); S. Duguid, 'The Policy of Unity: Hamidian policy in eastern Anatolia', *Middle Eastern Studies*, vol. IX, no. 2, 1973.

27. On the Ottoman exception in regard to the *asabiyya* phenomenon, cf. E. Gellner, *Muslim Society.*

28. Cf. A. Vali, 'Nationalism and Kurdish Historical Writing', *New Perspectives on Turkey*, 14 (1996), pp. 23-51.

29. The Kurdish nationalist intellectuals accused the tribes of being a stratum of the *mutegallibiyya*, i.e. the 'usurpers'. Cf. M. Selimbegi, 'Kürtlükte Terakki Cereyanlari', *Jîn* (1919, new edn by M. E. Bozarslan), vol. 4 (1987), pp. 745–751.

30. Michael Hudson suggested the concept 'tribal nationalism' in *Arab Politics, The Search for Legitimacy* (New Haven and London: Yale University Press, 1977). Gellner also noticed that a nationalism might have a double code, internal and tribal for the inside, ational for the outside E. Gellner, *Nations et nationalisme* (Paris: Payot, 1989), p. 195.

31. This is what M. Hroch defines as the phase C of small nations' nationalism; *Social Preconditions of National Revival in Europe: A comparative analysis of the social composition of patriotic groups among the smaller European nations* (Cambridge: Cambridge University Press, 1985), p. 23.

32. One should, however, underline that they did not contest the state for the same reasons as the Kurdish nationalist elite: they did it not because it was *Turkish* or *Arab* or *Persian*, but simply because it was *state*, i.e. a *central authority*. H. Bozarslan, 'The Kurdish Nationalism in Turkey: From the tacit contract to the rebellion (1919–1925)', in: A. Vali (ed.), *Essays on the Origins of Kurdish Nationalism* (Costa Mesa: Mazda, 2003), pp. 163–190.

33. For instance, in 1995, in Hakkari HADEP won 54.6% of the votes, thanks to the massive participation of two tribes: the Pinyasin and the Geylanis.

34. M. van Bruinessen, 'Les Kurdes, etats et tribus', *Etudes kurdes*, no. 1, 2000, pp. 9–31. Cf. also P. Bonte, 'Tribus et pouvoirs dans le monde arabe et ses périphéries', *La Pensée*, p. 59.

35. Cf. for some examples, however, H. Bozarslan, *Le Problème national kurde en Turquie kémaliste* (mémoire de diplôme de l'EHESS, Paris, 1986).

36. As L. Dillemann wrote after the Sheikh Said rebellion: 'As a general rule, the tribe acted according to its own laws. None of [the tribes] could pose a unified front to the adversaries. The [feeling of the] threat sharpened the opposition between clans and each time a chief tempted to resist the Turks, a rival rose up against him in order to supplant him with the help of the enemy'; *Les Français en Haute Djezireh* (CHEAM, n.d.), no. 50.538, p. 51.

37. Cf. R. Halli, *Genelkurmay Belgelerinde Kürt Sorunu* (Istanbul: Kaynak Yayinlari, 1992), vol. 1, pp. 67–68.

38. *Jash* means 'small donkeys'. Since the 1961 Barzani rebellion, this word has been used to designate the Kurds who collaborate with the Iraqi government.

39. Human Rights Watch, *Iraq's Crime of Genocide: The Anfal campaign against the Kurds* (New Haven and London: Yale University Press, 1995).

40. As N. Pope informs us, a village guard in Turkey earned, at the beginning of 1990s, a wage of 1,000 French francs (about £150), twice the national minimum wage (*Le Monde*, 30 July 1992).

41. Cf. H. Bozarslan, *Network-building, Ethnicity and Violence in Turkey* (Abu Dhabi: ECSSR, 1999).

42. For the Bucaks and their role in the complex web of underground economy and violence, cf. H. Bozarslan, 'The Kurdish Nationalism in Turkey'.

43. Former leaders of the True Path Party, respectively former president and prime minister of Turkey.

44. To my knowledge, at least, the leading branch of Bucaks has never used a religious or secularist (nationalist) *da'wa* to legitimize their *asabiyya*. The dissident branch, which has been marginalized, joined the Kurdish nationalists.

45. I suggest that in Hakkari the tribal agha's power and position rest in their ability

to manage the different resources of authority and power simultaneously; coercion, confiscating land and animals, the use of sheer violence against the central government's administrators, or local opposition through hirelings are as much a part of the agha politics as consolidating their position through affinitive links to rival aghas forming kirve relations [see note 147] with the local military officers, supporting the governmental party as well as Kurdish nationalist politics and having professional politicians and farmers simultaneously in the family. As it is difficult for one person to consistently carry out all these strategies simultaneously, there can be fluctuations in the careers of agha division of roles and ranking between them in term of "greatness" and "influence", all of which vary in the course of people's lives.' L. Yalçin-Heckmann, *Tribe and Kingship among the Kurds* (Frankfurt: Peter Lang, 1991), p. 131.

46. M. Seurat, 'Le Quartier de Bâb Tebbâné à Tripoli (Liban): étude d'une "asabiyya urbaine"', in: M. Zakaria, B. Chbarou, W. Charâra et al., *Mouvements communautaires et espaces urbains au Machreq* (Beirut: CERMOC, 1985), pp. 45–86.

47. In 1996 some Bucaks were arrested with 2,262,000 kilos of hemp. After a couple of days, the tribunal decided that it was not unlawful to have hemp at home and they were released. S. Hiçyilmaz, *Susurluk ve Kontrgerilla Gerçegi* (Istanbul: Evrensel Basim-Yayin, 1997), p. 22.

48. An enlarged family from Much province, whose activities covered the big Turkish metropolis. For the war between the Bucaks and the Söylemez during 1990s, cf. H. Bozarslan, *Network-building, Ethnicity and Violence in Turkey* (Abu Dhabi: ECSSR, 1999).

49. Cf. O. Sahin, *Firat'in Sirtindaki Kan: Bucaklar* (Istanbul: Kaynak Yayinlari, 1997).

50. One of high-ranking commanders of the death squads, Yesil, says: 'When I get bored, I go to Siverek. [Sedat Bucak] has all my sympathy. Nobody can touch Sedat Abi [grand brother]. Even President Demirel is involved [in this affair]. Let them touch him if they dare. Who offered [weapons to Sedat]? The state. There are written documents. How can they deny them?' *Aydinlik*, 14 June 1998.

51. For this concept, cf. I. M. Lapidus, 'Tribes and State Formation in Islamic History', in: P. S. Khoury and J. Kostiner, *Tribes and State Formation in the Middle East* (Berkeley, Los Angeles and Oxford: University of California Press, 1990), p. 34.

52. A kirve holds a boy during circumcision.

53. Kamil Atak, member of the MHP (Nationalist Action Party, radical right), head of the village guards and mayor of Cizre, has put it: 'if the state abandons us, we will serve those who give us weapons'; 'Silahi Kim Verirse Ona Hizmet Ederiz', *Hürriyet*, 17 December 1996.

PART THREE

Kurds in Iraq

Urbanization, Privatization, and Patronage: The Political Economy of Iraqi Kurdistan

Michael Leezenberg

Introduction

Analyses of the relations between the Kurds and the state in Iraq have tended to give pride of place to ethnicity as an explanatory factor. Such an ethnicity-based perspective, however, has difficulties explaining both the enduring conflict between the main Iraqi Kurdish parties and the political alliances between some Kurdish actors and their alleged ethnic opponents. Thus, to mention but the most famous of such apparent anomalies, the invasion by the combined forces of the Kurdistan Democratic Party (KDP) and the Iraqi army on 31 August 1996 and the subsequent (though temporary) ousting of the Patriotic Union of Kurdistan (PUK) from all of its strongholds in the region, left many observers bewildered. Most explanations of this dramatic development appealed to an alleged irrational and wholly personal rivalry between the KDP and PUK leaders, Masoud Barzani and Jalal Talabani; or to 'archaic' tribal divisions; or even to an allegedly primordial cleavage between speakers of the northern or Bahdinani and the southern or Sorani dialects; or at best to the cynicism of international power politics. Such attempts, however, risk conflating individual psychological motivations, processes of political decision-making and broader social developments; they tend to downplay the considerable autonomy the parties have achieved in acting out their political conflict. Thus, the infighting has misleadingly been portrayed as a conflict between the more rural Bahdinani-speaking northerners of the KDP and the more urban and sophisticated Sorani-speaking southerners of the PUK. Although at times the parties have indeed tried to mobilize the population along such quasi-ethnic lines, these attempts have not met with any serious response; sympathies for either KDP or PUK do not at all unambiguously match ethnic, educational or dialectal background.[1] But despite the parties' failure to mobilize the population along ethnic or tribal lines, the population has for its part not been able to pressure the parties into less violent policies. In other words, the problem to be explained is precisely how the Kurdish parties have been able to get away with pursuing policies that went against the interests and wishes of the population at large.

While part of the reason for the persistent political cleavages and antagonisms in the region has undoubtedly been the interference by neighbouring and other states, there are also domestic and structural causes of these cleavages and of the specific forms they have taken in recent years. It is on these local factors that I will focus here.[2] My perspective is informed by some of the theoretical concepts of political economy, in particular by the notion of patronage. The chapter's main emphasis lies with the transformation of systems of patronage in the contemporary cities of Iraqi Kurdistan; I shall try to describe how tribal and other 'traditional' structures have persisted, and even gained in importance, despite the enormous structural changes the region has undergone. Some of the main underlying socio-economic causes for this development have been, first, the rise of the private sector and the emergence of a form of state capitalism in Iraq from the 1970s onwards, and, second, the interaction between the region and the international market. The urban focus of the paper lies in the fact that the cities in Iraqi Kurdistan have become heavily dependent on state structures; tribal leaders and other patrons, I will argue, have become equally 'urbanized': they have turned these structures to their own advantage, accumulating wealth and power. After the 1991 uprising, they have been able to further extend their power. In other words, contemporary tribal and other divisions should not be seen as leftovers from traditional social structures, but as social strategies that have a function in a modern urbanized context as well. Given the lack of reliable quantitative social and economic source materials, however, I can do no more here than provide a preliminary and qualitative picture of these developments.[3]

Theoretical Background: Ethnicity, Economy, Patronage

The relative scarcity of substantial, social-scientific research on the Iraqi Kurds (as on the Kurds in general) is rather surprising, in view of the region's importance for the domestic and foreign policies of various countries. For the most part, both journalistic and academic Western-language writings pay predominant, if not exclusive attention to political factors; and few Kurdish authors have been in a position to publicize their views without the risk of being branded as biased towards one of the conflicting parties.[4] As said, however, numerous social, economic and even political developments do not at all fit in well with and may actually remain largely hidden from view in such a simplistic personality- and ethnicity-based perspective. A more theoretically informed discussion may open our eyes to less obvious developments and suggest a mode of explanation for events that may otherwise seem difficult to comprehend. For one thing, it leads to a de-emphasizing of an ethnic or nationalist confrontation between Kurds and Arabs as the prime mover of domestic developments. While such nationalistic political considerations undoubtedly played a role, there have also been more strictly social and economic aspects to Iraqi government policies.[5] More in general, an implicit 'mosaic model' of ethnic identity can be recognized in a good deal of writing (and especially in journalistic work) about contemporary Kurdistan: this is the idea that ethnic or sectarian groups like the Kurds or Arabs are immutable once and for all, and that social behaviour is determined primarily by one's being a Kurd or Arab or Sunni Muslim, etc. One should not, however, take ethnic groups such as 'the' Kurds as fixed and immutable. Ethnic, sectarian or tribal identity is not a fact of nature that unequivocally determines social behaviour; rather, it can itself be manipulated for social or political purposes.[6] Further, one should not overemphasize the role of the political sphere, or of individual decisions by those in power, in social developments: government policy decisions may in part be constrained or even thwarted by wider socio-economic developments. This is not to deny the overwhelmingly strong influence of the political sphere in Iraq: needless to say, Ba'ath policies have intruded in an often dramatic manner into citizens' everyday lives. Still, one should avoid giving too much weight to the role of the leaders' personalities in policy decisions.

It has been argued that a political economy perspective, which focuses on the development of class relations and the specific modes of production associated with each social formation, can help social studies of the Middle East get rid of outdated and Eurocentric assumptions.[7] For Iraq and Iraqi Kurdistan, the major study written from such a perspective is, of course, Hanna Batatu's monumental *The Old Social Classes and the Revolutionary Movements of Iraq*,[8] which describes the transformation of old status groups, like sheikhs and tribal leaders, into new social classes based on private ownership of land and mercantile capital. In analytical terms, such approaches mark major advances over the crude 'mosaic' models noted above, as they can in principle take the changing nature of ethnic and tribal loyalties in the face of social and economic transformations into account. A popular variety of such a political-economy approach is that of dependency theory, which emphasizes the importance of developing countries' being incorporated in the world market. This broader context of international capitalism leads to 'dependent development' in third-world countries, which is largely determined by foreign capitalist influences: they typically produce raw materials for the world market, and import technological know-how and industrial products from abroad. A dependency-theory perspective can yield important insights into the development of the Iraqi economy as primarily dependent on oil exports.[9] However, it tends to overemphasize external factors at the expense of internal economic and social dynamics. This is a particular problem in cases where state influence on the domestic economy has been as strong as in Iraq: it is the Iraqi state that since the mid-1970s has been the main economic actor, both as investor and as customer of privately produced goods; moreover, it very ably diversified its foreign sources of goods, arms and funding, and can thus be characterized as 'dependent' only in a rather generic sense.[10] More in general, the use of the classical categories of political economy leads to a relative neglect of other factors like ethnic, sectarian and tribal loyalties (although Batatu himself is well aware of these dimensions, and in his analysis rarely loses sight of them). Obviously, ethnic and sectarian categories are not just given; but one should also beware of dismissing them as merely ideological epiphenomena that only divert attention from a social reality assumed to be primarily driven by economic factors.[11]

A significant challenge for classical approaches of political economy is the fact that in Iraqi Kurdistan, class consciousness and primarily class-based social behaviour do not seem to have developed very much, despite the Marxist-inspired official ideology of many local parties and the still widespread appeal of vaguely socialist slogans (as elsewhere, the 1980s and 1990s have witnessed the increasing appeal of Islamist ideas, but these hardly refer to notions like class or even to economics at all). This will be a starting point of the present analysis. Its perspective is essentially that of political economy, but it pays specific attention to other factors that interfere with processes of class formation. These factors, it seems, can best be broadly indicated by the generic label of *patronage*. Patron–client relations are asymmetric power relations that differ as much from kinship-based organization as from power relations in centralized, lawful bureaucracies; unlike either, they are rarely perceived as wholly legitimate. They cut straight through class relations, and tend to occur 'where no corporate lineal group ... intervenes between potential client and potential patron' and 'where the formal institutional structure of society is weak and unable to deliver a sufficiently steady supply of goods and services'.[12] This characterization may seem at odds with the conditions pertaining in Ba'ath Iraq, which not only had strong and affluent state institutions until at least 1990, but also featured persistent tribal structures. I will argue, however, that both economic developments and state policies have actually *encouraged* the transformation of tribal loyalties into patron–client relations of a more restricted nature.[13]

On a consensus model of society, in which all relations and institutions are primarily taken as contributing to social integration, patronage forms a kind of mediation between the individual and the state (or, in the case of sheikhs and other religious patrons, the divine). Gilsenan[14] has argued, however, that patrons do not arise as a kind of 'social glue' or as mediators when 'gaps' appear in the social order, that is, when a genuine need for mediation between the individual and the state arises, but rather as the result of socio-economic transformations. In his view, patronage relations serve to maintain existing forms of political domination in the face of structural economic changes. Thus, contemporary patron–client relations should not be seen as just remnants of 'traditional' social relations, like tribal or religious loyalties, in a 'modern' state: they can actually be shaped by the specific characteristics of modern states. Neither is clientelism exclusive to 'poor' countries: there appears to be no direct relation between economic development and the strength of patron–client relations.[15] A final significant characteristic of patronage relations from a conflict perspective is the fact that they may well work against the best interests of the clients, in that they tend to perpetuate existing unequal divisions of material and other resources, and hence tend to keep the clientele dependent on patronage.

Now what is specifically urban about the problems to be discussed here? To begin with, Iraqi Kurdistan and, indeed, Iraq as a whole have become thoroughly urbanized in the decades following independence. This steady urbanization, which had already started in the 1930s, has constituted a momentous social transformation, but its effects have hardly been studied. At first, it was largely caused by the worsening conditions of living in the countryside, but it continued with the development of new opportunities for work, education and social mobility in the cities. Already by 1965, more than half of the Iraqi population was living in the cities; by 1980, this percentage had increased to over 70.[16] The Kurdish region lagged behind in this urbanization process: by 1977, 51 per cent of the local population was still rural.[17] The subsequent years, however, witnessed a continuing process of both voluntary and forced migration, mostly to cities and *mujamma'at* or resettlement camps in the region.[18]

It should be stressed that strictly ethnic or political considerations on the part of the government were only one among many factors that led to the urbanization of the Kurdish north. The progressive 1975 land reform was never fully implemented, and in any case, its effects were largely undone by the privatizations of the early 1980s, especially by the 1983 Law No. 35, which allowed for the leasing of large tracts of lands by Ba'ath party adherents.[19] Between 1975 and 1979, it was not only government policies of deportation but also the lack of rural development after the 1975 land reforms that forced many Kurds to migrate to the cities of northern Iraq.[20] After all, in Iraq as a whole, agricultural production has dropped dramatically since the early 1970s, and urbanization has been a nationwide phenomenon.

Already in the late 1970s, the failure of the successive land reforms had become apparent; much land had been lost for agricultural production, either through salinity or through deliberate destruction. At the same time, the city, as the main beneficiary of state spending, became ever more attractive for those seeking employment: in the 1970s and 1980s, urban wages, especially in the private sector, steadily increased. The cities were also attractive because of their much better developed health and education infrastructure. The displaced rural labour was largely absorbed in the 'notoriously unproductive' services sector, in which the state was an important employer.[21] In a sense, then, much present-day research on Iraqi Kurdistan must have an urban focus by default. Even studies on agricultural development cannot avoid paying attention to such specifically 'urban' phenomena as the commercialization of agrarian production, absentee landlordism, etc.[22]

Moreover, in their new urban context, patronage relations have arguably taken on a number of novel characteristics. Here, I will focus on the character of the (partly informal) social relations obtaining in the cities, in keeping with Lapidus,[23] who has argued that one should not study the 'Islamic city' itself, but rather focus on social forms and relations in such cities. In his view, informal ties of ethnicity, kinship and religion remain a constant factor amid the rapid economic transformations. While it remains to be seen how far such informal ties have themselves been influenced by economic developments, their very persistence indicates that one should remain wary of simple dichotomies between 'urban' and 'rural', 'traditional' and 'modern', and the like.

Urbanization, Class Structure and Patronage in Ba'ath Iraq

During the monarchic period, the traditional landowning and mercantile classes of Iraq largely failed to develop a class consciousness, mainly because of sectarian, ethnic and other divisions among themselves, but also because they had been insufficiently integrated into the Iraqi state to grasp the importance of the rapid socio-economic developments. In the 1950s new social trends emerged, such as the development of an urban proletariat and the upward social mobility – largely through the army – of the petty bourgeoisie. Oil revenues led to a steady rise in state income and autonomy. After the 1958 revolution, successive governments tried (with varying degrees of determination and success) to break the political power of the landlords, especially by promulgating and (at least partially) implementing several land reforms. The unstable 1960s witnessed a protracted power struggle among the different segments of the new ruling elites; the old landowning elites, by contrast, seemed to be losing ever more of their power base. After the coup of 1968, the new Ba'ath government carried through new land reforms, especially through laws no. 117 of 1970 and no. 90 of 1975, which aimed at further weakening the traditional landowners. Agriculture, however, was never a priority of the regime's economic policies. The nationalization of oil income in 1972 created unprecedented possibilities for state spending; most of the funds that became available were allocated in urban contexts, especially in industry and construction. Already during the 1970s, construction exceeded the share of agriculture and manufacturing in both the gross domestic product and government investment. The oil wealth and the rise of the state sector announced the speedy development of an affluent welfare state with a form of state capitalism: the private sector was not discouraged, and trade unions remained under strict political control.[24]

During the 1970s, accelerated urbanization, with its new potentials for education and social mobility, the land reforms and the increase in state power in general put unprecedented pressure on the landowners and tribal leaders. In fact, most observers at the time held that the rise of the Iraqi welfare state was likely to lead to a continuing decrease in the social importance of the traditional ruling strata. Thus, according to Batatu,[25] the power base (notably, the private possession of land) of these strata had largely been destroyed by the late 1970s. More in general, Iraqi social policy in the 1970s had the proclaimed aim of 'transferring political allegiance from kinship structures to the state'. It did not aim at eliminating class differences entirely, however, but rather at social reform within the framework of the welfare state.[26]

It seems, then, that rural tribal structures based on landownership were undergoing a serious crisis in the 1970s and early 1980s.[27] But this trend, if such it was, was reversed by the developments of the 1980s and early 1990s in Iraqi Kurdistan, and possibly in Iraq as a whole. By the late 1980s, part of the Kurdish tribal leadership had been given a new lease of life, but this time in an overwhelmingly urban context. The reassertion of tribal relations was encouraged by a combination of socio-economic and political factors. To begin with, the privatizations of the 1980s created advantageous conditions for private investment: tribal leaders loyal to the government now found new opportunities to increase their wealth as traders and as contractors for the profitable state-commissioned infrastructure projects. Many tribal leaders thus became urban entrepreneurs; construction projects were particularly lucrative, as they provided ample opportunities for corruption. These conditions helped the transformation of the erstwhile 'pre-capitalist' landowning stratum into a more strictly capitalist class; the possession of capital became a main source of power and prestige.

In this period, a large part of the urban population became directly or indirectly dependent on the state, either by being employed in the state services sector or by working for one of the private companies that carried out state-commissioned projects.[28] The mobilization of a large part of the male population for active military service created an acute shortage of personnel, and brought large numbers of women into the urban labour force. To some extent, an ethnic division of labour also developed: many foreign unskilled workers, especially from Egypt and Sudan, became employed in the urban informal sector (notably in construction, in shops and in restaurants), whereas Iraqi nationals more often worked in the state-related services sector. On the whole, the affluence that the nationalization of oil income in 1972 brought to society enabled the government to create a mixed economy, in which neither the state nor private capital predominated. These government policies have (whether or not intentionally) tended to prevent the development of a strong class consciousness among the population.[29] Thus, no serious class-based challenges to either the government or to the aghas-turned-entrepreneurs arose.

But there were also political factors that encouraged the reassertion of tribal and quasi-tribal structures. The most important of these were the outbreak of the Iran–Iraq war in 1980 and the subsequent renewal of large-scale Kurdish guerrilla activities. During the 1980s, the Iraqi government systematically reinforced tribal structures by installing so-called *mustashar* troops (Kurdish irregulars) and, paradoxically though this may seem at first blush, in the formation of new *urban* structures, the *mujamma'at*. The troops of irregulars were installed to protect the northern governorates without having to withdraw too many regular army forces from the war front. Tribal leaders could enlist their followers to form such a militia, and would receive generous rewards from the government. But also individuals without a specific tribal status could receive such awards if they brought together a number of armed men. Having or creating a quasi-tribal militia thus became a lucrative business: often, the numbers of those enlisted were wildly exaggerated, and not all of them countered the Kurdish guerillas as actively as they were supposed to do. According to McDowall,[30] quoting Masoud Barzani, the Kurdish parties to some extent even encouraged locals to join the irregular troops, as they argued they could not accommodate more guerrillas. To those enlisted, this system brought few financial awards, but at least they were exempted from front duty, and they could allay government suspicions by keeping up a semblance of loyalty. Among the many tribes who created such irregular troops or *jash* ('donkey foal', as Kurdish nationalists disparagingly called them) were the Surchi and the Bradost; but there were also men without a tribal background who acquired prominence by becoming *mustashar*, such as Mamand Qashqai and Tahsin Shawais. In other words, the *mustashar* system actually contributed to the creation of new quasi-tribal relations.

Deported Kurdish villagers were resettled in the quasi-urban *mujamma'at*. There, they were completely cut off from their former means of making a living, and became wholly dependent on state handouts. These were supplied primarily through the *mustashar* leaders, who were placed in charge of food redistribution. These could thus further reinforce their social and political position, once again with generous rewards and ample opportunities for corruption and clientelism.

The 1988 ceasefire brought a deep economic crisis to Iraq, which seriously threatened the repressive welfare state that had been created in the preceding years. The government had amassed enormous foreign debts, and the demobilization of large numbers of soldiers carried with it the risk of a steep rise in unemployment and social unrest. The depth of the crisis led the government to engage in a radical, if not reckless, reform programme that has been characterized (by Chaudhry[31]) as a form of economic 'shock therapy', as it seriously threatened the economic and social well-being of the urban population, which had already been under pressure owing to the vast war expenses. Price ceilings on basic foodstuffs were lifted, and numerous workers were fired. Apparently, the government tried to divert or channel the ensuing social unrest by initiating a violent campaign against foreign workers (primarily Egyptians), who were an easily identifiable target for local antipathies. Many of the Egyptian workers were chased out of the country in the winter of 1989–1990. According to Egyptian press reports at the time, armed Iraqi thugs killed between 1,000 and 2,000 Egyptian workers during this period. Local eyewitnesses at the time alleged that they had been instructed by the Iraqi government to scare the latter into leaving.

According to some analysts, such as Chaudhry, it was likewise economic factors, notably the crushing debt burden and the social upheaval caused by the economic reforms, that were among the main considerations leading to the Iraqi invasion of Kuwait in early August 1990. Subsequently, the UN imposed an economic embargo on Iraq; at once, the country's oil revenues were cut off. In order to stimulate the agricultural sector and thus enhance the country's economic self-sufficiency, the government then started leasing lands in the northern governorates to (often city-based) *mustashar*, who were thus further strengthened by the state.

The 1980s, then, marked the active encouragement of (quasi-)tribal social relations in Iraqi Kurdistan; but these relations were now reproduced in a largely urbanized environment and against the backdrop of an internationalized and commercialized economy. Why did the Ba'ath regime, with all its socialist and modernist rhetoric, not develop a more formal and less patronage-prone style of government? A main factor may have been its concern with political security, which was pursued by a policy of stick and carrot. Although the Ba'ath regime's merciless persecution of real and alleged opponents has been amply documented, the patronage-like complement to this repression has received rather less attention. Yet, in so far as any government can rule by the sheer terrorizing and atomization of its population at all, the Iraqi Ba'ath regime does not unambiguously fit this picture of a monolithic and purely repressive state power. In cities and countryside alike, as in the *mujamma'at*, the regime tried to create dependence on, and hence loyalty to, the state through middlemen who could rely on and strengthen and, in some cases, even create tribally-based claims to authority through the monopolization of food supplies. In other words, Iraqi government policies of the 1980s have stimulated a form of patronage imposed from above. This development does not fit in well with the more traditional conceptions of patronage as primarily emerging in the absence of a strong state. Likewise, in a tactic that is at odds with the picture of the Iraqi state as based on a near-total concentration of power in the hands of Saddam Hussein's extended family, the Iraqi government actually *delegated* power and means of coercion to locals with the implementation of the *mustashar* system. Even though the dubious loyalty of the *mustashar* was well known and well documented by the intelligence services, the government continued to rely on and even increase their local strength.[32]

The 1991 Uprising and the Attempts at Civilian Rule

The popular uprising that took place in the Kurdish regions in the aftermath of the Gulf War may have been a revolution in the political sense, but socially it left much as it was. In the days following the uprising, urban councils (*shuras*) had been established in Arbil and Sulaimaniya by communist-inspired groups; but these attempts at urban self-government quickly succumbed to the violence of the returning Iraqi army and to the pressure of the Iraqi Kurdistan Front (IKF) parties.[33] At the same time, the IKF announced a general amnesty for all former government collaborators; moreover, relief programs by the UN and others tended to use *mustashar* as middlemen for food distribution in the *mujamma'at*. Collaborators who had become rich in the preceding years were thus set to strengthen their economic position even after the uprising, even though many of them were politically discredited.

The IKF faced the dubious heritage of the strongly centralized and highly cost-inefficient (not to say corrupt) state apparatus on which a large part of the population had become dependent. At first, there were high hopes for a more democratic polity, but the May 1992 elections did not bring the population any concrete rewards. Humanitarian aid was largely concentrated on the rural sector, and directed towards the reconstruction of villages and the rehabilitation of subsistence farming; but the privatization and commercialization of agriculture in the 1980s, combined with the continuation of subsidized food imports by the UN and foreign NGOs and high local transport costs made the long-term success of these agricultural rehabilitation projects unlikely.[34]

Far fewer aid projects were aimed at generating jobs and income in the cities, where – as noted – the majority of the population was living. Attempts to get people to leave the relocation camps for their former villages could at best solve a fraction of the urban labour problems. The steadily worsening economic crisis had created a large urban proletariat or even sub-proletariat of unemployed and underpaid people. Not all of the new urban poor, however, belonged to the labour class: many were or had been civil servants, whose wages were now insufficient to cover the basic costs of living, others were internally displaced persons from Kirkuk and other government-held areas. Political events had caused the collapse of what little formal sector there was; because of the UN embargo and the Baghdad blockade, industry suffered badly. Factories had to reduce or even discontinue production for lack of spare parts and raw materials.[35]

At the same time, the informal sector expanded. In the cities, large numbers of small street vendors appeared. Many people resorted to selling part of their furniture or other possessions as a way of making ends meet; some even tore down part of their houses and resold the construction materials. But a much more momentous trend in the informal economy was the rapid development of cross-border trade. The semi-clandestine transport of petrol from Iraq to Turkey through the Kurdish-held Ibrahim Khalil border crossing was by far the most important activity; but the region also became a main transit zone for the smuggling of various luxury items (notably cigarettes, alcohol and narcotics) to Turkey, Iran and Iraq. In particular, the trafficking of refugees became a highly profitable business: people wishing to leave would pay up to US$5,000 to local 'travel agencies', and often had to pay hundreds of dollars for Turkish transit visas and bribes for Kurdish border officials.

These kinds of trade primarily benefited a small group of people who, often with the use of party networks and militias, could protect their business. The KDP and PUK quickly realized the economic potential of this cross-border trade, and both progressively tried to monopolize the profits that could thus be made. There have also been reports that a small group of party-backed entrepreneurs has gained control over the domestic markets and could thus influence consumer prices for basic foodstuffs and petrol. At one point in 1995, PUK leader Talabani optimistically announced that Iraqi Kurdistan was set to become a Middle Eastern equivalent of free-trade zones like Hong Kong. In fact, however, a model for Iraqi Kurdistan during this period is more readily found in Lebanon during the 1970s and 1980s, when the collapse of central government power equally enabled local warlords and military officers to engage in totally uninhibited smuggling and other profiteering activities.

The worsening economic crisis, the absence of a monopoly of violence and the KDP–PUK conflict that erupted in May 1994 created a climate of fear and uncertainty, in which assassinations were rife. While many of these assassinations seem to have been motivated by the political conflict between the KDP, the PUK and the Islamic Movement, some of them appear to have involved more strictly economic motives.[36]

Among these are the assassinations of an investigating judge who was engaged in bringing legal proceedings against several people accused of involvement in drugs trafficking in the Bahdinan area; the assistant general director of the Sulaimaniya cigarette factory; and a Sulaimaniya businessman with communist sympathies.[37] Equally, several trade union activists have been assassinated, especially in the Bahdinan region up to late 1994. Although the Bahdinan was the traditional KDP stronghold, that party by no means had the uncontested hegemony over the region, which was made insecure by the presence of large numbers of PKK guerrillas and by regular Turkish army incursions.

With the collapse of the strong Ba'ath state in 1991 and the ensuing economic crisis, the lower strata of the urban population became ever more dependent on patronage as a means for survival. The regional government had, for various reasons, not been able to replace the Ba'ath state institutions, let alone create new loyalties that transcended those to tribal chief, sheikh or party. But this very collapse of the state and of public security belies the view of patronage as a form of mediation between the individual and the state. Rather, local patrons have in large part created the dangers against which they subsequently offered to protect the population, and profited from the protection they offered citizens against real or self-created dangers, especially the dangers resulting from the rivalries between them. The main political parties, locked in fierce competition for political hegemony, not only engaged in attempts at clientelizing themselves; they also tried to co-opt rather than to replace or weaken the regional tribal leaders and other patrons.

Arbil

Because of its location and specific characteristics, Arbil has been a main arena of competition, not only between the KDP and the PUK but also for various other forces active in the region. Consequently, certain tendencies may have come out more clearly in this city than elsewhere; but the main points of this analysis also apply to the other major cities of Iraqi Kurdistan.

Since 1974, Arbil had been the seat of the regional government, and until late 1992, it could boast of the only university of the Kurdish region. In Arbil governorate, as opposed to Duhok and Sulaimaniya, there was no

clear majority for either the KDP or the PUK in the 1992 elections: the
KDP received 45.3 per cent of the vote, the PUK 44.2 per cent.[38] Civilian
government quickly appeared ineffective, especially in the face of the parties'
military might. In April 1993, the PUK politburo member Kosrat Rasoul,
a *peshmerga* leader who had maintained his own militia, and thus retained
an independent power base, replaced the civilian Fuad Ma'ssoum as prime
minister.[39] Until at least January 1995, when PUK troops ousted all KDP
personnel from the city, the two parties competed fiercely for political and
social hegemony. Ethnically, too, the population was more heterogeneous
than that of Sulaimaniya or Duhok: it consisted of Kurds, Arabs, Assyrians
and Turkmen. The numerical proportions of these respective groups are
difficult to assess; at present, however, the population of the city seems
predominantly, if not overwhelmingly Kurdish. Practically all Arabs, most
of whom had been employed as Ba'ath government officials, had left by
October 1991. The Assyrians in the city are largely confined to the 'Ain
Kawa suburb, while most Turkmen live in the older quarters. The Turkmen,
most of whom descend from the former Ottoman elite, are primarily active
in trade and crafts; as one elderly local Kurd put it, 'the Turkmen are the
capitalists, the Kurds are the workers'.[40] The Turkmen traditionally had high
social prestige but little political influence, and tended to loyalty towards
whatever authority was in power.

The city also had its slums, partly the direct and intended result of
Iraqi government policies, like the Jezhnikan, Baharka, Daratou and Bani
Slawa *mujamma'at* several miles to the north and south-east of the city,
where Anfal victims from various areas had been resettled by government
forces in the summer of 1988, without any provisions.[41] The aftermath of
the 1991 uprising witnessed a further influx of large numbers of internally
displaced persons, notably from Kirkuk governorate. Some of these settled
in temporary shelters on vacant spots in and around the city or in former
government buildings; the Kirkuk refugees, it appears, primarily resettled
in the Bani Slawa *mujamma'*. These internally displaced persons formed a
particularly vulnerable and destitute group; their presence placed a further
burden on the city's scarce resources and created the potential for social
conflicts.

In Arbil, the two main political parties behaved as the most important
patrons; the political conflict between them tended to mask their common
economic interests. The main political parties in Iraqi Kurdistan were
hardly marked off from each other by specific class interests or ideological
differences. The often-heard claim that the KDP is 'tribal' and the PUK is

more 'urban' should not blind us to the structural similarities between the two. After the 1991 uprising, especially after their 1992 election victory, both parties have been active in creating extensive patronage networks, at the cost of developing a more democratic polity. First and foremost, the parties have probably become the main employers in the region: enlisting as a *peshmerga* was practically the only employment option open for the large numbers of unemployed young males. The parties also bound the relatives of martyred *peshmerga* to themselves by giving them monthly allowances. Further, after both parties had emerged from the 1992 elections with 50 seats in the regional parliament, the party politburos forced an equal distribution of cabinet seats and indeed on all newly created posts for civil servants, notably policemen and teachers. This 'fifty-fifty' policy strengthened the hold of both parties on society at large, and tended to paralyse the elected political institutions. Parliament and government did not just consist of KDP and PUK straw men, however. In a special parliament session in August 1994, both party leaders were severely criticized by representatives for their inability to bring their armed conflict to an end. The outbreak of fighting in May of that year not only marked an escalation of the rivalry between KDP and PUK, but also reflected the increasing power imbalance between the elected structures and the party politburos.[42]

Most of the other parties had far fewer opportunities for such patronage. The Islamic Movement of Iraqi Kurdistan (IMIK) was the only other party that booked substantial successes in the mobilization and clientelization of the poorer urban population, especially through its various welfare activities.

Apart from these party-linked labour opportunities for *peshmerga* and civil servants, the parties also tried to increase their power base by associating themselves with former *mustashar* and with tribal chieftains in general. Already from 1991 onwards, they had became involved in an ever-stronger competition for alliances with local power brokers, whether tribal chieftains or men who had gained positions of importance only in the 1980s. In their attempts to instrumentalize existing patronage networks, they indirectly strengthened the position of these local patrons. The loyalties thus created were rather precarious, however: it occurred that one segment of a tribe sided with the PUK and another with the KDP (some tribes had simultaneously even maintained ties with Baghdad). Moreover, individual tribes could switch sides rather easily, if they had come to feel the other party had more to offer. Such switching sides was repeatedly the direct cause for the outbreak of major clashes between PUK and KDP: thus, the May 1994 infighting between both parties was triggered off by a land conflict near Qal'at Diza between tribal landowners and non-tribal peasants; and in November 1994, the fact that (part of) the Herki tribe switched allegiance from the KDP to the PUK was one of the main events that triggered the subsequent battle for control over Arbil.[43] In general, tribal leaders could profit most by maintaining an ambivalent position between the parties.

Between the KDP and the PUK, ideological differences and primarily class-based action hardly played a significant role in the political competition before and after the elections. Many communist groups had offices in Arbil (e.g. the ICP, the Toilers Party and various other Marxist–Leninist splinter groups, such as the Labour Party for the Independence of Kurdistan and the Communist Current) but their very number betrays the illusory character of these parties' attempts to take unified action on behalf of the poorer strata. Some of these parties have preferred to align themselves in various ways with the bigger parties in order to increase their political leverage.[44]

Even the Kurdistan Conservative Party, which was headed by Hussein Agha Surchi and received political and organizational support from Great Britain, can hardly be called a class-based party, despite the fact that its main proclaimed political aims were the preservation of the political role of the tribal leaders and, significantly, the attraction of foreign investment. It consisted mainly of those tribal chieftains who had been *mustashar* and were unable or unwilling to affiliate themselves with either the KDP or the PUK.

Two other parties played an important role in public life in Arbil. Both have been active in instrumentalizing the population's economic predicament to further their own ends (which partly coincided with those of their foreign sponsors). The Islamic Movement of Iraqi Kurdistan, backed by Iran and Saudi Arabia, created an extensive programme of support for urban orphans and those who took care of them, reconstructed mosques and stimulated Islamic education.[45] One of the Turkmen parties, the Iraqi National Turkmen Party (*Irak Milli Türkmen Partisi*, IMTP), received large sums from Turkey, and tended to work together with the Turkish Red Crescent. In order to strengthen its claim that most of the Arbil population is of Turkmen background, it opened schools and cultural institutes and created relief aid programmes open only to Turkmen or those who were willing to declare themselves Turkmen. In the dismal economic situation, such projects could have considerable success, as the urban population would turn for help to anyone with food or funds.

Apart from the political parties, other patrons emerged in Arbil: various urban entrepreneurs, tribal leaders and upstart *mustashar* leaders were able to turn the economic and political crisis to their advantage. Apparently, a number of the non-tribal entrepreneurs who had made their fortunes during the Ba'ath years left the city for Baghdad before the uprising; but others were able to continue their activities. During the 1980s, they had made their fortunes from trade in cigarettes, alcohol and foodstuffs, and some of them still maintained business offices abroad, e.g. in Turkey. Some of these (formerly) Arbil-based merchants still engaged in international trade; there was a story of one Baghdad-based merchant who managed to export dates from southern Iraq to Qatar by way of the Kurdish region and Iran, in violation of the UN embargo. Undoubtedly, there were many other cases of such continuing commercial activities.

The *mustashars* had been granted an amnesty after the uprising, and had maintained their armed forces. Consequently, some of them emerged as local warlords, both in the countryside and in the cities. Rather than trying to create a monopoly of violence, however, the KDP and PUK actively strengthened the position of such local warlords in their competition for alliances. The most famous (and most violent) of these urban warlords were Mamand Qashqai, a former *peshmerga* turned *jash*, who skilfully manoeuvred between the KDP and PUK, and maintained a large measure of control over the Azadi quarter of Arbil, until he was killed or, according to some sources, severely injured, in early 1995. Ali Galala, another earlier *mustashar* leader, was likewise associated with KDP; he was reportedly killed in a clash with PUK forces. But there were also local bosses who had sided with the PUK; one of them was a certain Faruq, nicknamed Faqa, in Kesnezan, who was killed by KDP militias.[46]

In a sense, one might with equal, if not better justification characterize numerous party officials as warlords, inasmuch as they actively profited from the economic stability and could maximize their profits using the military means at their disposal. But the very persistence and flourishing of these smaller independent bosses is indicative of the social anarchy into which the region was sliding. Details about the activities of these warlords are unknown, as are the activities of urban organized crime in general. There have been incidental reports, however, about the threat they posed to civilians. According to local informants, even cases of outright extortion occurred. Local gangs would visit the houses of the more prosperous families and threaten to kidnap or assassinate their children or relatives, unless a substantial amount of money was paid for protection. At one point in 1994, it was reported, one gang cut off water supplies in (part of) the Azadi quarter, and only reinstalled them after locals had made substantial payments. It seems that party militias themselves at times also engaged in extortion. There have been reports that, during the protracted fights for control over the access roads to the city, privately owned cars were confiscated at party checkpoints and sold off to Iran. The fights that raged during the summer of 1994 further increased the social chaos, and the crime rate rose even further. As the governmental police force collapsed, the Assyrian Democratic Movement, together with the Communists and the Toilers Party, then set up urban guards, which would patrol some quarters at night.[47]

Urban Protest and its Limitations

In the face of both parties and warlords, urban protest was bound to remain weak and ineffective. There have been various protest movements and organizations, which were not (or not primarily) party-linked or party-based, and in fact acted against the interests of the parties, but they faced an unequal battle. There is little information about their activities, precisely because they tried to operate outside the main party networks. At best, they were affiliated with the smaller parties, which on the whole were more concerned with the restoration of parliament and civil rule than the KDP and PUK (or, for that matter, the Islamic Movement and the IMTP).[48] In general, they were hampered by a severe lack of funds, and consequently did not have much to offer to their members. Here, I can give only a few examples.

In the face of the exceedingly high urban unemployment, which according to some may have been as high as 70 per cent, a Union of Unemployed was formed in November 1992.[49] Although it seems to have been based primarily in Sulaimaniya, there have been activities in other cities as well; the number of its members is unknown. The interests it defended repeatedly brought the Union into conflict with the governing parties, but it does not appear to have had any concrete social programme or plans of action: people joined it out of desperation, rather than because of any clear ideas about the realization of their social rights.[50] A Union of Refugees, which was active on behalf of internally displaced persons, seems to have faced similar difficulties.

The women's organizations in Iraqi Kurdistan had great difficulties in developing their own course of action, as they were for the most part linked to one of the political parties. Nonetheless, in September 1993, several organizations presented a petition with over 30,000 signatures to parliament, demanding an improvement in the legal status of women. The proposals never made it to parliament, however, because the KDP faction and conservative representatives refused even to have them discussed. In these and in other cases, a collusion of interests among the parties and the conservative elites carried the day against attempts to create greater social justice in the region through the elected bodies.

There were various forms of more restricted and ephemeral social protest. Between the summer of 1994 and the winter of 1995, numerous peace demonstrations were organized, but these were to no avail. During a special parliament session concerning the fraternal fights in August 1994, hundreds of people demonstrated in front of the parliament building for peace and the creation of new employment opportunities. Simultaneously, factory workers in Arbil (or at least those sympathetic to the ICP and the other organizing parties) went on strike. In August, hundreds of women organized a march from Sulaimaniya to Arbil. In January 1995, a group of intellectuals threatened collective and public self-immolation in protest against the urban clashes in which the PUK subsequently ousted the KDP from Arbil. According to the London-based daily *al-Hayat*, a further 10,000 people demonstrated against the renewal of fights. In other words, popular discontent with the parties' violent confrontation was widespread and vocal, but it failed to materialize into an effective organized protest. The various demonstrations had great popular support, but failed to change the parties' stance, which was becoming increasingly autonomous and indifferent to the population's wishes.

For the most part, then, urban protest organizations seem to have had restricted goals and short-term programmes, and were small and weak. Although they also addressed economic issues, they hardly featured any articulated class factor; as noted, most of the population had been employed in the state and private service sectors, and had developed no class outlook; by 1994, urban unemployment had become staggeringly high, and had led to an increasing dependence on the informal economy and on patronage. Moreover, the Marxist–Leninist movements in the region were themselves fragmented; and, as noted above, party affiliation or participation in party-specific activities is typically influenced by various other factors as well. Their lack of funds and the increasingly violent political climate, in which access to the media was severely restricted, made it difficult for such movements to gain a more influential position and to let their voices be heard by the outside world.

The predominant forms of social action in Iraqi Kurdistan, then, involved different levels of patronage: individuals could, or had to, seek support either from tribal leaders, urban entrepreneurs, or directly from the main political parties. To some extent, tribal leaders affiliated with one of the parties fulfilled a mediating function (e.g. in influencing voting behaviour during the 1992 elections); but in general, this 'mediation' tended to benefit the old and new power elites rather than the population at large. As long as the KDP–PUK conflict lingered on, numerous tribal leaders could maintain a power base of their own, in urban as well as in rural areas. Thus, the collapse of state power has led to a further decline in the mediating function of tribes, although this pattern was visible already in the earlier years of Ba'ath government; conversely, not all mediating practices disappeared overnight. As noted, the prime activity of party-related, tribal and other patrons has become capital accumulation, for which the establishment of an area under Kurdish political control created unprecedented potentials. In all kinds of economic activities (smuggling of goods and people, trade in foodstuffs, and the contracting of reconstruction projects), party structures and unquestioning tribal loyalties created considerable competitive advantages.

1996 and After: Curtailing Tribal Power?

In the new political constellation, the regional government appeared weak and ineffective. The main parties increasingly resorted to violence and, increasingly, their internecine fights hit civilian targets and led to civilian casualties; for example, in the battles for the Kesnezan checkpoint on the outskirts of Arbil, the nearby Rizgari hospital was severely damaged; there also were incidents of looting of hospital supplies and equipment and of the private property of local civilians.

This period of outright urban warfare was relatively brief, though. After the PUK ousted the KDP from Arbil in January 1995, it was better placed to impose an effective monopoly of violence in the city, and it appears that the position of these warlords gradually weakened in consequence. There seems to have been a crackdown on some of the (organized) criminal activities, and most of the strong men mentioned above seem to have been killed or ousted during this period. Clearly, the PUK takeover reduced the warlords' room for manoeuvre between the two parties that had until then been competing for supremacy in the city. This process of stabilization in Arbil and, indeed, in the Kurdish region as a whole appears to have largely continued following the events of August and September 1996. Some independent sources and foreign aid workers claim that the KDP rule over Arbil actually marked a further improvement over the PUK one-party administration in terms of efficiency; but such claims may be difficult to substantiate.

The anarchy between 1994 and 1996 repeatedly drove the political parties into armed conflicts with some of the larger tribes that had retained their independence. These conflicts, however, are not indicative of any wish on the parties' side to curtail tribal power in general, but of more restricted strategic goals. The tribal leaders, who had a long-standing claim to authority, differed in several respects from the local warlords, many of whom had risen to dominant positions only in the 1980s. The Surchis, one of the most important tribes in Arbil governorate, were not known for particularly violent behaviour in the city, but they had long been an important political force by virtue of their wealth, and after 1991 played a predominant role in the Conservative Party (KCP). In the 1980s, the Surchi chieftains had amassed fortunes by their activities in trade and construction and by supplying the government with large (and largely imaginary) forces of Kurdish irregulars. They had also accepted orders for government construction projects, which they would pass on to others, while themselves pocketing a fair amount of the allocated funds. After the uprising, they bought off the construction materials of the Bakhma dam site for an estimated 20 million dollars, and subsequently sold them, again with huge profits, to Iran. While Hussein Agha, the most important Surchi leader, does not himself appear to have been engaged in other forms of trade, some of his relatives had long been active in international trade, and even had offices in London.

The Surchis' local influence, however, was suddenly and violently crushed in the months preceding the KDP takeover of Arbil. In June 1996, KDP forces destroyed the Surchis' rural power base at Kilken, in the Harir plain north of Arbil. They killed Hussein Agha and an estimated 30 other members of the Surchi clan, destroyed the village and took numerous women and children hostage. At the time, local media such as the *Turkish Daily News* described this event as a clash between the KDP and the KCP *as parties*. However, although the precise course of events remains unclear, the incident does not appear to have been either a purely political confrontation or a more 'traditional' kind of tribal shootout. According to several observers, the KDP had clear strategic and economic motivations for its operation, notably the wish to gain control over the Surchis' traditional territory, the Harir plain, which linked the KDP headquarters at Salahuddin with their main military base at Spilk; and the prospect of control over the redistribution of supplies within the framework of the Food for Oil deal that had been reached between UN and Iraq in the preceding month. At the time, KDP propaganda denounced the Surchis as traitors for their alleged dealing with Baghdad, even though the KDP was itself less than three months away from openly collaborating with Iraqi government troops in its invasion of Arbil; but there are also indications that at the time, the Surchis were moving closer to the PUK, a move perceived by the KDP as a clear threat to its interests.[51]

Other tribal leaders themselves remained outside the urban context, and had their interests in the cities taken care of by close relatives; some of them appear to have continued to balance successfully between the different local political forces. Thus, Karim Khan Bradost, who himself continued to reside in his traditional rural stronghold near the Turkey–Iraq–Iran border triangle, was known to have maintained links with all the political forces in the region: KDP and PUK, as well as Turkey, Baghdad and the PKK. One of his sons had settled in Baghdad after the uprising, but another one became a member of parliament for the PUK. The latter could increase his fortunes by supplying a large percentage of the goods for foreign aid organizations active in Kurdistan.

In the years following the 1991 uprising, then, not only was the power base of these tribal chieftains not adversely affected, but it was actually strengthened. At least up until the establishment of two distinct and relatively stable zones under the de facto hegemony of, respectively, the KDP and the PUK, numerous tribal leaders and other middlemen were able to balance between the two rival parties, and even to exploit this rivalry to their own advantage. Subsequently, it appears, their role as economic middlemen returned to the foreground.

Following the establishment of effective one-party rule in Arbil, at first by the PUK and subsequently by the KDP, the worst urban anarchy seems to have abated. Indeed, the region as a whole regained a modicum of political stability and security. There are different reasons for this development. First and foremost, although popular discontent was in itself unable to stop the unprecedented violent urban infighting, it did lead to increasing support for parties like IMIK and the PKK, and among some even for the idea of a return of the Baghdad regime. In the face of such alternatives, the KDP and PUK could ill afford wholly to alienate the population at large. Economically, the conclusion and subsequent implementation of the Food for Oil deal between Iraq and the UN (a significant part of the revenues of which were earmarked for the Kurdish-held region) promised substantial new sources of income; but a measure of political and administrative stability was required for the commissioning and successful implementation of UN projects. The main Kurdish parties thus had both a clear political and economic interest in a return to a semblance of normality, though these interests did not lead to a more active pursuit of the restoration of the civilian, elected and joint government.

Following the PUK recapture of Sulaimaniya in October 1996, a demarcation line was established, which – despite various minor and some major skirmishes up to the autumn of 1997 – remained largely stable. In the course of 1996 and 1997, it appears, both parties realized they had more to gain by settling for a ceasefire than by a protracted armed confrontation. Following several further rounds of fighting, both party leaders – under intense American pressure – signed the so-called 'Washington Agreement' in September 1998, which was to initiate a process of normalization. Although this normalization process did not lead to the rehabilitation of the erstwhile regional parliament and government (in fact, both parties set up their own 'regional governments' in their respective spheres of influence), it did lead to a protracted period of relative calm and stability. Eventually, the parties managed to establish a more effective and less contested form of one-party rule. The most significant factor disrupting this new constellation was the emergence of new Islamist groups, such as the Islamic League and the Islamic Union Party. These distinguished themselves from the Islamic Movement by their rejection of armed tactics, and focused their attention on morals, welfare work and education. Apart from such concerns, however, they hardly appear to have had any substantial social or economic programmes.

Overall, the gradual implementation of the UN Food for Oil programme that got underway in the spring of 1997 has greatly reduced the hardship of the population; structurally, it marked no significant change in the existing distribution of economic power. These UN operations have often been criticized as highly cost-inefficient and corruption-prone; but they are probably no more so than the Iraqi form of state capitalism of the 1970s, of which they may be said to form a continuation or rehabilitation. The main risks associated with the UN programme have been the further erosion of local agriculture and continued dependence on external welfare.[52] Although party-related personnel appear to have profited most from the programme, some of the tribal chieftains could equally take advantage of the new opportunities by reverting to their prime economic activity of the 1980s, the contracting business. Likewise, former local (and party-affiliated) NGOs transformed themselves into private contracting firms without difficulty, which suggests an underlying continuity. The contractors served as local middlemen in a more restricted economic sense, working for the Iraqi state at first, and subsequently for the international humanitarian circuit. Since the implementation of the Oil for Food programme, new sources of local income were generated by the UN operations and their spin-off. Although undoubtedly a large proportion of the revenues was transferred to bank accounts abroad, the enormous profits increasingly had a local effect. The second half of the 1990s witnessed a new construction boom and a steady rise in the import of luxury goods, especially in cities close to the border, like Zakho and Duhok.

A word remains to be said about the underlying causes of the KDP–PUK conflict.[53] This conflict has been called 'suicidal'; but as disastrous as its consequences may have been for the population at large, the infighting has to some extent actually served the interests of the two parties. It should not be seen in overly personal terms; obviously, personal rivalries between Barzani and Talabani have played a role, but in themselves, these can hardly explain the tenacity and vicious character of the fights. There were simply too many people who had an active interest in maintaining a war economy and keeping the population weak and dependent, in order to maximize their profits. Some analysts have even suggested that the outbreak of internecine fights may actually have helped the parties to avert the outbreak of major social conflicts, by creating new dangers for the population at large.[54]

The division of border-trade profits was a main bone of contention between the Kurdish parties. At first, customs revenues were divided evenly among the IKF parties; after the elections, the KDP, PUK and the government each received a percentage of these revenues, and the other parties were excluded from this source of income. Starting with the May 1994 fights, the KDP kept all the funds collected at the Khabur border checkpoint for itself. All of a sudden, the PUK found itself severely short of funds, which was one of the reasons that it was initially more eager to push for peace than the KDP: it had the majority of the population, and in particular the urban areas with their large numbers of civil servants, under its control. As soon as it had found a new source of funding in Iran, however, it could take up a less compromising attitude towards the KDP. The KDP, in its turn, found that it had more to gain by maintaining good relations with Baghdad, especially because of the lucrative oil revenues from the Ibrahim Khalil border crossing, which it could thus keep for itself, rather than having to share them with the PUK, let alone the government.

Conclusion

The notion of patronage may open up fresh perspectives on the political economy of Iraqi Kurdistan; it allows for more analytical flexibility than relatively static macro-categories like ethnicity, or a rigid dichotomy between 'traditional' and 'modern'. If the present analysis can claim any degree of accuracy, it suggests a qualitative change in the nature of both tribes and political parties, even though existing patterns of loyalty have largely remained intact. Or, to put it more bluntly: the power elites of Iraqi Kurdistan have made extensive use of 'traditional' social structures and relations for wholly 'modern' purposes of capital accumulation. Perhaps the term 'patronage', which may imply a suggestion of mutual benefit that has been largely absent in practice, sounds too neutral as a catch phrase to characterize the kind of socio-political relations that have been developing in the region. But keeping in mind Gilsenan's critique[55] of patron –client relations, patronage may also be seen as involving the 'active creation and maintenance of dependence by those who have an interest in maintaining the existing division of power and resources'.[56]

Tribalism in Iraqi Kurdistan is not simply a survival from the past; neither are (quasi-) tribal relations opposed or complementary to the strength of the state. In the 1980s, relations of patronage (re-)emerged, not in order to fill any social gaps left open by a weak state, but as the direct result of the state's active intervention. Likewise, the patterns of patronage formed after 1991 can hardly be described as forms of mediation between the individual and the state, as the old state institutions had collapsed and a new bureaucracy could not develop. With the KDP–PUK competition, party patronage practically became institutionalized as the most profitable, or even the only viable option for many urban individuals. As patronage is usually defined as an informal relation, the expression 'institutions of patronage' may seem a contradiction in terms; but it should be kept in mind that patronage relations, no matter how openly they are formed, are never perceived as wholly legitimate; further, they are unstable, as clients may switch sides when they perceive or expect greater profits with another patron; finally, in the absence of an effective formal government bureaucracy, they are the most readily available and most advantageous means of creating support, or at least compliance, from the population.

Notes

1. The results of the 1992 elections are telling in this respect. Although the PUK did not make any significant inroads into the Bahdinan, the KDP's traditional mainstay (it received less than 10 per cent of the vote, the KDP over 80 per cent), the KDP drew a solid 30 per cent of the vote in the PUK heartlands, the Sorani-speaking Sulaimaniya region (cf. R. Hoff, M. Leezenberg, and P. Muller, *Elections in Iraqi Kurdistan: An Experiment in Democracy* (Brussels: Pax Christi International, 1992).

2. Also economically and socially, much of the region's predicament is, of course, conditioned by outside factors such as the UN embargo against Iraq as a whole, and by the internal blockade imposed in 1991 by the Baghdad government against the Kurdish-controlled area.

3. For an interpretation of local politics prior to the Arbil invasion, see: M. Leezenberg, 'Irakisch-Kurdistan seit dem 2. Golfkrieg', in: C. Borck et al. (eds), *Ethnizität, Nationalismus, Religion und Politik in Kurdistan* (Münster: LIT Verlag, 1997); for more detailed descriptions of new developments and long-term trends in the regional economy, see: Netherlands-Kurdistan Society, *Iraqi Kurdistan: Political crisis and humanitarian aid* (Amsterdam, 1996); M. Leezenberg, 'Humanitarian Aid in Iraqi Kurdistan', *CEMOTI*, 2000, no. 29, pp. 31–49; M. Leezenberg, 'Refugee Camp or Free Trade Zone? The economy of Iraqi Kurdistan since 1991', in: K. Mahdi (ed.), *Iraq's Economic Predicament* (London: Ithaca Press, 2002).

4. For some of the more important journalistic works, see L. Schmidt, *Wie teuer ist die Freiheit? Reportagen aus der Selbstverwalteten kurdischen Region 1991–93* (Cologne: ISP Verlag, 1994); C. Kutschéra, *Le Défi kurde; ou le rêve fou de l'indépendance* (Paris: Bayard, 1997); J. Randal, *After Such Knowledge, What Forgiveness? My Encounters with Kurdistan* (Boulder: Westview, 1999); for academic analyses see e.g.: M. Gunter, *The Kurdish Predicament in Iraq: A political analysis* (Basingstoke: Macmillan, 1999); F. Ibrahim, 'Die Genesis des kurdisch-irakischen Konflikts', in: *Perspectives of Southern Kurdistan in a Regional and Supraregional Context* (Bonn: Navend, 1999). Dagli focuses on the October 1992 fights between the Iraqi Kurdish parties and the PKK; F. Dagli, *Birakujî: Kürtlerin iç savaşi* [Fratricide: The civil war of the Kurds] (Istanbul: Belge Yayinlari, 1994). Aytar, in his book largely consisting of interviews with the protagonists, addresses the 1994 rounds of infighting between KDP, PUK, and IMIK; O. Aytar, *Kurdistana bi fiftî-fiftî* [Kurdistan fifty-fifty style] (Istanbul: Wesanên Nûjen, 1995). The numerous papers on Iraqi Kurdistan by Hamit Bozarslan (e.g. H. Bozarslan, 'Le Kurdistan: Economie de guerre, économie dans la guerre', in: F. Jean and J.-C. Rufin (eds), *Economie des guerres civiles* (Paris: Hachette, 1996) deserve mention for their analytical rigour and their thought-provoking perspectives.

5. Thus, for example, the land reform promulgated in Law no. 90 of 1975 did not exclusively, and perhaps not even primarily, target rural Kurdish strongholds as Kurdish nationalists claim, but also aimed at changing the class structure of Iraqi society in that it stimulated small peasants and cooperatives.

6. Leezenberg discusses how the ethnic identity of two heterodox and multilingual groups in Iraqi Kurdistan, the Shabak and the Kakais, has been a focus of competing political claims to hegemony; M. Leezenberg, 'Between Assimilation and Deportation: The Shabak and the Kakais in northern Iraq', in: B. Kellner-Heinkele et al. (eds), *Syncretistic Religious Communities in the Near East* (Leiden: Brill, 1997).

7. See, for example, S. K. Farsoun and L. Hajjar's 'The Contemporary Sociology of the Middle East: An assessment'; in H. Sharabi (ed.), *Theory, Politics and the Arab World* (London and New York: Routledge, 1990).

8. Princeton: Princeton University Press, 1978.

9. Thus, the chapter on economy and society since 1958 in Farouk-Sluglett and Sluglett's history of republican Iraq is clearly informed by the general concepts of dependency theory, without, however, being dogmatic in this respect; M. Farouk-Sluglett and P. Sluglett, *Iraq since 1958: From revolution to dictatorship* (London: I. B. Tauris, new edn 1990).

10. In fact, the very prosperity of Iraq and the other oil-producing nations presents something of an anomaly for a dependency-theory framework, according to which developing countries remain poor as a consequence of international capitalist development. Cf. Ismael on Kuwait as a comparable 'anomaly'; J. S. Ismael, 'Social Policy and Social Change: The case of Iraq', *Arab Studies Quarterly*, 1980, no. 2, pp. 235–248.

11. Thus, Haj while rightly criticizing essentialist views of sectarian cleavages and tribe–state relations, seems to overstate her case when she claims that tribal and ethnic divisions 'did not constitute discrete entities' in pre-colonial times, and are, as significant institutions, by and large the product of the British mandate period; S. Haj, *The Making of Iraq, 1900–1963: Capital, power, and ideology* (Albany: SUNY Press, 1997), pp. 146–147, 150.

12. See, for example: E. Wolf, 'Kinship, Friendship and Patron–Client Relations in Complex Societies', in: M. Banton (ed.), *The Social Anthropology of Complex Societies* (London: Tavistock, 1966), pp. 17–18; cf. E. Gellner and J. Waterbury (eds), *Patrons and Clients in Mediterranean Societies* (London: Duckworth, 1977); and L. Roninger and A. Günes-Ayata (eds), *Democracy, Clientelism amd Civil Society* (Boulder and London: Lynne Rienner Publishers, 1994).

13. These claims are in line with the observation that patronage is in itself a folk concept rather than a theoretical tool, and may have different characteristics in different socio-economic contexts.

14. M. Gilsenan, 'Against Patron–Client Relations', in: Gellner and Waterbury (eds), *Patrons and Clients*.

15. cf. M. J. Rooduijn, 'Politieke Patronage in Zuid-Italië' (PhD dissertation, University of Amsterdam, 1987); P. Arlacchi, *La mafia imprenditrice* (Rome: Il Mulino, 1983), Eng. trans. as *Mafia Business: The mafia ethic and the spirit of capitalism* (London: Verso, 1986).

16. Farouk-Sluglett and Sluglett, *Iraq since 1958*, p. 246.

17. cf. P. Marr, *Modern History of Iraq* (Boulder: Westview, 1985), p. 285.

18. These *mujamma'at* can be considered specifically urban structures insofar as their population has become totally dependent on state infrastructure and government handouts.

19. R. Springborg, 'Intifah, Agrarian Transformation and Elite Consolidation in Contemporary Iraq', *Middle East Journal*, 1986, no. 40, pp. 33–32; cf. Leezenberg, 'Irakisch Kurdistan', pp. 47–48.

20. Farouk-Sluglett and Sluglett, *Iraq since 1958*, p. 187.

21. J. Stork, 'State Power and Economic Structure: Class determination and state formation in contemporary Iraq', in: T. Niblock (ed.) *Iraq: The contemporary state* (London, 1982: 42).

22. For example, mechanized and commercialized agricultural labour is not autonomous with respect to the urban centres of wealth and power; farmers in present-day Iraqi Kurdistan are often (though by no means always) sharecroppers for landowners who themselves live in the cities.

23. I. Lapidus, *Muslim Cities in the Later Middle Ages* (Cambridge: Cambridge University Press, 1967).

24. This overview is largely based on Batatu; cf. Stork ('State Power and Economic Structure') and Farouk-Sluglett and Sluglett (*Iraq since 1958*, pp. 215–227).
25. *The Old Social Classes*, p. 1116.
26. J. S. Ismael, *Kuwait: Dependency and class in a rentier state* (Gainesville: University Press of Florida, 2nd edn 1980), pp. 241, 247–248. Article 42 of the Ba'ath Party constitution of 1947 explicitly states that 'the party aims at abolishing class differences and privileges' (Ismael, p. 237); but, as Farouk-Sluglett and Sluglett (*Iraq since 1958*, xv, ch. 7) note, Ba'athist policies in Iraq have never been genuinely socialist in practice.
27. There are indications that traditional loyalties were undergoing a change in character already in earlier years of the republican period. Rural Shabak, for example, remained loyal to their urban patrons in Mosul, no longer for ritual reasons, but for more restricted economic purposes . See: A. Rassam, '*Al-Taba'iyya*: Power, patronage and marginal groups in northern Iraq', in: Gellner and Waterbury (eds), *Patrons and Clients in Mediterranean Societies*.
28. Farouk-Sluglett and Sluglett (*Iraq since 1958*, p. 249), in fact, suggest that the state-sponsored private sector was the main urban employer at this time, even outdoing the massive state bureaucracy.
29. Springborg, 'Intifah, Agrarian Transformation', pp. 46, 51–52.
30. D. McDowall, *A Modern History of the Kurds* (London: I. B. Tauris, 1996), pp. 354–357.
31. K. A. Chaudhry, 'On the Way to Market: Economic liberalization and Iraq's invasion of Kuwait', *Middle East Report*, May–June 1991, pp. 14–23.
32. This development predates by a decade the trend towards 'neotribalism' which Baram sees emerging in the 1990s, as a result of Iraqi government policies in the face of the continuing UN embargo. See: A. Baram, Neo-tribalism in Iraq: Saddam Hussein's tribal policies 1991–1996', *IJMES*, no. 29, pp. 1–31.
33. L. Schmidt, 'Neue Wege der Politik und Organisierung: Soziale Bewegungen in den Städten der kurdisch verwalteten Region im Nordirak', in: J. Später, ... *Alles Ändert sich die ganze Zeit: Bewegungen im 'Nahen Osten'* (Freiburg: Verlag IZ3W, 1994), p. 160; cf. Leezenberg, 'Irakisch-Kurdistan seit dem 2. Golfkrieg', p. 53.
34. Moreover, the food distributions that were to be part of the Food for Oil deal concluded in May 1996 between the UN and the Iraqi government directly threatened this hard-won agricultural rehabilitation. The very announcement of the deal caused a marked fall in commodity prices, and led many farmers to reduce the amounts of seeds they purchased for the next harvest.
35. In any case, the industrial sector in the Kurdish region was far less developed than that in, e.g. Baghdad, Basra and Nineveh governorates (cf. Marr, *Modern History of Iraq*, pp. 269–270).
36. At times, the political motivations may be difficult to separate from the economic interests involved. Needless to say, the Iraqi government has been blamed for many of the assassinations and bombing assaults in the north.
37. Amnesty International, *Iraq: Human rights abuses in Iraqi Kurdistan*, Report MDE, 14 January 1995, pp. 89–98.
38. Hoff, Leezenberg and Muller, *Elections in Iraqi Kurdistan*, p. 29.
39. Kosrat quickly became the strong man of Arbil city and its surroundings. His rising political power led the KDP to accuse him of massive corruption after it had been ousted from Arbil, a charge that has regularly been levelled against people in power.
40. cf. Batatu (*The Old Social Classes*, p. 48), who points out that, during the monarchical period, several Kurdish villages surrounding Arbil were owned by urban Turkmen.

41. cf. Human Rights Watch/Middle East, *Iraq's Crime of Genocide: The Anfal campaign against the Kurds* (New Haven: Yale University Press, 1995), pp. 124–127.

42. Leezenberg, 'Irakisch-Kurdistan'; cf. Aytar, *Kurdistana bi fîftî-fîftî*).

43. Leezenberg, 'Irakisch Kurdistan', p. 66; cf. D. McDowall, *A Modern History of the Kurds*, pp. 386–387. The tribal dimension of these conflicts should not be seen, however, as the fundamental one; tribal divisions are but one of the potential fault lines in society that can be and have been instrumentalized for concrete goals. The specific alliance of the rival parties with, respectively, landowners and peasants in this specific conflict should not be seen as an indication of general ideological differences.

44. Thus, the Toilers Party, which holds that no industrial proletariat, and thus no labour class proper, exists in Iraqi Kurdistan, participated in a joint list together with the PUK. It split in 1994, after two of its four representatives in parliament joined PUK, following Talabani's appeal to all urban leftist groups to join together in a progressive front under PUK leadership.

45. In fact, however, IMIK has concentrated its activities in the area surrounding Halabja, which constituted its traditional heartlands. In 1997, it was given free reign in the area in the wake of an Iranian-brokered ceasefire with the PUK, and imposed *hudud* or strict Islamic legislation there.

46. Despite his violent character, the PUK are reported to have subsequently erected a monument for him. One Ghafa in Eski Kalak seems to be another local warlord who had sided with the PUK.

47. According to some sources, they were actually paid for doing so by inhabitants of the richer quarter.

48. Officials of these latter two parties paid lip service to the need for peace and normalization, but appeared to be more concerned with the pursuit of their own political agendas, which had little to gain by the restoration of the regional parliament. Significantly, an IMTP representative stated that putting an end to the KDP-PUK fights was 'not their business' despite the fact that the population of Arbil, which his party claims is predominantly Turcoman, was severely at risk (interviews, August 1994).

49. cf. Schmidt, *Wie teuer ist die Freiheit?*, pp. 170–177; Schmidt, 'Neue Wege der Politik', pp. 165ff.

50. Schmidt, *Wie teuer ist die Freiheit?*, p. 175.

51. For a description of events from the perspective of Hussein Agha's son Jawhar, see the London-based oppositional paper *Hetaw*, issues 4 and 5 (June–July 1996); cf. also McDowall, *A Modern History of the Kurds*, p. 451.

52. For an analysis of the development, constraints and consequences of humanitarian aid in the region from the first relief efforts in 1991 to the implementation of the Food for Oil programme, see Leezenberg (2000).

53. cf. Leezenberg, 'Irakisch-Kuridistan seit dem 2. Golfkrieg'.

54. R. Maro and R. Ofteringer, *Kurdistan: Ein Fotobuch* (Berlin: Edition ID Archive, 1995), p. 107.

55. M. Gilsenan, 'Against Patron–Client Relations', in: Gellner and Waterbury (eds), *Patrons and Clients in Mediterranean Societies*).

56. Of necessity, these patron-client relations have mostly been described from the patrons' side, as information about the city's poorer strata is sorely lacking.

Fayli Kurds of Baghdad and the Ba'ath Regime

Saad B. Eskander

Introduction

Until 1980, Fayli Kurds formed an important community in the city of Baghdad owing to their economic weight and political role. They had lived peacefully in that city for tens of years before the establishment of the Iraqi state in 1920–1921. Iraq's Pan-Arabists, notably the Ba'ath, unceasingly persecuted Fayli Kurds because of their political inclinations and their ethnic and cultural background. In the search for a scapegoat for their internal and external problems, the Ba'ath found an easy target in the Fayli community. Indeed, by the middle of 1980, the Ba'ath regime had deported almost one half of that community to Iran. This chapter seeks to identify the driving force behind the Ba'ath party's policy towards the Fayli community, since it seized power in July 1968. This policy was always pursued with fanatic determination to dismember that community.

One of the main weapons the Ba'ath used against the Fayli community was the complex issue of nationality and citizenship. Ever since the formation of the Iraqi state, the Pan-Arabists have distorted the modern principles of nation-state in theory and in practice. They have interpreted these principles with a view to depriving several ethnic and religious communities of their basic rights as equal citizens. We will explore the issue of citizenship insofar it affected Fayli Kurds' future in Iraq. To understand the Ba'ath Party's hatred of Fayli Kurds, we will examine the place of the Fayli community in the Ba'ath nationalistic ideology. It will be emphasized that Ba'ath relentless persecution of Fayli Kurds was both an extension to the old Pan-Arabists' anti-Fayli measures and an integral part of their policy of ethnic cleansing of Iraqi Kurds, which they have adopted since their seizure of power in 1968. Some light will also be shed on the position of the Fayli issue within the broader Kurdish question, when discussing the attitudes of the Kurdish nationalist parties towards that issue during their negotiations with the Ba'ath authorities in Baghdad between 1970 and 1991.

The Origins of the Fayli Kurds

Fayli Kurds are essentially Lesser Lurs in terms of their origins and dialect. Lesser Lurs form a significant section of the Kurdish people, who lived in the central and southern Zagros Mountains and the southernmost parts of Iraqi Kurdistan for centuries on end.[1] The larger portion of Lesser Luri regions lies in Iranian Kurdistan, whereas a smaller portion of it lies in Iraqi Kurdistan. This last point contradicts the existing misconception that Lesser Lurs were all emigrants from the modern Iranian districts of 'Ilam and Kermanshah, and that modern Iraq does not include any Luri region or Luri native population. In reality, some Luri regions are now part of Iraqi Kurdistan, and they form a substantial community in the districts of Diyalah, Kut and Amarah. A number of small Luri pockets used to exist in the districts of Hillah, Basra and Najaf.

That said, not all Lesser Lurs are called Fayli. It is only the Luri community of Baghdad who have been known as Fayli Kurds, whereas those Lesser Lurs who live in the southernmost parts of Iraqi Kurdistan (Khanaqin, Mandali, Shahraban, Badra-wa-Jasan, Zurbatiya, Qazil-Rubat, etc.) are not called Fayli. Neither the Luri inhabitants of the central and southern Zagros Mountains nor the Fayli community of Baghdad are familiar with the term 'Fayli'. An American scholar, Henry Field, maintains that the term 'Fayli' means 'rebel', whereas others believe that it means a 'large body'.[2] Unfortunately, none of these definitions is supported by any concrete evidence. There is no historical or linguistic source that might help us understand the origin of the term. It is worth noting that many of those Luri Kurds who emigrated from or were forced to leave their towns and villages in the southernmost parts of Iraqi Kurdistan and settled in Baghdad integrated into the Fayli community, and have also been called Fayli. 'Fayli' can thus be seen to be a loose and an ambiguous term that applies to those Shi'i Kurds who live in the city of Baghdad.

In his famous historical work *Sharafnama* (1596), the Kurdish historian, Sharafkhan Bitlisi, makes no reference to the term 'Fayli' when narrating the

history of some Luri dynasties of Lesser and Greater Luristan between the
mid-10th and the late 16th centuries.[3] This may strongly suggest that the term
'Fayli' appeared after the 16th century. Indeed, as far as the existing evidence
shows, the term 'Fayli' first appeared in the wake of Shah Nadir's murder in
1747, when some Kurdish tribes, who were called Fayli, took part in the civil
wars that engulfed all Persian provinces as well as eastern Kurdistan. Fayli
tribes played some part in Persian political life during the reign of the Zand
dynasty (1750–1779).[4] Later, some European travellers and commercial
representatives in the Ottoman and Persian provinces used the term 'Fayli'.
For instance, Claudius J. Rich, the representative of the East India Company
in Baghdad in the early 19th century, mentions in his book *Narrative of a
Resident in Kurdistan* that some Fayli families lived as refugees among the
Jaf tribes of the Sharazur region in southern Kurdistan.[5] In the same period,
a British traveller, Robert Ker Porter, made a reference to Fayli Kurds whom
he met during his travels in Mesopotamia and Iranian Kurdistan in the years
1818–1820.[6] It seems that by the late 18th or early 19th centuries the term
'Fayli' had become fairly common.

Historical Background and Cultural Characteristics of Fayli Kurds

In ancient times, Luri regions were wholly or partly coterminous with
some great states, notably Ilamid. The latter either invaded or were invaded
by neighbouring Mesopotamian dynasties. In the seventh century, all
Kurdish regions came under the control of the first Islamic–Arab Empire.
Subsequently, the central and southern Zagros Mountains were the scene of
several local rebellions. In the medieval era, around the mid-12th century,
Lesser Luristan gained autonomous status and was ruled by a native Luri
dynasty. The principality of Lesser Luristan, like other contemporary Kurdish
principalities, suffered from foreign invasions, notably those of the Mongols
and the Tatars. Owing to its strategic position overlooking the land route
between Persia proper and Mesopotamia, these invaders kept Lesser Luristan
autonomous under their nominal suzerainty. Lesser Lurs continued to enjoy
either independent or semi-independent status during the rise and fall of
several mighty powers, including the Safavid Empire. When Sharafkhan
Bitlisi completed his *Sharafnama* in the late 16th century, Lesser Luristan
still had its own principality.[7]

The protracted Ottoman–Safavid Wars between the 16th and 18th centuries gradually weakened the power of the reigning Luri dynasty. Lesser Luristan became one of the main theatres for these destructive wars because of its strategic position overlooking the route between Baghdad and Persia proper. As the Safavid Empire disintegrated, Lesser Luristan ceased to be the home of any autonomous principality. However, the successor states in Persia did not impose direct rule on Luri Kurds. Instead, they exercised their influence through local Kurdish chiefs who were the de facto rulers of Lesser Luristan until the collapse of the Qajar Empire in the early 1920s. It is worth noting that the Ottoman authorities extended their control to some of the Lesser Luri regions that became either part of the Baghdad Wilaya or the Sharazur Sanjaq. From time to time, some powerful Kurdish Mirs (princes) of the Baban principality brought certain Lesser Luri regions under their direct rule, such as Bajlan, Badra-wa-Jasan, Zahab and Zankbar.[8]

The Kurdish inhabitants of the central and southern parts of Zagros Mountains and the southernmost part of Iraqi Kurdistan are Shi'i Muslims. The conversion from the Sunni and Ahl-i-Haq to the Shi'i *mathhab* (school of law) took place some time after the establishment of the Safavid state in the early 16th century. Nowadays, around 15 per cent of Kurds are Shi'is.[9] The majority of the Kurds remained Shafi'i Sunnis. Many members of the smaller religious communities also kept their old faith, such as the Yezidis, Alevis and Ahl-i-Haq. It is highly likely that Luri Kurds converted to Shi'ism without any coercion, as there is no historical evidence to suggest otherwise. For instance, the Safavid, who sought to spread Shi'ism by both peaceful and violent means, did not organize military campaigns against Luri regions with a view to forcing their inhabitants to convert to Shi'ism. It seems that, before the 16th century, most Luri Kurds were Ahl-i-Haq, which is a religious group that venerates Imam Ali. This veneration of Imam Ali probably made it much easier for the Luri Kurds to convert to Shi'ism, which emphasized the right of Imam Ali's descendants to rule the Muslims. This process of conversion was speeded up by increasing contacts with Shi'i Iranian pilgrims who made frequent journeys to the Shi'i holy towns of Iraq, notably Najaf and Karbala. Persian pilgrim and commercial caravans mostly passed through Lesser Luristan. The continuing efforts of Sunni Ottomans to occupy Luri regions, which naturally incurred the hostility of their inhabitants, might have accelerated the process of conversion to Shi'ism. Since their conversion to Shi'ism, Fayli Kurds have shared with their Arab counterparts common religious practices, rituals and traditions, such as the Ashura ritual, commemorating the slaying of Imam Ali's son, Hussein, in the sixth century. All Shi'is consider the city of Najaf, the burial site of Imam Ali, to be the holiest place after Mecca and Medina. Fayli Kurds, like Shi'i Arabs, have buried their deceased relatives in Najaf's cemetery for decades. Some Fayli families established a small colony in the town of Kufa, very close to Najaf.

Another important, albeit controversial issue is when and why Fayli Kurds settled in the city of Baghdad. Since its foundation by the Abbasid caliph, Abu Ja'far al-Mansur, in the mid-eighth century, Baghdad has had a multi-ethnic composition and multicultural life. Baghdad's geographical location attracted non-Arab immigrants from neighbouring countries. It was, for instance, close to Kurdistan and Persia proper. One of the obvious consequences of frequent foreign occupations of Baghdad was the settlement of non-Arab elements in that city. One cannot deny that, while Baghdad was and is largely an Arab city, it has contained for most of its history non-Arab communities, such as Jews, Kurds, Persians, Turks, Armenians and Christians. In the 20th century, Baghdad mirrored modern Iraq's ethnic and cultural diversity. All ethnic and religious communities actively participated in the city's economic, political and cultural life.

It is extremely difficult to pinpoint a specific date when Fayli Kurds began to settle in Baghdad. Medieval Arab chroniclers mostly used the term 'Ajam' when referring to non-Arab elements in Baghdad, but it is impossible to say whether they meant Persians, Azerbaijanis, Turkmen or Kurds. Al-Sheikh Rasul al-Kirkukli, a Turkmen annalist, refers to the Kurds of Baghdad, who, like the rest of the inhabitants, suffered from starvation around 1736. He says nothing about their origins, jobs and activities. Since the commercial land route between Baghdad and Persia proper passed through Lesser Luri regions, it is logical to infer that some Luris (Faylis) decided to settle in Baghdad in order to pursue their commercial activities. In other words, the Fayli settlement in Baghdad was a direct consequence of increasing commercial relations between that city and the frontier regions where the Luri Kurds lived on both sides of the Ottoman–Iranian frontier. It is worth noting that Luri regions had much stronger economic and social relations with neighbouring Arab regions, situated to the west and the south, than with Persian regions. Mountainous Luri tribes sold their animal produce (such as wool, leather and meat) to neighbouring Arab towns, where they bought essential goods they needed (i.e. fabric, sugar and tea).

In an article on his journey from Baghdad to frontier regions in 1844, James Flex Jones, a senior member of a joint British–Russian commission to solve the Ottoman–Qajar frontier problem, maintains that the Luri regions of Khanaqin and Haj-Qara formed important trading outposts for the provinces of Baghdad and Kermanshah. He notices that many of the influential houses in Baghdad and Kermanshah had their commercial agents stationed in the towns of Khanaqin and Haj-Qara. He states that a British merchant, who accompanied him on his journey, sought to 'establish an agency for the collection of the produce of the Kurdish mountains, returning in exchange the manufactures of England'.[10] No doubt these commercial relations and the continuing contacts between Baghdad and the Luri regions induced many Faylis and their families to settle in Baghdad. Fayli settlement in Baghdad was then a long process; there is no evidence that it was the outcome of any military or political development, notably the repeated Persian occupations of Baghdad. Fayli Kurds thus had very old economic, social and cultural relations with Mesopotamian Arabs, especially those of Baghdad. However, unlike many Persians, Indians or Afghans who were Arabized by the passage of time, Fayli Kurds preserved their Kurdish cultural identity.

Social and Economic Conditions of the Fayli Community in the 20th Century

In the second and the third decades of the 20th century, only a handful of Fayli Kurds were merchants, whereas the vast majority were small traders, porters, artisans, labourers, etc. Some Fayli Kurds worked with Jewish merchants and benefited from their long experience in commerce. From the late 1940s and the early 1950s onward, Fayli Kurds were to be renowned for their role in Baghdad's commercial life. An important development took place in the early 1950s when the vast majority of the Jewish community were forced to emigrate from Iraq to the newly established Israeli state. Fayli Kurds quickly filled the considerable gap in the fields of commerce and retail industry left by the emigration of Jewish merchants and traders.[11] Fadhil al-Barrak, the former chief of the Iraqi Intelligence Service in the 1980s, claims in his book *Al-Madaris al-Yahudiya wa al-Iraniya fi al-Iraq* (The Jewish and Iranian Schools in Iraq) that emigrating Jewish merchants sold all their businesses to 'Iranian' merchants (Fayli Kurds) as part of an anti-Arab conspiracy.[12] Al-Barrak never mentions that the vast majority of Jewish businesses, properties and belongings were either destroyed and looted by local Arab mobs or confiscated by the Iraqi state. Therefore, very few Jews had any business interests left to sell to Fayli Kurds. In the circumstances and thanks to their own skills and hard work, Fayli Kurds began to play a significant part in Baghdad's commercial life from the 1950s onwards.

In the mid-1940s, Fayli merchants and some educated Fayli Kurds took an important initiative to establish Al-Jam'iya al-Fayliya (the Fayli Association). This association was the first of its kind, and aimed at bringing Fayli Kurds closer to each other as well as promoting education within the Fayli community. The Fayli Association founded two schools. Aziz al-Haj, a famous Fayli writer, argues that one of the School's aims was to prevent Fayli children from enrolling in Iranian schools.[13] Given Iraqi schools' refusal to enrol some Fayli children because their parents had no naturalization documents, the Fayli school was an educational necessity. At the time, Baghdad had very few schools, and they could not cope with the increasing demands for secular education. A few years later, the Fayli Association founded a club to promote sports activities among the members of the Fayli community. It is worth noting that Iraqi Arabs were allowed to enrol at the Fayli schools and to join the Fayli Club.

The Fayli Association did not promote isolationist tendencies, nor did it have any political objective. Most of the Faylis completed their primary and intermediate education at the Fayli schools and then continued their education at private and non-Kurdish secondary schools. The Fayli generations of the Republican era owed their good education to the existence of the Fayli Association. A high percentage of young Faylis completed their higher education in this period, and worked as doctors, lawyers, journalists, dentists, university and college teachers, etc. It is not an overstatement to say that from the 1960s onward, Fayli Kurds formed one of the most active and progressive elements in Baghdad's society in terms of their education, professions and political inclinations. Salman Shukur, an outstanding composer, Mustafa Jawad, an acclaimed writer and linguist, Kamil al-Basir, a well-known linguist, and Zahid Mohammad Zuhdi, a renowned poet, were all Fayli Kurds. There were also several outstanding Fayli sportsmen in various fields. Fayli Kurds, unlike other Iraqi Kurds, showed no interest in military professions. However, young Faylis served in the standing army as conscripts according to Iraq's compulsory military service law.

By the mid-1970s, most Fayli Kurds were either middle- or upper middle-class, and their social advancement expressed itself in their new residential areas. Before 1970, nearly all Fayli Kurds lived in the old quarters of Baghdad, notably Agd al-Akrad, Bab al-Sheikh, al-Fadal and Shurja. All these quarters lie in the eastern part of Baghdad. Now many Fayli families moved to new middle-class residential areas, such as Aqari, Shari'a Falastin and Jamilah. However, a considerable number of Fayli Kurds still lived in the old quarters of Baghdad, where their businesses were situated.

Citizens or Subjects

Ever since their formation, the new Middle Eastern nation states have faced a fundamental question on the concept of citizenship and equal rights for all people in societies that have been characterized by their ethnic and cultural diversity. The solution of the new native ruling strata in such states as Iraq and Syria has been to create a homogeneous society, instead of recognizing the existing ethnic and cultural diversity. Suspicions of ethnic and religious minorities prevailed over any sentiments of fraternity, as the concept of citizenship has been narrowly defined. In Iraq's case, during the monarchic period, the ruling political elite, which were essentially Sunni, Arab and pan-Arabists, defined the concept of Iraqi citizenship in ethnic, cultural and political terms. In other words, the ideal Iraqi citizen has to be an Arab, Sunni and politically loyal to the Iraqi state. This was reflected in Iraq's first citizenship law of 1924, which divided Iraqis into first- and second-class citizens according to their ethnic and cultural background. The vast majority of Fayli Kurds fell into the second category. It is ironic that the Ottoman citizenship law of 1869, on which the Iraqi citizenship was supposed to be based, was very liberal. Article 1 stipulated that any person born of Ottoman parents or of an Ottoman father was an Ottoman subject. According to article 2, any person born on Ottoman territory of foreign parents could, during three years subsequent to his majority, claim to be an Ottoman subject. Finally, article 3 provided that any foreigner who arrived at his maturity and who resided for five consecutive years could obtain Ottoman nationality.[14]

The extraordinary aspect of the issue of citizenship in Iraq since its establishment in 1921 was the arbitrary way in which various pan-Arab governments could arbitrarily deprive any Iraqi person of his or her citizenship. It was a common practice for Iraqi governments to deprive the leaders of the opposition of their citizenship as a 'lawful' and 'legitimate' punishment. Moreover, governments could at will strip a whole community of its Iraqi citizenship. In 1950, the cabinet of Tawfiq al-Swidi deprived all the members of the Iraqi Jewish community of their citizenship, even though the Iraqi Jews were considered in theory to be citizens of the first class. The government's measure was based on an old law known as the Mar Sham'un Law, which had been issued in 1933 immediately after the Assyrians' revolt of that year led by their religious leader, Mar Sham'un, and which deprived all Assyrians of their Iraqi citizenship. This law had not been implemented at that time because of British and French opposition.[15] As these examples show, the rights to legal equality and citizenship were not unconditional. Fayli Kurds, Iraqi Jews and Assyrians had always to prove their absolute loyalty and refrain from any oppositional political activity.

For the new generation of pan-Arabists who seized power in 1963, political loyalty of ethnic and religious minorities to the state and society has not been enough. These minorities have to espouse the cause of Arab nationalism as a sign of loyalty and allegiance; otherwise, they are regarded as an internal enemy. In this sense, Iraq has fallen short of being a modern nation-state, since it has renounced the modern principle of citizenship by granting equal legal rights to all Iraqis regardless of their ethnic and cultural backgrounds.

There is a common misconception among some scholars[16] and the Arab public concerning the legal status of Fayli Kurds. The pan-Arabists, particularly the Ba'ath, have been behind the dissemination of all forms of misinformation about the members of the Fayli community, including their historical background, as well as their cultural, economic and political activities in Baghdad.[17] The facts are, first, that the vast majority of Fayli Kurds had (and have) Iraqi citizenship, as they obtained the Iraqi nationality certificate (Jinsiya) in 1934, 1947 or 1957. Around 400,000 Faylis had Iraqi citizenship in 1980[18] and some 50,000 had residence permit ; the second wave of mass deportation of Fayli Kurds began under Ba'ath rule and about 200,000 were expelled, which involved both categories of naturalized and non-naturalized Fayli Kurds.[19] Second, the minority of Fayli Kurds who had permanent residence permits in Iraq, instead of the Jinsiya, who numbered more than 50,000 in the years 1971–1972, were mostly deported to Iran during the reign of President Ahmad Hasan al-Bakr. Finally, about 200,000 Faylis who have Iraqi Jinsiya still live in Iraq. The Ba'ath regime was unable to deport them probably because of the outbreak of the first Gulf war (1980–1988), followed two years later by the Iraqi invasion of Kuwait and then the outbreak of the second Gulf war.

There were several reasons why those Faylis who had permanent residency did not change or could not upgrade their legal status. Following the establishment of the Iraqi state in 1920–1921, these Faylis failed to see how important the issue of nationality was for their future in Iraq. It never crossed their minds that one day they would be one of the main targets of a pan-Arabist policy of imposing cultural and ethnic homogeneity. It was not only these Faylis who did not realize the extent to which Iraqi citizenship would be vital for their long-term interests in Iraq, but also many Shi'i Arabs. The same applies to some Iraqis who were of Persian, Asian or Afghan origin and who had lived in the Wilayas of Baghdad and Basra for decades, before the formation of the Iraqi state. No real effort was made by various Iraqi governments in the 1920s to explain to the majority of the population, who were overwhelmingly illiterate, the full political and legal implications of having Iraqi citizenship. In his memoirs, the great Iraqi poet Muhammad Mahdi Al-Jawahiri writes that his father, his grandfather, the clergymen of the holy city of Najaf and all the Arab tribes of the Euphrates did not know what the Jinsiya meant in practice. He emphasizes that almost all Iraqis did not know the new Jinsiya law.[20] This was the ground for his bitter criticism of that law, which divided the Iraqis into 'Othmani' (Ottoman) and 'Taba'iya' (alien subjects). Al-Jawahiri would have been one of the early victims of this law, had Sati al-Husri, the renowned pan-Arab ideologue, succeeded in his campaign against him.

Another misconception about the reasons why Fayli Kurds (and some Arabs, Asians, Afghans, etc.) did not upgrade their legal status from permanent residency to full citizenship, is that they did not wish to join the Iraqi army as conscripts (which was and still is compulsory for all young men at age 18. The fact is that the vast majority of young Faylis joined the army as part of their national duties. Only in exceptional cases did Faylis – or, for that matter, Arabs – try to avoid compulsory military service, although this duty was unpopular among Kurds and Arabs alike because it could last anything from four to 10 years. Certainly many people tried to avoid it by means of bribes, forging of their birth certificate or claiming disability.

Fayli Kurds viewed the pan-Arabists' seizure of power in the early 1960s as a very bad omen. When some Faylis decided to upgrade their status to full citizenship, they discovered that it was too late, as the Arif brothers regime (1963–1968) enacted new naturalization statutes. The old law stipulated that any person who was born in Iraq was entitled to become an Iraqi citizen at the age of 19, and that any person whose father was born in Iraq was entitled to Iraqi citizenship. The new law added the following conditions. First, the applicant had to prove that he or she faithfully served Iraq's interests. Second, the applicant had to prove that his or her father had been Iraqi and born in Iraq (this is known as al-Wilada al-Muda'afa, or 'dual birth'). Finally, the applicant would become an Iraqi citizen at the age of 20, only after the Minister of Interior accepted his or her application.[21] The last condition was of special importance, because the entitlement to Iraqi citizenship became subject to political and national security considerations, which the pan-Arabists had the exclusive right to define. Prior to the introduction of the new law, the head of the Department of Naturalization was in fact the only bureaucrat with the authority to endorse applications for citizenship. Under both the 'Arif and the Ba'ath regimes, Fayli Kurds who had permanent residency could not become full Iraqi citizens, even though they, their fathers and grandfathers had all been born in the country.[22] Moreover, during the 'Arif regime, several Fayli families were deported to Iran under the pretext that they did not have permanent residency status in the country.

The legal status and legitimate rights of Fayli Kurds who had Iraqi citizenship were considerably undermined by arbitrary measures. The latter considered the Shahadat al-Jinsiya (certificate of naturalization) as the only criterion for defining the legal status of Iraqis and their rights. This document had several grades of citizenship: first-, second- and third-class. A first-class citizen was considered to be 'Othmani' (i.e. a true Iraqi), whereas the remaining classes were 'Taba'iya' (foreigners). This was a rigid system under which no Fayli could upgrade his or her legal status, irrespective of the evidence he or she could present. Even if some Fayli Kurds had Ottoman grade, they would still be considered in practice as Taba'iya, i.e. aliens. Further, Fayli applications generally took several years to process. The Naturalization Department was in practice an integration centre under the supervision of the state security police. The Faylis' dread of pursuing their applications in that department got stronger as time passed. What usually happened was that departmental officials would tell them that their efforts to upgrade their legal status were futile, as they would always be identified as Iranians.

Among other anti-Fayli measures adopted by the Ba'ath regime was the restriction of the Faylis' right to inheritance, specifically their right to sell inherited property. Fayli Kurds could not become army officers or hold high positions in the bureaucracy or the government. Yet they had, by law, to serve as conscripts in the military. As time went on, various methods were invented for further restricting the freedom and civil rights of Fayli Kurds. Many Fayli teachers and lecturers were forced to resign their posts and leave the country. Young Faylis' admissions into the universities were restricted. Fayli Kurds were allowed to purchase property but not allowed to sell. Very few Faylis were able to have Iraqi passports. At the end, as the experience of the 1980 deportation illustrates, even those Faylis who had first-class citizenship were expelled from Iraq. On 7 April 1980, the Ba'ath Revolutionary Command Council (the highest legislative authority in the state) issued a new arbitrary decree (No. 666), stating that, first, any Iraqi who was of foreign origin would be deprived of his or her citizenship, if he or she were not loyal to 'the homeland, the people and the nationalistic and social objectives of the revolution'. Second, the Minister of the Interior must order the deportation of any person whose citizenship was withdrawn, unless the Minister was convinced for good reasons that his or her presence in Iraq was of legal and judicial necessity.[23] Iraqi Arabs were encouraged to divorce their 'Iranian' partners in exchange for material rewards and privileges. The second law (No. 1610), of 23 December 1982, consisted of the following provisions: first, any Iraqi woman married to a non-Iraqi man would be barred from registering her movable and immovable property in her husband's name or from taking any legal step that would transfer part or all of her property to her husband. Such action would be regarded as illegal. Second, upon the death of an Iraqi wife, her non-Iraqi husband had no inheritance rights. Third, upon divorce or separation, a Iraqi wife had the right to take all the property away from her non-Iraqi husband and his heirs. Finally, upon divorce or separation, an Iraqi wife would have custody of her children until they reached the age of maturity, if so she expressed that wish before the court.[24]

It is worth noting that Syria, which is ruled by another faction of the Ba'ath party, refuses to recognize almost 60 per cent of its Kurds as Syrian citizens. According to the Department of State in Washington, 'there is creditable evidence that the Syrian government has withdrawn Syrian nationality from between 90,000 and 120,000 Kurds, since the 1960s'.[25] In one of its reports, Middle East Human Watch (an American human rights organization) states that those Kurds who have no Syrian nationality are not permitted to study in Syrian universities or to get treatment in the government hospitals.[26] In Lebanon, where around 180,000 Kurds live, the complicity of its sectarian political system and its social structure have been responsible for depriving the vast majority of its Kurdish subjects, who are mostly Sunni Muslims, of all citizenship rights. According to Faroq Haji Mustafa, a Lebanese writer of Kurdish origins, only 20 per cent of Lebanese Kurds have been granted full citizenship status since the early 1990s, in spite of numerous promises made by the Lebanese authorities to grant all the Kurds full legal and political rights.[27] The issue of not recognizing the vast majority of Syrian and Lebanese Kurds as equal citizens has been the main reason for the emigration of hundreds of young Kurds to various western European countries.

In Iraq, between 1930 and 1980, the attitudes of various Iraqi governments towards the Fayli community had entered several phases. Under the monarchy, the pan-Arabist Rashid Ali al-Gaylani expelled a handful of Fayli families during his term as Minister of the Interior in the 1930s. There was a strong possibility that, had al-Gailani succeeded in ruling Iraq after the 1941 military coup, he would have embarked on a mass deportation campaign of all those communities whom pan-Arabists like himself viewed as an internal

enemy. During the pan-Arab rule of the Arif brothers (1963–1968), dozens
of Fayli families were deported to Iran under the pretext that they had no
legal status in Iraq. The Arif rule set the stage for future deportations of Fayli
Kurds by replacing the old Jinsiya law with a new one, which turned the
entitlement to Iraqi citizenship into political and national security matters.

In the years 1971–1972, the new Ba'ath regime of President Ahmad
Hasan al-Bakr carried out its first mass deportation of Fayli Kurds who
were not granted naturalization, even though they had enjoyed permanent
residency status in the country for decades. In April 1980, a few months
before the outbreak of the Iraq–Iran War, the Ba'ath regime waged a swift
mass deportation campaign against 200,000 Fayli Kurds. If a comparison is
made between the 1971–1972 and the 1980 deportation campaigns under
Ba'ath rule, one can identify some similarities and differences. First, both
expulsion campaigns coincided with a speedy and dangerous deterioration
in the bilateral relations between Iraq and Iran. In the early 1970s, the Ba'ath
regime told the representatives of the Kurdish nationalist movement, with
whom it entered into peace negotiations, that the Fayli Kurds were Iranians,[28]
and as such they posed a serious threat to Arab and Iraq's national security. In
1980, the Ba'ath regime was preparing an all-out invasion of Iran. Fayli Kurds
were the scapegoat.

Second, in 1971–1972 deportation was of a limited scale, because it
targeted those Fayli families who had only permanent residency status.
The regime kept a low profile. It did not resort to the state-controlled mass
media to wage a nation-wide propaganda campaign against Fayli deportees.
By contrast, the 1980 campaign was preceded by a nation-wide propaganda
onslaught. President Saddam Hussein himself took the lead in inaugurating
the new deportation campaign when he made a public appearance on state
television with threats to punish all 'Iranian' traitors who threatened Iraq's
security and stability. These 'Iranians' were alleged to be responsible for a
series of bomb explosions in Baghdad.

Finally, in the 1971–1972 deportation campaign, the expelled Faylis were
given a limited period to wind up their businesses, sell property and take
along their belongings. Generally, deportation was relatively 'humane', given
the Ba'ath regime's human rights record. Probably this cautious attitude had
to do with the weak influence the Ba'ath had at that period. By contrast, the
1980 deportation campaign was extremely ruthless; about 5,000 young Fayli
were kept as hostages in Iraqi prisons, while their families were deported to
Iran. Families were disunited; deportees were rounded up while at work,
unaware of the fate of their families. Some children were even at schools when

their parents were rounded up or deported. All properties and belongings were confiscated, including cash, jewellery and other personal valuables. Dispossessed, deportees were expelled to Iran, whose government was in not the least prepared to deal with such a sudden influx of people.

The Political Orientations of the Fayli Community

Fayli Kurds formed a close community, which was not, however, secluded or insulated. There was no history or evidence of any hostility or friction between Fayli Kurds and their Arab neighbours in Baghdad. Before the rise of pan-Arabism in the 1930s, Baghdad's ethnic and religious communities were seldom involved in communal violence. This changed from the late 1930s onwards. Fayli Kurds took a growing interest in Iraq's domestic politics. This was spurred by several important political developments, prominent among which were the growing tendencies towards ethnocracy. We have already mentioned the Rashid Ali al-Gailani episode. This coincided also with the expulsion of Jews and the government-instigated 'pogroms'.[29] Pan-Arabism was tainted by discrimination against non-Sunni Arabs, and was thus opposed to the liberal emphasis on citizenship and equality before the law irrespective of race, ethnicity, religion and gender. Perhaps the dramatic political developments that took place in Iraqi and Iranian Kurdistan, notably the Barzani revolt and the establishment of the Mahabad Republic in 1940s, politicized large swaths of Fayli Kurds, much to the distaste of the Baghdad central authority.

The political and cultural activities of Fayli Kurds had no communal leanings, nor any desire to form a sectarian political party; rather, they joined Iraqi or Kurdish political groups. As a general rule, Fayli Kurds were more left-leaning; they mostly joined the Iraqi Communist Party (ICP) and the Kurdistan Democratic Party (KDP). Ethnicity (being Kurds) and denomination (being Shi'is) were crucial in these political preferences. For them the ICP was a modernist political force advocating ethnic and cultural equality. Hanna Batatu notices a sudden increase in the number of Baghdadi Kurds who occupied middle-ranking positions in the ICP after 1947:[30] there were 49, mostly Faylis. In 1948, Aziz al-Haj became the first Fayli member of the ICP's Central Committee. He was a high-school teacher and the son of a Fayli merchant.[31] A few years later, the ICP's Central Committee had two Fayli members, while another Fayli became member of the ICP's Military Committee.[32]

In the last decade of the monarchical regime, Fayli quarters of Baghdad were the scene of massive activism, including a mass demonstration in support of the July 1952 revolt in Egypt.[33] Fayli support for the ICP reached its peak immediately after the outbreak of the July 1958 revolution. Enthusiastically, they took part in the ICP's activities, which were mostly directed against the pan-Arabists, especially the Ba'ath Party. Fayli Kurds supported the new republican rule and its symbol, General Qassim, who was Fayli on his mother's side. To persuade Qassim of the need to confirm the legal status of all Fayli Kurds as true Iraqi citizens, a Fayli delegation consisting of two senior members of the ICP and KDP held a discussion with the Premier Qassim, who promised, according to al-Haj, to resolve the Fayli issue.[34] He met his demise in 1963 before he could keep his promise.

The KDP was the other main party that attracted a considerable number of Faylis into its ranks. Fayli support for the Kurdish nationalist movement substantially increased after the formation of the KDP and the collapse of the Mahabad Republic in Iranian Kurdistan. Ja'far Mohammed Karim (1910–2000), a Fayli doctor, was one of the founders of the Kurdish Democratic Party (later renamed the Kurdistan Democratic Party). In 1946, he joined the Kurdish revolt in Iraqi Kurdistan and the Kurdish nationalist movement in Iranian Kurdistan respectively.[35] From the 1940s onward, Fayli Kurds were always to occupy senior positions within the leadership of the Kurdish nationalist movement. Habib Mohammed Karim became mullah Mustafa's personal aide and a member of the KDP's Central Committee. He was nominated by the KDP to be Iraq's vice-president in line with the terms of the March 1970 Peace Accord, also between the Ba'ath regime and the KDP leadership. Zakiya Isma'il Haqi, a Fayli lawyer, was elected the head of the Women's Union of Kurdistan, as well as a member of the Central Committee of the KDP. Razzaq Mirza was elected leader of the Youth Union of Kurdistan. Adil Murad became the General Secretary of the Student Union of Kurdistan. Young Fayli Kurds, male and female, joined these unions in huge numbers, especially in the 1960s and the early 1970s.

Following Qassim's suppression of the Kurdish nationalist movement, Fayli houses became the refuge for some fugitive Kurdish activists in Baghdad. Thus, in the new republican era, the Fayli Kurds were among the most active communities. When the Ba'ath Party and other pan-Arabists led by Abdul Salam Arif carried out their coup d'état in 1963, Fayli Kurds put up staunch resistance in the old quarters of Baghdad, which lasted several days after the summary execution of Qassim. In the wake of the coup, dozens of Fayli Kurds were arrested and tortured by the infamous Ba'ath paramilitaries, the National Guard.

The Kurdish Nationalist Movement, the Ba'ath Regime and the Fayli Issue

The issue of Fayli Kurds' legal status entered a new critical stage immediately after the Ba'athists carried out their military coup in July 1968. The new regime was determined to expel as many Fayli Kurds as it could from the country. However, the relative strength of the Kurdish nationalist movement, coupled with the political influence that the ICP still had, made it very difficult for the new regime to take drastic measures. In 1970, Kurdish newspapers began openly to debate the future of Fayli Kurds. They often exposed the racist nature of the Ba'ath attitude towards that community. During its negotiations with the KDP leadership in the early 1970s, and the Ba'ath insisted that the future of the Fayli community should not be discussed, claiming that it had no connection whatsoever with the broader Kurdish question in Iraq. In other words, the Ba'ath regime sought to separate the future of the Faylis from that of the rest of the Kurdish people, and to incorporate it into its general policy towards the Iranian regime, with which it had outstanding political and border disputes. The KDP leadership made some effort to establish that the future of Faylis must be interconnected with the solution of the Kurdish question. During these negotiations, the KDP proposed an amendment to article 10 in the nationality law. This would have made the court, not the Minister of the Interior, the only authority that could settle naturaliation cases. This amendment would have also prevented the Ba'ath regime from abusing the issue of the Fayli community's legal status. The regime was adamant in its attitude, and declined to amend the law.[36] Consequently, the 11 March Peace Accord of 1974 made no reference to the Fayli issue.

Nevertheless, Fayli Kurds extended support to the Kurdish armed revolt in Iraqi Kurdistan in 1974–1975. As in the past, Fayli merchants, businessmen, professionals and artisans made financial contributions to the KDP. Volunteers went to the mountains to participate in the armed struggle against the central authorities in Baghdad. Most of these volunteers included teachers, engineers, doctors, university graduates and students. If the KDP made some effort to improve the legal status of Fayli Kurds, the ICP leadership totally ignored that issue during its political alliance with the Ba'ath regime in the 1970s, even though a large number of the ICP members were Faylis.

In 1975, the Patriotic Union of Kurdistan (PUK) came into being immediately after the collapse of the revolt led by mullah Mustafa Barzani. Two educated Fayli Kurds were among the founders of the PUK, namely

Razaq Mirza and Adil Murad. The PUK was a broad political alliance, consisting of Kawmala (the League of Toilers), which was a Marxist group, Shurishgiran (the Revolutionaries) and the non-ideologically committed members, who were known as Khati Gishti (the General Line). The PUK attracted very quickly a number of young Faylis to its secret cells in Baghdad between 1976 and 1979. In 1976, a small clandestine network, known as Khuni Shahidan (the Blood of the Martyrs), whose members were mostly Faylis, decided to join Kawmala. As a result of the union between Khuni Shahidan and Kawmala in the city of Baghdad, a new organization came into being, named Halui Sur (the Red Hawks), and immediately attracted educated young Faylis to its ranks, especially university and college students. The main tasks of Halui Sur were to win people over to the Kurdish cause, to support the new armed revolt led by the PUK in the mountains of Iraqi Kurdistan and to wage urban guerrilla warfare within the city of Baghdad. Two years later, and after assassinating a well-known Kurdish collaborator, Othman Muhammad Faiq, a former Minister of Culture who was Saddam's close friend, most of the leaders of the new organization were arrested. They were either executed or imprisoned for life.

During its negotiations with the Ba'ath regime in 1984, the PUK leadership raised the case of Fayli Kurds, demanding the immediate release of all Fayli hostages, the return and the compensation of all deported Faylis and, most importantly, the granting of Iraqi citizenship to all Faylis. A main article concerning the Fayli issue was built into the PUK programme for the normalization of Kurdish relations with the Central Government.[37] The PUK suggested that the deported Faylis could resettle in Iraqi Kurdistan, like some other Kurds whom the regime had forced to leave their towns and villages. Eventually, the negotiations between the PUK and the Ba'ath regime collapsed, and fighting was resumed in 1985. In its 1991 negotiations with the Ba'ath regime, the Kurdistan Front (formed in the late 1980s and including major and minor Kurdish political parties) demanded that deported Faylis be permitted to return either to Baghdad or to Kurdistan, that they be fully compensated and, if incarcerated, to be released, and finally that they be recognized as full Iraqi citizens. Kurdish–Ba'ath negotiations ended in failure, and the future of Fayli Kurds, like that of the rest of the Kurdish people, remained uncertain.

Ethnic Groups in Ba'ath Political Thinking

The concept of Shu'ubiya has been an essential component of the Ba'ath Party's political thinking since its foundation in 1947. Ba'ath leaders borrowed this concept from the pioneers of pan-Arabism, such as Sati al-Husri, who first used it in the 1920s. The origins of the concept 'Shu'ubiya' go back to the Abbasid period when a literary movement by that name appeared in Mesopotamia. This movement promoted the cultural values of non-Arab Muslims, while criticizing Arab literary tradition for its lack of good taste and maturity. Nowadays, this concept cannot be easily defined as it has no equivalent term in English. Samir al-Khalil crudely defines Shu'ubiya as hatred or rejection of Uruba (Arabism) from within.[38] In reality, as another Iraqi researcher, Hassan 'Alawi, points out, the label 'Shu'ubi' (a person who is hostile to Arabism) has been used by Iraq's pan-Arabists against only those people who have been defined as 'Iranian' and 'Shi'i'.[39] Thus, from the pan-Arabists' viewpoint, Shu'ubiya has these two distinctive ethnic and sectarian connotations. It seems very odd that the pan-Arabists have not labelled the Turks as 'Shu'ubi', even though they blamed the long duration of Turkish domination for the economic and cultural backwardness of Arab societies.

As a political and historical concept, Shu'ubiya is the pan-Arabists' one-sided interpretation of past and contemporary events, in which Arabs' setbacks or weaknesses are attributed to the anti-Arab activities of certain alien elements living among them. These alien elements are distinguishable by their ethnic or cultural background, and by the notion that they form some sort of 'fifth column'. In Iraq's case, the pan-Arabists depicted Fayli community, among others, as such a fifth column, serving the interests of the Arabs' enemies.

As mentioned earlier, Al-Husri was the first to use the term 'Shu'ubiya', against the great Arab poet Muhammad Mahdi al-Jawahiri for a poem the latter wrote in praise of a mountainous resort he had visited in Iran. Ironically, al-Husri was born in Turkey and had a thick Turkish accent. Like other pan-Arabists, he was influenced by German nationalist theories based on race and by the success of the Turkish nationalist movement led by Mustapha Kemal Ataturk, who severely persecuted non-Turkish communities. In 1921, King Faysal brought him (as well as other Syrian and Palestinian pan-Arabist figures) to Baghdad. The figures who ran the affairs of Faysal's royal court were non-Iraqis, notably Rustam Hayder and Tahsin Qadri.[40] Al-Husri served as an adviser, and then as Director General of Education.[41] As the new nation-state consisted of different ethnic and cultural groups, which made extreme pan-Arab views not so appealing, the pan-Arabists accused foreign elements (i.e. non-Arab communities) of hindering Arab unity and independence. In retrospect, the divisive activities of the pan-Arabists that simply categorized Iraqis as pro- or anti-Arab actually undermined the fragile political unity of the young Iraqi state rather than strengthening it.

The Ba'athists further elaborated the concept of 'Shu'ubiya'. For them, hatred of Arabism takes several forms of subversive clandestine activity, including social, economic, political and cultural. In other words, the Ba'athists believe that their sacred efforts to unite all Arab peoples in a unitary state have been and will always be obstructed by the poisonous activities of the Shu'ubiya, which exists among Arabs as the agents of Western imperialism and hostile regional powers. It has become customary for the Ba'athists to label any force that opposes their extreme nationalism as Shu'ubiya, even if the accused is a true Arab. Their attitudes towards the Fayli community have some distinct characteristics. First, as far as the Shi'i Arabs are concerned, the concept 'Shu'ubiya' applies to individuals, not to the whole Shi'i community. By contrast, the Ba'athists considered the Fayli community as a whole to be Shu'ubi and agents of the Iranian enemy. Second, the Ba'athists have always refrained from using the words 'Fayli Kurds' in order to separate them from the rest of the Kurdish people in Iraq. Instead, they persistently employed the word 'Iranian' in their propaganda literature.[42] In this way, the Ba'athists succeeded, to a considerable extent, in preventing the Arab public from sympathizing with Fayli sufferings. Indeed, as soon as the Ba'ath regime waged its mass deportation campaign in April 1980, the Faylis found themselves totally isolated in Baghdad. This allowed the witch hunt of Fayli families to go almost undetected.

Fadil al-Barrak's book, *Al-Madaris al-Yahudiya wa al-Iraniya fi al-'Iarq* (Jewish and Iranian Schools in Iraq) is a true reflection of the manner in which the Ba'ath Party views the Fayli community. This book was published during the Iraq–Iran war in 1984.[43] Al-Barrak was the head of the General Security Directorate in the late 1970s. In 1982, Saddam Hussein appointed him as the head of the General Intelligence Service.[44] Al-Barrak was a well-educated Ba'athist, who obtained a doctorate in politics in Moscow. The core of his argument is that the 'Iranian' community and the Jewish community have served as a fifth column and have always conspired against Arab Iraq since ancient times. Throughout his book, he makes several comparisons between the evil deeds of the 'Iranians' and their co-conspirators, the Jews. To support his claim that there was an 'Iranian–Jewish' conspiracy against Arab Iraq, al-Barrak states that Jewish merchants who were forced to leave Iraq in the early 1950s sold all their businesses to 'Iranian' merchants, with a view to ruining Iraq's socialist economy.[45]

One of the main aims of al-Barrak's book is to defend the Ba'ath regime's deportations of Fayli Kurds and Shi'i Arabs. To justify the confiscation of naturalization certificates, passports or other legal documents by the regime, al-Barrak attempts to convince his readers that the deportees were of Iranian origin, who illegally crossed the Iran–Iraq international border, and illegally obtained Iraqi nationality.[46] Al-Barrak labels deportees as traitors and terrorists, who supported the political enemies of Arabism, such as the Islamic Da'wa, the ICP and the KDP.[47] Barrak stresses that these 'Iranians' illegitimately enriched themselves at the expense of their generous Arab hosts,[48] and sabotaged Iraq's socialist economy and ruined its financial institutions to serve Iran's interest.[49] All these illegal activities, Barrak claims, enabled the 'Iranians' to occupy vital positions in the economic, political and cultural life of the country, and thereby threatened Iraq's national security.

In retrospect, the Ba'ath had detailed plans to cleanse Baghdad and some other towns of Fayli Kurds. At the same time, the regime incorporated its anti-Fayli measures into its larger plan of ethnic cleansing in Iraqi Kurdistan. In 1968, the newly established Ba'ath regime closed down the Fayli Association, the Fayli Club and the Fayli School. In 1971–1972, as noted above, it deported Fayli Kurds who had permanent residency status in Iraq. Between 1972 and 1979, the regime, while proceeding with the sporadic deportation of Fayli families, made sure that Fayli Kurds would be excluded from occupying any high rank in the state and the civil service. It firmly rejected the KDP's nominee for the position of vice-president according to the March 1970 Accord, because he was a Fayli Kurd. The Ba'ath regime seemed to think that its acceptance of a Fayli Kurd as Iraq's vice-president would be tantamount to officially recognizing all members of the Fayli community as Iraqi citizens.

The information given by al-Barrak in his book clearly indicates that the Ba'athists had deportation plans against the Fayli Kurds as early as 1968. Barrak's book was based on the secret files of the Security Directorate; it contains endless details about the deportees: their names, numbers, addresses, businesses, properties and belongings.[50] It is worth mentioning that in 1978, at the trial of the members of the Halui Sur organization, who were mostly young Faylis, Muslim Hadi al-Jiburi, an old Ba'athist who presided over the court, called them traitors, agents of Iran and the fifth column. He shouted with excitement that the Ba'athists did not forget Fayli resistance to their coup d'état in February 1963, and that the Faylis would pay a heavy price for their disloyalty and hostility towards the Ba'ath Party.[51]

Notes

1. The other distinctive group of the Luri tribes, known as the Greater Lurs, is concentrated in the modern Iranian districts of Luristan.
2. A. Fayli, 'Min Hum al-Akrad al-Fayliyon' [Who are the Fayli Kurds?], *The Rozh Journal*, Stockholm, no. 1, June 1993, p. 5.
3. Sharafkhan Bitlisi, *Sharafnama*, part one, translated from Persian into Arabic by Mohammad Ali Oni, with an introduction by Yahya al-Khashab (Cairo: Dar al-Kutob al-Arabiya, 1962), pp. 35–55.
4. John Malcolm, *John Malcolm's History of Persia*, edited and adapted by M. H. Corrt (Lahur: 1888), p. 73.
5. Claudius J. Rich, *Narrative of a Resident in Kurdistan*, vol. 1 (London: Gregg International, 1968), p. 121.
6. Robert Ker Porter, *Travels in Georgia, Armenia, Ancient Babylon*, vol. 2 (London: Hurst, Rees, orma and Brown, 1822), p.204.
7. *Sharafnama*, pp. 35–55.
8. Al-Shaykh Rasul al-Kirkukli, *Dohat al-Wizara fiTarikh wa Waqa' Baghdad al-Zawra* [The Garden of Notables in the History of Baghdad City], trans. by Mosa Kadim Noras (Qom: Sharif al-Radi, h1413), pp. 146, 179, 229.
9. David McDowall, *A Modern History of the Kurds* (London: I. B. Tauris, 1996), p. 11.
10. Sections from the Records of the Bombay Government, no. XLII (Bombay, 1852), *Memoirs by Commander James Jones: Journey to the Frontier of Turkey and Persia through Part of Kurdistan* (April 1846), p. 143. Jones's memoirs were first published as a separate booklet under the title of *Narrative of a Journey through Parts of Persia and Kurdistan* (Baghdad, 1847).
11. Jirjis Fathalla, 'Kayfa Farratna bi Huquq al-Kurd al-Fayliyon' [How We Abandoned the Rights of the Fayli Kurds], *The Ilam Journal*, Gothenburg, no. 1, May 1993, p. 4.
12. Fadil al-Barrak, *Al-Madaris al-Yahudiya wa al-Iraniya fi al-Iraq* [The Jewish and Iranian Schools in Iraq] (Baghdad, 1984). Samir Al-Khalil (Kanan Makiya) provides a good analysis of al-Barrak's book in his work *Republic of Fear: the Politics of Modern Iraq* (London: Hutchinson Radius, 1989), pp. 16–20.
13. Aziz al-Haj, 'Al-Kurd al-Fayliyon: Masat Insaniya Yaloffoha al-Nisian' [The Fayli Kurds: A Forgotten Human Tragedy), *al-Ittihad*, no. 3347, 3 December 1999, p. 5.
14. British Documents on Foreign Affairs: *Reports and Papers from the Foreign Office, Confidential Print*, Part 1, Series B, The Near and the Middle East, 1856–1914, ed. David Gilland, vol. 6, *The Ottoman Empire in Asia*, 1860–1886 (University Publisher of America, 1984), Document 115, Inclusion in Document 114, Sir P. Francis to Sir H. Elliot, Constantinople, 1 July 1876, p. 201.
15. For more details see: Aziz al-Haj, *Baghdad Dhalik al-Zaman* [Baghdad in the Past] (Beirut: al-Mu'asasa al-Arabiya lil-Dirasat wa al-Nashr, 1999).
16. For instance, McDowall thinks that all Fayli Kurds lived in Baghdad without Iraqi citizenship. See: McDowall, *A Modern History of the Kurds*, p. 330.
17. Al-Barrak well expresses the Ba'ath party's view on the Fayli problem in his book *Al-Madaris al-Yahudiya wa al-Iraniya fi al-Iraq*, which will be discussed in due course.
18. This estimate is based on the fact that in 1980 almost one half of the Fayli community was deported to Iran. According to K. McLachlan and G. Joffe, 200,000 Faylis were deported in that year. See: K. McLachlan and G. Joffe, *The Gulf War: A Survey of Political Issues and Economic Consequences* (London: Economist Intelligence Unit, Special Report, no. 176, 1984), p. 34.

19. McDowall estimates the number of the deported Faylis as 50,000 in 1971–1972, whereas Samir Al-Khalil gives 40,000. See: McDowall, *A Modern History of the Kurds*, p. 336, and Al-Khalil, *Republic of Fear*, p. 19. According to Nushirwan Mustafa, who headed the Kurdish delegation during the peace process with the Ba'ath regime in 1991, the regime admitted the existence of 800,000 Kurds in the city of Baghdad. If a quarter of these Kurds were Faylis, Baghdad should have 200,000 Faylis remaining. Interview with Nushirwan Mustafa, August 1998.
20. Aziz al-Haj, 'Al-Kurd al-Fayliyon: Masat Insaniya Yaloffoha al-Nisian', p. 5.
21. Al-Barrak, *Al-Madaris al-Yahudiya wa al-Iraniya fi al-Iraq*, pp. 141–142.
22. Women, as mothers or wives, have no legal weight when the authorities decide the applicant's entitlement to Iraqi citizenship.
23. 'Human Rights Organisation for Fayli Kurds', *The Rozh Journal*, Stockholm, no. 1, June 1993, p. 16.
24. al-Haj, *Baghdad Dhalik al-Zaman*, p. 118.
25. US Department of State, 'Syria Human Rights Project, 1993', 31 June 1994.
26. Radio Station of 'Voice of America', the Kurdish Section, summer 1998.
27. Faroq Haj Mustafa, 'History and the Settlement of Kurds in Lebanon', *al-Hayat* newspaper, 30 August 2000.
28. Fathalla, 'Kayfa Farratna bi Huquq al-Kurd al-Fayliyon', p. 4.
29. Hanna Batatu, *Al-Tabaqat al-Ijtima'iya fi al-Iraq: Al-Hizb al-Shi'yo'i*, trans. by Afif al-Razaz (Beirut: Musasat al-Abhath al-Arabiya, 1992), vol. 2, p. 108.
30. Hanna Batatu, *Al-Tabaqat al-Ijtima'iya fi al-Iraq*, vol. 2, pp. 437–438.
31. In 1967, having separated from the ICP, Aziz al-Haj formed the Central Leadership that attracted a considerable number of Fayli Kurds to its ranks. It resorted to the strategy of armed struggle as a means of overthrowing the Ba'ath regime. The new organization disintegrated following the capture of its leaders in the early 1970s.
32. Batatu, *Al-Tabaqat al-Ijtima'iya fi al-Iraq*.
33. Al-Haj, 'Al-Kurd al-Fayliyon: Masat Insaniya Yaloffoha al-Nisyan', p. 5.
34. Al-Haj, *Baghdad Dhalik al-Zaman*, p. 118.
35. Zakiya Isma'il Haqi, 'Fi Arba'iniyat al-Doctor Ja'far Mohammad Karim [In memory of Dr Ja'far Mohammad Karim], *al-Ittihad*, no. 286, 8 September 2000, p. 14.
36. Fathalla, 'Kayfa Farratna bi Huquq al-Kurd al-Fayliyon', pp. 7–8.
37. The PUK Central Information Bureau in the liberated area of Iraqi Kurdistan published this programme in 1984.
38. Al-Khalili, *Republic of Fear*, pp. 18 and 153.
39. Hassan al-'Alawi, *al-Tathirat al-Turkiya fi al-Mashru' al-Qawmi al-Arabi fi al-Iraq* [Turkish Impacts on Arab Nationalism in Iraq] (London: Dar al-Zawra, 1988), pp. 12 and 144.
40. Hassan al-Alawi, *Dawlat al-Isti'ara al-Qawmiya* [The State of Nationalist Metaphor] (London: Dar al-Zawra, 1993), p. 12.
41. Al-Husri was deported and deprived of his Iraqi citizenship in the wake of the Rashid Ali coup in 1941, in which he was implicated. For more details concerning al-Husri's life and views see: Sati al-Husri, *Mudhakarati fi al-Iraq* [My Memoirs in Iraq] (Beirut, 1968), vol. 1, 1921–1927, and vol. 2, 1927–1941. See also: William J. Cleveland, *Sati al-Husri: min al-Fikra al-Othmaniy ila al-Uruba*, trans. by Victor Sahab (Beirut: Dar al-Sahab, 1983).
42. Al-Barrak's book uses the term 'Iranians' to describe all non-Arab or even non-Sunni groups, including Fayli Kurds; only once the term 'Fayli' is used in a footnote, on page 151.
43. On pp. 16–20, Al-Khalili provides a good analysis of al-Barrak's book.

44. In the early 1990s, Saddam murdered al-Barrak.

45. Al-Barrak, *Al-Madaris al-Yahudiya wa al-Iraniya fi al-Iraq*, pp. 147–148. He, like his leader Saddam Hussein, highlights Nebuchadnezzar's heroic achievements in the 6th century BC, when defeating Iraq's arch enemies, i.e. the Jews and the Iranian Ilamids.

46. Ibid., p. 143.

47. Ibid., pp. 143–146.

48. Ibid., pp. 156–158.

49. Ibid., pp. 149 and 153–155.

50. Ibid., pp. 151–158.

51. It is worth noting that al-Barrak headed the interrogation and the torture process of the Halui Sur's members. From an interview with R. B. Eskander, a former member of the Halui Sur, in February 2000.

Political Islam Among the Kurds

Michiel Leezenberg

Introduction

The theme of Islam is not very prominent or popular when it comes to writings about the Kurds. Political analyses of Kurdish nationalism tend, almost as a matter of definition, to downplay religious aspects, which the Kurds by and large have in common with their neighbours, and to focus on ethnic factors like language that mark off the Kurds.[1] Further, Kurdish nationalists tend to argue that the Kurds were forcibly converted to Islam, and that the 'real' or 'original' religion of the Kurds was the dualist Indo–Iranian religion of Zoroastrianism; this religion, it is further alleged, lives on in sects such as the Yezidis and the Kaka'is or Ahl-e Haqq, which are thus portrayed as more quintessentially Kurdish than the Sunni Islam to which most Kurds adhere. Likewise, foreign scholars often have a particular interest in the more exotic and colourful heterodox sects in Kurdistan, and have devoted a disproportionate amount of attention to groups like the Yezidis, the Ahl-e Haqq and the Alevis, not to mention the Christian and Jewish groups that live (or used to live) in the region. This is not to criticize such valuable and often very interesting research, but merely to state that many of the beliefs and practices of the Kurds, the vast majority of whom are of a more or less orthodox Sunni background, are still relatively uncharted territory.

Moreover, insofar as attention has been paid to Sunni Islam among the Kurds, it has mostly focused on the mystical varieties as exemplified by the local Sufi orders or *tariqas*; further, these orders, of both the Naqshabandiya and Qadiriya variety, have largely been studied in rural contexts.[2] The fact is, however, that most Kurds are not nowadays affiliated to Sufi networks, and are thoroughly urban rather than rural, as a result of both forced and voluntary processes of urbanization. Turkey has seen an enormous labour migration starting in the 1950s, and an equally momentous transnational labour movement from the 1960s onwards; in the 1990s, the destruction of thousands of Kurdish villages by the Turkish army drove further millions of Turkish Kurds to the cities. The social consequences of this rapid and chaotic forced urbanization are yet to be assessed, but they are likely to be dramatic. In Iraq, over 4,000 Kurdish and Assyrian villages have been destroyed in the 1970s and 1980s, and their population was relocated in *mujamma'at*, or collective towns, or in some cases exterminated. These violent episodes have to some extent masked the fact that Iraq as a whole was already predominantly urban by the late 1970s, the Kurdish areas lagging behind only slightly.[3] Next to such demographic developments, there has been another, equally momentous transformation in the means and channels of mass communication. Increasing numbers of people gained access to education, and literacy rates rose steadily (in Iraq at least up until 1990); and the products of printing and especially broadcasting became more widely available. It is precisely such factors, I will argue below, that have led to drastic changes in the character and role of religion in public and private life among the Kurds. These effects, moreover, have been rather different in Turkey and Iraq, to which I will restrict my attention here. The differences are in part due to the distinct political natures of the modern states of Turkey and Iraq, but also in part to important differences in what is usually called the 'public sphere' in these respective countries; that is, the arena or arenas where political, social, cultural and moral debates are acted out.

The heterodox groups and their relation to 'mainstream' Islam

Before embarking on the topic of contemporary Sunni Islam among the Kurds, however, I would like briefly to discuss the allegedly non- or pre-Islamic heterodox groups in Kurdistan. In fact, even these groups have an undeniable background in (folk-)Islamic traditions and cannot be adequately understood in isolation from this background. Claims about their alleged pre-Islamic origins or purely Kurdish character may have their uses for nationalist purposes, but in scholarly debates, they are seriously misguided, if not downright misleading.

As said, the most familiar and most widely studied of the heterodox groups in Kurdistan are the Yezidis, who have their religious centre at Lalesh in Iraqi Kurdistan, the Kaka'is or Ahl-e Haqq in Iranian and Iraqi Kurdistan, and the Alevis in Turkey. Of these, the only group that is exclusively Kurdish is that of the Yezidis. Many, if not most, Alevis are ethnically Turkish, and the Ahl-e Haqq sect has numerous Turcoman, Persian and to a lesser extent even Arab adherents. There has been a complex interaction of religious and linguistic factors in determining the ethnic adherence of these groups, especially in the face of the increasingly competing nationalisms trying to co-opt them, as will be argued below. Debates about the ethnicity – and hence claims as to the political loyalties – of these groups often take the form of discussions about their 'real origins', a question that has to some extent been encouraged by the preoccupations of Western linguistic and anthropological scholarship, especially the 19th-century tradition of historical and comparative linguistics and comparative religion. Such discussions often centre on the question of whether the religion or language of some Kurdish group displays a pre-Islamic or proto-Kurdish 'substratum'. These debates about origins and substrates are definitely important factors in contemporary contests for ethnic and political allegiance; but they are first and foremost claims to cultural and political legitimacy, and should not be confused with accounts of actual religious traditions and practices.

Among Kurdish nationalists, then, and to a lesser extent among academics, there is a tendency to overlook, downplay or even deny the folk-Islamic background that all of these groups unmistakably have. In fact, however, all of these groups display significant organizational, doctrinal and even terminological similarities with varieties of folk Islam. These features can by no means be brushed aside as mere later accretions or adulterations of originally non-Islamic faiths. Both organizationally and doctrinally, these groups emerged and developed against the backdrop of local varieties of folk Islam, especially *tariqa* Sufism. Undoubtedly, they have incorporated pre-Islamic doctrinal and ritual materials, but these cannot be seen as their essence or real origin. It is nothing unusual for a new religious tradition to incorporate, elaborate and reinterpret existing elements of religious and cultural traditions of its surroundings. Whatever their origin, then, these religious beliefs and practices are what they are today due to their embedding in folk-Islamic doctrines, rituals and organizations.

There is a good deal of historical evidence for such Sufi or folk-Islamic connections; I cannot discuss this claim in detail here, but a few remarks will suffice. Up until at least the 16th century, the Yezidis were considered a run-of-the-mill Sufi order, the doctrines and practices of which may have seemed dubious to some, but not as essentially or 'originally' un-Islamic. This becomes abundantly clear from a pamphlet against the Yezidis, written by the famous 14th-century Sunni apologist and polemicist Ahmad Ibn

Taimiyya (d. 1328 CE), who – as will appear below – is also a source of inspiration for present-day Islamic 'fundamentalist' figures and movements. Significantly, Ibn Taimiyya does not criticize the Yezidis (or *'Adawiyya* as he calls them) for any non-Islamic articles of faith like a Zoroastrian dualism or devil worship, but only for anthropomorphism (*tashbih*) and pantheism, or more precisely for their adherence to the – potentially pantheistic – doctrine of the 'unity of being' (*wahdat al-wujud*), which originates in the work of the equally famous muslim mystic Ibn 'Arabi (d. 1240 CE) and in *tariqa* Sufism. He also castigates them for an allegedly exaggerated veneration for Yazid, the sixth caliph, and for the family of sheikh 'Adi, the Yezidi sect's founder (who himself, significantly, was a Sufi from Lebanon). Ibn Taimiyya condemns the Yezidi practices in terms of 'heretic innovation' (*bid'a*) and 'exaggeration' (*ghuluww*) that were used for deviant tendencies within Islam, and does not brandish them as unbelievers with terms like *zandaqa*, which were used for clearly non-Islamic faiths such as Manichaeism and Zoroastrianism. In other words, Ibn Taimiyya does not for a moment appear to consider the Yezidis anything other than a Sufi sect gone astray, and he criticizes them as such.

Similar points apply to the other heterodox sects of allegedly non- or pre-Islamic character and origin. According to Ottoman documents, the Kaka'is or Ahl-e Haqq were still considered an unexceptional Sufi order, and thus as fully belonging to the Islamic community or *Umma*, up until at the very least the 16th century.[4] Likewise, the Alevis in Turkey were savagely persecuted in the 16th century by the Ottoman sultan Salim the Grim, not for any un-Islamic dualism or beliefs in reincarnation, but for possibly or actually constituting a fifth column for the heterodox Shi'i Safavid movement headed by Shah Isma'il, the founder of the Iranian Safavid Empire. For most of the subsequent centuries, the Ottoman authorities pretended the Alevis did not exist as a separate group, and classified them, if at all, as Bektashis, i.e. as members of yet another Sufi order, the practices of which may have been at least as heterodox as those of any other, but which was not politically suspect. For a long time, then, Alevis were considered Muslims pure and simple by the authorities, and possibly by their Sunni neighbours as well.

Similar points can be made concerning the doctrines of these groups. It has been argued by some scholars that some of their most clearly heterodox aspects, like the alleged Yezidi dualism and the Kaka'is belief in reincarnation, are not remnants of a pre-Islamic religious substratum, but rather a doctrinal innovation of more recent times, even though such a substratum of (partly Indo–Iranian) folk beliefs and practices is quite probably present.[5] Thus, the alleged devil-worshipping practices of the Yezidis show less affinity with the strict dualism of the pre-Islamic and Indo–Iranian religious tradition of Zoroastrianism, which acknowledges a principle of evil as being of nearly equal standing with the God of Good, than with the Islamic mystical vision of the devil or Iblis. In this vision, the devil is not so much the principle of evil, but, in fact, the most devoted of all God's servants, because in refusing to bow for Adam, he refuses the divine command but obeys the divine will, which forbids God's creatures to worship anything but Him. In other words, the devil is pictured as the strictest monotheist of all God's creatures, and it is precisely his tragedy that he will not regain his rightful place next to God until the end of time.[6] In short, some of the allegedly pre-Islamic religious 'substrata' of these groups may in fact be folk-Islamic interpretations or reinterpretations of existing materials.

Turkey

If we turn to the more orthodox Sunni forms of Islam, we see that vast changes have taken place in religious culture among the Kurds in both Turkey and Iraq. These have likewise had complex interactions with Kurdish ethnic identity. Traditionally, religious ethnic boundaries were considered more significant than linguistic ones; and despite being for the most part Sunni Muslims, the Kurds were to some extent distinguished from their Turkish and Arab neighbours in religious as well as linguistic terms. First, they belonged to the Shafi'i *madhhab* or school of law rather than to the Hanafi one like their Turkish and Arab neighbours; second, they were on the whole more inclined to the organized mystical forms of Islam, especially as practised in the Sufi orders or *tariqas*, especially of the Naqshabandiya and Qadiriya orders. In the 19th and early 20th centuries, it was the Sufi orders that were a prime vessel for social organization and mobilization, and it was primarily their charismatic leaders, the sheikhs, that were the leaders of the early Kurdish rebellions. The sheikhs were particularly well-placed to act as middlemen in conflicts, and hence to act as leaders or figureheads for broader Kurdish nationalist movements, as they were in a position to overcome the tribal divisions that had increased in importance since the Ottoman authorities had abolished the local Kurdish emirates in the mid-19th century. The most famous of these religious cum nationalist leaders is Sheikh Sa'id of Palu, who headed a large but unsuccessful revolt, co-organized with urbanized and secular Kurdish nationalists in 1925. Significantly, however, the leaders of this revolt did not succeed in wholly overcoming tribal and denominational differences: although it was primarily nationalistic in character, the participants were mobilized with (Sunni) religious slogans; as a consequence of this, the Alevi Kurds in the region, and other tribes that had been among the victims of the Sunni tribes that in the preceding decades had constituted the Hamidiyya cavalry or irregulars for the sultan, either abstained from participating in the rebellion or even actively opposed it.[7]

In the 1920s and 1930s, the staunchly secularist Kemalist government of the newly formed Turkish Republic took drastic measures against both Kurdish nationalist aspirations and religious leaders like the Sufi sheikhs. It pursued a radical and often violent secularization drive, inspired by the French idea of *laicité* as involving the outright banning of religion from the public sphere, as well as a French-inspired desire for a highly centralized style of government. At the same time that Kurdish was declared a forbidden language, all religious schools or *madrasas*, religious courts of law and Sufi lodges or *tekkes* were outlawed. Some of them continued on a clandestine basis, but the Sufi orders did lose much of their traditional role in Kurdish society. The aim of this programme, however, was less to eliminate religion than to impose strict state control over it, and to prevent anyone from trying to use religion as an instrument for political mobilization.

Although this laicist state policy was already toned down immediately after World War II, when party politics entered political life in Turkey, it was radically revised in the wake of the 1980 military coup. To counter the earlier left–right polarization, the generals now ordered a re-Islamization from above. Mosques were built at greater pace, and compulsory religious education was introduced in the school curricula. The importance the new rulers attached to these policies appears from the fact that, according to some sources, the Directorate for Religious Affairs (*Diyanet Isleri Baskanlıgı*) at some points had a higher budget at its disposal than the Ministry of Education.[8]

This re-Islamization policy coincided with, and indeed formed part of a neo-liberal revolution, which was initiated by the coup leaders and carried through in the whole of Turkish society under Prime Minister (later President) Özal. This revolution involved, among other things, the destruction of the more radical trade unions and the development of a new urban middle class that was as explicitly Islamic in its morality as it was consumerist in outlook. The Islamist Refah or Welfare Party, headed by Necmettin Erbakan, embodied this new outlook, but it was by no means the only political formation to do so; many of Refah's cultural and moral assumptions were also visible in Özal's Motherland Party and several other mainstream parties. It should be noted that these developments affected both the Turkish and the Kurdish parts of the population (Özal, it should be remembered, was of Kurdish descent, and repeatedly said so in public).

In their populist appeal to the masses, Refah leaders criticized the ostentatious display of wealth characteristic of the nouveaux riches, but its social and political programmes placed more emphasis on the improvement of morals and good manners than on the redistribution of wealth and property. Thus, Refah leader Erbakan, with his rhetoric of *adil ekonomik düzen*, or 'just economic order', blamed the plight of the poor in Turkey on the international economic constellation, in particular Turkey's heavy dependence on and indebtedness to the World Bank and the IMF; but given his ultimately conservative outlook, he did not call for radical economic reform or redistribution.[9] Thus, the Welfare Party is very much a party of the lower middle class and the newly arrived town dwellers, and its ideology reflects their hopes and aspirations for economic improvement and upward social mobility, as well as their concern with morality and honour.

The public sphere and the Kurds

In the early 1990s a significant liberalization of the economic and to some extent also the political sphere occurred. The appearance of private broadcasting channels alongside state-based broadcasting media had particularly important consequences. At the same time, there was a slight relaxation of the ban on the production and sale of Kurdish magazines, books and cassette tapes. These measures led to an increase in the variety of voices in the public sphere and a change in their character: at the expense of the more strictly political polarization between leftist and rightist groups that had marked the 1960s and 1970s, more openly nationalist (both Turkish and Kurdish) as well as religious (both Sunni and Alevi) voices emerged or re-emerged. The increasing presence of religious voices in the privatized mass media contributed to the weakening of the grip of the Kemalist dogma that religion should be banned from public life altogether. It also increased the leeway for the articulation of religion as independent from the state, and thus as a channel for political opposition.

The steady rise of the Islamist Welfare Party in the early 1990s, which promised an alternative to the Kemalist order and thus to the rigid Turkish nationalism and radical *laïcité* that characterized the Turkish Republic, carried a potential appeal to the Kurdish electorate. In its social and economical outlook, Refah was by and large a mainstream party, but in 1994, it was perceived as sufficiently oppositional and conciliatory to the Kurds (to whom it appealed in the name of Islamic brotherhood and of its vague concept of social justice expressed in the notion of *adil düzen*, or 'just order') to draw a massive Kurdish vote in the eastern provinces.[10] This sudden increase in Islamist voting behaviour, however, was less a sign of a sudden Islamization of Kurdish society in Turkey, though it was in part precisely that, than a widespread display of strategic voting among the Kurds. The votes for the Welfare Party would by and large have gone to the pro-Kurdish DEP, had that party not been banned from participating in the elections in the preceding months. In the wake of the DEP ban, many Kurds in the south-east perceived Refah as a good 'oppositional' alternative, even though in the west it ranked among the mainstream parties. But politically, this 'Islamist turn' has not been of an enduring character. Since Refah came to power in 1996, Kurdish enthusiasm for its policies and promises has waned considerably. In the 1998 local elections and in the 1999 parliamentary elections, Refah lost much of its earlier vote, while DEP's successor party, HADEP, which was not banned this time around, managed to gain a large percentage (and in some places the absolute majority) of the vote in the Kurdish east, although it still failed to take the 10 per cent hurdle nation-wide, and thus to secure representation in the national parliament.[11]

The rapid urbanization and the neo-liberal transformation of both the public sphere and the economy at large have equally affected the Alevi community. Between the 1950s and the 1970s, Alevism, which was not a unified religious doctrine but rather a collection of rural and largely orally transmitted religious traditions, seemed definitely on the wane. In the new urbanized context, it was next to impossible to maintain religious links with the traditional rural religious leaders or to continue the practice of specifically Alevi rituals like the *cem*, the periodical ceremonial gathering in which both men and women participate. By the late 1980s, however, public statements started appearing in which Alevis demanded recognition as a distinct and legitimate denomination. In part, this new public emergence of Alevism formed a reaction to the imposing of Sunni Islam as something of a state religion following the 1980 coup. The emerging Alevi movement maintained ambivalent if not contradictory relations with the state and with the Turkish and Kurdish nationalist movements.

Almost coinciding with, but largely independently from these developments, from 1990 onwards the PKK showed signs of gaining momentum as a mass movement. In order to increase its popular appeal and to counter Turkish propaganda charges that they were a bunch of 'Marxist atheists' and 'Armenian [i.e. Christian] terrorists', it started emphasizing its Sunni Islamic credentials. This populist move, however, led to renewed or increased antagonisms between them and some of the Alevi Kurds. For a good many of the latter, the term 'Kurd' meant *Sunni* Kurd by definition, so that Alevis are not and cannot be Kurds; a stronger emphasis on the Sunni religion of the Kurds at large was thus bound to alienate the Kurdish Alevis. Turkish propagandists eagerly picked up the idea that Alevism was an essentially Turkish folk variety of Islam, which to them implied that the very notion of 'Alevi Kurds' was something of a contradiction in terms. This was a serious challenge for Kurdish nationalists in Turkey, especially for the PKK, which mounted a large and concerted propaganda effort in magazines and manifestations (especially in European exile) and, increasingly, in the broadcasts of the Kurdish satellite television channel MED-TV, which argued that Alevism was an originally and authentically Kurdish religion.[12] At the same time, it intensified its guerrilla campaign in Dersim, the heartland of the Kurdish Alevis, with the aim of provoking intensified repression by the Turkish security forces that would increase the Kurdish national consciousness of the local population.[13]

In yet another largely unrelated development, the increasing visibility of the Alevis (who were usually perceived as leftist) in the public sphere led to increased tensions with circles that were more to the right of the political spectrum and which saw themselves as defenders of 'orthodox', that is, Sunni Islam. The rise of tensions led to several violent confrontations, the most notorious and bloody of which were the July 1993 arson attack on a hotel hosting an Alevi conference in Sivas and the March 1995 riots in the Gaziosmanpasha slums of Istanbul. In part, the tensions between the Alevi population and politicized Sunni Islam coincided with the Turkish–Kurdish divide; the population of Gaziosmanpasha consisted largely of Alevi Kurds from Tunceli area. But, more importantly, the riots reflected a general Alevi mistrust of the state and a hatred of the 'fascists' associated with it. With some justification, local Alevis perceived the police forces as strongly associated with the extreme right, especially the Nationalist Action Party (MHP), with Turkish nationalism and with Sunni Islam or Islamism.

At present, however, there is no unified Alevi political movement, and there is even more disagreement concerning the political and ethnic affiliation of the Alevi Kurds. The neo-liberal policies pursued by the successive governments have, in Turkey as elsewhere, led to a steady depoliticization among the poorer strata. Neither the traditional leftist parties nor the pro-Kurdish HADEP (Halkın Demokrasi Partisi, 'People's Democracy Party') have been able to mobilize significant numbers of either Alevi or Kurdish voters in the urban centres of western Turkey. But in any case, Turkish law no more allows for the creation of parties based on confessional particularisms like Alevism than of parties based on ethnicity, whether Kurdish or other. At present, the Alevis are as far from forming a unified social or political movement as ever. Kurdish ethnicity is but one among many cleavage lines among the Alevis, and perhaps not even a major one. With the demise of both mainstream and radical leftist parties, and with the failure of the Kurdish armed resistance, Alevi Kurds are presented with a range of new options. Alevis nowadays seem to move more towards the political centre and away from traditional leftist politics. Instead, they increasingly participate in various folklore organizations, which usually are relatively depoliticized, despite being in fierce competition with each other.[14] Numerous Alevi federations have emerged during the 1990s, at varying distances from the Turkish state. Likewise, Dersimis have founded organizations that aim at collecting, preserving and promoting the cultural traditions of their region of origin. The appearance of these *Dersim vakıfları*, or 'Dersim foundations', was primarily triggered, it seems, by the violent destruction of their traditional culture by the Turkish army in the autumn of 1994.[15] These activities are informed by an urgent sense of the importance of preserving local customs on the verge of disappearing forever, and far less by political, let alone territorial claims. The intensification of Alevi Kurdish initiatives of the late 1990s, then, is perhaps not an ethnic or confessionalist movement as much as a folklorist and regionalist one.

This new, literacy- and mass communication-based form of Alevism has been characterized as having dialectically developed out of a confrontation with 'scripturalist' (i.e. more scholastic, legalistic and doctrinal) forms of Islam;[16] but such claims downplay the massive changes that have taken place in 'mainstream' scripturalism as well. The development of these new varieties of Alevism reflects tendencies in the Islamic world at large. In Turkey, religious voices in the public sphere no longer are the monopoly of traditional religious leaders and institutions; increasingly, lay people with a higher (and state-based) education join in the debate. For these new intellectuals, such formerly significant institutions like *madrasa* education, the Shafi'i and Hanafi law schools, the Sufi orders and the Alevi *dedes*, have lost much of their relevance. Many people who publicly speak and write on such matters have had a state-based and often even secular education. Earlier, Islam could be used as a channel or instrument of separation; nowadays, it acts more often as a factor of integration and conciliation, especially between Turks and Kurds.[17] In short, the emergence or re-emergence of Islam on the

Turkish political scene from the late 1980s onwards took place in a radically reshaped cultural, social and economic landscape. The new forms of Islam do not appear to attach much importance to traditional distinctions between law schools and Sufi orders; they do, however, tend to emphasize more strongly than before the antagonism between Sunnis and Alevis. Moreover, they are far less conducive to political mobilization specifically, let alone exclusively, among the Kurds.

Iraq

Religious life among the Kurds of Iraq has run a rather different course. During the last decades, Sunni Islam may have been a less visible or prominent part of public life in Iraq, certainly in comparison with Arab and Kurdish nationalism, communism and 'Arab socialism', or even in comparison with Shi'i Islam; but it has never been absent. Iraq has never known the kind of radical attempts at secularization that were pursued in republican Turkey in the 1920s and 1930s. *Madrasas* and Dervish lodges were not closed, even though state-sponsored education was reformed along secularist and subsequently along nationalist and socialist lines from the mandate period onwards. Until the present day, the Sufi ritual of the *zikr* is carried out every week, even in the cities; it is clearly despised by the higher-class Kurds. Even in its most radically socialist (or apparently socialist) phase in the late 1960s and 1970s, the Ba'ath government never tried to antagonize religious groups as such. Despite its secularist and modernistic posturing, the Ba'ath often tried to co-opt as much as to coerce Islamic groups and leaders into political loyalty; this holds far more strongly for Sunni than for Shi'i groups.

One reason why Sunni Islam was never a dominant channel for political opposition as it was in, for example, Syria or Egypt is the simple demographic fact that the Sunni Arabs form a numerical minority in the country.[18] More in general, both Sunni and Shi'i Islam definitely seemed to be on the wane as a source of mobilization in the 1950s and 1960s. During these years, Iraqi politics was dominated by the largely, if not militantly secularist competing ideologies of Arab and Kurdish nationalism and communism. Sunni Islamic activities, the most important of which was probably the Iraqi branch of the Muslim Brotherhood, were small in scale and politically insignificant. The Iraqi Muslim Brotherhood was headed by one Mohammad Sawaf (1912–1992) and, significantly, by a Kurdish religious scholar, Sheikh Amjad al-

Zahawi;[19] in Iraq, that is, the Muslim Brotherhood could apparently mobilize
equally well among Kurds and Arabs. Not much is known about the history
of this branch, though, apart from the fact that it does not appear to have
ever had a large following.[20]

Apparently, the Iraqi Muslim Brotherhood was relatively autonomous
with respect to the Egyptian branch. Until the 1960s, it seems to have been
relatively open and even accommodating to the Shi'ites. This openness
apparently led to dissent (which Sawaf only with some difficulty could
contain) and, possibly, to infiltrations. In the late 1950s, according to some
sources, it lost much of the already small following it had, when it allegedly
appeared to have been infiltrated by the CIA; Sawaf reportedly left Iraq
for Saudi Arabia in 1959, never to return. From the late 1960s onwards,
therefore, it became more secretive, and had a closed membership.[21] Even
though he was in exile, Sawaf continued to be seen by many as the legitimate
religious if not organizational leader of the Iraqi MB.

More importantly, perhaps, the Muslim Brotherhood does not appear
to have taken an oppositional stand against any of the succeeding Iraqi
governments, all of which were dominated by Arabs from the Sunni belt.
Especially the Arif brothers appear to have had close ties to the MB. In late
1964, the then Iraqi president, 'Abd al-Salam Arif, is alleged to have intervened
with the Egyptian government on behalf of the MB intellectual Sayyid Qutb
and to have invited him to settle in Iraq. Qutb, however, remained in Egypt
and subsequently was arrested once again and hanged in August 1966.

In its turn, the Ba'ath regime is said to have tolerated and perhaps even
encouraged the activities of the Muslim Brothers in return for their loyalty to
the regime and abstention from any political activities. Upon coming to power
in 1968, the new Ba'ath regime appointed a Muslim Brotherhood member,
one 'Abd al-Karim Zaydan, as a cabinet minister. Information concerning
the subsequent development of relations between the government and
the Iraqi MB is extremely scanty, but except for a few isolated incidents, it
does not appear to have ever had the character of a violent confrontation.[22]
Given its rejection of armed *jihad*, even the more oppositional figures of
the contemporary Iraqi MB do not reject out of hand the possibility of a
dialogue with the Iraqi government.[23] Reportedly, in the late 1990s the
Ba'ath government has even delegated social (and political) control of some
of the popular quarters of southern Baghdad to MB groups. Being Sunni and
relatively loyal, these may help it in keeping the large and potentially restive
Shi'i segments of the urban population at bay. In short, with the exception
of the bloody confrontations with Iraqi Shi'is in the late 1970s, social and

political conflicts in Iraq were usually articulated in terms of class, ethnicity and nationalism, rather than in religious terms. Before addressing the radical changes on this front, which occurred from the 1980s onwards, however, I would like briefly to summarize developments among the heterodox minority groups in Iraqi Kurdistan.

The Yezidis and the Kaka'is in Ba'ath Iraq

Developments within the heterodox groups dwelling among the Kurds of Iraq have been rather different from those among the Alevi Kurds in Turkey. Although in Iraq urbanization has been no less massive and probably even more destructive than in Turkey, it has had totally different effects on such existing social networks as the tribes and religious orders. In Turkey, the destruction of such independent loci of power and organization was an integral element of Kemalist domestic policies until World War II. The successive Iraqi governments, by contrast, including the Ba'ath government that has ruled Iraq since 1968, have never been as unambiguously opposed to these ties and networks, but more typically tried to exploit them for their own ends. From the early 1980s onwards, they were even actively strengthened in Iraqi Kurdistan. The Ba'ath government enlisted (or even created) tribal leaders to act as paramilitary chieftains, but also middlemen for the distribution of food, goods and service in the relocation camps, or *mujamma'at*, to which thousands of rural Kurds had been deported.[24] Tribal and religious leaders could thus maintain or even strengthen a degree of leverage with the central government, but this position as middlemen at times required rather delicate balancing acts.

Minority groups like the Yezidis, the Shabak and the Kaka'is maintained an ambiguous ethnic position, and some of them were less than fully committed to the Kurdish nationalist movement. In the 1980s, the Iraqi government increased the pressure on these groups, either by simply declaring them to be Arabs by fiat, or by forcing them, notably in the 1987 census, to describe their ethnicity as either Arab (which implied political loyalty to the regime) or Kurdish (which could, and on several occasions did, result in condemnation by the regime as being 'oppositional'). In this period, the question whether the members of these groups were 'really' Kurds or Arabs became more central for the government, the group members and their leaders. The fact that many Kaka'is are multilingual (speaking Sorani Kurdish, Arabic, Turcoman and/or a variety of Hawrami locally called 'Macho') has made the question of their 'real' national identity even more intractable.[25]

The competing claims to ethnic and political allegiance have led to
various splits in these groups. Their members have also suffered at the
hands of the government, especially in 1988, when many of their villages
were destroyed and their inhabitants were deported.[26] Following the 1991
uprising, competition for political and ethnic allegiance did not abate,
however, but shifted to the local Kurdish parties, and increasingly to Turkish
and Turcoman organizations.[27] The most destructive years of the 1980s
are over, but the ethnic and political position of these groups remains as
ambiguous and precarious as ever. Although it remains unclear how the more
recent developments of the 1990s have affected these groups, especially in
government-held territory, there are indications that their leaders have been
able to maintain or even strengthen their position as middlemen, either with
the government in Baghdad or with the local Kurdish party in control.[28]
There are also scattered reports that, with the rise of political Islam in the
region, the Yezidis have increasingly been the target of criticisms and attacks
by Islamic activists, but it is difficult to give a reliable assessment of such
claims.

Political Islam in Iraqi Kurdistan

To outside observers, one of the most significant and surprising developments
in Iraqi Kurdistan after the 1991 uprising against Saddam Hussein's regime
seemed to be the apparently sudden emergence of a vigorous and influential
Islamist movement. Foreign Islamic charity organizations soon started
engaging in substantial welfare programmes of a distinctly Islamic character,
which were most clearly visible in the quick spread of newly constructed
mosques, in cities and countryside alike.[29] But also local Islamist organizations
emerged, at first sight almost out of the blue. Their emergence did not square
well with the often-heard claim, eagerly repeated by secularized Kurdish
nationalists, that traditionally the Kurds were less strict in observing religious
practices and duties than their Arab neighbours.[30] The most significant of
these was the Islamic Movement of Iraqi Kurdistan (Bizutnewey Islami
Kurdistani 'Iraq) led by mullah Othman bin Abdulaziz from Halabja; in
later years, other organizations, notably the Islamic League (Rabitay Islami),
an Islamist welfare organization, and an affiliated political party, the Islamic
Union (Yekgirtuy Islami) gained prominence.[31] Here, I will restrict my
attention to the Islamic Movement; further, given the lack of detailed and
reliable information, the present account is no more than a first sketch.

In secularized nationalist circles and among foreign aid workers (many of whom were affiliated to Christian charity organizations), the Islamic Movement has received a rather consistently negative press; it has been accused of numerous assassinations, threats against rival party members and against secularized women, and even of carrying out bombing campaigns against ladies' hairdressers. But, whatever the truth of such accusations, violent methods and the attempt by political parties to influence every part of the public and private life of the population are by no means new to Iraq's Kurds, who have suffered under the Ba'ath party's totalitarian rule for decades, and who have likewise experienced violent tactics and attempts at dominating public life by the other local Kurdish parties in the 1990s. What is new, however, is the specifically Islamic discourse in which the new movement's actions are couched; moreover, it appears totally different in character and organization from Islamist movements in neighbouring Turkey. Unlike the Welfare Party, for example, the Islamic Movement propagates an armed struggle or *jihad* against the Iraqi regime and other enemies. It is a guerrilla movement rather than a civilian political party; apparently it recruits most of its active cadre from tribal warriors, and possibly youths from the urban destitute classes.

The explanation for the rise of political Islam in Iraqi Kurdistan often given by educated locals is that, following the upheavals of the Gulf War and its aftermath, many Kurds have turned to religion as a source of consolation and security. Political Islam would thus be an expression of disappointment with the Kurdish nationalist movement and of anguish about the dire social and economic conditions obtaining since the 1991 Gulf war and the subsequent uprising against the Iraqi regime.[32] But this folk explanation can hardly account for its activist and, at times, violent character, or for its essential novelty. Moreover, Islamist activities in the region go further back in time than is often thought, and well predate the infighting and corruption of the nationalist Kurdish leadership of the 1990s. The first Islamist-type assaults of which I am aware were said to have occurred in Sulaimaniya around 1983, when Muslim conservatives allegedly conducted a campaign of throwing acid on the exposed legs of urban women wearing skirts they considered too short. This kind of Islamist action is by no means simply a reassertion of traditional Islamic values and practices: acid assaults are not a traditional Islamic way of punishment or combat.[33] The new Islamic movements are not a straightforward outgrowth of the older Sufi orders, either; rather, their intellectual and organizational origins appear to lie with more recent developments in the Islamic world at large. Likewise, the Islamic Movement has regularly been accused of receiving funds from, and thus being no more than a straw man of Saudi Arabia and Iran, but it should not be considered simply an agent for these states (between the two of which, it should be noted, there is a bitter rivalry on the international Islamist stage). And indeed, there are indications that the Islamic Movement depends at least as much on relatively informal and less state-based networks as on direct state patronage. The most important of these networks are those of the Muslim Brotherhood and of Pakistani organizations like the Jama'at-i Islami, as I will argue below.

In the Kurdish north, it seems that Sunni religious leaders as such were not typically at odds with the Ba'ath regime. As noted, Sunni Islam, especially of the kind preached and practiced by the MB, apparently was a source of accommodation rather than confrontation with the Baghdad regime. Hence, it is not surprising that the future leader of the Islamic Movement of Iraqi Kurdistan (IMIK), mullah Othman Abdulaziz, who was a member of the Iraqi MB, does not appear to have taken a strongly oppositional stance vis-a-vis the Iraqi regime until the late 1980s. In the same period, mullah 'Ali, his brother and heir to the IMIK leadership, was a *peshmerga*, but for the secular–nationalist PUK rather than any Islamic organization. In the 1950s, both brothers had moved from their native village of Hasanawa to the nearby town of Halabja, where they became the imams of the Othman Pasha mosque; subsequently, they opened a *madrasa* or religious school in the Kani Ashqan quarter. According to some sources, Othman was educated at the famous al-Azhar Islamic university in Cairo, but IMIK spokesmen deny this. Whatever the truth of this, he had and has maintained close links with the Muslim Brotherhood, especially, it seems, through the good offices of its Iraqi leader, Sawaf.[34]

There are conflicting claims as to the founding date of the Islamic Movement. Some sources speak of 1978, some of 1986 or 1987, and yet others argue that it did not emerge as a full-fledged party until after the 1991 Gulf war. There may be a measure of truth to all these claims: they point to the gradual formation and transformation of an organized urban religious group centred around mullah Othman into an armed political organization, a process that apparently had not yet quite finished by the time of the 1992 regional elections. Be this as it may, in Iraq, as elsewhere, Islamist ideas and movements received a great boost with the successful Islamic Revolution in Iran in 1979. Even during the early 1980s, it is reported, some of the conservative Muslim leaders in the Sulaimaniya and Halabja areas more actively and explicitly fulminated against Kurdish nationalists and communist activists than against the government. The turning point, at least as far as the emerging Islamic Movement was concerned, seems to have occurred in 1987. In May of that year, it appears, mullah Othman called for a *jihad* or holy war against the Iraqi regime, in reaction to the destructions and chemical attacks on Kurdish villages in the region. These operations had been stepped up after Saddam's cousin 'Ali Hasan al-Majid had been appointed the head of the Ba'ath party's 'Directorate of Northern Affairs'; they had forced numerous people from the surrounding countryside to flock to the city of Halabja. Demonstrations or possibly a full-blooded revolt against Saddam Hussein's regime then broke out in some parts of the city. The extent of these protests is somewhat unclear, as is the question to what degree they were spontaneous and how far a response to mullah Othman's call for a *jihad*; but the regime reacted swiftly and violently. In retaliation for the demonstrations, al-Majid ordered the destruction of the entire Kani Ashqan quarter of Halabja where the demonstrations had taken place, and where mullah Othman's *madrasa* was located.[35] Unknown numbers of demonstrators were arrested.

Mullah Othman, together with his brother mullah 'Ali and a number of followers, fled to Iran, a move that subsequently tended to be given a religious meaning: party representatives pictured it as a *hijra* or flight of the kind the prophet Mohammad had made when leaving Mecca for Medina in 622. But an even stronger catalyst for the emergence of an Islamic opposition movement among the Kurds was the Iraqi regime's notorious chemical attack on the very same city of Halabja in March 1988.[36] This attack, in which some 5,000 Kurdish civilians perished, was widely publicized thanks to the reports of foreign journalists brought in by the Iranian army. It galvanized an entire generation of Kurds into renewed action. In the more secularized and nationalist Kurdish circles, it was represented as an expression of the Ba'ath regime's racist or fascist character. In more pious religious circles, by contrast, it was interpreted as an act of unbelief (*kufr*) by a secular nationalist regime. In other words, the cataclysmic events of 1988 were given a religious significance and mobilized a large number of more conservative (and, possibly, until then relatively quietist) Kurds, as becomes clear from the biographies of some of the Islamic Movement's leading cadres. A number of Kurdish activists also appear to have switched allegiance from especially the PUK to the Islamic Movement, possibly as a result of the PUK's ambiguous and fateful role in the Iranian occupation of Halabja, which had provoked the bombing.

Both the 1987 call for *jihad* and the 1988 attack against Halabja were grounds for estrangement from the Muslim Brotherhood, the main international network to which mullah Othman belonged. First, the MB rejected violent methods such as armed struggle against local governments,

and second, the Kurdish Islamists were bitterly disappointed by the failure of
the Arab MB branches to condemn the Halabja attack. Reportedly, mullah
Othman continued to be a member of the Iraqi Muslim Brotherhood, but
increasingly went his own way. In Iranian exile, the fledgling organization
had ample occasion to organize its people; but it seems to have drawn its
inspiration at least as much from Pakistan and Afghanistan. In Pakistan,
IMIK's closest allies apparently were the Jama'ati Islami founded by Abu 'Ala
al- Maududi and the Jama'at al-'Ulama al-Islami headed by Maulana Fazlur
Rahman.[37] In Afghanistan, IMIK seems to have maintained especially close
ties with Burhanuddin Rabbani, who also belonged to the Jama'at-i Islami
network; they strongly disapproved of the violently anti-Shi'i methods of the
Taliban.[38] A considerable part of its cadre appears to have been educated in
Islamic education centres in Pakistan, such as the University of Sind and the
Islamic universities of Peshawar and Islamabad. Apparently, these links were
established primarily through the networks of the Muslim Brotherhood,
especially through Sawaf (who apparently had been living in Saudi Arabia
ever since leaving Iraq), but also through more activist *jihad* groups, which
were fighting the Russian occupation of Afghanistan. Peshawar in particular
was a focus for Islamist activities in nearby Afghanistan. It was primarily the
Muslim Brotherhood and the Pakistani Jama'at-i Islami that were the local
organizational centres of these activities. There were numerous Arabs in this
area, the so-called 'Afghans' in their countries of origin.[39]

A particular source of inspiration for the Islamic Movement's conception
of *jihad* appears to have been the Palestinian Abdallah Azzam (killed in
Afghanistan in 1989), who was a member of the Muslim Brotherhood
and a key figure in Arab–Afghan activities. Ideas and quotations from
Azzam's writings repeatedly appear in some of the statements of Islamic
Movements spokesmen, together with those of Said Hawa, one of the leaders
of the Syrian branch of the Muslim Brotherhood.[40] Reportedly, there were
significant numbers of veterans from the Afghan war among the fighters of
the Kurdish Islamic Movement. Several leading IMIK members maintained
close personal contacts with Azzam. In other words, the 1980s brought Iraqi
Kurdish Islamists closer to the so-called *salafi-jihadi* or 'fundamentalist holy
war' groups in the Islamic world, i.e. activist groups, mostly with links to
the Afghan war, who keep their distance from both Saudi Arabia and the
Muslim Brotherhood. Azzam was a main theorist for these groups, with his
call for more active struggle against foreign invaders of Islamic lands.[41] An
older source of inspiration for the *jihadi* groups is the very same Ibn Taimiyya
mentioned above, who fiercely fought the Mongol occupation of Islamic

territory, with both the pen and the sword. In its interpretation of *jihad* as armed struggle, the Islamic Movement differs from the contemporary Muslim Brotherhood at large and from the Rabita in Iraqi Kurdistan, which do not have an armed wing and emphasize peaceful means such as education and public morality, and which seem to mobilize among the more educated urban groups.

Perhaps remarkably for a contemporary *salafi-jihadi* movement, however, the IMIK is not strongly or dogmatically anti-American. Reportedly, it has been much criticized by its fellow groups for this attitude. As such, the IMIK would seem to be indicative, if not emblematic of the serious rupture among the Islamist movements that was caused by the 1990 Gulf crisis and the ensuing Gulf war pursued by a coalition of states against Iraq.[42] To the dismay of its traditional supporter, the Wahhabi state Saudi Arabia, the Muslim Brotherhood declared itself in support of Saddam Hussein. The Kurdish IMIK, having called a *jihad* against the Iraqi regime, could not of course take this stance, so organizational links with the Muslim Brotherhood were further loosened. IMIK representatives have repeatedly declared that they would not negotiate with the Iraqi regime, and claimed that their movement aims at overthrowing the Ba'ath regime and replacing it with an Islamic state, but in practice, it did not appear to have taken much military action against Iraq either before or after the 1991 uprising. In the 1990s it was more often engaged in local conflicts with other Kurdish parties, especially (but not exclusively) the PUK, which it repeatedly accused of being 'communist', a sign of a competition for local authority or, alternatively, of continuing Iranian interference in the Kurdish parties' relations.

After the 1991 uprising, the Islamic Movement quickly filled the vacuum left behind by what was left of the Iraqi welfare state. It did much grassroots work among the urban destitute, who tended to be ignored by the other Kurdish parties and by the international humanitarian agencies alike. By the 1992 elections, it had become the largest political party in Iraqi Kurdistan after the KDP and PUK, taking some 5 per cent of the vote. Closer analysis of the election results shows that IMIK was especially strong in the Ranya area where it had its headquarters, the urban centres of Arbil and Sulaymania, and of course in Halabja, mullah Othman's mainstay (here, it drew votes in numbers comparable to those of the PUK and KDP); moreover, its electorate was overwhelmingly urban. Remarkably, IMIK received less than 2 per cent of the vote in the northern Bahdinan region, which is less urbanized and often considered more tribal and less 'modernized' than the regions further South. It may be precisely this alleged 'backwardness', however, that accounts for the lack of the Islamic Movement's appeal in the north. Bahdinan is a traditional KDP stronghold, and tribal structures and Sufi orders have remained relatively strong. Subsequently, it was the Rabita rather than the Islamic Movement that made inroads in this area, but once again, and significantly, primarily in urban areas like Duhok.[43]

In December 1993, and again from May to August 1994, the Islamic Movement was engaged in a bloody confrontation with the PUK, in which both sides were alleged to have committed serious human rights violations against captured fighters.[44] IMIK spokesmen, like those of other parties, routinely denied having committed any such offences.[45] In late 1995, a settlement between the two parties was reached thanks to Iranian mediation. In April 1997, however, new rounds of fighting between PUK and IMIK occurred along the Iranian border; on 16 May, a truce was signed, reportedly again under strong Iranian pressure. Since the early 1990s, IMIK appears to have lost some of its urban constituency, in part because of its violent methods. In the March 2000 municipal elections in the PUK area, it was the Islamic Unity Party (*Yekgirtuy islami*) rather than IMIK that gained a significant percentage of the votes; in all, Islamic groups received some 30 per cent of the votes in the Sulaimaniya area. But the Halabja area remained strictly IMIK territory. The movement imposed *hudud* (Islamic penal code) in this area in 1997, and was the uncontested ruler here until all militant Islamist organizations were ousted from the border area during the 2003 war.

In June 2001, however, a serious rift occurred in the IMIK ranks, when Ali Bapir (who was alleged to have been approached earlier by Iran to form an Islamist organization of his own) split off and formed his own group by the name of 'Islamic Association of Kurdistan' (Komalay Islami Kurdistan), which concentrates its activities in his mainstay, the Ranya area; the remaining IMIK branch continued under the name of 'United Islamic Movement of Kurdistan'. According to some sources, mullah Krekar (an Afghan veteran and former IMIK guerrilla leader), together with one Mohammad Barzinji, effectively formed a third Islamist splinter party in the city of Sulaimaniya, called the 'Centre Group' (Jama'at al-markaz). It is too early to make any predictions about the future of these respective Islamist groups.

Not much is known about the doctrines or the dynamics of mobilization in the Halabja area; but IMIK representatives often take pains to distance themselves from the Wahhabi movements with their strong dislike of Shi'is, Sufis and saint worship. Such remarks do not seem to be mere window dressing, aimed at legitimizing the existing links with Iran. Similarly, in the Halabja area, the IMIK does not seem to be strongly opposed to local tribes and *tariqas*. On the contrary, some of its leaders are linked through intermarriage to the descendants of the famous Sheikh Othman of Tawila, and it seems to continue the mediation in tribal conflicts that had made Othman a locally respected leader. Some local observers even perceive a strong continuity between IMIK and the Jaf tribal confederation, which used to be very strong locally; but such characterizations, although not entirely baseless, are too sweepingly reductionist.

Conclusion

What, then, should we make of the emergence of political Islam among the Kurds in Turkey and Iraq? One should beware of treating both simply in terms of a generic 'resurgence of Islam': although there are factors common to both countries (rapid urbanization, the demise of communism and other secular political doctrines, and neo-liberal reforms of the economy, not to mention a prolonged armed conflict between Kurdish nationalists and the respective governments), these have had rather different effects. Turkey has rather more of a public sphere or perhaps an entirely differently structured public sphere from Iraq: especially in the 1990s, more room was created for civilian party politics, privatized mass communication channels and local charity work. Consequently, political Islam in Turkey is by and large civilian, especially if we disregard the case of the notorious Kurdish Hizbullah, a shady organization which for years appears to have been largely tolerated, if not actually supported, by the Turkish security apparatus.[46] The developments in party politics and the reshaping of the media landscape in the 1990s have allowed a plurality of voices to be heard. Ba'ath Iraq, by contrast, with its long-standing monopolization of all institutions of civil society and mass communication, has not (or possibly not yet) witnessed the emergence of durable institutions of civil society. Given the Ba'ath rigorous ways of dealing with any form of political opposition, it was natural, if not inevitable, that a Kurdish opposition, whether Islamist or secular, should take the form of guerrilla organizations. Following the 1991 uprising, several factors created room for Islamist organizations like IMIK, Rabita and Yekgirtu to gain social and political influence: the collapse of the hitherto strong state apparatus; the ensuing social, political and economic chaos; and the gradual erosion of Kurdish nationalism as a mobilizing force.

In contradistinction to the relatively pluralist character of the public sphere and the political domain in Turkey, the threat or use of armed action and violent methods have been more characteristic and effective political strategies in Iraqi Kurdistan, as have ties of patronage and tribal links. Iraq has witnessed the reproduction and strengthening of patronage mechanisms, especially in the face of the radical retreat of the state welfare system from the late 1980s onwards. Almost all Kurdish parties in Iraq tend, or are tempted to monopolize public debate, or at least to co-opt possible sources of dissent. This seems to be a heritage from the Leninist tradition that identifies party and state, which also informs Ba'ath political practice, but does not originate with it. Moreover, it seems that in Iraq, Islamist networks are personalized rather than purely doctrinal; ideological differences, like those over the Gulf war or the attitude towards the United States, may not be wholly irrelevant, but they do seem of secondary importance.

Turkey has a very diversified and largely privatized public sphere, within which all kinds of debates and rivalries are acted out by non-violent means. It also has its own autonomous Islamist networks, which are largely unrelated to those of the Muslim Brotherhood. There have been and are some contacts between the different Islamic groups. Afghanistan was one cause that united Sunni Muslim activists; more recently, Chechnya has been another. But these isolated and largely symbolic causes do not allow us to speak of a unified Sunni internationalist movement: the apparent lack of any substantial contacts between Kurdish Islamists in Iraq and Turkey is a case in point. For the most part, the Islamist organizations work within a national framework, and acquire many of the traits that other parties in their respective countries have. They may even have a strongly local character, witness the Islamic Movement of Iraqi Kurdistan, which, following its earlier successes in the entire region, appears to have fallen back on its traditional stronghold, the Halabja area.

Notes

1. There are some studies, however, of the complex interaction between nationalist and religious factors, especially M. van Bruinessen, *Agha, Sheikh, and State: The social and political structures of Kurdistan* (London: Zed Press, 1992), chs 4, 5.
2. The most famous and detailed of these studies is, of course, van Bruinessen, *Agha, Sheikh, and State*, especially ch. 4.
3. P. Marr, *The Modern History of Iraq* (Boulder: Westview), p. 285.
4. cf. M. van Bruinessen, *Mollahs, Sufis, and Heretics: The role of religion in Kurdish*

society (Istanbul: Isis Press, 2000), p. 283.

5. See: R. Lescot, *Enquête sur les Yezidis de Syrie et du Djebel Sindjâr* (Damascus: Institut Français, 1938), p. 43; van Bruinessen, *Mollahs, Sufis, and Heretics*, pp. 249–250.

6. P. Awn, *Satan's Tragedy and Redemption: Iblis in Sufi psychology* (Leiden: Brill, 1983).

7. See: van Bruinessen, *Agha, Sheikh, and State*, ch. 5, pp. 143–158, for more details on the nationalist and religious dimensions of the Shaykh Said rebellion.

8. For more on the Directorate, see: D. Shankland, *Islam and Society in Turkey* (London: Eothen Press, 1999), pp. 28ff., who, incidentally, questions the budget claim.

9. cf. Shankland, ibid., pp. 209–214 for translations from Erbakan's 1994 pamphlet of the same title.

10. See: B. Duran, 'Approaching the Kurdish Question via Adil Düzen: An Islamist formula of the Welfare Party for ethnic co-existence', *Journal of Muslim Minority Affairs*, no. 18, pp. 111–128.

11. In fact, not only the electorate but also party personnel moved back and forth between the parties relatively freely. There are numerous Kurdish politicians at both the local and national levels who switched or switched back from the Islamist Refah to the pro-Kurdish HADEP (*Halkın Demokrasi Partisi*, 'People's Democracy Party') in the 1998 and 1999 elections.

12. In later years, PKK propaganda has shifted to a more accommodating multiculturalist discourse, which has emphasized the rich and colourful diversity of the Mesopotamian heritage.

13. See: M. Leezenberg, 'Kurdish Alevis and the Kurdish Nationalist Movement in the 1990s', in: P. J. White and J. Jongerden (eds), *Turkey's Alevi Enigma* (Leiden: Brill, 2003).

14. See: K. Vorhoff, 'Alevism, or Can Islam be Secular?', *Les Annales de l'autre Islam*, no. 6, pp. 135–151.

15. According to a 1995 report by the Netherlands Kurdistan Society, *Forced Evictions and Destruction of Villages in Dersim (Tunceli) and the Western Part of Bingöl*, the Turkish army conducted a concerted campaign of village destructions between September and November 1994, which led to the evacuation or destruction of about one third of the villages in Tunceli province.

16. Notably by M. van Bruinessen in his 2000 inaugural lecture, 'Muslims, Minorities, and Modernity: The transformation of heterodoxy in the Middle East and Southeast Asia', published in part in *ISIM Newsletter*, no. 7.

17. Dorronsoro and Cizre-Sakallioglu likewise emphasize the fact that, with the demise of the Sufi orders, religion has lost much of its salience as a catalyst or organizational channel for Kurdish ethnic or nationalist movements; G. Dorronsoro, 'L'Islam kurde dans le sud-est de la Turquie', *Les Annales de l'autre Islam*, no. 6, pp. 115–134; Ü. C.-Sakallioglu, 'Kurdish Nationalism from an Islamist Perspective: The discourses of Turkish Islamist writers', *Journal of Muslim Minority Affairs*, no. 18, pp. 73–90.

18. One should beware, however, of the still widely prevalent reductionist analyses of Iraqi society that perceive the ethnic cleavages between Sunnis and Shi'ites and between Kurds and Arabs as unambiguous, rigid and all-determining.

19. A relative of Zahawi, one Fadil Muhammad Salah Zahawi, appeared on top of the 1992 electoral list of the Islamic Movement, albeit as an independent candidate.

20. I owe much of what scant information I have on the development of political Sunni Islam in Iraq to interviews with anonymous Iraqi informants. See also: T. H. al-Azami, 'The Emergence of the Contemporary Islamic Revival in Iraq', pp. 123–141, and 'The Islamic Party and the Political Future of Iraq: An interview with Dr Osama

Takriti', pp. 155–164, both in *Middle East Affairs Journal*, no. 3, 1997; S. F. Karikar, 'A Comprehensive Analysis of the Kurdish Cause', *Nida' ul-Islam* (www.islam.org. au), September–October 1997.

21. See: al-Azami, 'The Emergence of the Contemporary Islamic Revival', pp. 134–135, 140 n. 46.

22. There are reports from MB sources, however, which mention repeated waves of mass arrest of Iraqi MB members.

23. See: T. H. al-Azami, 'The Islamic Party', p. 163.

24. Cf. M. Leezenberg, 'Irakisch-Kurdistan set dem zweiten Golfkrieg', pp. 49–50.

25. Such contestations of the Kakais' ethnic allegiance were also acted out in theological terms. Government sources argued that the Kakais, being descendants of the Shi'i and Arab Imam 'Ali, were by definition Arabs themselves. Kurdish nationalist religious specialists of the Kakais retorted that their leaders were reincarnations rather than direct descendants of Ali, and could thus very well be Kurds.

26. Cf. M. Leezenberg, 'Between Assimilation and Deportation: History of the Shabak and the Kakais in northern Iraq', in: B. Kellner-Heinkele et al. (eds), *Syncretistic Religious Communities in the Near East* (Leiden: Brill, 1997).

27. Thus, all the *ghulat* or heterodox Shi'i groups were suddenly claimed to be 'really' Turkish, as part of the – preposterous – claim that Iraq counted some 2.5 million Turkmen. Members of these groups were given food rations and financial assistance by Turkish welfare organizations on condition that they sign a declaration that they were Turkish. All of these measures were obviously part of a campaign to counter Kurdish nationalist claims to the region.

28. M. Leezenberg, 'Between Assimilation and Deportation'; cf. F. A. Jabar, 'Shaykhs and Ideologues: Detribalization and retribalization in Iraq, 1968–1998', *Middle East Report*, 2000, no. 215, pp. 28–31, for the general pattern of retribalization in Iraq in the 1990s.

29. It should be added that numerous European and American Christian charity organizations active in the region were equally engaged in proselytizing.

30. There are reasons to doubt the validity of such claims also for earlier periods. Thus, Batatu quotes figures from the 1947 census, which lists a total of 4,828 urban and 769 rural religious institutions; H. Batatu, 'Iraq's Underground Shi'a Movements: Characteristics, causes and prospects', *Middle East Journal*, no. 25, p. 582. Most urban institutions are in Shi'i territory, but the vast majority of the rural ones (714) appear to be in the Kurdish-inhabited area. The organized religiosity of the rural Kurds thus outstripped that of both Sunni and Shi'i rural Arabs.

31. The Rabita, much like the IMIK leadership, seems to be an offshoot of the Iraqi branch of the Muslim Brotherhood; its aims are similar to IMIK's, but it wants to reach these through education and welfare work rather than through violent tactics.

32. Cf. M. Leezenberg, 'Irakisch-Kurdistan seit dem zweiten Golgkrief', for a characterization of the political and social instability in the region up until early 1996.

33. I suspect that these assaults are an import of South Asian (perhaps Pakistani) origin, where throwing acid in enemies' (and especially women's) faces has become a sadly widespread practice; but I must admit I have insufficient knowledge about these matters.

34. Cf. al-Azami, 'The Islamic Party', p. 162.

35. See Document no. 7 in Middle East Watch's collection of Ba'ath documents captured in the 1991 uprising, *Bureaucracy of Repression* (1993)

36. For more details see: M. Leezenberg, 'Genocide and Responsibility: The chemical

attack against Halabja and the Iran–Iraq war', paper originally presented at the international conference Halabja 1998: 10. Jahrestag der Giftgas-Angriffe auf Kurdistan–Irak, Berlin, March 1998, in preparation.

37. Interestingly, the Jama'at al-Ulama also appears to have maintained close ties with the Baghdad regime, from which it received funds during the Iran–Iraq war, because of its strongly anti-Shi'i and thus anti-Iranian stance. See: M. Ahmad, 'The Politics of War: Islamic fundamentalism in Pakistan', in: J. Piscatori (ed.), *Islamic Fundamentalisms and the Gulf Crisis* (n.pl.: American Academy of Arts and Sciences, 1991), p. 168.

38. Thus, an IMIK spokesman expressed his disapproval of the establishment of a Shi'i Hussainiya in the staunchly Sunni city of Sulaimaniya, which his party perceived as a provocation by the PUK at the behest of Iran; but he said his party would not let itself be provoked into taking action against it.

39. Cf. B. Rubin, 'Arab Islamists in Afghanistan', in: J. L. Esposito (ed.), *Political Islam* (Boulder and London: Lynne Rienner, 1997); O. Roy, 'Sunnitische Internationale aus dem Niemandsland', *Le Monde diplomatique* (German edition), October 1998; G. Kepel, *Jihâd: Expansion et déclin de* l'Islamisme (Paris: Seuil, Kepel 2000.

40. It is not clear how far mullah Othman developed his views on *jihad* independently from these authors, as some IMIK spokesmen claim.

41. Cf. Kepel, *Jihâd*.

42. See: J. Piscatori (ed.), *Islamic Fundamentalisms*, for some early analyses.

43. A university was founded in Duhok in 1992, in which subsequently a Faculty of Theology, sponsored by Saudi Arabia, was opened. The Rabita is often alleged to mobilize especially among these theology students.

44. Amnesty International, *Iraq: Human Rights Abuses in Iraqi Kurdistan* (London: Amnesty International, 1995), Report MDE 14/01/95.

45. Interviews, Iraqi Kurdistan, August 1994.

46. Cf. G. Dorronsoro, 'Les Mouvements Islamistes au Kurdistan', *L'Etat du monde*, 1996, pp. 102–104; 'L'Islam kurde dans le sud-est de la Turquie', *Les Annales de l'autre Islam*, 1999, no. 6, pp. 129–131.

Note: An earlier version of this paper was drafted for publication in German in 2001; by a bizarre coincidence, it was actually submitted for publication on the morning of 11 September 2001. Since then, political Islam in Iraqi Kurdistan has become a focus of international journalistic attention, especially in the light of claims, never substantiated, that mullah Krekar's offshoot of IMIK, *jund al-islam* (later reorganized, and renamed *ansar al-islam*), provided the missing link between the Iraqi regime and the al-Qa'ida network; of Krekar's arrest in Holland and subsequent expulsion to Norway; and of course of the events surrounding the 2003 war in Iraq and ousting of Saddam's regime. It appears that as a result of these developments, political Islam – whether civic or more militant in character – is, at present, past its prime in Iraqi Kurdistan. Unfortunately, these developments could not be taken into account for the present paper.

PART FOUR

Post-conflict Iraq

Federalism and the Kurds of Iraq: The Solution or the Problem?

Michael M. Gunter

Introduction

An artificial state cobbled together by British imperialism following World War I,[1] Iraq may well prove to be a failed state. The interim constitution – known as the Transitional Administrative Law (TAL)[2] – promulgated on 8 March 2004 for a democratic federal Iraq proved only a temporary compromise given the majority Shi'ites' insistence on what they saw as their right to unfettered majority rule. Thus, United Nations Security Council Resolution 1546 of 8 June 2004, which authorized Iraq's new interim government, failed even to mention the TAL and federalism as a solution for the Iraqi Kurdish problem. Grand Ayatollah Ali al-Sistani, the de facto Shi'ite leader and spokesman, in general felt that the TAL should not tie the hands of the Iraqi parliament elected in January 2005 and specifically objected to Article 61(c) in the TAL, which gave the Kurds an effective veto[3] over the final constitution that was to be adopted later in 2005.

Many Arabs consider the Kurds traitors for having supported the United States in the 2003 war. On the other hand, many Kurds see the Arabs as chauvinistic nationalists who oppose Kurdish rights because they would end up detaching territory from the Arab patrimony. The only thing Nechirvan Idris Barzani, the prime minister of the Kurdistan Regional Government in Irbil, and Condoleezza Rice, the US National Security Adviser, could agree upon concerning federalism, when they met at the White House in October 2004, was that federalism did not mean separatism. The future of Iraq, moreover, has become even more uncertain given the virulent insurgency against the interim Iraqi government and its US ally. The purpose of this article is to analyse the Kurdish future in Iraq after the elections held on 30 January 2005.

Background

Into the first half of the 19th century, the traditional decentralized Ottoman state and millet system of religious communities in effect offered the various nations of the Ottoman Empire autonomy.[4] Some might see this millet system as a type of indigenous embryonic federalism. Beginning in the 1830s, however, the Ottoman Empire began to centralize in an attempt to modernize itself and stave off the Western onslaught.[5] This process of centralization eliminated the autonomy long enjoyed by the Kurdish emirates.[6]

Following World War I, modernization policies continued with the demise of the Ottoman Empire and the development of modern states in Turkey, Iran, Iraq[7] and Syria. The price to be paid for a modernized state, however, was a highly centralized government that sought to assimilate its minorities.[8] Such a vision of modernity had no place for a Kurdish identity. This process has been termed 'official nationalism': 'The leaders of the most powerful nations ... impose[d] their nationality on all their subjects –of whatever religion, language or culture ... As they saw it ... they were strengthening their state by creating within it a single homogeneous nation.'[9]

Indeed, in Iraq the Ba'athist state of Saddam Hussein eventually unleashed a genocidal assault on its Kurdish minority in the guise of its so-called Anfal campaign of chemical warfare and mass murder.[10] In Turkey, the Kurds were targeted to lose their identity as Mountains Turks in need of assimilation.[11] The modernization policies in Iran of Reza Shah Pahlavi and his son, Muhammad Reza Shah Pahlavi, ended the Kurdish tribes' nomadism and thus much of their identity.[12] Even more, the Ayatollah Ruhollah Khomeini's Islamic Revolution had no place for a separate Kurdish identity in its Islamic Republic.[13] Finally, in Syria, the government went so far as to deny some of its Kurdish population citizenship in its dictatorial modern state.[14]

Only Saddam Hussein's monumental miscalculation in bringing down upon himself the United States-led attack during the Gulf war in 1991 and the subsequent safe haven protected by a no-fly zone enabled a de facto Kurdish state to emerge in northern Iraq.[15] No one, however, recognized this state because it threatened to destabilize the existing regional state system.[16] Despite the relative prosperity it began to enjoy after 1997 from its 13 per cent of Iraq's renewed oil sales, the future of this de facto Kurdish state ironically depended upon Saddam Hussein's remaining in power. Once he was gone, it was unlikely the United States would continue to protect it from a post-Saddam Iraqi government.[17] Indeed, the United States and the regional states all insisted that Iraq's territorial integrity be protected. There would be no independent Kurdish state. Turkey even declared that any attempt to implement such a state would be a casus belli.

Faced with such harsh realities, the Iraqi Kurds turned to federalism as their best realistic hope in a post-Saddam Hussein Iraq. If some type of federalism were to work, however, the Iraqi Kurds and their fellow Iraqi Arab compatriots were going to have to learn how to implement what by definition would be a complicated and sophisticated division and sharing of powers between a central (national or federal) government and its regional (state or constituent) components. Moreover, the pluralism implicit in federalism would have to depend on a deeply imbued democratic ethos Iraqis lacked. Despite the democratic edifice they had built after 1991, for example, even the Iraqi Kurds had fallen into internecine conflict between 1994 and 1998. In the end, therefore, many Iraqi Arabs viewed federalism as simply another step towards the Kurdish independence they feared and would not accept.

Visionary future

Federalism was first seriously broached as a solution to the Kurdish problem in Iraq following the Gulf war in 1991. On 4 October 1992 the parliament of the de facto Kurdish state in northern Iraq declared Iraqi Kurdistan a constituent state in a federal Iraq. Both of the two main Iraqi Kurdish leaders endorsed the concept. Queried over the meaning of what had been declared, Masoud Barzani, the leader of the Kurdistan Democratic Party (KDP), declared that a federation 'is a more advanced concept than autonomy but is not outside the framework of Iraq'.[18] Jalal Talabani, the leader of the Patriotic Union of Kurdistan (PUK), elaborated: 'The federal state will be like the State of California in the United States'.[19] Iraqi opposition conferences at Vienna, Austria (16–19 June 1992) and Salah al-Din in northern Iraq (late October 1992) also adopted the principle of federalism as a solution for the Kurdish problem, but without implementing any specific constitutional formulas.[20]

Over the years Ba'athist Iraq had supposedly countenanced a wide range of attitudes toward the Iraqi Kurds' relationship with the rest of Iraq.[21] Yet even when the Ba'athists spoke about the Kurds as a nation (*qawm*) possessing national rights and aspirations, they were careful to declare that these rights were given to a people, not to the territory, because rights to the territory implied secession. In addition, these rights were given by proclamation (*bayan*), rather than agreement (*ittifaq*). This choice of terms meant that the Ba'athist state was the sole sovereign power unilaterally awarding certain privileges to the Kurds and thus, of course, could withdraw them at any time.

Finally, the designation Kurdistan (usually employed by the Kurds when referring to their geographical homeland) was seldom used by the Ba'athists. Instead, the Ba'athists used such terms as region, zone, northern region, our north or the autonomous area. For their part, the Kurds have strongly objected to the concept that Iraq is part of a pan-Arab union because this would reduce them to an obscure minority. According to the Kurds, the proper way to visualize Iraq would be as a state consisting of two parts, Iraqi Kurdistan and Arab Iraq. Only the latter would be part of the Arab union or homeland.

As Dr Barham Salih, the prime minister of the Kurdistan Regional Government in Sulaimaniya and subsequently the deputy prime minister of the interim Iraqi government, explained in reference to the accomplishments made by the Kurds over the past decade: 'These achievements should be celebrated as a model for the rest of Iraq. Indeed, we Kurds are willing to give up our dreams of an independent Kurdistan in order to bring our expertise in governing to a new democratic Iraq.'[22] To further explore the Kurdish future in Iraq after the January 2005 elections, this article will next analyse the draft constitutions prepared by the Iraqi Kurds in 2002 for the Iraqi Kurdistan Region and the Federal Republic of Iraq. These draft constitutions reveal what for the Kurds are their optimal desiderata.

Draft Constitution[23]

Preamble

The draft 'Constitution of the Iraqi Kurdistan Region' opens with a preamble that attempts to justify what the Kurds seek to accomplish: 'The Kurds are an ancient people who have lived in their homeland of Kurdistan for thousands of years, a nation with all the attributes that entitle it to practise the right of self-determination similar to other nations and peoples of the world.' United States President Woodrow Wilson's Fourteen Points issued during World War I, the relevant provisions of the Treaty of Sèvres in 1920 and British promises that 'officials of Kurdish origin should be appointed to the administration of their own land and that Kurdish should be the language of education, the courts and for all services rendered' are also mentioned. Nevertheless, 'Southern [Iraqi] Kurdistan was annexed in 1925 to the newly created state of Iraq.'

The preamble continues by noting that when Iraq was admitted to the League of Nations, it made a statement on 30 May 1932 that 'includes a number of international obligations and sets out guarantees for the rights of the Kurds that Iraq is not allowed to amend or abolish ... These obligations have been transferred to the United Nations Organization and are still in effect to this day.' The preamble also mentions the interim constitution for the Republic of Iraq issued in 1958 which 'stated in Article 3 that Arabs and Kurds are partners in the Iraqi state', as well as the agreement reached on 11 March 1970 between the Kurds and the Iraqi government that 'recognized autonomy for the people of Kurdistan within the Iraqi Kurdistan Region'.

Having listed these constitutional and legal precedents, the preamble concludes that, 'in spite of this, successive Iraqi governments have turned their backs on these obligations to the Kurds and instead have practised a racist and chauvinistic policy of ethnic cleansing and destruction by all political and military means.' The Anfal campaign, Halabja and the Fayli Kurds, among others, are specifically mentioned.[24]

The preamble then goes on to detail United Nations Security Council Resolution 688 of 5 April 1991, which established the Safe Haven for the Kurds and gave the Kurds the 'opportunity to elect their first parliament on 19 May 1992 and to establish the Kurdistan Regional Government'. The Kurdish parliament then chose 'the federalism formula ... as an ideal solution for the ethnically pluralistic Iraqi society that would safeguard its unity and would ... satisfy the legitimate aspirations of the people of Iraqi Kurdistan as this formula will guarantee their participation in the making of decisions while protecting the integrity and unity of Iraq.' Finally, the preamble also broaches the necessity for 'sufficient international guarantees' for the proposed draft constitution 'so that all sides to the agreement will abide by it and respect its terms'.

General matters

The draft constitutions for the Iraqi Kurdistan Region and the Federal Republic of Iraq would set up a form of federalism in which the Kurds and Arabs each establish their own regional governments and then delegate specific limited powers to a central government. The Kurdistan Regional

Government would have its own elected assembly and president, write its own laws, control the budget for the region, raise taxes, have its own police and defence forces, run the region's schools and universities, own the region's natural resources and receive a proportionate share of Iraq's vast oil wealth. The Federal Republic of Iraq would control foreign affairs, collect customs duties and issue a currency.

The draft constitution foresees 'a multiparty, democratic, parliamentarian, republican political system' for the Kurdistan Region, which would consist 'of the provinces of Kirkuk, Sulaimaniya and Erbil in their administrative boundaries prior to 1970 and the province of Duhok along with the districts of Aqra, Sheikhan, Sinjar and the sub-district of Zimar in the province of Ninevah, the district of Khaniqin and Mandali in the province of Diyala, and the district of Badra in the province of Al-Wasit'. The region's people would 'consist of the Kurds and the national minorities of Turkmen, Assyrians, Chaldeans and Arabs', while Kirkuk[25] would be the capital of the Kurdistan Region. 'Kurdish shall be the official language' and 'official correspondence with the federal and regional authorities shall be in both Arabic and Kurdish'. It would be 'compulsory' to teach Arabic in the region, while 'Turkmen shall be considered the language of education ... for the Turkmen ... [and] Syriac shall be the language of education and culture for those who speak it in addition to the Kurdish language'.

Basic rights

An entire part or section of the draft constitution guarantees that 'citizens of the Kurdistan Region are equal before the law in their rights and responsibilities without discrimination due to race, colour, sex, language, ethnic origin, religion or economic status'. In addition, 'women shall have equal rights with men'. Another specific article guarantees 'freedom of expression, publication, printing, press, assembly, demonstration and forming of political parties, unions and associations'. In addition, 'freedom of religion ... is guaranteed'.

This part of the draft constitution also declares that 'all types of torture, physical or psychological, are prohibited'. In addition, 'the privacy of postal, cable and telephone communications is guaranteed' and similarly 'the right of ownership'. Finally, the draft speaks to the rights of education, work, social security benefits, public health and political refugees.

Governmental institutions

Part III of the draft constitution would establish a regional assembly,[26] president[27] and judiciary. The assembly would be 'elected through direct secret, general ballot' and 'fair representation of national minorities shall be observed'. Parliament's term would run for five years or less if it 'does not give a vote of confidence to the Council of Ministers in three successive votes'.

The draft constitution states that 'the President of the Kurdistan Region ... is the highest executive authority and ... represents the President of the Federal Republic of Iraq in the region and substitutes for him/her on state occasions and coordinates between the federal and regional authorities'. The president 'is elected by direct, secret, general ballot by the people of the region' in a manner that 'shall be regulated by law' for a term of 'five years'. If the office of the president falls vacant, 'the President of the Kurdistan Regional Assembly shall assume responsibilities of the President until such time as a new President is elected'.

In addition to the president, 'the Kurdistan Region Council of Ministers is the highest executive and administrative authority in the region; it carries out its executive responsibilities under the supervision and guidance of the Kurdistan Regional President'. The Council of Ministers or Cabinet is to consist of the prime minister and no more than 15 ministers. While the prime minister must be a member of the Regional Assembly, his ministers may be members or need only 'meet the necessary qualifications for membership in the Assembly'. The Cabinet shall include 'representation of the national minorities, Turkmen, Assyrians and Chaldeans' and meet with the approval of both the president and assembly.

The draft constitution also speaks of 'the region's court system in all its levels' as being 'independent with no power above it except the law itself'. It is to possess 'general jurisdiction over all public and private entities and individuals except those stipulated in a law'. This exception pertains to 'the non-Muslim communities [which] have the right to establish religious, "spiritual", legal bodies in accordance with a special law'. In a manner suggestive of the former Ottoman millet system, 'these bodies shall have the right to look into all personal matters of citizens belonging to those communities, matters which are not included in the competence and responsibility of the "Muslim" religious courts.'

Administrative and fiscal

Part IV of the draft constitution provides for various local governmental institutions, while Part V deals with fiscal matters. The regional government 'can levy and collect taxes and duties within the region', but 'export and import duties (customs) are the responsibility of the federal authority'. Special attention should be given to the provision that the 'Kurdistan Region's share of natural resources, in particular, oil, and revenue from the sale of its products in and outside the country, as well as grants, aid [and] foreign loans made to the Federal Republic of Iraq [shall be] in a proportion based on the relation of the region's population to the total population of Iraq.'

Ultimate matters

Disputes among the Kurdistan regional authorities over the interpretation of the draft constitution 'shall be referred to the Cassation Court of the Kurdistan Region'. The Federal Constitutional Court shall adjudicate constitutional conflicts that might arise between the Kurdistan region and the Arab region or the Federal Republic of Iraq. Finally, given the past Kurdish history of unfilled rights, the draft constitution declares near its end that if it is 'changed without the consent of the Kurdistan Regional Assembly ... this shall afford the people of the Kurdistan Region the right of self-determination'. This, of course, means the right to become an independent state.

Draft Constitution of the Federal Republic Of Iraq[28]

Preamble

The preamble of the draft constitution of the Federal Republic of Iraq declares in its opening section that Iraq 'has not enjoyed peace and security' because it has been 'characterized by a high degree of centralization'. This centralization and 'the indifference of decision makers ... are the basic reasons for the Kurds being deprived of their legitimate rights under the successive Iraqi governments'. Federalism 'would be more consistent with the pluralist nature of the Iraqi community made up of the two primary nationalities, Arabs and Kurds, in addition to other national minorities present among the population ... and is a suitable basis for solving the Kurdish problem in Iraq.' In addition, federalism 'affords the Kurdish people the enjoyment of their legitimate national rights and internal independence within the region of Kurdistan and within the framework of a single Iraqi state and without disrupting the unity of that state.'

The preamble also mentions the necessity of 'giving women their full rights

... of their equality with men under the law, ... national religious tolerance, ... and human rights ... in accordance with the provisions of the Universal Declaration of Human Rights and other related international treaties and conventions'.[29] Finally, the new Iraqi state is to be 'founded on a democratic, parliamentarian, federal system'.

Basic rights

Many democratic guarantees of the proposed draft constitution of the Federal Republic of Iraq are virtually verbatim repetitions of the draft constitution for the Iraqi Kurdistan Region cited above and therefore need not be repeated here.

The Federal Republic of Iraq will consist of two territorial regions that are constitutionally defined: an Arabic region and a Kurdish region. 'Power is inherent in the people as they are the source of its legitimacy.' The draft constitution establishes Baghdad as the capital, declares that Iraq 'shall have a flag, an emblem and a national anthem that shall reflect the union between the Kurds and the Arabs', states that 'the state religion is Islam', and that 'Arabic is the official language of the federal state and the Arab region. Kurdish shall be the official language of the Kurdistan Region'. The draft also specifically declares that 'citizens are equal under the law without discrimination due to sex, race, colour, language, religion or ethnic origin'.

Institutions

The federal parliament will consist of two chambers: the National Assembly (Chamber of Deputies) and the Assembly of the Regions. Although not specifically detailed, it would seem that the National Assembly would represent the people of Iraq according to their population, while the Assembly of the Regions would represent the two regions on an equal basis despite the differences in population. It also should be noted that each chamber 'participates on an equal footing' with the other. The federal parliament would serve a five-year term, and no individual could hold a position in more than one federal, regional or local legislative body at the same time.

The President of the Federal Republic of Iraq would 'be elected through direct ballot for a period of five years and may stand for re-election once'. In an attempt to ensure an ethnic balance between the two regions, the draft constitution provides that the President and the Prime Minister must be from different regions. Furthermore, the Council of Ministers (Cabinet) 'shall represent both regions in proportion to the regions' populations'.

The membership of the High (Constitutional) Court shall be evenly divided between members from each region. It shall have the duty of interpreting the federal constitution, conflicts over its meaning between the federal and regional levels and conflicts between the regions.

Responsibilities

The draft constitution specifically declares that the federal government shall assume the following responsibilities: declaring war and concluding peace; setting out foreign policy and diplomatic and consular representations; concluding international treaties and agreements; defending the country; issuing currency and planning monetary and banking policy; defining standards for weights and measures and designating salary policy; drafting general economic planning aimed at development in the regions in the areas of industry, commerce and agriculture; ordering federal general audits; overseeing federal security affairs; and concerning itself with citizenship, residency and foreigners' affairs, oil resources and nuclear power.

The draft constitution also specifically states that 'each region shall have a share of the revenues from the oil wealth, grants and foreign aid and loans in proportion to its population in relation to that of the total population of the country'. In addition, each region shall have the authority to levy taxes on income, inheritance, agricultural land and property taxes, property registration fees, court fees, licence fees and water and electricity charges.

Ultimate matters

The final part of the federal draft constitution seeks to guarantee the rights and powers of the Kurds and the Kurdistan Region. 'Citizens of the Kurdistan Region shall be appointed to the various positions in the federal ministries and other bodies both inside and outside the country and in particular in the deputy minister, director general or other high-level positions according to the ratio of the regional population to the total population of the Federal Republic of Iraq.' This proportionality principle applies even to student fellowships and student admissions to all schools both inside and outside the country.

Another specific article seeks to 'redress the effects of Arabization and deportations that took place in some parts of the Kurdistan Region' in such areas as Kirkuk and several other places. Kurds 'should return to their previous homes in those areas', while 'the Arab citizens who were brought by the authorities into those areas at any time since 1957 should return to their original homes'. In addition, Kurdish '*peshmerga* forces and their various divisions shall constitute a part of the Armed Forces of the Federal Republic of Iraq.'

The federal draft guarantees that the borders of the Kurdistan Region cannot be altered 'except with the approval of the Assembly of the region concerned'. The Kurds are given a veto over amendments to the federal constitution by the provision that 'the terms of this [Federal] Constitution cannot be amended unless through a two-thirds majority vote by members of both the Federal and Regional Assemblies'. Another article of the draft constitution declares that the new Federal Republic of Iraq 'shall be accountable to the United Nations Organization for guaranteeing the rights, the boundaries and powers of the two regions designated in this Constitution and the Regional Constitutions'.

Mirroring the draft constitution of the Kurdistan Region, the federal draft ends by granting the Kurds 'the right of self-determination' if either the regional or federal constitutions is unconstitutionally altered. This final provision clearly implies the right of the Kurds to become independent. Yet as Dr Barham Salih, the prime minister of the Kurdistan Regional Government in Sulaimaniya, concluded: 'We Kurds are championing a federal, pluralist democratic Iraq that cannot again brutalize its citizens and threaten its neighbours. The final irony may be that the Kurds, the perennial victims of the Iraqi state, will turn out to be its saviour.'[30]

Theoretical Analysis of Federalism

At this point it would seem appropriate to analyse the theoretical possibilities federalism entails. By way of general definition, federalism is a form of government in which power is divided and shared between the central (national or federal) government and the constituent (state or regional) governments. Individuals are citizens of both the central and constituent governments, and they elect at least some parts of both governments. A federal form of government is covenantal. This means that the authority of each level of government – central and constituent – derives from the constitution, not from the other level of government. Thus, neither level of government can take away the powers of the other. As such, federalism would most likely require a written constitution that upholds the constitutional rights of each level of government and provides a means of adjudicating differences between them. Federal forms of government also normally entail a bicameral legislature consisting of one chamber representing the people according to their population and the other chamber representing the constituent parts of the federal system. Given the sharing of power that federalism entails, implicit in a true federal system is democracy or at least some form of pluralism.[31]

There are many different variations of federalism. Some are majoritarian in the sense that they do not constrain the overall majority living throughout the entire country. Such federal systems would also tend to be mono-national in the sense that they seek to impose one single national standard upon the entire population of the country. Despite recent lip-service to ethnic diversity, for example, the United States federal system was clearly established on a national, not a multinational basis because of the relatively homogeneous character of its original population (minus, of course, the African slaves and Native Americans). Indeed, as the United States expanded from its original largely homogeneous 13 colonies, no new states were added until their original populations were outnumbered by WASPs (White Anglo-Saxon Protestants). As noted by Nathan Glazer, this is the reason that the US federal system manifests 'little coincidence between ethnic groups and state boundaries'.[32]

Just because one particular model might work well in, say, the United States, Belgium, Canada or Germany does not necessarily mean that it would also work well in Iraq. Each individual state must find the particular form that suits its own unique characteristics best. As a national minority within Iraq, clearly the Iraqi Kurds would not want to establish a majoritarian, mono-national federal system within Iraq. This is because the Arab or Shi'ite majority, if it so chose, then would be in a position to threaten the Kurdish political, cultural, linguistic and/or economic identities.

A federal form of government can blunt majoritarian effects, however, by institutionalizing power-sharing arrangements in the central levels of government and incorporating separation of powers, bills of rights and courts, etc., that are insulated from the immediate power of an overall majority in the entire central state. The United States, Australia and Canada, for example, allow equal representation to each of their constituent parts in their Senate, resulting in such large constituent parts as California, New South Wales and Ontario and such small ones as Rhode Island, Tasmania and Prince Edward Island, each having the same representation in most basic respects.

Federal systems also differ in how they distribute powers within the central government. The US Senate, for example, is arguably the more powerful chamber in the national bicameral legislature, while the upper chambers in

Belgium, Canada and India are much weaker. Some federal systems like that of the United States elect their executives separately, while others elect their executives in the lower house of their legislature. There are also single-person and plural executives.

Federal forms of government further differ in how powers are divided between the central and constituent governments. In the United States, for example, the central government possesses the delegated powers listed in the constitution, while the states have the reserved powers not specifically denied them by the constitution.[33] In Canada, on the other hand, it is the opposite. The provincial governments possess the delegated powers, while the central government in Ottawa has the reserved powers. In the German federal system, the *Länder* (constituent) governments enjoy considerable administrative powers independent of the central government, particularly as to the raising of revenue.

Given the central government's repressive track record in Iraq, it would be to the Kurds' advantage, of course, to establish a central Iraqi government with precise, limited powers, while constitutionally guaranteeing themselves a maximum amount of public policy making on the constituent level of government. Despite their historic position of power in Iraq, the Arab Sunnis presumably would now favour federal arrangements similar to those preferred by the Kurds. For their part, of course, the Shi'ites presumably would now favour a central government with strong and widely based powers, while seeking to constrain the prerogatives of the constituent governments.

However, Adeed Dawisha and Karen Dawisha have argued that the new Iraqi federation should be built around the pre-existing 18 governorates of Baathist Iraq.[34] Donald L. Horowitz maintains that such an arrangement would tend to dilute the strength of any one ethnic group by creating constituent governments that would encourage inter-ethnic cooperation.[35] Such an arrangement, of course, would be certain to be opposed by the Iraqi Kurds, who would see their very national existence diluted by it. Rather, the Iraqi Kurds would seemingly seek some form of ethnic or multinational federalism, which would allow them to pursue their ethnic identity.

Unfortunately, Iraq's influential neighbour, Turkey, fears the demonstration effect on its own restless Kurds of any Kurdish entity on the Turkish border. Indeed, General Ilker Basbug, Turkey's deputy chief of staff, declared that 'if there is a federal structure in Iraq on an ethnic basis, the future will be very difficult and bloody'.[36] Turkish Prime Minister Recep Tayyip Erdogan accused the Iraqi Kurds of 'playing with fire'[37] by trying to annex the oil-rich Kirkuk area to their prospective federal state. Turkish opposition to ethnic or multinational federalism in Iraq reflects its long-standing security fears that any decentralization there – especially in favour of the Kurds – will inevitably encourage the Kurds in Turkey to seek autonomy and eventually separation. Thus, in the name of stability, Turkey remains an inveterate opponent of an ethnically based or multinational federal system in post-Saddam Hussein Iraq.

The most Turkey seems willing to grant is some type of geographic federalism based on a variation of that proposed by the Dawishas above. Such an arrangement would tend to dilute Kurdish ethnic strength and its perceived challenge to Turkey. Turkey also has argued that geographic federalism would dampen ethnic animosities that might be aroused by ethnic federalism by encouraging multi-ethnic and multi-sectarian civic nationalism.[38] Some, of course, have noted the inconsistencies of this Turkish aversion to ethnic federalism in Iraq with Turkey's demand for ethnic-based federalism in Cyprus. When the present author brought this inconsistency up at a scholarly conference held at the Eastern Mediterranean University in northern (Turkish) Cyprus in April 2003, he was sharply informed by his Turkish interlocutors that there was no inconsistency. This was because the Turkish position in Cyprus had been guaranteed by the international treaty that had originally established a bi-national Cypriot state in 1960. No such treaty, of course, existed on behalf of the Iraqi Kurds.

Based on the above, it is clear that the mono-national US federal system would not be to the advantage of the Iraqi Kurds. Instead, the Iraqi Kurds would be favoured by a multinational or ethnic federal system that ideally would seek 'to unite people who seek the advantages of a common political unit, but differ markedly in descent, language and culture'.[39] A multinational federal system rejects the integrationist and assimilationist goals of a national federal system in favour of promoting the existence of two or more separate nations. Advocates of multinational federalism maintain that it is possible for the people living in such federations to possess dual loyalties, one to the overall central government and the other to the constituent government. Further, they see no reason why ethnically based constituent states in a multinational federation could not protect the rights, say, of such minorities as the Turkmen, Assyrians or Yezidis in a putative Kurdistani constituent state that was part of a federal Iraq.

Scholars have advocated multinational federations both as a means to hold nations together as well as to maintain the territorial autonomy of historic national minorities such as the Kurds.[40] Switzerland and Canada, currently two of the world's longest-lasting states, are examples of contemporary functioning multinational federations. In recent years, however, other multinational federations have either disintegrated or failed to protect democratic rights. The Soviet Union, Yugoslavia, Czechoslovakia and Eritrea's secession from Ethiopia are prime examples.[41] In the Arab world, even the mono-national United Arab Republic uniting Egypt and Syria lasted only from 1958 to 1961, while the United Arab Emirates is clearly a mono-national federation and also not a democracy.

Federacy

Although the Kurds seek to enter a multinational federal system in Iraq, they cannot impose such a federation upon unwilling partners. A federacy might be an imaginative solution to this problem. Under such a system, Iraqi Kurdistan could enter a federal arrangement with the central Iraqi government, while the rest of the country would *not* be federally organized. Federacy might satisfy the Kurds' desire for federalism while accommodating the Arabs' wish to maintain elements of a unitary state if that is what they want.

Will federalism work?

The best-laid plans, of course, can fail to materialize. As Liam Anderson and Gareth Stansfield have noted, Iraq lacks a democratic tradition. For one to develop requires the existence of an implicit consensus on the legitimacy of the underlying order and trust on the part of the minority that the majority will not abuse its power. These, however, are the very ingredients that have 'mostly been in pitifully short supply' in modern Iraq.[42] Moreover, as already noted, federalism is a sophisticated division and sharing of powers between a central government and its constituent parts that would probably demand, as a prerequisite for its successful implementation, a democratic ethos. Trying to establish federalism in Iraq before that state is able to imbue a democratic tradition may be placing the cart before the horse.

Advocates of a federal solution for the Kurds of post-Saddam Hussein Iraq might draw at least five lessons from recent multinational federations that have failed.[43] 1) *Coercion.* These federal systems were coerced arrangements, not voluntary agreements. The former Soviet Union is a prime example. 2) *Authoritarianism.* These federal systems lacked a democratic tradition and when one was suddenly foisted upon them, it simply created the opportunity for secession to occur. The breakup of the former Yugoslavia is an example. 3) *Maltreatment of smaller nations*. These federal systems were not able to solve problems between the historically dominant nation and the smaller one. The Malays and the Chinese in Malaysia may be an example of this problem. 4) *Economic distributive conflicts*. These federal systems failed to construct or continue economic distributive mechanisms promoting economic policy, taxation, revenue sharing and public expenditures, which were regarded as fair by all the concerned nations. Czechoslovakia is an example. 5) *Centralizing coups*. Authoritarian attempts to centralize the federal systems led to their breakdown. The Serbs in former Yugoslavia are an example of this pattern.

The implications of these lessons of failure for a successful multinational federation in post-Saddam Hussein Iraq are obvious. 1) A successful Iraqi federation must be a voluntary arrangement, not one regarded as being imposed by the United States or some other outside power. Thus, the federation must be ratified by its various constituent parts. For the Kurds, this must mean a free referendum within Kurdistan. The fact that unofficial but democratically held referenda in February 2004 and again in January 2005 almost unanimously opted instead for independence illustrates the inherent difficulties federalism faces among the Kurds, not to mention the Arabs, many of whom resent what they see as any challenge to their territorial patrimony. 2) A federal Iraq must be democratic with the full panoply of liberal democratic rights and institutions so egregiously lacking in Iraq's history. 3) Positive constructive relations based on mutual trust and recognition must be built among the Kurds, Sunni Arabs and Shi'ite Arabs, as well as the smaller minorities of Turkmen, Christians and others. Although developments within the Kurdish region since 1991 offer some encouragement for implementing this requirement, even here the intra-Kurdish warfare that occurred between 1994 and 1998, not to mention the long history of hostile relationships with the rest of Iraq, offer strong doubts. 4) Although oil and water resources as well as educational traditions would seem to offer some hope regarding economic distributive possibilities, much new ground will have to be developed before one might reasonably hope for success on this score too. 5) There must be strong constitutional guarantees with accepted judicial conflict settlement procedures to prevent efforts to sabotage the federal arrangement in favour of an authoritarian centralization. In the end, therefore, there must be an accepted default mechanism that would allow the Kurdistan constituent region to opt for independence if its constitutional status in a federal Iraq is challenged. Some type of international protection through a treaty sanctioned by the United Nations with United States support would probably be highly important on this score. Given the failure of attempts to guarantee Kurdish rights in Iraq via international pacts in the past, such legal devices remain problematic.

Reasons for the success of such multinational federal systems as Belgium, Canada, India and Switzerland might also hold lessons for those seeking to implement a federal system for the Iraq.

1) Multinational federal systems sometimes succeed thanks to the presence of one large nation that has the power to prevent secession but feels secure enough to countenance the rights of smaller nations within the federation. The historically oppressed Shi'ites, however, have no experience that encourages one to believe they might be able to assume this role of a protective majority nation. On the other hand, the now embattled former ruling, but numerically minority Sunnis are also unlikely to be in the generous mood required by this scenario.

2) Lacking such a compassionate unifying nation, multinational federal systems should possess cross-national, power-sharing practices in the central government. Such consociational practices would present alternatives to smaller nations that otherwise might choose secession. Whether the brief power-sharing experiences the post-Saddam Hussein Iraqi Governing Council and its successor Iraqi Interim Government provided are apropos here remain to be seen.

3) Non-interventionist neighbours on the international borders of the multinational federal system are also necessary. Otherwise, such neighbours would disrupt the successful operation of the federation. This means, of course, that Turkey, Iran, Syria and Saudi Arabia must learn to accept a federal Iraq. So far, this route has not been taken, because Iraq's neighbours view a federal Iraq as a destabilizing influence in their region. Indeed, the institutionalization of de facto statehood in the Kurdistan Regional Government since 1992 and even more since the fall of Saddam Hussein has inspired Kurds in Iraq's neighbours to demand greater rights for themselves. Previously unheard-of Kurdish unrest in Syria in the spring of 2004 is a good example of this situation. For such very reasons, Turkey has viscerally opposed the concept of a Kurdish federal state, going so far as to declare that it would be a casus belli.

Turkey's decision not to join the United States in the 2003 war to remove Saddam Hussein, however, allowed the Iraqi Kurds, as the sole ally of the United States on the northern front, to strengthen their position. As a result, Turkey has had no other choice but to accept very grudgingly this development. Indeed, continuing instability in post-Saddam Hussein Iraq in time may lead Turkey to see a multinational federal Iraq or even an independent Iraqi Kurdistan as the best possible stabilizing influence. For Turkey to support a federal or even independent Iraqi Kurdistan, however, other alternatives must first prove to be totally unacceptable. If they become so, then Turkey – for the sake of its own best interests of existing in a stable region – may come to accept and even defend a federal Iraq or, if this proves impossible, an independent Iraqi Kurdistan.

4) Once again it must be emphasized that an authentic multinational federal system must be democratic. Democracy would allow the representatives of the various constituent parts of the federal system to engage in dialogue and bargaining that would facilitate political and constitutional cooperation. A genuine democratic ethos would protect individual and collective rights and thus inhibit actions against national minorities. Such a situation in turn would encourage inter-ethnic and/or inter-religious cooperation. Again, however, given Iraq's historic lack of a democratic tradition, its institutionalization now would seem at best difficult.

5) In considering the possibilities of federalism for the Iraqi Kurds, Kurdish divisions, most noticeably between the Kurdistan Democratic Party (KDP) and Patriotic Union of Kurdistan (PUK), have up to now been glossed over with the easy assumption that the two will somehow end their long struggle against each other and join forces to create a Kurdistan federal state. A close study of history and the current situation, however, might quickly disabuse one of such notions. Indeed, their inveterate competition and disunity spilled over into a bloody civil war during the mid-1990s and many underlying divisions still remain. Serendipitously, 'the divided system which emerged in the summer of 1996 allowed the KDP and PUK to govern the region without the problems of internal competition, and without antagonising the neighbours'.[44] Might some type of federalism that gave separate institutional recognition to these two separate Kurdish statelets within an independent Kurdistan be the ironic answer to their disunity?

Elections

A number of other problems face a prospective Kurdish federal state. As noted above, unofficial referenda held in February 2004 and again in Jaunuary 2005 almost unanimously called for independence[45] despite the opposition of the KDP and PUK leaders, who argued that independence would not be practical. In maintaining this position, Masoud Barzani and Jalal Talabani run the risk of losing control of the Kurdish 'street' and thus their long-term grip on power. Indeed, in October 2004, an internal party conclave apparently obliged Talabani to share more of his authority within the PUK, following a dispute between him and the next two senior PUK leaders (Kosrat Rasoul and Nechirvan Mustafa Amin) over their position in Baghdad when dealing with the United States. As for the KDP, Nechirvan Idris Barzani, the nephew of the KDP leader Masoud Barzani, has clearly emerged as his heir apparent. Given the volatility of events, whether these two mainline parties and leaders can continue to maintain their position remains to be seen.

In an effort to maintain their control of events, the KDP and PUK joined 15 other smaller Kurdish groups to form a single list of candidates for the seats to be chosen both in the Iraqi national and Kurdish regional elections held on 30 January 2005. The two main Kurdish parties argued that such a single list would avoid splintering the potential Kurdish strength at a time when no Arab electoral group offered to support Kurdish demands. What was not as readily admitted, however, was that such a single list would be most likely to guarantee continuing KDP and PUK dominance of Kurdish politics because those chosen for the two parliaments would be the KDP and PUK candidates listed highest on the single all-Kurdish list.

In the immediate aftermath of the national elections held on 30 January 2005 for an interim parliament that would choose a new interim government and write a new constitution for Iraq, 'the Kurds seemed to hold the balance of power'.[46] To form the necessary two-thirds majority coalition government, the religiously sanctioned Shi'ite coalition approved by Grand Ayatollah Ali al-Sistani and known as the United Iraqi Alliance would most likely have to accept the Kurdish demands for strong Kurdish rights in a democratic federal Iraq. These demands included the so-called Kurdish veto over approving or amending any future Iraqi constitution that would establish a democratic federal Iraq; a Kurd (probably Talabani) to be chosen interim president of Iraq; a limited role for Islam; the rights of women; no Arab troops in Kurdistan; and Kirkuk. The Kurds also decided that Barzani would become president of the unified Kurdistan Regional Government. If these demands were not accepted, the Kurds could simply maintain their de facto independence. On paper, it seemed a win/win situation. Only time, of course, would tell if this strong theoretical position could be maintained in practice.

Kirkuk

Kirkuk is situated along the line where the Kurdish and Arab populations of Iraq meet. It also possesses enormous oil reserves. Thus, the Iraqi government and the Kurds have never been able to agree on whether or not it should be included in a Kurdish autonomous region. The uncompromising position Barzani and Talabani seem to be taking on Kirkuk as part of Kurdistan is probably at least in part a result of their fear of losing control of the Kurdish 'street', which considers Kirkuk to be the Kurdish 'Jerusalem'.

Kirkuk voted against Faisal's becoming king of Iraq during the referendum of 1921. Turkey also claimed it until the League of Nations finally handed it over to Iraq, as part of the former Ottoman *vilayet* of Mosul, in 1926. Indeed, the 1957 census indicated that Kirkuk city (as distinguished from Kirkuk province or governorate) had a slightly larger Turkmen (39.8 per cent) than Kurdish (35.1 per cent) population. The Arabs (23.8 per cent) constituted only the third largest group. The 1957 census, however, also showed that Kirkuk province had a Kurdish majority of 55 per cent, while the Arabs numbered only 30.8 per cent and the Turkmen 14.2 per cent.[47]

During the 1960s and 1970s, Kirkuk was perhaps the most important point of disagreement between mullah Mustafa Barzani (Masoud Barzani's legendary late father) and the Iraqi government. Illustrating how strongly he felt about the issue, the elder Barzani reputedly declared that, even if a census showed that the Kurds were only a minority in Kirkuk, he would still claim it. Showing his ultimately poor judgment on the matter, Barzani also stated that he would allow the United States to exploit its rich oilfields if the United States would support him.[48] Thus, the Iraqi government had reason to believe that – given the Kurdish links to the United States, Israel and then pro-Western Iran – handing Kirkuk to the Kurds would, in effect, be giving it and its rich oil reserves back to the West.

Given its oil and geo-strategic location, Kirkuk's Kurdish majority was diluted over the decades by Saddam Hussein's Arabization policies, so that when Saddam Hussein fell from power in 2003, the city had roughly equal populations of Kurds, Arabs and Turkmen, as well as a considerable number of Christians. Indeed, the census that had been taken in 1977 even showed that Kirkuk province had an Arab plurality of 44.41 per cent, while the Kurds numbered 37.53 per cent and the Turkmen 16.31 per cent.[49] Saddam Hussein accomplished this demographic legerdemain by expelling and killing many Kurds, replacing them with Arab settlers and gerrymandering the province's boundaries. The Iraqi government even officially renamed Kirkuk as Tamim (Nationalization), supposedly in honour of the nationalization of the oilfields in 1972.

In a theoretical victory for the Kurdish position, Article 58 of the TAL declared that 'the Iraqi Transitional Government ... shall act expeditiously to take measures to remedy the injustice caused by the previous regime's practices in altering the demographic character of certain regions, including Kirkuk, by deporting and expelling individuals from their places of residence, forcing migration in and out of the region, settling individuals alien to the region, depriving the inhabitants of work and correcting nationality.' The TAL, however, was not able to settle on a time schedule to implement these decisions, speaking only of 'a reasonable period of time' and declaring that 'the permanent resolution of disputed territories, including Kirkuk, shall be deferred until ... a fair and transparent census has been conducted and the permanent constitution has been ratified'.

Although tens of thousands of Kurds have returned to Kirkuk and filed claims for homes and property lost when they were expelled, by the beginning of 2005 no claims had been settled. As for taking a census, the Kurds, of course, argue that one should be taken only *after* all the expelled Kurds have been allowed to return to Kirkuk and the Arab newcomers returned to their original homes. To summarily oust the new Arab population after it has lived in Kirkuk for some 30 years, however, would simply create new injustices. In addition, the Turkish military has suggested that it would take it only 18 hours to reach Kirkuk if the Kurds insisted on tampering with the city's population to their own benefit and to the detriment of the Turkmen.[50] In a stunning victory for the Kurds, the Independent Electoral Commission of Iraq authorized some 100,000 Kurds to return to Kirkuk and vote in the elections held on 30 January 2005. The result was a resounding Kurdish electoral victory in the Kirkuk municipal elections. On the cusp where most of Iraq's ethnic and sectarian divisions meet, Kirkuk is a microcosm of Iraq's ethnic and sectarian tensions and a likely place for a possible civil war to be ignited, especially given the failure of any group – including most noticeably the Kurds – to manifest a willingness to compromise on their maximal demands.

Tentative conclusion

Based on the above analysis, it would be very difficult for the Kurds to obtain the type of federalism that would satisfy their demands. Moreover, even if the Kurds were able to achieve some type of meaningful federalism in theory in the final version of the new constitution, Iraq's lack of a democratic culture would make actual federalism very difficult to implement.

Independence?

If, for any of the reasons analysed above, a federal Iraq proves impossible to construct, why not an independent Iraqi Kurdish state? What would be so sacred about the territorial integrity of a failed state like Iraq that was becoming increasingly unstable?[51] Indeed, within the past decade, both the Soviet Union and Yugoslavia broke up into numerous new states. Earlier, Singapore split off from Malaysia, Bangladesh from Pakistan and, more recently, Eritrea broke away from Ethiopia and East Timor from Indonesia. The United Nations also has in the past officially approved self-determination for the Palestinians[52] and black South African majority.[53]

Why do the Arabs so rightfully demand a state for the Palestinians, but so hypocritically deny one for the Iraqi Kurds? Why do the Turks demand self-determination for the Turkish Cypriots, but deny the same for the Iraqi Kurds? For the Kurds and their supporters, the current situation is neither fair nor logical. Indeed, a strong case can made that the injustice done to the Kurds contributes to the instability in the Middle East.

The Iraqi Kurds, however, would be well advised to proceed with the consent of the United States, Turkey and the other involved regional neighbours, because without their consent an independent Iraqi Kurdistan would prove impossible to sustain for obvious geopolitical reasons. The first step to achieve this seemingly impossible task is for the Iraqi Kurds to be seen giving their all in trying to make a democratic federal Iraq work. If such an Iraq proves impossible to achieve, the Iraqi Kurds then would be seen as having the right, in the name of stability that also would benefit the United States, Turkey and other neighbouring states, to move towards independence.

At that point, the Iraqi Kurds must convince these states that in return for their support for Iraqi Kurdish independence, an independent Iraqi Kurdistan would not foment rebellion among the Kurds in neighbouring states either directly or indirectly. These states' guarantee of an independent

Iraqi Kurdish state would be a powerful incentive for the Iraqi Kurds to satisfy them on this point. Furthermore, the Iraqi Kurds must proceed in a manner that their neighbours, including the Iraqi Arabs, would perceive to be fair to them. This will probably mean compromise on the Kurdish demand for oil-rich Kirkuk as the capital of Iraqi Kurdistan.

In addition, the Iraqi Kurds should encourage Turkey's grudging democratic reforms that will help lead to eventual Turkish membership of the European Union (EU) and thus help solve the Kurdish problem in Turkey without secession. If Turkey joins the EU, its fears about an independent Iraqi Kurdish state would most likely gradually abate, since EU membership would guarantee Turkish territorial integrity. Furthermore, once Turkey joins the EU, the influence of the Turkish military on political decisions regarding such issues as the Iraqi Kurds would diminish, a work already in progress as Turkey's EU candidacy proceeds. A more civilian-directed Turkish government within the EU would be less likely to fear an independent Iraqi Kurdish state.

On the other hand, if Turkey were kept out of the EU, Turkey would be more likely to continue to view the Kurdish issue in the context of traditional national security issues hostile to an independent Iraqi Kurdish state. Cast adrift from both the EU and the United States, Turkey would be more likely to seek succour from Syria and Iran, both of which remain hostile to any concept of an independent Iraqi Kurdish state.

The stability achieved by an independent Iraqi Kurdish state supported by Turkey would also encourage stronger economic relations between the two. These relations have been suffering for years because of the instability caused by Iraq's wars against Iran and the United States, as well as the US-led sanctions against Iraq that in turn have hurt Turkey. Improved economic relations between Turkey and the Iraqi Kurds would also help benefit the Kurds in Turkey who so badly need a better economic situation.

In conclusion, Turkey should come to realize that, as the more powerful partner by far, it would become the natural leader and protector of an independent Iraqi Kurdistan, a state that would also serve as a buffer between Turkey and any lingering instability to the south. Historic Turkish fears of a Kurdish *kukla devlet* (puppet state) are anachronistic and will only help create a self-fulfilling prophecy. The late Turkish president Turgut Özal's imaginative initiatives towards the Kurds during the early 1990s illustrate that these arguments concerning Turkish–Kurdish cooperation are not divorced from reality.

Notes

1. On this point, see Toby Dodge, *Inventing Iraq: The failure of nation building and a history denied* (New York: Columbia University Press, 2003).
2. See the text of the Transitional Administrative (TAL) Law in the appendix.
3. Article 61(c) of the TAL – the so-called 'Kurdish veto' – declares that 'the general referendum will be successful and the draft constitution ratified if a majority of the voters in Iraq approve and if two-thirds of the voters in three or more governorates do not reject it'. Since Iraqi Kurdistan consists of three governorates, this provision gives the Kurds an effective veto over the final constitution. Iraq's Sunni Arabs could also use it.
4. In general, see: Kemal Karpat, *An Enquiry into the Social Foundations of Nationalism in the Ottoman State: From social estates to classes, from millets to nations* (Princeton: Center of International Studies, 1973); Halil Inalcik, *The Ottoman Empire: The classical age, 1300–1600* (London: Weidenfeld & Nicolson, 1973); Stanford Shaw and Ezel Shaw, *History of the Ottoman Empire and Modern Turkey,* vol. II: *Reform, Revolution and Republic: The rise of modern Turkey, 1805–1917* (Cambridge: Cambridge University Press, 1977); and more specifically, see: Paul White, *Primitive Rebels or Revolutionary Modernizers? The Kurdish national movement in Turkey* (London: Zed Books, 2000), pp. 56–57. I published earlier portions of this article as 'Kurdish Future in a Post-Saddam Iraq', *Journal of Muslim Minority Affairs*, 23, April 2003, pp. 9–23.
5. Bernard Lewis, *The Emergence of Modern Turkey*, 2nd edn (London: Oxford University Press, 1968).
6. David McDowall, *A Modern History of the Kurds* (London: I. B. Tauris, 1996), pp. 38–65.
7. For a detailed history of modern Iraq's earlier decades, see: Stephen H. Longrigg, *Iraq, 1900 to 1950: A political, social and economic history* (London: Oxford University Press, 1953). More recently, see: Phebe Marr, *Modern History of Iraq*, 2nd edn (Boulder: Westview, 2004); and Charles Tripp, *A History of Iraq*, 2nd edn (Cambridge: Cambridge University Press, 2000). For further background, see Majid Khadduri, *Socialist Iraq: A Study in Iraqi Politics Since 1968* (Washington: The Middle East Institute, 1978); and Marion Farouk-Sluglett and Peter Sluglett, *Iraq since 1958: From revolution to dictatorship* (London: Kegan Paul International, 1987).
8. For an excellent discussion of this point, see: Andreas Wimmer, *Nationalist Exclusion and Ethnic Conflict: Shadows of modernity* (Cambridge: Cambridge University Press, 2002), pp. 156–195.
9. Hugh Seton-Watson, *Nations and States: An Enquiry into the Origins of Nations and the Politics of Nationalism* (Boulder: Westview, 1977), p. 148. For more important work on how modern states have sought to create nations, see: Ernest Gellner, *Thought and Change* (London: Weidenfeld & Nicholson, 1964); and Benedict Anderson, *Imagined Communities: Reflections on the Origin and Spread of Nationalism* (London: Verso, 1991).
10. Human Rights Watch/Middle East, *Iraq's Crime of Genocide: The Anfal campaign against the Kurds* (New Haven: Yale University Press, 1995); and Kanan Makiya, *Cruelty and Silence: War, tyranny, uprising and the Arab world* (New York: W. W. Norton & Company, 1993), pp. 151–199. Also see: Samir al-Khalil (Kanan Makiya), *Republic of Fear: The politics of modern Iraq* (Berkeley: University of California Press, 1989).

11. Michael M. Gunter, *The Kurds and the Future of Turkey* (New York: St. Martin's Press, 1997), p. 6.
12. McDowall, *Modern History of the Kurds*, pp. 66–86, and 214–283.
13. Nader Entessar, *Kurdish Ethnonationalism* (Boulder: Lynne Rienner, 1992), pp. 29–48; and Farideh Koohi-Kamali, *The Political Development of the Kurds in Iran: Pastoral nationalism* (Basingstoke: Palgrave Macmillan, 2003).
14. Mustafa Nazdar (Ismet Cheriff Vanly), 'The Kurds in Syria', in: Gerard Chaliand (ed.) *A People without a Country: The Kurds and Kurdistan* (New York: Olive Branch Press, 1993), pp. 194–201; and Ismet Cheriff Vanly, 'The Kurds in Syria and Lebanon', in: Philip G. Kreyenbroek and Stefan Sperl (eds), *The Kurds: A contemporary overview* (London: Routledge, 1992), pp. 143–164.
15. For a discussion see: Michael M. Gunter, *The Kurds of Iraq: Tragedy and hope* (New York: St Martin's Press, 1992), pp. 49–95.
16. Michael M. Gunter, *The Kurdish Predicament in Iraq: A political analysis* (New York: St Martin's Press, 1999), pp. 111–126; Gareth R. V. Stansfield, *Iraqi Kurdistan: Political development and emergent democracy* (London and New York: RoutledgeCurzon, 2003); and Kerim Yildiz, *The Kurds in Iraq: The past, present and future* (London and Ann Arbor, MI: Pluto Press, 2004).
17. Michael M. Gunter, 'United States Foreign Policy toward the Kurds', *Orient*, 40, September 1999, p. 433.
18. Cited in 'KDP's Barzani Interviewed on Federation Plans', *Al-Akbar* (Cairo), 22 November 1992, p. 4; as cited in *Foreign Broadcast – Information Service Near East & South Asia*, 1 December 1992, p. 25. 'Autonomy' had been the official, earlier goal of most Iraqi Kurdish parties, but, given its results, most now felt that it had been a terrible failure. For analyses of this earlier period, see: Edmund Ghareeb, *The Kurdish Question in Iraq* (Syracuse: Syracuse University Press, 1981); Sa'ad Jawad, *Iraq and the Kurdish Question, 1958–1970* (London: Ithaca Press, 1981); Edgar O'Ballance, *The Kurdish Revolt, 1961–1970* (Hamden: Archon Books, 1973); and Ismet Cheriff Vanly, 'Kurdistan in Iraq', in Gerard Chaliand (ed.), *A People without a Country: The Kurds and Kurdistan* (New York: Olive Branch Press, 1993), pp. 139–193.
19. Cited in 'Kurdish Officials Interviewed', Ankara Kanal-6 Television Network in Turkish, 1730 GMT, 19 October 1992; as cited in *Foreign Broadcast Information Service – West Europe*, 22 October 1992, p. 72.
20. For analyses of these earlier Iraqi opposition conferences, see: Michael M. Gunter, 'The Iraqi National Congress (INC) and the Future of the Iraqi Opposition', *Journal of South Asian and Middle Eastern Studies*, 19, Spring 1996, pp. 1–20; Michael M. Gunter, 'The Iraqi Opposition and the Failure of US Intelligence', *International Journal of Intelligence and Counter-Intelligence*, 12, Summer 1999, pp. 135–167; and Robert G. Rabil, 'The Iraqi Opposition's Evolution: From conflict to unity?', *Middle East Review of International Affairs (MERIA) Journal*, 6, December 2002, 17 pp.; online journal, http://meria.idc.ac.il
21. The following discussion is largely based on Ofra Bengio, *Saddam's World: Political discourse in Iraq* (Oxford: Oxford University Press, 1998), pp. 109–120.
22. Barham A. Salih, 'Give us a Chance to Build a Democratic Iraq', *New York Times*, 5 February 2002.
23. The following citations are taken from the draft obtained by the present author from the authorities of the Kurdistan Regional Government. Nouri Talabany, an Iraqi Kurdish jurist living in London, also drew up a useful draft constitution for the Iraqi Kurdistan Region in 1992. See: *The Kurdish View on the Constitutional Future of Iraq* (London, 1999). Also of interest is the stillborn 'Autonomy Draft Law' that resulted

from Barzani and Talabani's negotiations with the Iraqi government in the spring of 1991. See: M. Gunter, *Kurds of Iraq*, pp. 63–70. For an earlier scholarly proposal, see: Ali Allawi, 'Federalism', in: Fran Hazelton (ed.), *Iraq since the Gulf War: Prospects for democracy* (London and Atlantic Heights, NJ: Zed Books, 1994), pp. 211–222.

24. For details on these specific events, see: Gunter, *Kurds of Iraq*, pp. 17, 43–45 and 87–88.

25. For an analysis of the problems caused by Kirkuk, see below.

26. Multiparty elections were held for the Kurdistan Regional Parliament (Assembly) on 19 May 1992, but only the KDP and the PUK received more than the 7 per cent of the vote necessary to enter the legislature. After the votes of the smaller parties were proportionately distributed, the KDP won 50.22 per cent and the PUK won 49.78 per cent. Following lengthy negotiations, the two main parties agreed to split 50 seats apiece. The remaining five seats were given to the Christian minority. The Turkmen had chosen not to participate.

During the KDP–PUK civil war from 1994 to 1998, the entire assembly was unable to meet, and rival KDP and PUK governments existed in Arbil and Sulaimaniya. In October 2002, as plans began to materialize for a post-Saddam Iraq, the full assembly finally met. As of this writing (February 2005), the two Kurdish administrations are scheduled to be unified with Masoud Barzani as president and Nechirvan Idris Barzani as prime minister. Jalal Talabani is in line to become interim president of Iraq. Of course, only time will tell if these plans materialize.

27. During the elections for a parliament on 19 May 1992, the Kurds also voted for a supreme leader (president). Barzani won 466,819 votes, while Talabani tallied 441,057. Two other candidates won much smaller numbers. Since no one won a majority, however, a run-off election was necessary. As a result of Kurdish divisions, such an election was never held and no president was chosen.

28. The following citations are taken from the draft constitution obtained by the present author from the authorities of the Kurdistan Regional Government.

29. These provisions concerning women's rights and the role of religion conflict with the positions taken by many (but certainly not all) Iraqi Arab Shi'ites and Sunnis, and therefore portend possible future basic constitutional crises.

30. Barham Salih, 'A Kurdish Model for Iraq', *Washington Post*, 9 December 2002.

31. For background, see: Daniel Elazar, *Exploring Federalism* (Tuscaloosa: University of Alabama Press, 1987); Preston King, *Federalism and Federation*, 2nd edn (London: Frank Cass, 2001); and Ronald Watts, 'Federalism, Federal Political Systems, and Federations', *Annual Review of Political Science*, 1, 1998, pp. 117–137. The writings on federalism by Brendan O'Leary are particularly important for the Kurdish issue. See, for example, his 'Multi-National Federalism, Federacy, Power-Sharing and the Kurds of Iraq', paper presented to the conference on Multi-Nationalism, Power-Sharing and the Kurds in a New Iraq, George Washington University, Washington, DC, 12 September 2003. See also: Brendan O'Leary, Ian S. Lustick and Thomas Callaghy (eds), *Right-Sizing the State: The politics of moving borders* (New York: Oxford University Press, 2001).

32. Nathan Glazer, 'Federalism and Ethnicity: The American solution', in Nathan Glazer (ed.), *Ethnic Dilemmas, 1964–1982* (Cambridge: Harvard University Press, 1983), p. 276.

33. Through implied powers and generous constitutional interpretations over the years, of course, the central government has grown immensely in power relative to the state governments in the United States.

34. Adeed Dawisha and Karen Dawisha, 'How to Build a Democratic Iraq', *Foreign*

Affairs, 82, no. 3 (May/June 2003), pp. 36–50.

35. Donald L. Horowitz, *Ethnic Groups in Conflict* (Berkeley: University of California Press, 1985), pp. 563–652.

36. Cited in Daniel Williams, 'Iraqi Kurdish Leader Demands Guarantees: Minority seeks Autonomous Region, Expulsion of Arabs under New Government', *Washington Post*, 18 January 2004.

37. Cited in 'Turkey's Growing Uneasiness over Iraqi Kurds' Federalist Aspirations', *Briefing* (Ankara), 19 January 2004, p. 7.

38. For further analysis, see: M. Hakan Yavuz, '*Provincial* not *Ethnic* Federalism in Iraq', *Middle East Policy*, no. 11 (Spring 2004), pp. 126–131.

39. Murray Forsyth (ed.), *Federalism and Nationalism* (Leicester: Leicester University Press, 1989), p. 4.

40. See, for example, Michael Hecter, *Containing Nationalism* (Oxford: Oxford University Press, 2000).

41. For background analyses, see: Ronald L. Watts, *Comparing Federal Systems in the 1990s* (Kingston, Ontario: Institute of Intergovernmental Relations/Queen's University, 1996); Ursula K. Hicks, *Federalism, Failure and Success: A comparative study* (London: Macmillan, 1978); and Thomas M. Franck, *Why Federations Fail: An inquiry into the requisites for successful federation* (New York: New York University Press, 1968).

42. Liam Anderson and Gareth Stansfield, *The Future of Iraq: Dictatorship, democracy or division?* (New York: Palgrave Macmillan, 2004), p. 10. For the counter view, 'that Iraq and its people do not necessarily suffer from an immutable democratic deficit', see: Adeed Dawisha, 'Democratic Attitudes and Practices in Iraq, 1921–1958', *Middle East Journal*, no. 59 (Winter 2005), p. 11.

43. The following discussion is based largely on cogent points made by Brendan O'Leary in his paper 'Multi-National Federalism, Federacy, Power-Sharing and the Kurds of Iraq', pp. 13–18.

44. Stansfield, *Iraqi Kurdistan*, p. 175.

45. Peter W. Galbraith, 'As Iraqis Celebrate, the Kurds Hesitate', *New York Times*, 2 February 2005.

46. Gareth Smyth, 'Kurds "Hold Balance of Power" in Iraq', *Financial Times*, 1 February 2005.

47. Directorate of Population, Ministry of Interior, *Iraq's General Statistical Census for 1957.*

48. On these points, see Gunter, *Kurds of Iraq*, pp. 17 and 28.

49. Nouri Talabani, *Mantikat Kirkuk Wa Muhawalat Taghyeer Wakiiha Al-Kawmy* [The Kirkuk District and Attempts at Changing Its National Reality] (London, 1999), p. 81.

50. 'Military Issues Dire Warning on Iraq', *Briefing* (Ankara), 8 November 2004, p. 11.

51. See, for example: Ralph Peters, 'Break Up Iraq Now!', *New York Post*, 10 July 2003; Leslie H. Gelp, 'The Three-State Solution', *New York Times*, 25 November 2003; Peter W. Galbraith, 'Iraq: The bungled transition', *New York Review of Books*, 23 September 2004; and Christopher Catherwood, 'Everything about Iraq Says: Chop it in three', *The Times* (London), 26 December 2004.

52. See, for example, UN General Assembly Resolutions 2672 C (XXV), in *UN Chronicle*, 1971, no. 1, p. 46; 3236 (XXIX), in *UN Chronicle*, 1974, no. 11, pp. 36–74; and 33/23, in *UN Chronicle*, 1978, no, 11, p. 80.

53. See, for example: UN General Assembly Resolutions 2396 (XXIII), in *UN Chronicle*, 1969, no. 1, p. 94; and 31/61, in *UN Chronicle*, 1976, no. 1, p. 79.

Finding a Dangerous Equilibrium: Internal Politics in Iraqi Kurdistan – Parties, Tribes, Religion and Ethnicity Reconsidered

Gareth Stansfield

Introduction

The Kurds in Iraq now enjoy a level of attention from Iraqi politicians and the international community at large considered unattainable in previous decades. No longer are the Kurds an isolated, provincial, perhaps even politically unsophisticated minority, of interest only to academics or humanitarian-minded organizations. They are now the centre of attention: not only is the President of Iraq (Jalal Talabani) a Kurd but also the leader of one of the two most prominent parties representing the Kurds in Iraq. Further, the Kurdish demand to govern themselves is finally being heard through an electoral process, which, while far from perfect, was still more representative than any previous such event in Iraq's tortured history. The Kurds also have a relatively capable military force (at least when compared with the fragile formations of the post-Saddam Iraqi military and with the limited militias operated by the principle Shi'i political parties) and have the most institutionalized administrations within the territorial confines of Iraq in the shape of the Kurdistan regional governments (at the time of writing, it appears that the use of the plural is correct as the two Kurdish governments, one based in Erbil and the other in Sulaimaniya, have still not unified). Put quite simply, for once the Kurds matter when considering the future development of Iraq. It is now impossible (or, at least, very difficult and worryingly bloody) to imagine the Kurds being forcibly reintegrated back into a unitary Iraqi state governed from an all-powerful Baghdad. It is similarly hard to imagine that Iraq can continue to exist within its current territorial confines as anything other than a federal state with an autonomous 'Kurdistan' entity within it – if only because this is the minimum demand of the newly important Kurds.[1]

There are, however, important issues to address with regard to the recent political history of 'Kurdistan' and the factors underlying its new-found importance. In keeping with the majority of the post-Saddam discourse on Iraq, it is increasingly common to find, both in media publications and academic works, sweeping generalizations regarding the Kurds, their aims and the methods by which their objectives are to be achieved. This is similarly so when the Shi'i are discussed, and when the forces of the so-called Arab Sunni insurgency against coalition forces and the institutions of the new Iraqi government are considered. These generalizations are quite spectacular and can result in counter-factual analyses. The history of animosity that exists between the Kurdistan Democratic Party (KDP) and the Patriotic Union of Kurdistan (PUK) is routinely discussed *ad infinitum*, yet it is also argued that such animosity is now somewhat irrelevant, on the grounds that a common position, devoid of competition and suspicion, has been reached in the Kurds' efforts to secure a position of influence, if not dominance, in the future constitutional structure of Iraq. As if this level of generalization was not enough, it is also often assumed that the labels 'the Kurds' and 'the KDP/PUK' are almost synonymous. This is understandable to a certain extent – after all, the KDP and PUK dominate political activity in the two administrations and across the region. But it is a statement that belies the reality of the detail on the ground, and is in danger of ignoring other political and social actors of considerable real or potential influence.

Such generalizations suggest that this obvious dominance of the KDP and PUK in Kurdistan is omnipotent and popular in nature. Yet other formations are re-emerging in the post-Saddam environment, including once-powerful Kurdish tribes and political Islamist organizations. Furthermore, new formations have also appeared, which I will refer to as 'ultra-nationalist', and which are a source of increasing concern to the leadership of the two established parties as they struggle to maintain their popular support base in a rapidly changing environment.

The aim of this chapter is to provide an analysis of the development of the Kurdish political position in post-Saddam Iraq. While other chapters in this collection focus upon what may be called 'the Kurdish position in Baghdad' and how the unified Kurdish position on federalism has developed (particularly evident in the erudite writing of Michael Gunter), this chapter focuses upon Kurdistan itself and the development of internal politics and transformation of political life since 2003. It proposes that the political conditions found in Iraqi Kurdistan on the eve of Saddam's removal from power were, in effect, the product of a series of anomalous situations that, since 1990, had engulfed Iraq and impacted upon the Kurdistan region. In brief, the continued survival of Saddam Hussein's regime in a weakened state served to allow the Kurdistan region to develop in relative isolation from the rest of Iraq while concomitantly providing the leadership of the KDP and PUK with an opportunity to consolidate their hold on power. They achieved this by taking advantage of or generating a range of opportunities, such as (i) Saddam seeking to develop and maintain his economic ties through Kurds; (ii) anti-Saddam forces (including those of the Iraqi opposition, in addition to foreign powers such as the US) depending upon Kurdish goodwill (and territory) to operate against Baghdad in the 1990s; and (iii) neighbouring powers (including Turkey and Iran) benefiting from alliances with Iraqi Kurdish parties in defence of their own national interests. The removal of Saddam's regime in effect removed the foundations of the conditions that maintained the delicate forces allowing the autonomous Kurdish region to survive and prosper unchallenged. With the anomaly of Saddam Hussein's regime removed, the political balance in Kurdistan has been altered. Old animosities have resurfaced and new ones have joined them.

The argument proceeds by addressing four inter-related aspects that have affected recent Iraqi Kurdish politics. The first section addresses the situation of the Kurds on the eve of Saddam's removal, describing the development of the delicate balance that had emerged over the previous decade. The second section traces the historical evolution of the new and old dynamics that have now emerged in Kurdistan. The 'new' trends can mainly be classified as a distinctly Kurdish nationalist movement, which, unlike the positions adopted by virtually all Iraqi Kurdish parties including, the KDP and PUK, at a minimum demands that the Kurds should have the choice as to whether they remain in Iraq or not; at a maximum that the Kurds should, as a policy aim, pursue secession from Iraq and the establishment of an independent Kurdish state. The 'old' trends are perhaps more threatening to the continued hegemony of the KDP and PUK, as they build upon well-established notions of loyalty and/or kinship. The groups that characterize these 'old' trends are previously subdued tribes, held in place by the dominance of the KDP in particular and the PUK to a lesser extent, now reinvigorated by the changes occurring in Iraq and the possible removal of the conditions that maintained the hegemony of the KDP and PUK. Such tribes, in particular the Baradostis, the Zebaris and the Mizouris, have traditionally displayed little support for the

Barzanis, the KDP and the PUK (indeed, they often displayed considerable antipathy). Other groupings in this category of 'old' trends include Islamist organizations (including the Yekgurtu Islami Kurdistan (Kurdistan Islamic Union – KIU) and the Islamic United Movement of Kurdistan (IUMK), and more radical organizations including the now infamous Ansar al-Islam) and, to a lesser extent, the parties of the left. The final section returns to the situation in Iraq and Baghdad and analyses the Kurdish position in the elections of January 2005 and the subsequent formation of the transitional Iraqi national assembly and government. I argue that it is during this period that the previously glossed-over differences between the KDP and the PUK again hint at resurfacing, as the arrangements for Kurdish involvement in Iraq (which includes seeing a Kurd as president of Iraq in the form of PUK Secretary-General Jalal Talabani) introduce new tensions into the Kurdish political scene because the PUK is forced to act in an 'Iraqi' nationalist manner, whereas the KDP (whose president, Masoud Barzani, is appointed president of the Kurdistan Region) moves toward a more 'Kurdish' nationalist position. Issues relating to the balance of roles in the Kurdistan Regional Government (KRG) have emerged as potentially destabilizing conditions while, in Baghdad, it is far from clear that the promises made to the Kurds by other Iraqi political formations while in opposition will indeed be honoured.

Iraqi Kurdistan on the Eve of Saddam's Downfall

By 1988, the Kurds had seemingly been eradicated as a political force in Iraq. From being in a state of permanent rebellion since 1961, the Kurds were devastated by the impacts of two quite different changes in bilateral relations between Iran and Iraq. The first of these changes occurred in 1975. Since 1970, the Kurds had enjoyed a heightened degree of autonomy from Baghdad, as enshrined in the March Manifesto of that year, which allowed for the establishment of Kurdish institutions of administration covering the governorates of Erbil, Dohuk and Sulaimaniya, but not Kirkuk. Later, the principal Kurdish negotiator of that time, the late Sami Abdul Rahman, reflected that the Kurds had gained nothing from that arrangement but 'paper autonomy'. The disgruntlement was readily apparent by 1974, as the *peshmerga* of the KDP (under the leadership of mullah Mustafa Barzani) again took up arms against the Iraqi government in response to the passing of the Autonomy Law (which attempted further to institutionalize this 'paper autonomy' and lack of control of Kirkuk). Benefiting from significant Iranian support, the *peshmerga* scored a string of victories against Iraqi forces. The success was short-lived, however, as Saddam secured a strategic agreement at Algiers with the Shah of Iran, in which Iraq ceded control of the Shatt al-Arab waterway in the south of the country, in exchange for Iran's curtailing of support of the Kurdish rebels. The *peshmerga* were routed, Barzani was forced out of Iraq never to return to Kurdistan alive, and the Kurds were weakened by their division into two camps – the newly formed leftist PUK of Jalal Talabani and the regrouped KDP under the leadership of mullah Mustafa's sons, Idris and Masoud.

Worse was to come with the second change in bilateral relations between Iran and Iraq following the Islamic Revolution of 1979, which witnessed the deposal of the Shah and the rise to power of Ayatollah Khomeini. Taking advantage of what was considered to be a weakened Iran, Saddam invaded in 1980, hoping for a quick and relatively trouble-free victory over what was considered to be his antithesis. It was not to be. The Iran–Iraq war soon developed into a catastrophic war of attrition for both sides. Caught between these two warring powers, the Kurds once again took up arms against Baghdad. This time, Saddam responded with a level of violence that shocked even the most informed observers of his brutal career. The now infamous Anfal campaign of 1987–1988, resulting in the systematic depopulation of the rural areas of Kurdistan and the deaths of an estimated 100,000 people, combined with the brutal military assault on Halabja, was an almost successful attempt to destroy the Kurds as a political force (if not even in an absolute sense) once and for all. Saddam very nearly succeeded. More than 4,000 villages were razed, untold numbers of people killed and deported, and the *peshmerga* forced to evacuate with their leaders to Iran.

It was to take an event of spectacular proportions to allow the Kurdish parties to recover from the blows received in the 1970s and 1980s. Saddam's invasion of Kuwait in 1990 and the subsequent defeat of Iraqi forces by a US-led coalition in 1991 were followed by a spontaneous *intifada* in the south of Iraq, and then a *rapareen* in the Kurdish north. Although still debated, it appears that the involvement of the KDP and PUK in the planning of the *rapareen* was, at best, limited. If any political organization can claim to have instigated the *rapareen*, it was the Kurdistan Socialist Party. Indeed, it would take the leadership of the KDP and PUK several days to bring the *peshmerga* into the Kurdish cities of Iraq and organize the emergency administration of the Kurdish region. While short-lived, because Saddam was unable to turn the remnants of his military forces against the poorly equipped rebels, the northern uprising heralded the emergence of a Kurdish-dominated de facto state. Aware that it would be a damaging drain upon precious resources, Saddam withdrew his officials, funding and military forces from Kurdistan and placed the region under an internal economic embargo. The leadership of the Iraqi Kurdish Front (IKF – an umbrella organization of the most prominent Kurdish parties, including the KDP and PUK) responded not by declaring independence, as was expected, but by making plans to hold multi-party elections for a regional assembly within the territorial confines of Iraq.[2]

The emergence of autonomous Kurdistan in Iraq in 1991 was therefore due to the presence of anomalies within the Iraqi political system. The weakness of the central government, combined with the same government's need to find mechanisms by which to trade with neighbouring states, meant that the Iraqi Kurds found their geopolitical position in the mountains of the Turkish, Iraqi and Iranian border area to be, for once, advantageous. Iraqi Kurdistan was placed under double sanctions, one set from the UN imposed on the entirety of Iraq, the other from Saddam placing an internal embargo against the renegade region. However, the internal embargo was selective at best, as Saddam needed to deal with the Iraqi Kurds in order to smuggle illicit oil products from 'Iraq proper' into Turkey. Iraqi Kurdistan therefore became a useful gateway to the outside world. It also became a viewing point for outside powers to look inside Iraq. Officially, the Kurdish region existed under the same stringent economic constraints as the rest of the country. Unofficially, however, as the international community (and particularly the US) had a peculiar relationship with the Kurds (they were 'Iraqis' but were seemingly opposed to the regime of Saddam), a blind eye was turned to the questionable legality of Kurdish actions facilitating trade between Iraq and the rest of the region. A further anomaly, related to the continued presence of Saddam in Baghdad, was the establishment of Operation Northern Watch (the 'no-fly' zone), whereby the airforces of the US, Britain and France protected the area north of the 36th parallel from possible Iraqi transgressions.[3] The fact that at least half of Kurdish-controlled Iraq (principally the governorate of Sulaimaniya) is, in fact, south of the 36th parallel begs the question as to what, exactly, the military planners would have done if Sulaimaniya had been attacked (indeed, Erbil, which lies just north of the 36th parallel, was invaded by Saddam's forces in 1996, resulting in nothing more than limited cruise missile strikes in the south of Iraq).

With Kurdistan placed as a convenient economic link between Iraq and the rest of the world, and the airforces of several nations charged with protecting the Kurds against the aggression of Baghdad, it was left to the Kurdish leadership to walk a narrow path between administering the Kurdistan Region of Iraq to a level benefiting its inhabitants, yet not being so successful as to raise fears in regional capitals that the Kurds would move towards seceding from Iraq. Regional capitals had little to fear, however, as the deeply engrained rivalry between Barzani and Talabani engulfed the early years of the fledgling entity and saw a civil war rend Kurdistan into two de facto statelets from 1994 onwards.

Somewhat unexpectedly, after Kurdistan was partitioned between the KDP and PUK in 1994, the division was consolidated (though not codified) in 1996. While the division emphasized the inherent antipathy and distrust between the PUK and KDP, which was obvious for all to see, the political system stabilized considerably and socio-economic and security conditions in the two Kurdish regions improved markedly, especially when compared with conditions in the rest of Iraq. The KDP administered its region (Erbil and Dohuk) from Erbil, while the PUK administered Sulaimaniya and Darbandikhan, and both regions began to prosper economically from 1997 onwards, but especially the KDP-controlled area with its lucrative border crossing with Turkey at Ibrahim Khalil.

By 2003, the Kurdistan Region had achieved a degree of semi-permanency in the minds of many regional capitals (possibly even in Ankara), and international actors were increasingly viewing the region in a similar way. Indeed, the UK Foreign and Commonwealth Office (FCO) took the unprecedented step of issuing separate travel advice for Kurdistan and Iraq in April 2005.[4] While not an official recognition, it illustrates clearly that Kurdistan is considered in quite different terms from the rest of Iraq.

These differences between Kurdistan and the rest of Iraq can be seen very clearly on the ground. Whatever the failings of the Kurdistan regions, under the leadership of the KDP and PUK, they had become an institutionalized feature of the political landscape and culture of the population of Kurdistan, to the extent that the word 'government' now refers to 'Kurdish government', rather than 'Iraqi'. Kurdish, rather than Arabic, is now the standard language. Indeed, at this time English is perhaps a more popular second language than Arabic for Kurds and there is a drive to replace Arabic as the second language of every Kurdish university. The economy, while linked to Baghdad, operates independently of it. To all intents and purposes, the people of Kurdistan (or, at least the Kurdish majority there), long distinct in their ethnic identity, have developed a vibrant Kurdish nationalism and few are willing to be labelled

'Iraqi' any longer.[5] Complicating an already decidedly complex picture is the question of which political party will head what is rapidly emerging as a popular political movement demanding an independent Kurdish state. As we shall see later, this question is again exercising the leaderships of the KDP and PUK as they attempt to place themselves in positions of influence, whether in Baghdad or Erbil, which will keep all options open to them in the future months and years.

Old and New Mobilization

It is difficult to exaggerate the levels of authority enjoyed by the KDP and PUK in their respective administrative zones. It is also very easy to criticize the governing tendencies of both parties, and indeed several observers discuss the KDP and PUK administrations as though they are little better than what existed under Saddam's regime.[6] This view often fails to take into account both the advances made in Kurdistan, under the leadership of these two parties, and the environment in which the advances took place. However, within both regions of Iraqi Kurdistan there remains an increasingly vocal public criticism of the achievements of the KDP- and PUK-dominated administrations of Erbil and Sulaimaniya. Often, the criticisms are aimed at a personal level, at the leaders of the parties and governments. Commenting on a recent defence of the achievements of the KRG by Bayan Sami Abdul Rahman, Dr Showan Khurshid begins his letter to the often anti-KDP/PUK website www.kurdishmedia.com by stating that, '[t]he obvious problem of Kurdistan presently is that the parties are even more important than people and the leaders of the parties are more important than anyone else.'[7] Such criticism has become more apparent in Kurdistan, especially since the removal of Saddam; many claim that the leadership of the KDP and PUK wasted the opportunity to secede from Iraq and move towards independence. However, its roots are in fact deeper, and, as with most political developments in Kurdistan, complex.

It is only in relatively recent times that the political system of Iraqi Kurdistan has been so overwhelmingly dominated by the KDP and PUK. Even in the 1980s, for example, there were many parties operating in the mountains of Kurdistan, against the forces of the Iraqi government and often against each other. The KDP and PUK were certainly important, but other groups, including the Kurdistan Socialist Party (KSP) and the Kurdistan

Communist Party (PASOK) were also very powerful. In addition to these political parties, Kurdish society continued to be tribal in nature, and political organization was often structured around tribal groupings. These tribes would act according to tribal interests, rather than any notion of allegiance to a political party or a national movement, and would be motivated more by economic advancement than by any promotion of a particular ideology. This meant that many tribes would find common cause with those powers that could improve their immediate, local situation. Therefore, some Kurdish tribes fell into the habit of dealing with the Iraqi government to provide security in their areas, often against their fellow Kurds. When these opportunities of economic advancement also matched the divisions of a particular intra-Kurdish tribal dispute, then the dispute would be heightened. This scenario explains, to a considerable extent, the animosity that developed between the KDP and several very prominent and powerful Kurdish tribes, including the Surchi, Zebari and Baradosti. Of course, it is perhaps inaccurate to suggest that the competition was with the KDP – it was really with the Barzanis – but the KDP came to be seen as the vehicle by which the Barzani tribe would dominate the political life of Kurdistan.

With the establishment of the KRG in the early 1990s, the KDP and PUK were positioned to consolidate their positions of prominence because (i) the more powerful tribes were often associated with providing military irregulars for the Iraqi government (the so-called *jash*), and thereby suffering in the 1990s as Kurdish nationalism began to grow in the largely urban population of Iraqi Kurdistan,[8] and (ii) the KDP and PUK found themselves at the head of an extensive network of patronage by quickly dominating the administrative offices of the de facto state. Some tribes (including the Surchi and the Herki) rebelled against the new arrangements, while others became tied to the economic strings of the two parties and received financial assistance from them, and yet others withdrew and reconsolidated their finances and networks, including the Baradosti and the Mizouri. Now, as the tribes in the rest of Iraq are becoming increasingly empowered because of the chaotic conditions that have existed since the removal of Saddam Hussein's government, and as the future of Iraq and of Kurdistan is openly negotiated, these tribes are once again beginning to realize that developments across Iraq may threaten the continued predominance of the KDP and PUK. It remains difficult, however, to imagine how these once-powerful tribes can challenge the KDP and PUK. Some of these tribes are indubitably endowed with considerable wealth (particularly the Baradosti and the Mizouri), yet they are quite simply unable to counter the gains made by the PUK or, especially, of the KDP over the last decade in terms of accumulation of resources; expansion of military force; and the building of a support base in urban Kurdish society. The 'old' tribes also have to contend with the fact that their members themselves have been influenced to varying degrees by the existence of a de facto Kurdish state. Many tribal members have become urban businessmen, building upon their families' connections to establish impressive networks and lucrative businesses in Erbil, Sulaimaniya and Dohuk. By doing so, they have been brought into close contact with KDP and PUK officials and the strength of popular opinion towards the Kurdish nationalist position. It would now be (almost) unheard of for individuals operating in this regard to consider taking up arms for tribal interests against the KDP, PUK or the Barzanis, for example. As such, various tribal leaders have been forced to accept that the time to challenge the established powers for heightened political influence in Kurdistan has passed. However, they exist as powerful and influential formations, which the leadership of the KDP and PUK cannot ignore.

Operating at a broader level, the KDP and PUK have had to contend with a rise in the activities of Islamist organizations. In common with the region, Iraqi Kurdistan has not been immune to the heightened role of Islam within society. Although it remains comparatively secular compared to the rest of Iraq or immediate neighbours, a growing number of mosques and institutions have been built and organizations formed in Iraqi Kurdistan, and religious conservatism in society has noticeably increased. Again, this change is not new and can be traced, in an organizational sense, to the formation of the Islamic Movement of Kurdistan (IMIK) in the late 1970s. The KDP and PUK have a long and bitter history of interaction with the IMIK, the IMIK having been heavily involved in the intra-Kurdish civil war of the 1990s. However, it would be the poles of political Islam that would cause the leadership of the KDP and PUK far more cause for concern in the run-up to regime change in Baghdad. On the one hand, the emergence of a moderate Islamist party (the Yekgirtu Islamiya Kurdistan – Kurdistan Islamic Union) made inroads into the popular support base of both parties, especially the KDP, as it offered a new, non-military alternative to the KDP and PUK, and leaders untainted by the problems associated with Barzani and Talabani. The KIU, under the leadership of Salahadin Ba'ahadin, was officially formed in January 1994 and grew quickly in the chaotic mess created by the inter-factional fighting between the KDP and the PUK. Its reputation of being a non-partisan and conciliatory organization was further enhanced when it played a key role in the creation of the Committee of Peace and Fraternal

Relations, a gathering of the smaller parties meeting in order to facilitate the development of relations between the KDP and PUK. An acknowledgement of the popular support base of the KIU came with the formation of the Third Cabinet of the KRG in Erbil, when a KIU representative, Hadi Ismael, became Minister without Portfolio and later Minister of Justice. These gains were further reflected in the student elections of 1999. While the KDP and PUK student organizations were victorious in Dohuk and Salahadin (Erbil) universities (for the KDP), and Sulaimaniya (for the PUK), the KIU came second in every ballot, emphasizing their rise to prominence. Indeed, their securing of 36 per cent of the vote in Dohuk forced Barzani to recognize that he had a potential serious challenge from the KIU in what had previously been considered to be the undisputed KDP heartland.

At the other extreme was the aggregation of various extremist fundamentalist groupings, which came together to form the ultra-violent Jund al-Islam – the forerunner of the now infamous Ansar al-Islam. It is possible to trace the formative moments of the Jund al-Islam to 2001, when divisions began to appear in the military wing of the IMK. The principal opponent to the leadership of the IMK was the young mullah Ali Bapir, who, on 30 May 2002, established of the Islamic Group of Kurdistan (IGK), effectively breaking up the IMK. However, Bapir could not control his new followers and, at the same meeting that saw the formation of the IGK, a group of ultra-fanatical members demanded that a *jihad* be launched against the KDP and PUK. As a result of Bapir's refusal, the extremists formed the Jund al-Islam on 31 August 2001. With the Jund as a focal point, other groupings soon joined, including Kurdish HAMAS, Islamic Tawhid and Hezi Du Soran (Soran Second Force). Together, and with funds reportedly supplied by Osama bin Laden, they formed Ansar al-Islam.[9]

The emergence of tribal interests and the spreading influence of Islam in Kurdistan are two characteristics of Kurdish society that have reappeared as political circumstances in both Kurdistan and Iraq. A third grouping has also emerged, its origin being in the experience of living outside the strictures of Baghdad since 1991 – this grouping can best be described as the 'neo-nationalists'. By heading a Kurdish state in all but name, the leadership of the KDP and PUK heightened aspirations and hopes among Kurds in Iraq. While the experiences of living in Iraqi Kurdistan in the 1990s were, at times, difficult, the population of the region had only the experience of living in Saddam's Iraq for comparison, and it was a comparison that put the Kurdish 'democratic experiment' in a favourable light. As the decade progressed, the memory of living under the authority of the Iraq government was also steadily eroded, as Kurds who were infants in 1990 began to mature and take a deeper interest in their political condition. By 2000, these Kurds were teenagers and young adults and had developed a very strong notion of their Kurdish identity and often an unwillingness to refer to themselves as 'Iraqi'. Growing throughout the 1990s, therefore, was a pool of support for any party that would adopt a vibrant Kurdish nationalist position. The KDP and PUK often flirted with embracing this trend, but, as heads of governments, were also aware of the dangers involved in offending Turkey, or even Iraq, if the sentiments of 'the Kurdish street' were reflected in their official policies. Barzani and Talabani may have been describing their actions as 'realistic', but, for many Kurds, they were a betrayal.

When analysing 'the Kurds', it is necessary to make a distinction between the two major parties of the KDP and PUK, on the one hand, and Kurdish society on the other. The distinction is important, as it is apparent that there is an increasing disconnect between the two parties and society at large. The KDP and PUK have long had links with successive Iraqi governments and have been operating under the assumption that secession from Iraq is not, as yet, a possibility. Kurdish society, however, which has been traumatized considerably by successive Iraqi governments, is reacting in a more radical manner. Unwilling to be held within a state dominated by Arab nationalists, the Kurds have developed a strong Kurdish nationalist position, which has deep roots in Kurdish society.[10] However, the Kurds are not yet unified. Different trends are apparent within political parties and within civil society. These trends span the gamut of political motivations, from those seeking outright independence and the declaration of a Kurdish state to those wishing to promote a federal arrangement within Iraq. These positions often overlap, and the holders of them are capable of changing position or holding several at the same time. For example, it is extremely difficult to find any Kurd who does not believe that independence is 'the dream of every Kurd'. However, many recognize that such an aim is perhaps too remote at present and a more realistic proposition would be to seek a federal arrangement in Iraq. The problem with regard to these trends is that the 'realists' are increasingly found in the ranks of the political parties (particularly the KDP and PUK), whereas the maximalist position, which demands the independence of the entire Kurdish region of Iraq, is becoming prominent in civil society and grass-roots political opinion, creating a gulf between Kurdish society and its current crop of political representatives.[11]

This problem grew rapidly following the removal of Saddam. With the dissolution of the Iraqi government and army, the KRG and the Kurdish military found themselves as the pre-eminent administrative and military organizations in the state, in terms of their efficiency and organizational coherence. For many Kurds, this was the ideal time to declare independence from Iraq, as there was simply no force in Iraq that could prevent them from doing so. The KDP–PUK leadership, however, remained extremely wary of aligning themselves with this position, again because they believed that this would provoke Turkey into invading the north of Iraq and destroying the institutions that had been established over the previous decade. Although the position taken by Barzani and Talabani was (and remains) eminently sensible when the context of regional politics is considered, to many younger Kurds it seemed that Barzani and Talabani were yet again acting in their own immediate interests, rather than in the interests of the Kurds. As both leaders engaged with the occupying powers and took positions in the Iraqi Governing Council (IGC) in 2003, a new movement began to form. This movement, which became known as the Kurdistan Referendum Movement (KRM), has unclear beginnings. Some speculate that the KDP and PUK were intrinsic in its establishment, as it would be useful to have evidence of secession-minded Kurds growing in number in Kurdistan in order to promote the KDP and PUK as the parties of moderation – the only organizations preventing Iraq from disintegrating. This position would then be used to force through the Kurdish federal model with the Coalition and the post-Saddam Iraqi government in Baghdad. This argument may have some validity. Two of the primary leaders of the KRM, Hawlkat Abdulla and Dr A. K. Bukhari, are based in Sulaimaniya and Erbil respectively and have strong contacts in the offices of the PUK and KDP; and there are suggestions that two pro-PUK individuals (Nouri Talabani and Jamal Abdul) both played a role in establishing the movement in Sulaimaniya. Others contend that the party emerged when several Kurdish academics and observers, some based in the diaspora, became increasingly disappointed with the actions of the KDP and PUK. Whatever the truth of the matter, the reality would seem to be that the KRM is no longer under the control of either the KDP or the PUK and is now something of a loose cannon in the politics of Iraq and Kurdistan.

The greatest victory of the KRM was to hold an unofficial referendum on the day of the Iraqi elections (30 January 2005). In this referendum, 1,998,061 people voted. Of these, 1,973,412 (98.8 per cent) voted for the Kurdistan Region of Iraq to become independent.[12] If these figures are correct, and there is little to suggest that they are not, then this is a spectacular repudiation of the notion that Kurds remain committed to the notion of the integrity of the Iraqi state. As with the tribes and moderate Islamist groups, however, it is very difficult to imagine the KRM being able to mobilize enough political and economic resources by which to challenge the hegemony of the KDP and PUK. The status quo in Kurdistan seems to be secure, and is threatened only by the (increasingly limited) activities of Ansar al-Islam or by foreign intervention (particularly from Turkey).

The Kurds and Post-election Iraq

With so many developments, new dynamics emerging and old ones reappearing, it is understandable that attention has moved away from the perennial destabilizing issue in Iraqi Kurdistan in modern times – the competition between the KDP and PUK leaderships for undisputed hegemony in Kurdistan. After 1998, the disagreements between the two parties did not disappear, by any means, but were instead managed by a combination of internal agreements (including the Shaqlawa–Koysanjaq series of meetings) and external initiatives – most notably the Washington Agreement of 1998, sponsored by the US. Iraqi Kurdistan did not unify as a result of these initiatives, but a relative warming of relations and a normalization of some activities occurred, although the atmosphere between the two parties remained one of distrust, manifested, at times, in public statements of enmity.

When it became apparent that the US was seemingly intent upon removing Saddam's regime following 11 September 2001, the KDP and PUK began to operate in closer harmony, but still remained highly suspicious of each other. Their differences could be seen clearly in the way they related to the other parties of the Iraqi opposition. Talabani's PUK strongly supported the political platform developed by Chalabi's INC, whereas Barzani's KDP sought alliances with Allawi's Iraqi National Accord (INA) and Shi'i parties including the Supreme Council for Islamic Revolution in Iraq (SCIRI) and Hizb al-Da'wa. However, even though each party felt more comfortable with different ensembles of Iraqi opposition groups, they both remained committed to the same aim – of removing Saddam from power and remaking Iraq into a federal state, home to an autonomous Kurdistan unit.

To their credit, the KDP and PUK maintained this front during the difficult days following Saddam's deposal. There was, to be frank, too much happening in Iraq as a whole for them to be concerned about the balance of power in Kurdistan, particularly as Turkey remained watchful of any attempt by any Kurdish party to promote independence. The 'realist' position currently adopted by the KDP and PUK recognizes the inherently difficult theatre of international relations in which Iraqi Kurdistan exists. With Turkey to the north, Iran to the east, Syria to the west and Iraq proper to the south, the geopolitical position of Kurdistan is complex and thorny. Academics generally believe that the emergence of an independent Kurdish state in Iraq (or, indeed, anywhere) would conflict with the national interests of all these states, especially Turkey.[13] Most analyses insist that, with considerable Kurdish populations of their own, Turkey, Iran and Syria all have reason to prevent Iraq fragmenting and a new State of Kurdistan emerging within the current borders of Iraq, as this could provoke separatist Kurdish tendencies within their own borders. However, the cohesiveness of the Kurdish political front was weakened following the elections of January 2005. Although the unified Kurdish list did remarkably well (securing 75 seats in the Iraqi national assembly and totally dominating the Kurdistan National Assembly), disputes have emerged between the KDP and PUK over how to divide their successes. Providing a release to what could have been a most destabilizing situation, the high Kurdish turn-out in the elections, combined with very low turn-out in Arab Sunni areas, placed the leaders of the Kurdish list (in effect, Barzani and Talabani) in the role of king-makers in Baghdad. The Shi'i United Iraqi Alliance (UIA) list achieved a plurality (which later became a majority of 51 per cent), but the Transitional Administrative Law (TAL) of Iraq specified that a two-thirds majority was needed in order to form a government. The UIA therefore needed the Kurds. In return, the Kurds gained several important positions in the new government of Iraq, including that of president, which went to Jalal Talabani. The appointment of Talabani to what is seen as the highest (if symbolic) position in the Iraqi state allowed the Kurds a degree of flexibility when it came to Kurdistan. With Talabani safely in position in Baghdad, Barzani would take the role of president of Kurdistan Region, thereby ensuring a degree of parity between the two parties. It was also envisaged that the two Kurdistan Regions would, at last, unify (they had been doing so, very slowly and half-heartedly, in the areas of public service provision) under the premiership of Nechervan Barzani, with, it was hoped, Kirkuk as capital of the Kurdistan Region.

Notwithstanding the legion of problems involved with bringing Kirkuk into the Kurdistan Region, the sleeping animosity between the KDP and PUK has been reawakened as each side believes the other to be attempting to position itself to take advantage of different opportunities. The PUK, with its strong representation in Baghdad and its close links with the Shi'i political organizations (particularly since Ahmed Chalabi was appointed deputy prime minister), are obviously in a position of immense influence, and may be able to control Iraq's future evolution and the position of Kurdistan within it. However, they risk losing the support of both the emergent 'ultra' Kurdish nationalists, who consider Talabani to be an 'Iraqi' rather than a 'Kurdish' nationalist, and even members of the PUK who are have moved more towards the Kurdish nationalist position. Conversely, Barzani's position, which does not appear to be quite so strong on paper, allows him to broaden and consolidate his support base in Kurdistan by adopting a stronger 'Kurdish nationalist' position than that available to Talabani. Indeed, it seems that Barzani has been doing exactly this.

If such actions served to awaken the suspicions of each side, then their concerns were confirmed by a series of disagreements that emerged between the KDP and PUK over the details of Barzani's presidency over Kurdistan and Talabani's presidency of Iraq. Although details are sketchy, it appears that serious differences have emerged relating to the duration of positions, the appointing of deputies and the command of the *peshmerga*. Furthermore, at the time of writing, there is little evidence to suggest that the ministries which *are* meant to be unified actually act in a unified manner. Indeed, the situation in Kurdistan appears to be rather chaotic. The Kurdistan National Assembly had still not convened three months after it had been elected, possibly reflecting the lack of progress made in the formation of the government of Iraq, and, while the unification of the Kurdistan administrations has been promised (for several years), it is still far from clear that it will happen other than in name only. The appointment of the PUK's ex-security head, Omer Fattah, to be Nechervan Barzani's deputy indicates that some of these issues are perhaps being resolved, but the signs are that it will be quite a long time before the political situation in Kurdistan is normalized.

Conclusion

The political forces that allowed the Kurdistan Region to develop as a quasi-independent entity in Iraq in the 1990s have been removed and the future of both the Iraqi state and the Kurdish region are yet to be codified. However, the existence of a Kurdistan state in all but name has introduced new dynamics, which are dangerous if not impossible to ignore. The first is that new realities have been created on the ground. Kurds (younger Kurds in particular) do not consider themselves to be Iraqi, but Kurdish. The second is that political culture and institutions have developed in a very different manner compared to the rest of Iraq. The third is that the KDP and PUK have themselves changed from being parties with extensive networks and support bases to de facto governments in their own right, with access to the resources of the Kurdistan Region and the ability to patronize or coerce as they see fit. This is a great deal of power to expect them to relinquish voluntarily.

With Saddam removed, old political forces in Iraq have resurfaced and new ones joined them. The once-powerful Kurdish tribes, which have a natural animosity particularly towards the KDP and to a lesser extent also towards the PUK, are chafing at their subordinate position with the Kurdistan Region, but it is unrealistic to expect them to be able to challenge what is now the overwhelming power of the two governing parties. They will, however, become important allies or political opponents in future months, and have already expanded considerably into sectors of the Kurdish and Iraqi economies. Islamist organizations are similarly growing, but the moderate parties operate in a political system in which the 'rules of the game' are controlled by the KDP and PUK. Quite simply, they will never be allowed to develop into a position where they could challenge the hegemony of either party. Similarly, the KRM represents a vocal and popular opinion in Kurdistan, but it will be pushed into obscurity as the KDP (possibly) continues to move more towards a position espousing Kurdish nationalism itself.

In short, the greatest threat to the continued prosperity of the Kurdistan Region in Iraq is the seemingly irreconcilable differences between the leaderships of the KDP and PUK, which continue to simmer beneath the surface of the glossy exterior. These differences were not forgotten during the regime change process, but were ignored. Now that competition has started for political control in Baghdad and, by extension, Kurdistan, it would seem that all is not well between the two parties. It is too early to suggest that the devastating conflicts of the 1990s are about to reappear – indeed, I would still consider this unlikely because of the continued focus upon securing federalism in the new Iraqi constitution – but the KDP and PUK are certainly not now conjoined in a union of brotherly admiration. As always, a dangerous balance needs to be found between two parties that are competing for the same prize – to head the Kurdistan national movement in Iraq. Currently, one party (the PUK) believes this can be achieved from Baghdad. The other (the KDP) is moving towards a 'Kurdistan'-based approach. Far from being evidence of a complementary position, these moves could merely be the latest in the game of political control between the KDP and PUK.

Notes

1. For the purposes of this chapter, I will refer to a 'Kurdistan' region rather than a 'Kurdish' region. I choose to do this not because I support the notion that a 'Kurdistani' identity has emerged, as some academics claim, but that the region that would form an autonomous region in the north of Iraq, which would at least be based upon the current boundaries of the territory is administered by the Kurdistan regional governments. 'Kurdistan' refers to a geographic area in which many peoples live – Assyrians, Turkmen and Arabs – whereas the more ethnically weighted term 'Kurdish' is rather exclusive in meaning. Problems of definition obviously remain, as many Turkmen in particular would claim to live in Turkmenali (Land of the Turkmen) rather than 'Kurdistan'. Assyrians equally struggle to accept that the area in which they live is 'Kurdistan'. It is impossible to use a term that does not offend anyone at all, but I contend that 'Kurdistan region' is the better and more accurate option.

2. See: Gareth Stansfield, *Iraqi Kurdistan: Political development and emergent democracy* (London: RoutledgeCurzon, 2003).

3. See Tim Niblock, *Pariah States and Sanctions in the Middle East: Iraq, Libya, Sudan.* (Boulder, CO: Lynn Reinner, 2003); Sarah Graham Brown, *Sanctioning Saddam: The Politics of Intervention in Iraq.* London. I B Taurus, 1999.

4. 'British FCO Travel Advice Changes to Reflect Differences in the Region Administered by the Kurdistan Regional Government', 11 April 2005, posted at http://www.kurdistancorporation.com

5. Liam Anderson and Gareth Stansfield, *The Future of Iraq: Dictatorship, democracy or division?* (New York: Palgrave Macmillan, 2004), p. 177.

6. See, for example: Kyle Madigan, 'Corruption instead of Development in Iraqi Kurdistan', *Radio Free Europe/Radio Liberty*, 30 April 2005, listed at http://www.kurdishmedia.com/news.asp?id=6751. For the response of the KRG (Erbil) to this article, see: Bayan Sami Abdul Rahman, 'KRG's Comments on the "RFE/RL" Article: "Corruption instead of Development in Iraqi Kurdistan", 1 May 2005, posted at http://www.krg.org/

7. Showan Kurshid, 'The Need for Neutral Arbitration Institutions between the KDP and PUK', 2 May 2005, listed at www.kurdishmedia.com/reports.asp?id=2603.

8. Phebe Marr, 'Iraq "The Day After": Internal dynamics in post-Saddam Iraq', *The Naval War College Review*, Winter 2003.

9. See: Michael Rubin, 'The Islamist Threat in Iraqi Kurdistan', *Middle East Intelligence Bulletin*, 3, December 2001, p. 12; Gareth Stansfield, 'The Kurdish Dilemma: The golden era threatened', in: Toby Dodge and Steve Simon (eds), *Iraq at the Crossroads: State and society in the shadow of regime change*, International Institute for Strategic Studies Adelphi Paper no. 354 (Oxford and London: IISS/Oxford University Press, 2002), pp. 131–148; International Crisis Group, 'Radical Islam In Iraqi Kurdistan: The mouse that roared?', *Middle East Briefing*, 4, February 2003, p. 7.

10. For an analysis of the development of Kurdish nationalism in Iraq, see: Denise Natali, 'Manufacturing Identity and Managing Kurds in Iraq', in: Brendan O'Leary, Ian Lustick and John McGarry (eds), *Right Sizing the State: The politics of moving borders* (Oxford: Oxford University Press, 2001), pp. 253–288.

11. Associated Press, 'Kurds Disillusioned by Main Parties', 11 October 2004, listed at http://www.kurdishmedia.com/news.asp?id=5580.

12. Kurdistan Referendum Movement – International Committee, 'Press release', London,

8 February 2005, listed at http://www.kurdishmedia.com/news.asp?id=6235

13. For analyses of Kurdistan's geopolitical position, see: Robert Olson (ed.), *The Kurdish Nationalist Movement in the 1990s: Its impact on Turkey and the Middle East* (Lexington: University Press of Kentucky, 1996).

Arab Nationalism Versus Kurdish Nationalism: Reflections on Structural Parallels and Discontinuities

Faleh A. Jabar

Introduction

Arabs and Kurds entered the age of nationalism almost on equal ground. Up to 1917, these two ethnic groups were essentially subjects of the multi-ethnic, multi-cultural, multi-religious Ottoman 'sacred' Empire. Like Arabs, Kurds did not and could not achieve nation-statehood. The ideal Arab nation, presumably extending from the ocean to the Gulf (from Morocco to Iraq), envisaged during the 1910s in the Mashraq or the larger Arab nation, and the lofty dream of the Arabists in the 1940s, remained as remote as ever. Arabs, however, manufactured several territorial states or had had such territorial states manufactured for them. They enjoyed statehoods; the Kurds did not. Much of the Kurdish failure can be explained by the very success of territorial states that their neighbours, Turks, Iranian, and the Arabs in Iraq, created. But the Arab failure to go beyond the territorial states has structural parallels with the Kurdish failure to achieve nation-statehood.

In the preceding chapters, Kurdish nationalism and/or ethnicity was the focus of attention in sociological, cultural and historical terms. This was theoretically embedded in two different approaches, the one with the nation as the conceptual reference point, the other taking ethnicity as the focus of analysis.

In this concluding chapter, Arab nationalism forms the subject-matter of our examination: its modalities, changing over space and time hand-in-glove with socio-cultural change, serve to bring into bold relief the amorphous yet structural parallels between the two neighbouring but conflicting nationalisms. Both nationalisms grew out of the Ottoman era. Ottoman centralization and constitutionalism fostered embryonic ethnic self-consciousness. The rise of Turkish nationalism in the late nineteenth century spread the idea of nation-ness regionally. Arabs and Kurds were among the first emulators. Paradoxically, Kurdish activists and thinkers contributed to the construction of Ottoman, Turkish and Arab nationalisms in terms of ideas and elitist movements. The name Abdul-Rahman al-Kawakibi, a Kurd from Aleppo, Syria, is central.

We begin with some general remarks on the nature of nation, nationalism and nation-statehood, and then move to the common ancestry: Turkish nationalism. The sections that follow deal with the modalities of Arab nationalism, that nationalism's relation to religion, to Sufi orders and to social change.

General Remarks

Nationalist imagining usually tends to project its national community far back in historical time; and languages, cultures and religions, that may serve as national markers, have such longevity. But neither languages nor religions are nations, let alone nation-states. Nations and nationalism are young phenomena in the context of world history. In modern times, however, nations, nationalism and, for that matter ethnicity, have become the universal form of political organization.

This organization implies a congruence of national (or ethnic) and political borders, so the norm runs.[1] The paradox, however, is the regular breach of this norm.

Nationalist or ethnic boundaries are defined, created or invented along many cultural lines. National communities are defined by culture; culture in turn is based on language, religion or race.

If ethnicity is differentiated by culture, culture itself is too elusive to define. In the domain of nationalism, culture appears in the form of language (as a system of communicating and accumulating knowledge); or religion (unified religion: e.g. Islam, Christianity, Judaism) or sectarian religion (reformed religion, such as Protestantism versus Catholicism, or reformed Islam versus mystical, Sufi Islam); or race (Gellner argued in the case of black African nationalism that there were homogeneous linguistic and religious cultures uniting whites and blacks, and that since no tribal or other African group was capable of creating a unifying high culture, Africans looked for race as a trait, an identifying and differentiating means).[2]

If nations or ethnicities are defined purely in linguistic terms (leaving aside other cultural markers) there should be some 8,000 or so nationalisms worldwide; whereas there are in fact hardly 200 nation-states; and only a few can claim ethnic homogeneity. Actual or dormant nationalisms are fewer in number.

If we accept Gellner's criteria and calculations, the ratio between actual nation-states and potential nationalism is 'only one effective nationalism for ten potential ones'.[3]

This may entail further actual or potential national struggles ahead, at a time when the waves of nationalism seem almost to be coming to a halt, following the disintegration of ex-Yugoslavia and the ex-Soviet Union.

Numerous nation-states were born out of ancient, sacred empires; others evolved from random conquest by modern colonial administrations; some grew out of pre-political tribal confederations; in all cases, however, the new, often industrially based, administrative-political unit has become universal, or, in the words of Hegel, world history is composed of numerous particular national spirits, each of which should be seen as a real individual.[4] Nation-state building seems a continuous, wave-like process in which latecomers emulate already existing models – an act of 'piracy' in the Andersonian sense.

This differentiation between nation-statehood and nationalism seems to suggest that not only could nationalism be differentiated from the nation-state, but that the two may well diverge in time. As a concept, theory, movement or ideology, nationalism appears to have emerged after, rather than before, the actual emergence of the world's first nation-state models, namely the English and the French. Theorization and discursive representations of nation-ness came even later. This may well pose the question whether the first builders of nation-statehood were aware of the nature of the enterprise they were carrying out – one thinks of the pre-Archimedean boats that actually floated without the help of any cognitive theory of object-liquid weight-volume correlation.

In the eighteenth- and nineteenth-century European context, the French started the process of nation-building, leading to nationalism; the Germans, Americans and the Italians reversed the process; but the rise of nationalism came first.

Theorization of these processes came, as it were, *post-festum*. If the approximate date of the genesis of the nation-state is generally accepted;

the 'precise date of the genesis of nationalism is a matter of dispute: [Hans] Kohn tends to favour 1642, [Lord] Acton the 1772 Partition of Poland, [Elie] Kedourie 1806, the date of Fichte's famous Addresses to the German Nation ... Most opt for 1789 [the French Revolution]'.[5]

In the Western context, the Germans, Italians and Americans were latecomers: the Germans and Italians in the nineteenth century, the Americans a century earlier. For Asia and Africa (later on), nationalism was, and for some still is, an a-priori construction, a scheme preceding the actualization of nation-statehood.

Hence the idea that those nations are 'invented', artificial constructions, or anthropologically 'imagined'. The random nature of territorial spaces of a vast number of nations, conditional as they were on a host of factors, reinforced the artificiality or invented-ness of these modern communities; the cultural heterogeneity of the latter would add weight to the artificiality theory. Nations are imagined or hypothesized to be an ideal model of the congruence of political and cultural (national) borders, as noted earlier. Many existing, potential or latent nations represent a sociological zoo in terms of cultural markers of national or ethnic boundaries, such as language, religion, race or any other differentials. This applies clearly to the imagined Arab or Kurdish nation; and Martin van Bruinessen provides interesting evidence in this volume on the nuances of heterogeneous cultural markers of ethnicity in the Kurdish case. Both nationalisms also seem a-priori constructions, predating statehood.

It is also generally agreed that the rise of proto-types of nation-states occurred first in Europe (in the sixteenth to nineteenth centuries) and is presented as a break from traditional, agrarian or feudal societies; or the same process is presented as the rise of industrial, modern or capitalist society. This society triggered new, socio-economic and cultural dynamics conducive to the creation of a fluid division of labour, larger markets, standardized culture, the fostering of vernacular languages, secularization or the weakening ties of church and sect: in a word, a new society that went beyond the local confines of agrarianism was created. In this sense nation-states and nationalism are correctly envisaged as recent historical products of the industrial age.

This contrasts sharply with the ethnic or nationalistic imagining of an eternal historical existence of nations from time immemorial. Arabs and Kurds are no exceptions. Contrary to actual history, Arab nationalist theoreticians construct a hypothetical narrative in which the Arab nation and Arab nationalism appear to date back to antiquity. In this conception of things nationalistic, the relation of nation to individual appears as natural as his or her having limbs, eyes, nose or brains.[6] This temporal extension of nationhood beyond history is challenged by the Islamist conception of the Umma defined as a religious community, that is, the nation of Islam.

The main body of the neo-Islamists usually denies the existence of nationalism and nation-state in early, medieval or modern (late nineteenth-century) Islam, both in terms of conceptual categories and of actual organization. On the other hand, neo-Islamists claim that the Muslim nation, based, as it was and should be, on religious rather than ethnic, cultural or other bonds, existed in the glorious past and is about to re-emerge in the near future.[7] What the Islamists dismiss is not the imagined eternal character of nationalism as such, but a certain type of nationalism, based on ethnicity rather than creed.

While secular nationalists of both communities accuse the colonial West of hindering the creation of a pan-Arab or a pan-Kurdish state, Islamists accuse the West of introducing, in fact transplanting, nationalism simply to destroy the erstwhile united Islamic Umma. Arab and Kurdish nationalism seem to be irreconcilably counter-posed to Islam as a cultural marker; or the other way round, with Islam counter-posed to pan-Arab or pan-Kurdish nationalism. Non-religious markers of ethnicity (Islam) seem in disharmony with the religious *differentia specifica*.[8]

This uneasy symbiosis characterized the development that Arab nationalism has charted: it may also characterize Kurdish nationalism now and in the future.

Nationalism, Secularism and Religion

A thorough assessment of the relationship between Arab or Kurdish nationalism and Islam, or even between nationalism and religion, entails a journey beyond the realm of politics into the role of religion and/or secularization in fostering the creation of nation-states in the Arab world or even beyond.

According to Benedict Anderson, the dawn of European nationalism was also the dusk of religion.[9] The implication is that secularization and the creation of nation-states go hand in hand as indispensable, integrated components, asserting new loyalties and a novel socio-economic and political organization, that stand over and above other forms of allegiance and political association, whether these are wider or narrower than the ethnic-political units embedded in the dynamism of the newly emerging, highly mobile, culturally standardized, modern or industrial society. Is this regularity universal? Definitely not.

The sociology of nationalism (if such a branch of study did indeed exist)[10] suggests, in a different analysis, that reformation of religion, or in the words of Gellner the universalization of clerisy or high culture in which reformed religion was in certain cases instrumental, is the cultural cornerstone of the new stage, the industrial society and, with a transition to the new unit, the nation-state.[11]

If both Anderson's and Gellner's conclusions are valid, and we believe they are conditionally, the inference has to be drawn that no fixed essence could ever be ascribed to monotheistic world religions, Islam included, an eternalized essence that, in and of itself, promotes or hinders the rise of nation states.

In the role given to homogenized culture in nation-building there is a place reserved for religion, either as a trait or *differentia specifica*. This applies to certain forms of contemporary nationalism, the Pakistani, the Israeli and the Persian, to name but few.

Even in the early stages of nation-state-building in Western Europe (the Euro-centric model), reformed theology itself was instrumental in creating national churches, defying, as they were, the cosmic, supra-national loyalty of Christendom, and fostering the generalization of vernacular languages, the very medium of homogenized culture. Of course, it cannot be denied that this led to a theological schism that was, in turn, in many cases and at different points in time conducive to religious cleavages detrimental to national homogeneity.

It seems that the role culture plays, in whatever definition it is conceived (there are more than one hundred and fifty definitions of culture), is that of identification, which is at one and the same time a process of differentiation: A is A and A is not B.

For example, when we describe an object or a phenomenon as being *non-white* (not B), it does not follow from this that it is red, white, yellow or green or whatever (also not C, not D, not E, not Z, etc.). But determination of an object as being black (Gellner used the metaphor 'blue') would totally negate all other possible colour-related adjectives. This may explain the dilemma of those nationalists who use culture in a negative way, that is, to determine their specific trait, in an inverted manner, to establish identity by way of negation, on the model of the German philosopher Fichte, for whom the world is 'Nicht Ich' ('Not I').

Pre-national Ottomans: Religion, Sufism and Proto-type Nationalism

Arabs and Kurds emerged from the sacred Ottoman Empire. Their cultural and territorial destinies were intertwined by the very transition from this supra-national, and in fact pre-national polity, to the modern nation-state.

The pre-national, mostly sacred empires were the ideal political formation: the Roman Empire, and later the Holy Roman Empire, the Muslim Empire (Ummayid and later Abbasid), the Ottoman Empire. Terms like Christendom and Islamdom, so often read in this era, were the conceptual expressions of pre-modern or agrarian forms of organization and allegiances.

Within these seemingly greater political blocs, loyalty or affiliation was linked with different forms of sub-political organization: feudal fiefs and their lord, city-states, dynastic principalities, religious groups or sects, tribal confederations, and the like. Paul Hirst describes this world as one of endless and multiple authorities that modern states abhor.[12]

In the world of Islam one may speak of allegiances to tribe, clan, family, religious groups (Muslims, Christians, Jews, Hindus and so on) or various religious sects within one and the same religion (Shi'i, Sunni, or Sufi orders) and, of course, ruling dynasties.

The mega unit we call empire was then highly fragmented from within: its various constituent parts lacked the organic links that bring cohesion to modern societies, and each community in fact lived under the empire in 'centuries of solitude'.

Both the wider unit (the empire, or the centre) and the subunits, in whatever manner defined, are inherent in the conceptualization, say, of Islam and the organizational forms this religion took (Sufi orders, or central institutions of Mufti or Mujtahid, and so on).

By dint of its very function the religious establishment at the centre had to advocate universal claims, representing Islam as a universal faith, one which is directed at all Muslims, if not at all humans, as slaves or worshippers of the almighty God. Without such a claim to universality (which always existed, potentially or otherwise, in Islam) the legitimacy of Ottoman rule would have collapsed in the eyes of the Muslims they governed. To put the same idea in a more universal form: 'All great classical communities conceived of themselves as cosmically central by the medium of sacred language linked to a supra-terrestrial order of power.'[13]

Centrally institutionalized religion played an important role in Arab, Turkish and Persian nationalisms, both as protector or threat. In the case of the Kurds, Sufi orders were crucially instrumental. These orders had a similar role in local nationalisms across the Arab world, in the Sudan (Khatmiya and Ansar), Algeria (Qadiriya), and Libya (Sanusi order).

Sufi orders in the nineteenth and twentieth centuries were diverse in terms of social space and modes of organization. We may distinguish rural from urban orders, on the one hand, and high and low orders, that is, elitist and popular, urban orders, on the other hand. Urban orders were divided according to lines of occupation, artisans, soldiers, and so on.

Popular urban and rural-tribal orders with their saint worship and personal mediation of the Sheikh and, by extension, the saint, were particularistic by definition, that is, pre-national, sub-national, or even anti-national. They were the product of fragmentation and the isolation of socio-economic and cultural formations. Even when the high, universal, central culture has, like its low, particularistic, fragmented counterpart, the same Sufi inclination, as was really the case during much of the Ottoman period, the difference between the two was more than obvious when we contemplate the reason why saint worship was missing from the high culture while representing the focal point of the low, Sufi Islam of the village, the tribe and the guild.

Few scholars contend that the universal character of Islam (addressing all humanity) contradicts the particular claims of nationalism, Arab and Kurdish, as nationalism is directed at a specific ethnic group.[14] If this were true, how could a particularistic model of Islam like Sufi orders spread across ethnicities, regions and groups, and develop nationalistic urges?

The actual history of nation-state building in Arab lands, in Turkey, Iran and to some extent in Pakistan in the twentieth century provides ample evidence that the major obstacle to modern nation-state building was particularist Sufi Islam: the fragmented units protected were by their Sufi culture, not universal Islam. It was reformed, universal Islam that countered Sufi fragmentation and paved the way for the cultural forging of national rather than subnational communities.

The Kurdish case offers an exact opposite. Bruinessen has testified in this volume to the crucial role Sufi orders and networks played in the enhancement of the early Kurdish prototype nationalist rebellions in Iraq.[15]

Reformed Islam could create a cementing culture that superseded and overcame tribal and bedouin segmentation and fragmentation long before the creation of unifying modern systems, such as bureaucracy, currency, fixed borders, standing armies or specialized, state-controlled educational systems relying on high-tech communication and transportation systems.[16]

But Islam's universalism, on the other hand, could be and has actually been instrumental in fostering pan-national loyalties throughout the twentieth century. At the same time, universal Islam could function, as it does today, as the theoretical basis for the claim of a pan-Islamic nation and nationalism.[17]

Viewed from the vantage point of the nineteenth-century 'sacred' Ottoman Empire, nationalism seems a divisive force. The rise of several nation-states in its stead is thus a new political organization with two edges directed simultaneously against the greater, cosmically central community (Islamdom, or Christendom) and against the internal segmentation of the same large cosmic community. In short, nationalism and nation-building involve cessation and unification, integration and disintegration, centrifugal and centripetal tendencies.

The Ottoman Empire and Turkish Nationalism

In the preceding sections we noted that the rise of nationalism followed the creation of the first wave of nation-states, but that nationalism preceded that of the second and third waves. In all cases, nationalism, nationhood and national statehood were the outcome of the transition from agrarianism to industrialism.

Not only did Arab and Kurdish nationalism precede the construction of Arab or Kurdish nation-states, but also these nationalisms preceded any transition to industrialism. They were thus responsive nationalisms; reacting against and responding to external dynamics. Ottoman reforms and Turkish nationalism were among these dynamics.

In his *The History of Arab Peoples*, Albert Hourani points out that:

> Turkish and Arab nationalism at this stage [the second half of the nineteenth century] were not primarily directed against the encroachment of the European power as much as towards problems of identity and political organization of the empire: what were the conditions on which the Ottoman Muslim community could continue to exist?

He also adds that:

> Egyptian, Tunisian, and Algerian nationalism were different in these ways. All three were faced with specific problems of European rule, all three were concerned with these problems

within a clearly delimited country. Egypt and Tunisia had been virtually separate political entities for a long time, first under their own dynasties, then under British or French rule; Algeria too had been a separate Ottoman territory and had now been virtually integrated into France.[18]

The Ottoman Empire was a multi-national, multi-ethnic, multi-religious organization, stretching over almost all the modern Arab world (with the exception of Morocco) and covering considerable territories in eastern and middle Europe. Apart from Anatolia, the remaining Ottoman Arab provinces were ruled by alien dynasties descending from the military elites, with a great measure of autonomy culminating in virtual independence (Egypt, Algeria, Tunisia, Yemen, Hijaz in Arabia) or ruled by local notable tribal chieftains or religious families (Ashraf, that is. the noble, presumably descendants from the prophet Muhammad's family or tribe). Some exceptions existed: certain provinces were ruled by governors directly appointed by the Sublime Porte in Istanbul.[19]

In this polity, individual citizens, secular law, the sovereignty of the nation, territorial state and other aspects of modern nation-statehood were simply wanting; in their stead were primordial or traditional groups (tribes, clans, religious groups ,urban artisan and merchants guilds represented by their notables and chieftains) the Shari'a (Islamic law), the patrimonial rule of the sultan coupled with a degree of direct representation of groups and sects by their elders and notables; and the boundaries of the empire extended to wherever possible: in a word, this was a pre-modern world.

At the turn of the twentieth century, and even long before, the empire had been disintegrating, unable either to successfully challenge the superior, encroaching West, or to sustain its domination over rising nationalism in its European sectors, or even decentralization tendencies in some Arabic parts (Egypt, Algeria, Tunisia, the Arabian Peninsula, the Sudan).

The need to hold together a teetering empire from within, coupled with other urgent needs in facing challenges from European industrial powers, imposed on sections of the Ottoman civil and military elites and functionaries a drive to modernize the state, starting with the military. Rivalries among European powers enhanced this process. In the eyes of state functionaries, modernization was an absolute necessity. But the reformers conceived of modernity in military and political terms, simply as a reorganization of state agencies.

The first attempts to reorganize the military (abolishing the Janissary and creating a standing army equipped with modern, if imported, military technology) were met with stiff resistance from both the traditional Janissary and some religious circles.[20]

In the meantime, Western powers were penetrating the markets of the empire, relying on networks of domestic trade agents, often non-Muslims. At a later stage, Western pressures from Britain, France and Austria for political, legal and economic reforms, above all guaranteeing the modern rights of property and abolishing the poll tax imposed according to the Shari'a on non-Muslims, were increased. With such reforms, perhaps even earlier, came Western ideas, notably those of the French Revolution: nationalism and constitutionalism were on the agenda. A similar, perhaps more vigorous, development took place in Egypt under Muhammad Ali.[21]

The history of European influence on Ottoman rulers and state functionaries goes back to the eighteenth century, with the Ottoman ambassadors or travellers to Europe channeling back their admiration of the new industrial and advanced civilization, as compared with their stagnant, backward world. As a result of their literary works, the Ottomans heard for the first time of manufactures, printing machines (introduced in 1726), man-made laws, modern military organization, and the like.[22]

The emergence of the Young Ottomans, a secret liberal society formed in 1865 to establish a constitutional state, marked a new historical era.[23] Highly influenced by the French thinkers (for example, Rousseau and Montesquieu) whose works had been translated into Turkish a century earlier they also came under the influence of German and Italian nationalist movements working towards for their belated nationhood.

The liberal nationalism of the Young Ottomans was still intertwined with the religious matrix of Islamic traditional thought. Ali Suavi, one of the Young Ottoman's ideologues, called for 'religious reform as the starting point of a revival of Islamic state and law'.[24]

Loving one's country, the Young Ottomans asserted in citing sayings of the Prophet Muhammad, is part of religious belief; and constitutionalism is but the Islamic *Shura* principle (consultation). Ali Suavi was labelled a 'liberal theologian' and a 'turbaned revolutionary'. Yet it was he who after the Franco-Prussian War broke with the idea of Ottomanism, or Ottoman nationalism, and adopted for the first time the concept of 'Turkish as distinct from Islamic Ottoman loyalty'.[25]

Logically, constitutionalism presupposed the transfer of sovereignty from the God-ordained sultan to the worldly people. This in turn implied seeds of nationalism, positing the question who are the people and how are they defined.

At this stage Turkish nationalism was not yet clearly defined, nor had it a mature secular form. Constitutionalism encountered fierce opposition from Sultan Abdulhamid and the religious establishment, the Grand Mufti, who were reviving the title of the caliphate, an old religious office giving its bearer both a political and religious status and control over all Muslims. Thus the ruling dynasty and its clerical establishment threw Islam into a political battle with both constitutionalism and, later on, nationalism.

Secularization of laws, of the educational system and of other areas was gaining momentum, weakening the seven pillars of the caliphate wisdom. The fate of the Young Ottomans was bleak, and finally ended with the collapse of constitutional reform, with the dissolution of the first Ottoman parliament in February 1878, after a short lifespan of eleven months. But the constitutional-nationalist revolution was only a decade ahead. The movement known as the Young Turks was started by four students (paradoxically some of them were Kurds by ethnic origin) in 1889, grew rapidly and gained military muscles by winning over officers in the standing army. The movement developed two trends: one was liberal and stood for decentralization of the empire, by giving more autonomous rights to ethnic groups, including the Arabs and Kurds; the other (the Union and Progress) advocated a constitutional polity with central Turkish authority.

The printed word, telegraph and railway systems – the modern communication networks – not only provided the physical means to organize and agitate for the new ideas, but enabled interaction throughout the region. The development of the modern educational system and the new, standing army offered another social agent for change. It was the Young Turks movement that inspired, organized and led the constitutional revolution against Caliph Abdulhamid II in 1908. Both movements, the Young Ottomans and later the Young Turks, left deep marks on Islamic traditional structures and thought, and encouraged urban elites of other Muslim groups, Arabs and Kurds, to embrace the new discourse of nationalism.

The year 1906 should also be remembered. It was the year of the constitutional revolution (*Mashruta*) in Qajar, Iran, in which a significant element of the clergy played an important part, advocating the Persian variety of constitutionalism shrouded, as it were, in a secular-religious form of Persian nationalism. The Shi'i clerisy was divided, and a liberal wing strongly endorsed constitutionalism.[26] Among the most interesting features was that the Qajar Shah called for an *Islamic 'majlis'* (assembly); while it was the anti-Shah clergy who demanded a *National* Assembly ('*Majles-i Melli*').[27] The name of Muhammad Na'ini figures high as the clerical ideologue of the

Iranian constitutional revolution.

The First World War brought the dismemberment of what was left of the Ottoman Empire, releasing Turkish, Arab and Kurdish nationalism in search of identity and statehood.

Literary Nationalism, Islamic Nationalism and Ethnic Arab Nationalism

There are two different but widely accepted representations of the genesis of Arab nationalism. The first refers to the revival of Arab literature in the mid-nineteenth century; the second to the 1917 Arab Rebellion led by Sharif Hussein of Mecca against the Ottomans. Both views overlook the third phase in between these two, namely the work and role of the great Muslim reformer Jamal Al-Din al-Afghani (d. 1989), in promoting anti-Western nationalist urges. At the same time, both representations falsely emphasize an Arab–Turkish conflict. These three intertwined moments require elaboration.

Arabs and Turks

Under the Sublime Porte, Arabs and Kurds lived in what Holt terms a 'peaceful symbiosis' with the Turks. Turkish was the language of administration, Arabic that of state religion.[28] Both were linked by a common religious loyalty, that of Islam. In fact, the Arabs played an important part in the circles that surrounded the Ottoman governors of Arab provinces, in addition to their existence in the higher echelons of the Ottoman standing army and administration, which testifies that little attention was paid to Turkish–Arabic linguistic and ethnic distinctions. Yet this symbiosis was not altogether free of rivalries, contradictions and even animosities.

Arab nationalistic or ethnic self-consciousness, a predecessor of political nationalism proper, began, like its Kurdish counterpart, in the form of literary nationalism as early as the mid-nineteenth century. The ideals of the French Revolution had already influenced many Arab thinkers and intellectuals.

In this period literary nationalism involved a group of Arab writers and intellectuals, the majority of whom were Christian Arabs from the Levant, in search of equality of citizenship under the influence of Western discourses of nationalism. For them, Arabism would override the religious hierarchy of the Ottoman millet system. Prominent among the 'cultural nationalists' were Nasif Al-Yaziji, Butrus Al-Bustani, Jurji Zaydan and other late nineteenth-century writers. They expressed pride in the Arab language, in Arab history and heritage, sowing thereby the seeds of an Arab cultural nationalism that would sooner or later develop into political, though elitist, doctrine.

But these were individual cases, isolated by illiteracy and weak communication, and inhibited by religious divisions.[29]

Afghani and the politicization of nationalism

In most studies of the origins of Arab nationalism, the Islamic thinker and reformer Jamal Al-din Al-Afghani (1839–97) is almost dismissed. Afghani (or Asad Abadi, according to Nekkie Keddie)[30] is invariably presented as a religious reformer rather than a nationalist thinker. Keddie's book on Afghani adopted the interesting title *An Islamic Response to Imperialism*.

A closer look at his writings and activities may well justify concluding that Afghani is the precursor of both Islamic and Arab nationalism, or the father of both secular and religious forms of nationalism. Quoting W. C. Smith, Keddie says that Afghani was '[T]he first to stress the 'Islam–West' antinomy and the first important figure with nostalgia for the departed earthly glory of pristine Islam.' Smith further notes that Afghani stressed both internal reform and external defence, encouraged both nationalism and pan-Islam, and advocated borrowing from the West, bringing a new vitalistic activism.[31]

Afghani, a stateless citizen, constant traveller and practising militant, presented no systemized view on nationalism or even pan-Islamism. His main concern was agitation for an anti-imperialist drive in India, Persia, Egypt and Ottoman Turkey during his active life in the second half of the nineteenth century. In part, his religious reform, the essence of which was a return to rationalism and the exaltation of reason, was devised to strengthen the Islamic world against the encroaching West.

It is interesting to note, as Keddie has asserted, how Afghani, during his Indian period, laid emphasis on *nationalism*: 'There is no happiness except in nationality, and there is no nationality except in language, and language cannot be called a language except if it embraces all affairs that those in manufacture and trade need for explanation.' He further adds that human bonds are twofold: 'one is ... the unity of language of which nationality and national unity consist ... the other is religion'. But a single people with 'one language in the course of thousands of years changes its religion two or three times without [changing] its nationality'.[32]

In later periods Afghani kept this duality of religion–nationalism, but he began to put emphasis on pan-Islamism more than ever. Two factors may explain this: first, Afgani's view of the civilizational role of religion; and, second, the practical needs of his activities and alliances against the British, which varied in different parts of the Islamic world.

To save the lands of Islam from falling into the hands of Britain and other colonial powers, it was necessary, he thought, first to reform Islam on Protestant lines, install constitutional democracy and forge an Islamic unity of action between Ottoman Turkey, Qajar Iran, Egypt (before the British occupation) and Afghanistan. His call for political and intellectual modernization was based on a reinterpretation of the tenets of Islam against traditional, medieval scholasticism, which was fatalist in nature and rigid in structure, and which rejected and resisted change.

His lectures at the Al-Azhar mosque school in Egypt and in Istanbul focused, among other things, on exalting the primacy of human reason, rationality and the need for *Ijtihad* (independent ruling in matters of religion). To Afghani, religion was the driving force of civilization and the moral stimulator of human actions. No society was conceivable without religion.

Yet it was, in his opinion, the fatalist nature of current Islam (its submissive otherworldliness) that caused the backwardness of the Muslims, and he set out on a new trajectory to rationalize Islamic dogmas in order to cope with the challenges of the time. To that end he revived medieval rational Islamic philosophy and theology ('*Mutazilite*') which had 'exalted reason above literalist revelation'.[33]

Afghani combined nationalism with constitutionalism, and tied both to religious reform.[34] If he had held aloft the Islamic League as a supreme goal in the hope that this would unite the Muslim states and peoples of the time against the imperial West (Britain, in fact), he did not underestimate the role of nationalism, notably Arabism: 'There is no way to distinguish one nation from another but by language ... The Arab nation is Arabic before being affiliated to any religion or sect'.[35] He praised the role of Arabs and Arabic as the people and language of early, triumphant Islam, and severely criticized the Turks for having no cultural contribution similar to that of the Arabs. He even lamented the fact that the Turks could have, in his opinion, created a nation held together by the two most powerful of all human bonds, religion and ethnicity.[36]

In his interesting call to the Afghans and the Persians to unite, he wrote: '[the] Germans differed in their Christian religion the way Iranians and Afghanis differ in their confessions. When Germany saw its national unity threatened, it prioritized patriotic unity and became the master of Europe'.[37]

Nations, he said on another occasion, 'are formed by two cementing forces, that of *Jins* (nationality) based on solidarity and cohesion, and on religion, which performs the same function ethnicities do in uniting the people'.[38]

Divided disciples: Kawakibi and others

Afghani left deep marks on the first manifestations of nationalist action in Iran and Egypt, and his influence was felt even in the high Shi'i clerical circles in Iraq (Samara), with many of whom he had correspondence.

The religious–ethnic duality of his doctrine gradually dissolved into its two elementary components; and these components were, so to speak, divided among his disciples in the wider Middle East. Religious reformation, the reformation of traditional political culture and the structure of the religious establishment was task taken up by both Muhammad Abdu (1849–1905), who ultimately became the Grand Mufti of Egypt, and the Syrian constitutional Arabist thinker Abdul Rahman Kawakaibi (d. 1903, in Cairo).

Whereas Abdu's nationalism took on an Egyptian character, that of Kwakibi was pan-Arabist. Later on, Abdu's heritage developed into a secular–constitutional Egyptian nationalism (Saa'd Zaghlool and Lutfi al-Sayid) and a traditional pan-Islamic form of nationalism, developed by the Cairo-based Syrian disciple of Abdu, the fundamentalist Rashid Ridha.

Kawakibi, a Kurd from Aleppo, was the real and actual founding father of the first concept of Arab nationalism. In his two major works, *The Nature of Despotism* and *The Mother Of Towns*, Kawakibi examines two intertwined notions, that of tyranny, in this case Turkish, and of Arab unity on the basis of patriotism (*Watani,* meaning ethnic or nationalist) not religion. To him, religious tyranny is the basis of political and other forms of despotism. And the basis of religious tyranny is passive fatalism.[39] He calls upon Arabs to unite in a nation 'like the nations of America and Australia which science has led to patriotic rather than religious union, national [Jinsi] rather than religious communal and political rather than administrative allegiances ... Long live the nation [Umma], longlive the *fatherland,* let us live *free*'.[40]

The Arab nation Kawakibi speaks of includes the Fertile Crescent and Egypt: the Maghrib (Morocco, Algeria, Tunisia and Libya) is almost always excluded from the term 'Arab lands' in the writings of this period down to the middle of the twentieth century. According to Kawakibi, the cornerstone of the Arab nation is the shift of the caliphate from the Turks back to the

Arabs. The idea of the caliph being an Arab from Quraish, the clan of the prophet Muhammad, is as old as Islamic theology and jurisprudence; yet it reappears here in Kawakibi's writings in a constitutional garb, devoid of any worldly power of governance. Kawakibi's caliph is merely a symbol for Islam in general, and a reintroduction of the Arabs into the highest seat of power in defiance of the Ottomans, whose ruler, Sultan Abdulhamid, claims the caliphate for himself and his own political designs.

Hourani says of Kawakibi's notion:

> The centre of gravity must move back to Arabia: there should be an Arabian caliph of the line of Quraish, *elected* by *representatives of the Umma*; he should have religious authority throughout the Muslim world, and be assisted in the exercise of it [religious authority] by a consultative body nominated by the Muslim rulers. If he has any temporal authority [here political] it is confined in Hijaz [in Arabia].[41]

Not only does the concept of the caliphate advocated by Kawakibi differ from that of Sultan Abdulhamid, but it constitutes its direct opposite. It was constitutionalist, void of political power and distanced from the Turks or any non-Arab contender.[42]

Kawakibi's theory owes much to the Italian nationalist thinker Alfeiri, whom he had read in Turkish in Istanbul during his civil service there. The idea of restoring the caliphate to the Arabs, it should be mentioned, was in the air. It had been propagated on a very limited scale by Napoleon Bonaparte during his short-lived conquest of Egypt,[43] encouraged by the various Egyptian khedives by old Egyptian–Ottoman rivalries; and was actually put on the agenda by the British and the French on the eve of the First World War.[44] But Kawakibi's aim for the caliphate was to see it abolished, not restored: he was more concerned with constitutional nationalism.

At the time of Kawakibi's teachings, attempts to free Arab nationalistic thought from its religious matrix had already been started, though on a very limited scale, by some Christian Lebanese and Syrian writers, within what we have termed cultural nationalism. Further attempts at secular nationalist ideas took place in the hands of two prominent Christian Arab intellectuals, Adib Ishaq (1856–85), a Syrian from a mercantile family in Damascus, and Najib Azouri (d. 1916). Unlike Kawakibi, both were French-educated Christians, but, like him, both lived in exile in Egypt, and were alienated from the Ottomans. With Arab (Syrian) grievances in the background, together with concern over the fate of Arab Christians within the hypothetical Arab nation if and when based on 'religious ethnicity', an anti-Turkish Arabism with secular tones was bound to emanate from their sentiments, writings and activities.[45]

In Adib Ishaq's articles 'can be seen the first full expression of the feelings which had now gathered around the concept of the nation and formed the state of mind called "nationalism"'.[46]

Hourani adds that Ishaq, in his support and cooperation with the anti-British 'Urabi revolt in Egypt towards the end of nineteenth century, emphasized 'the importance of national unity [which] ...included Copts and Muslims'.[47]

According to Azouri, the Turks had destroyed civilization and no reform should be expected from Sultan Abdul Hamid II: hence independence should be sought, but with the help of foreign powers. His French involvements were suspected, and Azouri spent the rest of his life in Paris, whereas Adib Ishaq was banished by the Egyptian khedive, only to be placed behind bars in Constantinople.

It is interesting to note that Azouri's political scheme related only to the Fertile Crescent, excluding Egypt and the Maghrib, both under British and French control. Adib Ishaq, on the other hand, envisaged an all-embracing Arab unity, containing all Arab-speaking people in the Mashraq and Maghrib. His anti-Western colonialism was paramount.[48] But the political ideas of both were anchored in French liberal ideas of constitutionalism and religious freedom.

Ishaq was nearer to the pulse of Christian Arabs sensing a need for a unity transcending religious allegiance; Azouri was more willing to show due consideration to traditional Muslim thinking and the Egyptian rulers, whence sprang his adherence to the idea of restoring the Arab caliphate.

A New Era: Post-Independence Secular Nationalism and the German Paradigm

By the end of the First World War, the old religious solidarity with, or ethnic alienation from, the Ottomans had gone with the wind, though the secular and religious forms of solidarity of the subcommunities were present in Arab societies and developing both within the newly emerging nation-states (Iraq, Egypt) and in those countries which were still under colonial control.

In this period nationalism took further steps in developing a clear distinction from religion; the separation of the one from the other was now achieved by the non-Christian theoretician Sati' al-Husri (d.1968).

With the collapse of the Ottoman Empire, whose administration he served and in whose Turkish language he was versed, Husri shifted loyalties, as many Arab-Ottomans elites did, from the Ottoman Islamic League to Pan-Arabism, basing himself not on French but on German classical thought, notably that of Fichte.[49] The nation, according to Husri, is a spiritual entity, standing above race, sect, religion and history itself: it is a 'natural' phenomenon. Common language and history are the very essence of nationalism, any nationalism. In his own words, the nation is a living organism endowed with life and sensibilities; language is the life of the nation, and history is its sensibility.[50]

To avoid any misconception, Husri sets rigid and well defined limits to differentiate nations and nationalism from state, and fatherland (territorial boundaries) from patriotism. This non-congruence of nation and state is bizarre, given the fact that the unity of the two is the ideal to which nationalism strives.

For Husri, however, each category (nation and state) constitutes a different entity or aspect of human societies and their political organization. Why this odd separation of, at the least, the nation from the state, or of fatherland (as a geographical setting) from nationalism? The answer lies in the reality of the Arab nation to which he expounded his theory, and for whose unity he went on striving with the help of Syria (under King Faisal), Iraq, and later Egypt under Nasser: it did not have a state of its own, but was rather a multitude of territorial-administrative states with their own native nationalism (or patriotism).[51]

The language-nation theory was in contrast to many states and nations worldwide, as is the case of Spanish or Portuguese-speaking Latin-American countries, or multi-lingual Switzerland and Belgium. Husri would answer that these are states, not nations, and support his view with the philosophical argument that man, as a species, is a speaking animal rather than a social or political animal.[52]

Husri's option for the German theory of nationalism, notably that of Fichte whose work he praised highly (even more than Herder's and Hegel's), could be attributed to the fact that the German theory of nationalism, as we observed in Section One, was authoritarian in nature. It defined nation as *Stamme* (the German word for tribe or clan), which is a primordial definition lending a birth-imposed natural togetherness to the national community.

The French notion of nationalism was liberal, anchored in the will of togetherness, involving free choice, and bonding mutual interest, as the nineteenth-century French thinker E. Renan reiterated.[53] Husri opposed the French concept, and searched for a theory of nationalism, like that of the German Romantics,[54] that could match the Arabs' divided polities. Perhaps the revival of Germany in the 1930s deepened the admiration of the Arab nationalists for the vitality of German nationalism; certainly in this period the nationalists of the Middle East showed their preference for Germany and even Fascist Italy as a way of expressing their antipathy towards the French and the British, their colonial oppressors. In plain words Husri said in 1930: 'The model we should endeavour to achieve is that of fascism not Bolshevism.'[55]

With Husri, the secular, authoritarian, theoretical model of Arab nationalism reached its peak. Later, Ba'thism was to be almost a replica, at least in practice.

Husri's secular tones were highly praised,[56] particularly by the Soviet scholar Techonova.[57] However, his authoritarian model of monolithic nations, following the German model, left a negative legacy of assimilative Arabism in Iraq and Syria. As a result, the Kurds in these two countries suffered from the conflict between the German paradigm, embraced by a nationalist Arab government, and the French paradigm, aspired to by non-Arab ethnic groups. Husri's authoritarian ethnic legacy still lingers on.

Populist Nationalism: the Ba'ath

If, in the nineteenth century, the former generation of nationalist thinkers was composed of individuals from traditional backgrounds – traditional families, notables, mercantile households and religious nobility – the next generation of Arab nationalist ideologues, in the second half of the twentieth century, descended from new social strata, the middle and lower middle classes, in a society moving towards modernization. Husri was a transitional figure in an interim period. The older generation moved within a very limited circle of literate elites of a traditional society, using printed media against a vast ocean of illiteracy and isolated rural areas where the bulk of population worked and lived, a society where social discourses were metaphysical in the Comtian[58] sense of the word, a pre-Copernican cosmos.

Outside the elitist salons of the nobles and notables, modern political parties and societies emerged, extending deep roots among the urban classes and beyond. A new movement emerged that focused on imperialist hegemony and social aspects of modernization, such as agrarian reform and industrial relations.

The world saw the rise and brief success of Fascism and Nazism, the victory of the Allies, the growing prestige of the Soviet Union and Marxism, the rise of national liberation movements in Asia (Vietnam, China and India) and later in Africa. The war of liberation marked a turning point from earlier nationalism, from autonomy under British or French control to full independence. Such was the general context under which a new popular and populist wave of pan-Arab nationalism grew, namely Ba'thism and Nasserism.

Among the new generation of nationalist thinkers and leaders many names, mostly Syrians, appear: Zaki Arsouzi, an Alawite intellectual from Alexandria; Akram Hourani, a Sunni Muslim landowner; and Michel 'Aflaq, an Orthodox from a Damascene mercantile family; and Salah al-Din al-Bitar, a Muslim Sunni intellectual. Although Ba'thism was associated with the name of Michel Aflaq (c. 1989), it was the brainchild of these four middle-class Syrian intellectuals. Hourani brought to the movement his 'rural socialism'; Aflaq added the nationalization of Islam; Arsouzi introduced an esoteric spiritualism; and Bitar brought his French teachings on nationalism.

In the interwar period, Arabs lost independence; Syria was colonized by the French; Alexandria was the object of Turkish irredentism; and Palestine was lost to Zionism. This was conceived as nationalist decline; and the ruling conservative and traditional nobles and notables were held to blame.

Ba'thism had to face three political and ideological challenges, that of traditional Islamism, which now took a political form (the Muslim Brotherhood, spreading from Egypt and backed by Saudi Arabia); the Marxist movement, which was gaining some momentum in Syria and Iraq; and the pre-independence, traditional nationalism.

In its founding statement, the BASP said:

> We represent the Arab spirit against materialist communism.
>
> We represent the living Arab history against the dead history of the reactionaries [i.e., the Muslim Brothers]
>
> We are against the verbal, false nationalism [i.e. traditional landlords].[59]

In *Towards Renaissance*, Aflaq says: 'The religious reactionary is in the same camp as the social reactionary.'[60]

Husri's theory, as observed earlier, distinguished nationalism and the nation from the state; Husri also defined the cultural content of nationhood in the secular ethnic terms of language and history. Aflaq, by contrast, turned his back on the universal character of ethnic nationalism, and reintroduced Islam to the national spirit, stating that: 'Islam is an Arab movement; it means the renovation and perfection of Arabism ... the message of Islam is to create an Arab humanism.'[61]

Aflaq nationalized Islam, yet this led to the reintroduction of religion into theory. Husri fought such inclusion all the way long. He was a pedagogue and an acute theoretician with weak political instincts. Aflaq was a political writer with weak theoretical instincts, and a Christian who feared religious isolation. Yet Aflaq and his circle had some philosophical affinity with Husri. The latter was German-educated; the former French-educated. The German philosophical influence, however, crept through the French admirers and disciples of Nietzsche. The Will to power Aflaq speaks of echoed Nietzsche's Zarathustra. Aflaq's conceptualized the Will as creator of the world, as a self-sustained essence that determines its determinants. The Will as essence is eternal, unchangeable; it is the carrier of many predicates which may change and even whither away, but the bearer would retain its eternal nature.

This is reflected in his definition of the nation. To him the nation is first and foremost a Will, an idea that existed in the past and should be rediscovered in the present. Nationalism, on the other hand, is 'first and foremost love'.[62] Or, 'Our nationalism is not a theory but the source of all theories, it is not the offspring of thought but its mother. ... Should we encapsulate nationalism in a very limited space of consciousness, imprison it in a narrow definition as did theology with religion in the past?'[63]

The nation is a will and idea, eternal in nature, nationalism is love, and Islam is the national Arab agent. The fourth and perhaps most important element in Aflaq's views is that of the Arab's *Khosusiya*, that is, his originality or exclusive, unique nature. We are different, says Aflaq. We are *not* like the West: we differ from the rest of the world. This difference is not defined in the sense of what exactly the Arabs are like, but rather the other way round: what the Arabs are *not*. Logic states that definition (or determination) is negation. To Aflaq, negation is definition.

The mystical elements in Aflaq 's ideas (as with Arsouzi) belong to a whole period, when the nation was conceived as a spiritual entity or essence transcending, like superman, time and space in the reality of the supra-terrestrial.

The Mashriq and the Maghrib

Nationalistic concepts and doctrines in the Mashraq were secular and ethnic, with minor Islamic motifs; those in the Maghrib were Islamic in character; in Egypt the two coexisted. This is a major differential distinguishing Arab from Kurdish nationalism as far as the uneasy symbiosis of religion and nationalism is concerned. But this differential also shows that different forms of nationalism may develop among a single ethnic community, as Abbas Vali argues in this volume, and as I do below.

In the Mashraq, nationalistic sentiments and notions developed in direct opposition to the Ottomans. The need to break with common religious identity and bring forth ethnic differences was felt by native political activists. Christian Arabs were also inclined to supersede religious divisions with their co-ethnic Muslim Arabs.

In the Maghrib, by contrast, lack of religious or ethnic uniformity between the colonizers and the colonized rendered ethnic difference directly manifest in Islam. Islam was a marker of the Arabic speaking community in as much as the Arabic language was a marker of Islam. And both could easily stress the native nationalism that characterized the administrative and political units the Ottomans had created, Algeria, Tunisia, for example. The presence of French colonial settlements reinforced the cultural duality that was, per se, conducive to that version of pre-modern responsive nationalism.

When Arabism made its appearance in the Maghrib, the notion was already a part of Islam. Even nowadays, Islam is equated with Arabism, and the man in the street would hardly believe that an Arab is not a Muslim.[64]

Gradually, responsive proto-nationalism was embedded in reformed Islam: Bin Badis (d. 1940) in Algeria, or Tha'alibi, the founder of the Constitutionalist party (d. 1944) in Tunisia, took the nationalist initiative to heart.

Bin Badis's couplet became the war cry:

> The People of Algeria
> Are Muslims
> And to Arabism they belong
> [*Sha'b al-jaza'iri Muslimun*
> *Wa Ila al-'Urobati Yantasib*]

Egypt was a unique, more complex, case, combining Islamic nationalism with native, Egyptian nationalism throughout the nineteenth and the first half of the twentieth centuries, only to add pan-Arabism to its history. It was a country with a definite territorial space, a ruling dynasty, and a measure of tension with Constantinople. When Napoleon Bonaparte invaded Mamluk Egypt in the early nineteenth century he could not find any trace of the Arabism his German mentor and philosopher, Leibniz, had advised him to win over if he wanted to turn Arabs against the Turkish Ottomans. Instead he found a strong Islamic identity, and, out of sheer opportunism, he converted to Islam.[65]

Responsive nationalism, however, soon began to surface in reaction to the British occupation and Ottoman pressures. Perhaps Muhammad 'Abdu best illustrated these two facets. He speaks of the tyrannical Sultan Abdulhamid II as 'the greatest murderer in this epoch',[66] but adds that 'Arabs deserve having a glorious state of their own ... but the Turks would fight them ... When both the Turks and the Arabs are weakened, the European powers would jump to subjugate both or the weakest.'[67]

The programme of the Egyptian National (*Watani*) Party, formulated in part by Abdu himself, conveys a sense of what nationalism (here Egyptian) is and is not: 'The National Party is a political not religious organization; it includes men of different creeds and dogmas, all Christians and Jews, and *any person who toils on the land of Egypt and speaks its language*.'[68]

The programme also envisaged good relations with the Sublime Porte, the Khedive and European powers, namely France and England.[69]

'Abdu was the father of Egyptian secular and liberal nationalism. But the other part of his activity and writings were concerned with the reformation of Islam. Like his mentor, Afghani, he held that Islam was the true driving force of civilization. It is this latter part of Afghani-Abdu's heritage that would be the mainspring of the Islamic cultural nationalism led by the next generation of their disciples, beginning with the fundamentalist Rashid Ridha (d. 1935). His concepts were partly an ideal continuation of Abdu's Islamic reformed themes; but also a discontinuation. Unlike his predecessor he rejected modernity and advocated Islamic particularism.

According to Hamid Enayat, Ridha was the first to coin the concept of the 'Islamic state', on the eve of the abolition of the caliphate in 1924.

Ridha's Islamic state was not meant to be an alternative to the caliphate, but to the modern state. The traditional concept of the caliphate envisages a union of religion and the politics. The liberal modernist followers of Abdu (such as Ali Abdul Raziq of Egypt) denied the caliphate as an imperative of faith.[70] Ridha took the opposite position; he 'made a direct assault on two vital issues: the principle of popular sovereignty and the possibility of man-made laws'.[71]

Ridha was thus the precursor of contemporary fundamentalism, which soon made its appearance in Egypt in 1928 in the hands of Hassan al-Banna. It is this trend that would gradually mould the Islamic form of cultural nationalism that we know today.

Hassan Banna, the founder of the Muslim Brotherhood, attempted the Islamization of the modern concepts of patriotism, nationalism and Arabism, lending them a traditional legitimacy. Banna saw in the concept of patriotism two conflicting aspects, one positive and acceptable, namely loving one's own country, the second secular and unacceptable, namely the idea that patriotism is the source of allegiance tying individuals to a territorial state. Islam, in Banna's view, is the boundaries of the *'watan'* (homeland), not the geographical limits set by patriotism, *Wataniya*. In addition to idealizing national borders, Banna finds a similar duality in the concept of patriotism: a positive aspect conducive to a search for glory, endeavour to work and struggle; and a negative one composed of elements of *Jahiliya* (barbarism), such as glorifying race, aggression against weaker races (a reference to Italy and Germany) and deserting the creed of Islam, not to mention the abolition of the Arabic language in writing and letters, a reference to Kemal Ataturk's decision to replace the Arabic with the European alphabet. Banna also made Arabism a predicate to Islam, not the other way round, as was the case with secular Arab nationalists. In his view, however, Egyptianism and Arabism were micro-allegiances; the major allegiance is the Islamic nation, the universal realm of Islam. If Banna combined these three levels of identity, the main cohesive element of all is Islam as a faith, culture and polity. The unity of religion and state in the form of adopting the Shari'a was his paramount ideal.[72]

Neo-Fundamentalism and Nationalism

The rise of Islamic fundamentalism came in the wake of the Arab defeat in the June war of 1967. The defeat of Pakistan in 1971 and the secession of Bangladesh had similar effects. The Iranian revolution in February 1979, which assumed an Islamic character, was another factor in the neo-Islamic boom.

As far as nationalism is concerned, sociologists such as Emanuel Sivan jumped to the conclusion that neo-Islamism is bidding nationalism farewell. The reason why this divorce is so emphatically asserted is the internecine ideological battle between secular nationalist and Islamists.

I would argue that the neo-Islamist movements are, in the main, a reproduction of nationalist movements and trends of the 1950s, operating this time at a more sophisticated level of political motivation, mobilization and militancy, but with a different political debate. The new Islamic movements combine the various layers of political, economic and cultural nationalism into one coherent whole. The cultural component seems crucial.

In his de-nationalizing of the fundamentalist movements, Sivan relied heavily on the examples of the Muslim Brothers (MB) in Egypt and Syria in the 1960s, when they refused to cooperate with the ruling national regimes in their war against Israel. This, in fact, is the general position of almost all neo-Islamic movements in the Mashraq, even after the Arab debacle in 1967. For example, the MB leadership in the West Bank considered the defeat a divine revenge exacted on Nasser and his allies for the execution of the prominent MB leader Sayyid Qutb in Egypt in 1965.[73]

The reaction in the Maghrib may have been dissimilar. At least we can quote the Tunisian neo-Islamist leader, Jorshi, who, along with his movement, criticized the Bourqaiba regime for *not* taking part in the Arab struggle against Israel. The other, more traditional-minded leader of the same trend in Tunisia, Rashid Ghanooshi, said loud and clear: 'I was an advocate of Nasserism because I hated Bourgiba, the enemy of Arabism and Arab-speaking people, I loved Nasser because he was the symbol of Arabism and Islam.'[74]

We have argued earlier that Arabism and Islamism were combined together in the Maghrib; in the Mashraq, they developed separately, and sometimes in opposition to each other. The effects of the two Gulf Wars (1980 and 1990-1) helped the mixture in the Mashraq to coalesce.[75]

In a search for a common ground, the secular nationalist and Islamic movements began to explore and reinvent their positions. One example is the forty-six successive nationalist–Islamist conferences held between 1980 and 1990. These events revealed a great deal of ideological rapprochement between the thinkers and leaders of the two wings. Reading the documented minutes of their meetings, both groups extended mutual recognition of each others' themes as true and complementary. It was argued by the Islamists (Hasan Turabi of Sudan) that Islamic unity is inconceivable without Arab unity.[76]

In addition to despotism and social injustice, three main nationalistic themes were highlighted by the Islamists: the threat of Westernization and dependency, the hazards posed by Israel, and, lastly, the urgent need for Arab and Islamic unity.[77] What this rapprochement may well signify is the existence of a measure of nationalistic continuity.

Burgat maintains that political Islam is the voice of 'the South' against 'the North'. He views neo-Islamism as the third phase of the nationalistic drive to eliminate colonialism. Muslims, he thinks, began with political independence as a first stage, moved to economic independence as a second, and they are now heading towards cultural independence as the third and perhaps the last stage.[78] This culturalist representation is typically French.

Cultural alienation from the West forms the main feature of Islamic nationalism, but cultural nationalism is hardly bereft of political and economic nationalism.

Ethnic nationalism stands in contrast to Islamic nationalism in that the former recognized the community as the focus of allegiance, and, if it was liberal, it would also recognize the people as the source of sovereignty and legislation. These themes are abhorred by Islamists; they see the sovereignty of the people and placing allegiance with mundane, mortal beings as an encroachment upon God's glory.

Ethnic, secular nationalism, whether pan-Arab or local, poses the problem of other ethnic groups, such as the Berbers, notably in Algeria, the African-Christian group in south Sudan, and the Kurds in Iraq and Syria. Islamic nationalism, on the other hand, excludes non-Muslims and recognizes no ethnic community, Kurds or otherwise.

The shift to Islamic nationalism signifies the defeat of the left and of secular nationalists. A similar path cannot be altogether dismissed in the case of the Kurds. In Iraqi Kurdistan there is a partly active, partly dormant Islamic challenge.

Notes

1. Ernest Gellner, *Nations and Nationalism*, p. 1 (Blackwell, 1992).
2. Ibid.
3. Ibid., p. 45.
4. W. F. Hegel, *Philosophy of Right*, trans. T. M. Knox, , p. 126 (Oxford: Oxford University Press, 1967).
5. A. D. Smith, *Theories of Nationalism*, p. 27 (Duckworth, 1971).
6. Michael Aflaq, *Towards Renaissance*, 4th edn, p. 58 (Beirut, 1963).
7. Ayatollah Muhamad Shirazi, *Towards a One-thousand Million Muslim Government*, Qum: n.d., p.17–19. See also his treatise, 'Governance in Islam', Qum, n.d.

8. Analysed in the realm of ideological debate or of party-political conflict, this largely ideological cleavage made scholars such as Sivan jump to the conclusion that Islamism is bidding farewell to nationalism. Emanuel Sivan, *Radical Islam*, pp. 20, 31 and *passim* (New Haven and London: 1985).

9. Benedict Anderson, *Imagined Community*, p. 19 (London: Verso, 1985).

10. Sami Zubaida, 'Theories of Nationalism', in G. Littlejohn (ed.), *Power and State*, , pp. 52-3 (Cromhelm, 1978).

11. Gellner, *Nations and Nationalism*, pp. 41, 51, 52.

12. Paul Hirst and Thompson, *Globalization in Question* (Cambridge: Polity Press, 1999).

13. Anderson, *Imagined Community*, p. 20.

14. E.g. Hamid Enayat, *Modern Islamic Political Thought*, p. 126 (London: Macmillan, 1988).

15. See Martin van Bruinessen, *Agha, Shaikh and State: The Social and Political Structures of Kurdistan* (London: Zed Books, 1992).

16. For a detailed description of this period see *The History of Saudi Arabia*, London: Saqi Books; and M. Rasheed, *A History of Saudi Arabia* (Cambridge: Cambridge University Press, 2002).

17. Edward Mortimer, *Islam, Power and Faith*, p. 186 and *passim* (London: Faber and Faber, 1982).

18. Albert Hourani, *The History of Arab Peoples*, pp. 309–10 (London, 1990).

19. Ibid., pp. 217, 251; see also H. A. R. Gibb and Harold Bowen, *Islamic Society and the West,* vol. 1 (Oxford, 1950, pp. 48–53).

20. Bernard Lewis, *The Emergence of Modern Turkey*, pp. 83, 88 (Oxford, 1961); Hourani, *History of Arab Peoples*, p. 272.

21. P. M. Holt, *Egypt and the Fertile Crescent, 1516–1922: A Political History*, p. 52 (London: Longmans, 1966) ; Lewis 'Awadh, *The History of Modern Egyptian Thought*, 4th edn, pp. 73–4 (Cairo, 1987) ; see also Lewis, *Emergence of Modern Turkey*, p. 148; Hourani, *History of the Arab Peoples*, p. 273.

22. Khalid Ziyada, *The Discovery of European Progress*, Beirut, 1981, pp. 34, 37, 39, 41, 43.

23. Lewis, *Emergence of Modern Turkey*, p. 148.

24. Ibid., p.151.

25. Ibid., p. 152.

26. Ha'iri, Abdul Hadi, '*Shi'ism and Constitutionalism in Iran: A Study of the Role Played by the Persian Residents of Iraq in Iranian Politics* (Leiden: E. J. Brill, 1977).

27. Ervend Ibrahamian, *Iran between Two Revolutions*, pp. 85, 86–92 (Princeton: Princeton University Press, 1982)

28. Holt, *Egypt and the Fertile Crescent*, p. 256.

29. Hourani, *Arabic Thought in the Liberal Age*, pp.103–29; Nekkie Keddie, *An Islamic Response to Imperialism*, pp. 3–4, 20 (Berkeley and Los Angeles: University of California Press, 1983).

30. Keddie, *An Islamic Response*, pp. 6–7.

31. Ibid., p. 4, n. 1.

32. Afghani's essay is entitled 'The Philosophy of National Unity', quoted in Keddie, *An Islamic Response*, p. 56.

33. Keddie, *An Islamic Response*, p. 18; Hourani, *Arabic Thought*, pp. 119–25; also Afghani's criticism of the materialists, trans. Keddie, pp. 130, 140, 144–7, 167.

34. Emile Toma, *The History of Modern Arab Peoples*, Beirut, 1981, p. 91.

35. Jamaludin al-Afghani, *Political Writings*, Beirut, 1981, p. 313.

36. Ibid., p. 320.

37. Ibid., p. 263.

38. Ibid., p. 37.

39. Toma, *History of Modern Arab Peoples*, p. 89.

40. Ibid., p. 97 (author's italics).

41. Hourani, *Arabic Thought*, p. 273.

42. Ibid.

43. Awadh, *History of Modern Egyptian Thought*, p. 66.

44. Hourani, *Arabic Thought*, pp. 269–72.

45. Holt, *Egypt and the Fertile Crescent*, p. 258, Hourani, *Arabic Thought*, pp.195, 277; see also Ilias Khouri (ed.), *Christian Arabs*, 2nd edn, Beirut, 1975, pp. 64–6.

46. Hourani, *Arabic Thought*, p. 196.

47. Ibid.

48. Toma, *History of Modern Arab Peoples*, pp. 102–3.

49. Sati' al-Husri, *Ideas and Discourses in Arab Nationalism*, Beirut, 1959, p. 128.

50. Ibid.

51. William L. Cleveland, *The Making of an Arab Nationalist: Ottomanism and Arabism in the Life and Thought of Sati' al-Husri,* pp. 80, 88, 140–1 (Princeton: Princeton University Press, 1971) ; T. P. Techonova, *Sati' al-Husri, the Pioneer of Secularism in Arab National Thought*, pp. 55, 77 (Moscow, 1987).

52. Husri, *Selected Essays on Arab Nationalism*, 2 vols, p. 26 (Beirut, 1974).

53. Techonova, *Pioneer of Secularism*, p. 46; Sati' al-Husri, *What is Nationalism?*, pp.125–7 (Beirut, 1959).

54. Cleveland, *Making of an Arab Nationalist*, p. 164.

55. Ibid., p. 234.

56. Husri, *Selected Essays*, vol.1, p. 46.

57. Techonova, *Pioneer of Secularism*, p. 41.

58. August Comte, the founder of sociology.

59. *The Struggle of the BASP: National Command*, Damascus, 1978, p. 15.

60. Aflaq, *Towards Renaissance*, p. 55.

61. Ibid., p. 51.

62. Ibid., p. 44.

63. Ibid., pp. 41, 43.

64. The author's personal observation in Tunisia, Algeira and Libya. Native sociologists confirm this was a characteristic of normative conceptions in the Maghrib.

65. Awadh, *History of Egyptian Thought*, p. 21 and *passim*.

66. Muhamad Abdu, *Collected Works*, 2nd edn, vol. 1, p. 736 (Beirut, 1972).

67. Ibid., p. 735.

68. Ibid., p. 369 (author's emphasis).

69. Ibid., p. 368.

70. Ali Abil Raziq, *Islam and the Foundations of Governance*, pp. 37, 174 (Beirut, 1972).

71. Enayat, *Modern Islamic Political Thought*, p. 77.

72. Rif'at al-Sa'id: *Hassan al Banna, The Founder of Muslim Brothers Group*, 5th edn, p. 54 and *passim* (Cairo, 1984).

73. A.Yassin, 'The Role of HAMAS in the Islamic Phenomenon in the West Bank and Gaza', in *The New Jordan Review*, no. 11, 1988, p. 45 ; and Sadiq Jala al-Azim, *A Criticism of Religious Thought*, 5th edn, p. 97 and *passim* (Beirut, 1982).

74. François Burgat, *L'Islamisme au Maghreb*, p. 113 (Cairo, 1992).

75. Faleh A.Jabar, 'The Gulf War and Ideology: The Double-edged Sword Of Islam', in

Haim Bresheeth and Nira Yuval Davis (eds), *The Gulf War and the New World Order*, p. 213 (London: Zed Books, 1991).

76. Sa'ad Eddin Ibrahim, *The Islamic Awakening and the Concerns of the Arab Nation*, pp. 313, 318, 323 (Jordan, 1988).

77. Ibid., pp. 85, 92, 98.

78. Burgat, *L'Islamisme au Maghreb*, pp. 80, 85.

Appendix

Coalition Provisional Authority
Law of Administration for the State of Iraq
for the Transitional Period
8 March 2004

Preamble

The people of Iraq, striving to reclaim their freedom, which was usurped by the previous tyrannical regime, rejecting violence and coercion in all their forms, and particularly when used as instruments of governance, have determined that they shall hereafter remain a free people governed under the rule of law.

These people, affirming today their respect for international law, especially having been amongst the founders of the United Nations, working to reclaim their legitimate place among nations, have endeavored at the same time to preserve the unity of their homeland in a spirit of fraternity and solidarity in order to draw the features of the future new Iraq, and to establish the mechanisms aiming, amongst other aims, to erase the effects of racist and sectarian policies and practices.

This Law is now established to govern the affairs of Iraq during the transitional period until a duly elected government, operating under a permanent and legitimate constitution achieving full democracy, shall come into being.

Chapter One – Fundamental Principles

Article 1

- (A) This Law shall be called the 'Law of Administration for the State of Iraq for the Transitional Period', and the phrase 'this Law' wherever it appears in this legislation shall mean the 'Law of Administration for the State of Iraq for the Transitional Period'.
- (B) Gender-specific language shall apply equally to male and female.
- (C) The Preamble to this Law is an integral part of this Law.

Article 2

(A) The term 'transitional period' shall refer to the period beginning on 30 June 2004 and lasting until the formation of an elected Iraqi government pursuant to a permanent constitution as set forth in this Law, which in any case shall be no later than 31 December 2005, unless the provisions of Article 61 are applied.

(B) The transitional period shall consist of two phases.

(1) The first phase shall begin with the formation of a fully sovereign Iraqi Interim Government that takes power on 30 June 2004. This government shall be constituted in accordance with a process of extensive deliberations and consultations with cross-sections of the Iraqi people conducted by the Governing Council and the Coalition Provisional Authority and possibly in consultation with the United Nations. This government shall exercise authority in accordance with this Law, including the fundamental principles and rights specified herein, and with an annex that shall be agreed upon and issued before the beginning of the transitional period and that shall be an integral part of this Law.

(2) The second phase shall begin after the formation of the Iraqi Transitional Government, which will take place after elections for the National Assembly have been held as stipulated in this Law, provided that, if possible, these elections are not delayed beyond 31 December 2004, and, in any event, beyond 31 January 2005. This second phase shall end upon the formation of an Iraqi government pursuant to a permanent constitution.

Article 3

(A) This Law is the Supreme Law of the land and shall be binding in all parts of Iraq without exception. No amendment to this Law may be made except by a three-fourths majority of the members of the National Assembly and the unanimous approval of the Presidency Council. Likewise, no amendment may be made that could abridge in any way the rights of the Iraqi people cited in Chapter Two; extend the transitional period beyond the time frame cited in this Law; delay the holding of elections to a new assembly; reduce the powers of the regions or governorates; or affect Islam or any other religions or sects and their rites.

(B) Any legal provision that conflicts with this Law is null and void.

(C) This Law shall cease to have effect upon the formation of an elected government pursuant to a permanent constitution.

Article 4

The system of government in Iraq shall be republican, federal, democratic and pluralistic, and powers shall be shared between the federal government and the regional governments, governorates, municipalities and local administrations. The federal system shall be based upon geographic and historical realities and the separation of powers, and not upon origin, race, ethnicity, nationality or confession.

Article 5

The Iraqi Armed Forces shall be subject to the civilian control of the Iraqi Transitional Government, in accordance with the contents of Chapters Three and Five of this Law.

Article 6

The Iraqi Transitional Government shall take effective steps to end the vestiges of the oppressive acts of the previous regime arising from forced displacement, deprivation of citizenship, expropriation of financial assets and property, and dismissal from government employment for political, racial or sectarian reasons.

Article 7

A) Islam is the official religion of the State and is to be considered a source of legislation. No law that contradicts the universally agreed tenets of Islam, the principles of democracy or the rights cited in Chapter Two of this Law may be enacted during the transitional period. This Law respects the Islamic identity of the majority of the Iraqi people and guarantees the full religious rights of all individuals to freedom of religious belief and practice.

(B) Iraq is a country of many nationalities, and the Arab people in Iraq are an inseparable part of the Arab nation.

Article 8

The flag, anthem and emblem of the State shall be fixed by law.

Article 9

The Arabic language and the Kurdish language are the two official languages of Iraq. The right of Iraqis to educate their children in their mother tongue, such as Turkmen, Syriac or Armenian, in government educational institutions in accordance with educational guidelines, or in any other language in private educational institutions, shall be guaranteed. The scope of the term 'official language' and the means of applying the provisions of this Article shall be defined by law and shall include:

(1) Publication of the official gazette, in the two languages;

(2) Speech and expression in official settings, such as the National Assembly, the Council of Ministers, courts and official conferences, in either of the two languages;

(3) Recognition and publication of official documents and correspondence in the two languages;

(4) Opening schools that teach in the two languages, in accordance with educational guidelines;

(5) Use of both languages in any other settings enjoined by the principle of equality (such as bank notes, passports and stamps);

(6) Use of both languages in the federal institutions and agencies in the Kurdistan region.

Chapter Two – Fundamental Rights

Article 10

As an expression of the free will and sovereignty of the Iraqi people, their representatives shall form the governmental structures of the State of Iraq. The Iraqi Transitional Government and the governments of the regions, governorates, municipalities and local administrations shall respect the rights of the Iraqi people, including those rights cited in this chapter.

Article 11

(A) Anyone who carries Iraqi nationality shall be deemed an Iraqi citizen. His citizenship shall grant him all the rights and duties stipulated in this Law and shall be the basis of his relation to the homeland and the State.

(B) No Iraqi may have his Iraqi citizenship withdrawn or be exiled unless he is a naturalized citizen who, in his application for citizenship, as established in a court of law, made material falsifications on the basis of which citizenship was granted.

(C) Each Iraqi shall have the right to carry more than one citizenship. Any Iraqi whose citizenship was withdrawn because he acquired another citizenship shall be deemed an Iraqi.

(D) Any Iraqi whose Iraqi citizenship was withdrawn for political, religious, racial or sectarian reasons has the right to reclaim his Iraqi citizenship.

(E) Decision Number 666 (1980) of the dissolved Revolutionary Command Council is annulled, and anyone whose citizenship was withdrawn on the basis of this decree shall be deemed an Iraqi.

(F) The National Assembly must issue laws pertaining to citizenship and naturalization consistent with the provisions of this Law.

(G) The courts shall examine all disputes arising from the application of the provisions relating to citizenship.

Article 12

All Iraqis are equal in their rights without regard to sex, sect, opinion, belief, nationality, religion or origin, and they are equal before the law. Discrimination against an Iraqi citizen on the basis of his sex, nationality, religion or origin is prohibited. Everyone has the right to life, liberty and the security of his person. No one may be deprived of his life or liberty, except in accordance with legal procedures. All are equal before the courts.

Article 13

- (A) Public and private freedoms shall be protected.
- (B) The right of free expression shall be protected.
- (C) The right of free peaceable assembly and the right to join associations freely, as well as the right to form and join unions and political parties freely, in accordance with the law, shall be guaranteed.
- (D) Each Iraqi has the right of free movement in all parts of Iraq and the right to travel abroad and return freely.
- (E) Each Iraqi has the right to demonstrate and strike peaceably in accordance with the law.
- (F) Each Iraqi has the right to freedom of thought, conscience and religious belief and practice. Coercion in such matters shall be prohibited.
- (G) Slavery, the slave trade, forced labour and involuntary servitude, with or without pay, shall be forbidden.
- (H) Each Iraqi has the right to privacy.

Article 14

The individual has the right to security, education, health care and social security. The Iraqi State and its governmental units, including the federal government, the regions, governorates, municipalities and local administrations, within the limits of their resources and with due regard to other vital needs, shall strive to provide prosperity and employment opportunities to the people.

Article 15

- (A) No civil law shall have retroactive effect unless the law so stipulates. There shall be neither a crime, nor punishment, except by law in effect at the time the crime is committed.
- (B) Police, investigators or other governmental authorities may not violate the sanctity of private residences, whether these authorities belong to the federal or regional governments, governorates, municipalities or local administrations, unless a judge or investigating magistrate has issued a search warrant in accordance with applicable law on the basis of information provided by a sworn individual who knew that bearing

false witness would render him liable to punishment. Extreme exigent circumstances, as determined by a court of competent jurisdiction, may justify a warrantless search, but such exigencies shall be narrowly construed. In the event that a warrantless search is carried out in the absence of an extreme exigent circumstance, the evidence so seized, and any other evidence found derivatively from such search, shall be inadmissible in connection with a criminal charge, unless the court determines that the person who carried out the warrantless search believed reasonably and in good faith that the search was in accordance with the law.

(C) No one may be unlawfully arrested or detained, and no one may be detained by reason of political or religious beliefs.

(D) All persons shall be guaranteed the right to a fair and public hearing by an independent and impartial tribunal, regardless of whether the proceeding is civil or criminal. Notice of the proceeding and its legal basis must be provided to the accused without delay.

(E) The accused is innocent until proven guilty pursuant to law, and he likewise has the right to engage independent and competent counsel, to remain silent in response to questions addressed to him with no compulsion to testify for any reason, to participate in preparing his defence and to summon and examine witnesses or to ask the judge to do so. At the time a person is arrested, he must be notified of these rights.

(F) The right to a fair, speedy and open trial shall be guaranteed.

(G) Every person deprived of his liberty by arrest or detention shall have the right of recourse to a court to determine the legality of his arrest or detention without delay and to order his release if this occurred in an illegal manner.

(H) After being found innocent of a charge, an accused may not be tried once again on the same charge.

(I) Civilians may not be tried before a military tribunal. Special or exceptional courts may not be established.

(J) Torture in all its forms, physical or mental, shall be prohibited under all circumstances, as shall be cruel, inhuman or degrading treatment. No confession made under compulsion, torture or threat thereof shall be relied upon or admitted into evidence for any reason in any proceeding, whether criminal or otherwise.

Article 16

(A) Public property is sacrosanct, and its protection is the duty of every citizen.

(B) The right to private property shall be protected, and no one may be prevented from disposing of his property except within the limits of law. No one shall be deprived of his property except by eminent domain, in

circumstances and in the manner set forth in law, and on condition that
he is paid just and timely compensation.

(C) Each Iraqi citizen shall have the full and unfettered right to own real
property in all parts of Iraq without restriction.

Article 17

It shall not be permitted to possess, bear, buy, or sell arms except on licensure
issued in accordance with the law.

Article 18

There shall be no taxation or fee except by law.

Article 19

No political refugee who has been granted asylum pursuant to applicable law
may be surrendered or returned forcibly to the country from which he fled.

Article 20

(A) Every Iraqi who fulfils the conditions stipulated in the electoral law has
the right to stand for election and cast his ballot secretly in free, open,
fair, competitive and periodic elections.

(B) No Iraqi may be discriminated against for purposes of voting in elections
on the basis of sex, religion, sect, race, belief, ethnic origin, language,
wealth or literacy.

Article 21

Neither the Iraqi Transitional Government nor the governments and
administrations of the regions, governorates and municipalities, nor local
administrations may interfere with the right of the Iraqi people to develop the
institutions of civil society, whether in cooperation with international civil
society organizations or otherwise.

Article 22

If, in the course of his work, an official of any government office, whether in the
federal government, the regional governments, the governorates and municipal
administrations or the local administrations, deprives an individual or a group of
the rights guaranteed by this Law or any other Iraqi laws in force, this individual
or group shall have the right to maintain a cause of action against that employee
to seek compensation for the damages caused by such deprivation, to vindicate
his rights and to seek any other legal measure. If the court decides that the official
had acted with a sufficient degree of good faith and in the belief that his actions

were consistent with the law, then he is not required to pay compensation.

Article 23

The enumeration of the foregoing rights must not be interpreted to mean that they are the only rights enjoyed by the Iraqi people. They enjoy all the rights that befit a free people possessed of their human dignity, including the rights stipulated in international treaties and agreements, other instruments of international law that Iraq has signed and to which it has acceded, and others that are deemed binding upon it, and in the law of nations. Non-Iraqis within Iraq shall enjoy all human rights not inconsistent with their status as non-citizens.

Chapter Three – the Iraqi Transitional Government

Article 24

(A) The Iraqi Transitional Government, which is also referred to in this Law as the federal government, shall consist of the National Assembly; the Presidency Council; the Council of Ministers, including the Prime Minister; and the judicial authority.

(B) The three authorities, legislative, executive and judicial, shall be separate and independent of one another.

(C) No official or employee of the Iraqi Transitional Government shall enjoy immunity for criminal acts committed while in office.

Article 25

The Iraqi Transitional Government shall have exclusive competence in the following matters:

(A) Formulating foreign policy and diplomatic representation; negotiating, signing and ratifying international treaties and agreements; formulating foreign economic and trade policy and sovereign debt policies;

(B) Formulating and executing national security policy, including creating and maintaining armed forces to secure, protect and guarantee the security of the country's borders and to defend Iraq;

(C) Formulating fiscal policy, issuing currency, regulating customs, regulating commercial policy across regional and governorate boundaries in Iraq, drawing up the national budget of the State, formulating monetary policy and establishing and administering a central bank;

(D) Regulating weights and measures and formulating a general policy on wages;

(E) Managing the natural resources of Iraq, which belongs to all the people of all the regions and governorates of Iraq, in consultation with the governments of the regions and the administrations of the governorates, and distributing the revenues resulting from their sale through the national budget in an equitable manner proportional to the distribution of population throughout the country, and with due regard for areas that were unjustly deprived of these revenues by the previous regime, for dealing with their situations in a positive way, for their needs and for the degree of development of the different areas of the country;

(F) Regulating Iraqi citizenship, immigration and asylum; and

(G) Regulating telecommunications policy.

Article 26

(A) Except as otherwise provided in this Law, the laws in force in Iraq on 30 June 2004 shall remain in effect unless and until rescinded or amended by the Iraqi Transitional Government in accordance with this Law.

(B) Legislation issued by the federal legislative authority shall supersede any other legislation issued by any other legislative authority in the event that they contradict each other, except as provided in Article 54(B).

(C) The laws, regulations, orders and directives issued by the Coalition Provisional Authority pursuant to its authority under international law shall remain in force until rescinded or amended by legislation duly enacted and having the force of law.

Article 27

(A) The Iraqi Armed Forces shall consist of the active and reserve units, and elements thereof. The purpose of these forces is the defence of Iraq.

(B) Armed forces and militias not under the command structure of the Iraqi Transitional Government are prohibited, except as provided by federal law.

(C) The Iraqi Armed Forces and its personnel, including military personnel working in the Ministry of Defence or any offices or organizations subordinate to it, may not stand for election to political office, campaign for candidates or participate in other activities forbidden by Ministry of Defence regulations. This ban encompasses the activities of the personnel mentioned above acting in their personal or official capacities. Nothing in this Article shall infringe the right of these personnel to vote in elections.

(D) The Iraqi Intelligence Service shall collect information, assess threats to national security and advise the Iraqi government. This Service shall be under civilian control, shall be subject to legislative oversight and shall operate pursuant to law and in accordance with recognized principles of human rights.

(E) The Iraqi Transitional Government shall respect and implement Iraq's international obligations regarding the non-proliferation, non-

development, non-production and non-use of nuclear, chemical and
biological weapons, and associated equipment, materiel, technologies
and delivery systems for use in the development, manufacture, production
and use of such weapons.

Article 28

(A) Members of the National Assembly; the Presidency Council; the
Council of Ministers, including the Prime Minister; and judges and
justices of the courts may not be appointed to any other position in or
out of government. Any member of the National Assembly who becomes
a member of the Presidency Council or Council of Ministers shall be
deemed to have resigned his membership in the National Assembly.

(B) In no event may a member of the armed forces be a member of the National
Assembly, minister, Prime Minister or member of the Presidency Council
unless the individual has resigned his commission or rank or retired from
duty at least eighteen months prior to serving.

Article 29

Upon the assumption of full authority by the Iraqi Interim Government in
accordance with Article 2(B)(1), above, the Coalition Provisional Authority
shall be dissolved and the work of the Governing Council shall come to an end.

Chapter Four – the Transitional Legislative Authority

Article 30

(A) During the transitional period, the State of Iraq shall have a legislative
authority known as the National Assembly. Its principal mission shall
be to legislate and exercise oversight over the work of the executive
authority.

(B) Laws shall be issued in the name of the people of Iraq. Laws, regulations
and directives related to them shall be published in the official gazette and
shall take effect as of the date of their publication, unless they stipulate
otherwise.

(C) The National Assembly shall be elected in accordance with an electoral
law and a political parties law. The electoral law shall aim to achieve
the goal of having women constitute no less than one-quarter of the
members of the National Assembly and of having fair representation for
all communities in Iraq, including the Turkmen, Chaldo-Assyrians and
others.

(D) Elections for the National Assembly shall take place by 31 December
2004 if possible, and in any case no later than by 31 January 2005.

Article 31

(A) The National Assembly shall consist of 275 members. It shall enact a law dealing with the replacement of its members in the event of resignation, removal or death.

(B) A nominee to the National Assembly must fulfil the following conditions:

(1) He shall be an Iraqi no less than 30 years of age.

(2) He shall not have been a member of the dissolved Ba'ath Party with the rank of Division Member or higher, unless exempted pursuant to the applicable legal rules.

(3) If he was once a member of the dissolved Ba'ath Party with the rank of Full Member, he shall be required to sign a document renouncing the Ba'ath Party and disavowing all of his past links with it before becoming eligible to be a candidate, as well as to swear that he no longer has any dealings or connection with Ba'ath Party organizations. If it is established in court that he lied or fabricated on this score, he shall lose his seat in the National Assembly.

(4) He shall not have been a member of the former agencies of repression and shall not have contributed to or participated in the persecution of citizens.

(5) He shall not have enriched himself in an illegitimate manner at the expense of the homeland and public finance.

(6) He shall not have been convicted of a crime involving moral turpitude and shall have a good reputation.

(7) He shall have at least a secondary school diploma, or equivalent.

(8) He shall not be a member of the armed forces at the time of his nomination.

Article 32

(A) The National 'Assembly shall draw up its own internal procedures, and it shall sit in public session unless circumstances require otherwise, consistent with its internal procedures. The first session of the Assembly shall be chaired by its oldest member.

(B) The National Assembly shall elect, from its own members, a president and two deputy presidents of the National Assembly. The president of the National Assembly shall be the individual who receives the greatest number of votes for that office; the first deputy president the next highest; and the second deputy president the next. The president of the National Assembly may vote on an issue, but may not participate in the debates, unless he temporarily steps out of the chair immediately prior to addressing the issue.

(C) A bill shall not be voted upon by the National Assembly unless it has been read twice at a regular session of the Assembly, on condition that at least two days intervene between the two readings, and after the bill has been placed on the agenda of the session at least four days prior to the vote.

Article 33

(A) Meetings of the National Assembly shall be public, and transcripts of its meetings shall be recorded and published. The vote of every member of the National Assembly shall be recorded and made public. Decisions in the National Assembly shall be taken by simple majority unless this Law stipulates otherwise.

(B) The National Assembly must examine bills proposed by the Council of Ministers, including budget bills.

(C) Only the Council of Ministers shall have the right to present a proposed national budget. The National Assembly has the right to reallocate proposed spending and to reduce the total amounts in the general budget. It also has the right to propose an increase in the overall amount of expenditures to the Council of Ministers if necessary.

(D) Members of the National Assembly shall have the right to propose bills, consistent with the internal procedures that are drawn up by the Assembly.

(E) The Iraqi Armed Forces may not be dispatched outside Iraq, even for the purpose of defending against foreign aggression, except with the approval of the National Assembly and upon the request of the Presidency Council.

(F) Only the National Assembly shall have the power to ratify international treaties and agreements.

(G) The oversight function performed by the National Assembly and its committees shall include the right of interpellation of executive officials, including members of the Presidency Council, the Council of Ministers, including the Prime Minister, and any less senior official of the executive authority. This shall encompass the right to investigate, request information and issue subpoenas for persons to appear before them.

Article 34

Each member of the National Assembly shall enjoy immunity for statements made while the Assembly is in session, and the member may not be sued before the courts for such. A member may not be placed under arrest during a session of the National Assembly, unless the member is accused of a crime and the National Assembly agrees to lift his immunity or if he is caught *in flagrante delicto* in the commission of a felony.

Chapter Five – the Transitional Executive Authority

Article 35

The executive authority during the transitional period shall consist of the Presidency Council, the Council of Ministers and its presiding Prime Minister.

Article 36

(A) The National Assembly shall elect a President of the State and two Deputies. They shall form the Presidency Council, the function of which will be to represent the sovereignty of Iraq and oversee the higher affairs of the country. The election of the Presidency Council shall take place on the basis of a single list and by a two-thirds majority of the members' votes. The National Assembly has the power to remove any member of the Presidency Council of the State for incompetence or lack of integrity by a three-fourths majority of its members' votes. In the event of a vacancy in the Presidency Council, the National Assembly shall, by a vote of two-thirds of its members, elect a replacement to fill the vacancy.

(B) It is a prerequisite for a member of the Presidency Council to fulfil the same conditions as the members of the National Assembly, with the following observations:

(1) He must be at least forty years of age.

(2) He must possess a good reputation, integrity and rectitude.

(3) If he was a member of the dissolved Ba'ath Party, he must have left the dissolved Party at least ten years before its fall.

(4) He must not have participated in repressing the *intifada* of 1991 or the Anfal campaign and must not have committed a crime against the Iraqi people.

(C) The Presidency Council shall take its decisions unanimously, and its members may not deputize others as proxies.

Article 37

The Presidency Council may veto any legislation passed by the National Assembly, on condition that this be done within fifteen days after the Presidency Council is notified by the president of the National Assembly of the passage of such legislation. In the event of a veto, the legislation shall be returned to the National Assembly, which has the right to pass the legislation again by a two-thirds majority not subject to veto within a period not to exceed thirty days.

Article 38

(A) The Presidency Council shall name a Prime Minister unanimously, as well as the members of the Council of Ministers, upon the recommendation of the Prime Minister. The Prime Minister and Council of Ministers shall then seek to obtain a vote of confidence by simple majority from the National Assembly prior to commencing their work as a government. The Presidency Council must agree on a candidate for the post of Prime Minister within two weeks. In the event that it fails to do so, the responsibility of naming the Prime Minister reverts to the National Assembly. In that event, the National Assembly must confirm the nomination by a two-thirds majority. If the Prime Minister is unable to nominate his Council of Ministers within one month, the Presidency Council shall name another Prime Minister.

(B) The qualifications for Prime Minister must be the same as for the members of the Presidency Council except that his age must not be less than 35 years upon his taking office.

Article 39

(A) The Council of Ministers shall, with the approval of the Presidency Council, appoint representatives to negotiate the conclusion of international treaties and agreements. The Presidency Council shall recommend passage of a law by the National Assembly to ratify such treaties and agreements.

(B) The Presidency Council shall carry out the function of commander-in-chief of the Iraqi Armed Forces only for ceremonial and protocol purposes. It shall have no command authority. It shall have the right to be briefed, to inquire and to advise. Operationally, national command authority on military matters shall flow from the Prime Minister to the Minister of Defence to the military chain of command of the Iraqi Armed Forces.

(C) The Presidency Council shall, as more fully set forth in Chapter Six below, appoint, upon recommendation of the Higher Juridical Council, the presiding judge and members of the Federal Supreme Court.

(D) The Council of Ministers shall appoint the Director-General of the Iraqi National Intelligence Service, as well as officers of the Iraqi Armed Forces at the rank of general or above. Such appointments shall be subject to confirmation by the National Assembly by simple majority of those of its members present.

Article 40

(A) The Prime Minister and the ministers shall be responsible before the National Assembly, and this Assembly shall have the right to withdraw its confidence either in the Prime Minister or in the ministers collectively or individually. In the event that confidence in the Prime Minister is withdrawn, the entire Council of Ministers shall be dissolved, and Article 40(B), below, shall become operative.

(B) In the event of a vote of no confidence with respect to the entire Council of Ministers, the Prime Minister and Council of Ministers shall remain in office to carry out their functions for a period not to exceed thirty days, until the formation of a new Council of Ministers, consistent with Article 38, above.

Article 41

The Prime Minister shall have day-to-day responsibility for the management of the government, and he may dismiss ministers with the approval of a simple majority of the National Assembly. The Presidency Council may, upon the recommendation of the Commission on Public Integrity after the exercise of due process, dismiss the Prime Minister or the ministers.

Article 42

The Council of Ministers shall draw up rules of procedure for its work and issue the regulations and directives necessary to enforce the laws. It also has the right to propose bills to the National Assembly. Each ministry has the right, within its competence, to nominate deputy ministers, ambassadors and other employees of special grade. After the Council of Ministers approves these nominations, they shall be submitted to the Presidency Council for ratification. All decisions of the Council of Ministers shall be taken by simple majority of those of its members present.

Chapter Six – the Federal Judicial Authority

Article 43

(A) The judiciary is independent, and it shall in no way be administered by the executive authority, including the Ministry of Justice. The judiciary shall enjoy exclusive competence to determine the innocence or guilt of the accused pursuant to law, without interference from the legislative or executive authorities.

(B) All judges sitting in their respective courts as of 1 July 2004 will continue in office thereafter, unless removed from office pursuant to this Law.

(C) The National Assembly shall establish an independent and adequate budget for the judiciary.

(D) Federal courts shall adjudicate matters that arise from the application of federal laws. The establishment of these courts shall be within the exclusive competence of the federal government. The establishment of these courts in the regions shall be in consultation with the presidents of the judicial councils in the regions, and priority in appointing or transferring judges to these courts shall be given to judges resident in the region.

Article 44

(A) A court called the Federal Supreme Court shall be constituted by law in Iraq.

(B) The jurisdiction of the Federal Supreme Court shall be as follows:

(1) Original and exclusive jurisdiction in legal proceedings between the Iraqi Transitional Government and the regional governments, governorates and municipal administrations, and local administrations.

(2) Original and exclusive jurisdiction, on the basis of a complaint from a claimant or a referral from another court, to review claims that a law, regulation or directive issued by the federal or regional governments, the governorates or municipal administrations, or local administrations is inconsistent with this Law.

(3) Ordinary appellate jurisdiction of the Federal Supreme Court shall be defined by federal law.

(C) Should the Federal Supreme Court rule that a challenged law, regulation, directive or measure is inconsistent with this Law, it shall be deemed null and void.

(D) The Federal Supreme Court shall create and publish regulations regarding the procedures required to bring claims and to permit attorneys to practise before it. It shall take its decisions by simple majority, except decisions with regard to the proceedings stipulated in Article 44(B)(1), which must be by a two-thirds majority. Decisions shall be binding. The Court shall have full powers to enforce its decisions, including the power to issue citations for contempt of court and the measures that flow from this.

(E) The Federal Supreme Court shall consist of nine members. The Higher Juridical Council shall, in consultation with the regional judicial councils, initially nominate no fewer than eighteen and up to twenty-seven individuals to fill the initial vacancies in the aforementioned Court. It will follow the same procedure thereafter, nominating three members for each subsequent vacancy that occurs by reason of death, resignation or removal. The Presidency Council shall appoint the members of this Court and name one of them as its presiding judge. In the event an appointment is rejected, the Higher Juridical Council shall nominate a new group of three candidates.

Article 45

A Higher Juridical Council shall be established and assume the role of the Council of Judges. The Higher Juridical Council shall supervise the federal judiciary and shall administer its budget. This Council shall be composed of the presiding judge of the Federal Supreme Court, the presiding judge and deputy presiding judges of the federal Court of Cassation, the presiding judges of the federal Courts of Appeal and the presiding judge and two deputy presiding judges of each regional Court of Cassation. The presiding judge of the Federal Supreme Court shall preside over the Higher Juridical Council. In his absence, the presiding judge of the federal Court of Cassation shall preside over the Council.

Article 46

(A) The federal judicial branch shall include existing courts outside the Kurdistan region, including courts of first instance; the Central Criminal Court of Iraq; Courts of Appeal; and the Court of Cassation, which shall be the court of last resort except as provided in Article 44 of this Law. Additional federal courts may be established by law. The appointment of judges for these courts shall be made by the Higher Juridical Council. This Law preserves the qualifications necessary for the appointment of judges, as defined by law.

(B) The decisions of regional and local courts, including the courts of the Kurdistan region, shall be final, but shall be subject to review by the federal judiciary if they conflict with this Law or any federal law. Procedures for such review shall be defined by law.

Article 47

No judge or member of the Higher Juridical Council may be removed unless he is convicted of a crime involving moral turpitude or corruption or suffers permanent incapacity. Removal shall be on the recommendation of the Higher Juridical Council, by a decision of the Council of Ministers, and with the approval of the Presidency Council. Removal shall be executed immediately after issuance of this approval. A judge who has been accused of such a crime as cited above shall be suspended from his work in the judiciary until such time as the case arising from what is cited in this Article is adjudicated. No judge may have his salary reduced or suspended for any reason during his period of service.

Chapter Seven – the Special Tribunal and National Commissions

Article 48

(A) The statute establishing the Iraqi Special Tribunal issued on 10 December 2003 is confirmed. That statute exclusively defines its jurisdiction and procedures, notwithstanding the provisions of this Law.

(B) No other court shall have jurisdiction to examine cases within the competence of the Iraqi Special Tribunal, except to the extent provided by its founding statute.

(C) The judges of the Iraqi Special Tribunal shall be appointed in accordance with the provisions of its founding statute.

Article 49

(A) The establishment of national commissions such as the Commission on Public Integrity, the Iraqi Property Claims Commission and the Higher National De-Ba'athification Commission is confirmed, as is the establishment of commissions formed after this Law has gone into effect. The members of these national commissions shall continue to serve after this Law has gone into effect, taking into account the contents of Article 51, below.

(B) The method of appointment to the national commissions shall be in accordance with law.   .

Article 50

The Iraqi Transitional Government shall establish a National Commission for Human Rights for the purpose of executing the commitments relative to the rights set forth in this Law and to examine complaints pertaining to violations of human rights. The Commission shall be established in accordance with the Paris Principles issued by the United Nations on the responsibilities of national institutions. This Commission shall include an Office of the Ombudsman to inquire into complaints. This office shall have the power to investigate, on its own initiative or on the basis of a complaint submitted to it, any allegation that the conduct of the governmental authorities is arbitrary or contrary to law.

Article 51

No member of the Iraqi Special Tribunal or of any commission established by the federal government may be employed in any other capacity in or out of government. This prohibition is valid without limitation, whether it be within the executive, legislative or judicial authority of the Iraqi Transitional Government. Members of the Special Tribunal may, however, suspend their employment in other agencies while they serve on the aforementioned Tribunal.

Chapter Eight – Regions, Governorates and Municipalities

Article 52

The design of the federal system in Iraq shall be established in such a way as to prevent the concentration of power in the federal government that allowed the continuation of decades of tyranny and oppression under the previous regime. This system shall encourage the exercise of local authority by local officials in every region and governorate, thereby creating a united Iraq in which every citizen actively participates in governmental affairs, secure in his rights and free of domination.

Article 53

(A) The Kurdistan Regional Government is recognized as the official government of the territories that were administered by that government on 19 March 2003 in the governorates of Dohuk, Arbil, Sulaimaniya, Kirkuk, Diyala and Neneveh. The term 'Kurdistan Regional Government' shall refer to the Kurdistan National Assembly, the Kurdistan Council of Minister, and the regional judicial authority in the Kurdistan region.

(B) The boundaries of the eighteen governorates shall remain without change during the transitional period.

(C) Any group of no more than three governorates outside the Kurdistan region, with the exception of Baghdad and Kirkuk, shall have the right to form regions from amongst themselves. The mechanisms for forming such regions may be proposed by the Iraqi Interim Government, and shall be presented and considered by the elected National Assembly for enactment into law. In addition to being approved by the National Assembly, any legislation proposing the formation of a particular region must be approved in a referendum of the people of the relevant governorates.

(D) This Law shall guarantee the administrative, cultural and political rights f the Turkmen, Chaldo-Assyrians and all other citizens.

Article 54

(A) The Kurdistan Regional Government shall continue to perform its current functions throughout the transitional period, except with regard to those issues which fall within the exclusive competence of the federal government as specified in this Law. Financing for these functions shall come from the federal government, consistent with current practice and in accordance with Article 25(E) of this Law. The Kurdistan Regional Government shall retain regional control over police forces and internal security, and it will have the right to impose taxes and fees within the Kurdistan region.

(B) With regard to the application of federal laws in the Kurdistan region, the Kurdistan National Assembly shall be permitted to amend the application of any such law within the Kurdistan region, but only to the extent that this relates to matters that are not within the provisions of Articles 25 and 43(D) of this Law and that fall within the exclusive competence of the federal government.

Article 55

(A) Each governorate shall have the right to form a Governorate Council, name a Governor and form municipal and local councils. No member of any regional government, governor or member of any governorate, municipal or local council may be dismissed by the federal government or any official thereof, except upon conviction of a crime by a court of competent jurisdiction as provided by law. No regional government may dismiss a governor or member or members of any governorate, municipal, or local council. No governor or member of any governorate, municipal or local council shall be subject to the control of the federal government except to the extent that the matter relates to the competences set forth in Article 25 and 43(D), above.

(B) Each governor and member of each Governorate Council who holds office as of 1 July 2004, in accordance with the law on local government that shall be issued, shall remain in place until such time as free, direct and full elections, conducted pursuant to law, are held, or unless, prior to that time, he voluntarily gives up his position, is removed upon his conviction for a crime involving moral turpitude or related to corruption, or upon being stricken with permanent incapacity, or is dismissed in accordance with the law cited above. When a governor, mayor or member of a council is dismissed, the relevant council may receive applications from any eligible resident of the governorate to fill the position. Eligibility requirements shall be the same as those set forth in Article 31 for membership in the National Assembly. The new candidate must receive a majority vote of the council to assume the vacant seat.

Article 56

(A) The Governorate Councils shall assist the federal government in the coordination of federal ministry operations within the governorate, including the review of annual ministry plans and budgets with regard to activities in the governorate. Governorate Councils shall be funded from the general budget of the State, and these councils shall also have the authority to increase their revenues independently by imposing taxes and fees; to organize the operations of the governorate administration; to initiate and implement province-level projects alone or in partnership with international and non-governmental organizations; and to conduct other activities insofar as is consistent with federal laws.

(B) The Qada' and Nahiya councils and other relevant councils shall assist in the performance of federal responsibilities and the delivery of public services by reviewing local ministry plans in the afore-mentioned places; ensuring that they respond properly to local needs and interests; identifying local budgetary requirements through the national budgeting procedures; collecting and retaining local revenues, taxes and fees; organizing the operations of the local administration; initiating and implementing local projects alone or in conjunction with international and non-governmental organizations; and conducting other activities consistent with applicable law.

(C) Where practicable, the federal government shall take measures to devolve additional functions to local, governorate and regional administrations, in a methodical way. Regional units and governorate administrations, including the Kurdistan Regional Government, shall be organized on the basis of the principle of decentralization and the devolution of authorities to municipal and local governments.

Article 57

(A) All authorities not exclusively reserved to the Iraqi Transitional Government may be exercised by the regional governments and governorates as soon as possible following the establishment of appropriate governmental institutions.

(B) Elections for governorate councils throughout Iraq and for the Kurdistan National Assembly shall be held at the same time as the elections for the National Assembly, no later than 31 January 2005.

Article 58

(A) The Iraqi Transitional Government, and especially the Iraqi Property Claims Commission and other relevant bodies, shall act expeditiously to take measures to remedy the injustice caused by the previous regime's practices in altering the demographic character of certain regions, including Kirkuk, by deporting and expelling individuals from their places of residence, forcing migration in and out of the region, settling individuals alien to the region, depriving the inhabitants of work and correcting nationality. To remedy this injustice, the Iraqi Transitional Government shall take the following steps:

(1) With regard to residents who were deported, expelled or who emigrated; it shall, in accordance with the statute of the Iraqi Property Claims Commission and other measures within the law, within a reasonable period of time, restore the residents to their homes and property or, where this is unfeasible, shall provide just compensation.

(2) With regard to the individuals newly introduced to specific regions and territories, it shall act in accordance with Article 10 of the Iraqi Property Claims Commission statute to ensure that such individuals may be resettled, may receive compensation from the state, may receive new land from the state near their residence in the governorate from which they came or may receive compensation for the cost of moving to such areas.

(3) With regard to persons deprived of employment or other means of support in order to force migration out of their regions and territories, it shall promote new employment opportunities in the regions and territories.

(4) With regard to nationality correction, it shall repeal all relevant decrees and shall permit affected persons the right to determine their own national identity and ethnic affiliation free from coercion and duress.

(B) The previous regime also manipulated and changed administrative boundaries for political ends. The Presidency Council of the Iraqi Transitional Government shall make recommendations to the National Assembly on remedying these unjust changes in the permanent constitution. In the event the Presidency Council is unable to agree unanimously on a set of recommendations, it shall unanimously appoint a neutral arbitrator to examine the issue and make recommendations. In the event the Presidency Council is unable to agree on an arbitrator, it shall request the Secretary-General of the United Nations to appoint a distinguished international person to be the arbitrator.

(C) The permanent resolution of disputed territories, including Kirkuk, shall be deferred until after these measures are completed, a fair and transparent census has been conducted and the permanent constitution has been ratified. This resolution shall be consistent with the principle of justice, taking into account the will of the people of those territories.

Chapter Nine – the Transitional Period

Article 59

(A) The permanent constitution shall contain guarantees to ensure that the Iraqi Armed Forces are never again used to terrorize or oppress the people of Iraq.

(B) Consistent with Iraq's status as a sovereign state and with its desire to join other nations in helping to maintain peace and security and fight terrorism during the transitional period, the Iraqi Armed Forces will be a principal partner in the multinational force operating in Iraq under unified command pursuant to the provisions of United Nations Security Council Resolution 1511 (2003) and any subsequent relevant resolutions. This arrangement shall last until the ratification of a permanent constitution and the election of a new government pursuant to that new constitution.

(C) Upon its assumption of authority, and consistent with Iraq's status as a sovereign state, the elected Iraqi Transitional Government shall have the authority to conclude binding international agreements regarding the activities of the multinational force operating in Iraq under unified command pursuant to the terms of United Nations Security Council Resolution 1511 (2003) and any subsequent relevant United Nations Security Council resolutions. Nothing in this Law shall affect rights and obligations under these agreements or under United Nations Security Council Resolution 1511 (2003) and any subsequent relevant United

Nations Security Council resolutions, which will govern the multinational force's activities pending the entry into force of these agreements.

Article 60

The National Assembly shall write a draft of the permanent constitution of Iraq. This Assembly shall carry out this responsibility in part by encouraging debate on the constitution through regular general public meetings in all parts of Iraq and through the media, and receiving proposals from the citizens of Iraq as it writes the constitution.

Article 61

(A) The National Assembly shall write the draft of the permanent constitution by no later than 15 August 2005.

(B) The draft permanent constitution shall be presented to the Iraqi people for approval in a general referendum to be held no later than 15 October 2005. In the period leading up to the referendum, the draft constitution shall be published and widely distributed to encourage a public debate about it among the people.

(C) The general referendum will be successful and the draft constitution ratified if a majority of the voters in Iraq approve and if two-thirds of the voters in three or more governorates do not reject it.

(D) If the permanent constitution is approved in the referendum, elections for a permanent government shall be held no later than 15 December 2005 and the new government shall assume office no later than 31 December 2005.

(E) If the referendum rejects the draft permanent constitution, the National Assembly shall be dissolved. Elections for a new National Assembly shall be held no later than 15 December 2005. The new National Assembly and new Iraqi Transitional Government shall then assume office no later than 31 December 2005, and shall continue to operate under this Law, except that the final deadlines for preparing a new draft may be changed to make it possible to draft a permanent constitution within a period not to exceed one year. The new National Assembly shall be entrusted with writing another draft permanent constitution.

(F) If necessary, the president of the National Assembly, with the agreement of a majority of the members' votes, may certify to the Presidency Council no later than 1 August 2005 that there is a need for additional time to complete the writing of the draft constitution. The Presidency Council shall then extend the deadline for writing the draft constitution for only six months. This deadline may not be extended again.

(G) If the National Assembly does not complete writing the draft permanent constitution by 15 August 2005 and does not request extension of the deadline in Article 61(D) above, the provisions of Article 61(E), above, shall be applied.

Article 62

This law shall remain in effect until the permanent constitution is issued and the new Iraqi government is formed in accordance with it.

http://www.cpa-iraq.org/government/TAL.html

Contributors

Joyce Blau is Professor Emeritus at the Institut National des Langues et Civilisations Orientales. At present she is an administrator of the Kurdish Institute of Paris. She is chief editor of the journal *Etudes kurdes* and with Professor Keith Hitchins co-edits the *Journal of Kurdish Studies*. Joyce Blau is the author of numerous papers on the Kurdish language, literature and civilization. Among her books on the Kurds are (with Veysi Barak) *Manuel de Kurde: Kurmanji* (Paris: Harmattan, 1999) and *Méthode de Kurde: Sorani* (Paris: Harmattan, 2001).

Hamit Bozarslan is co-director of IISMM (Institut d'Etudes de l'Islam et des Sociétés du Monde Musulman) and associate professor at the Ecole des Hautes Etudes en Sciences Sociales (EHESS). He is a former visiting fellow at the Centre Marc Bloch (Berlin) and the University of Princeton. He is the author of *100 mots pour dire 'violence' au Moyen-Orient* [100 Words for Saying 'Violence' in the Middle East] (Paris: Maisonneuve-Larose, 2005) and *From Political Contest to Self-Sacrifice: Violence in the Middle East* (Princeton: Marcus Wiener, 2004).

Martin van Bruinessen is an anthropologist who has carried out extensive fieldwork in various parts of Kurdistan since the mid-1970s. He is the author of *Agha, Shaykh and State: The social and political structures of Kurdistan* (London: Zed Press, 1992) and numerous articles on the Kurds and their neighbours. He is affiliated with the International Institute for the Study of Islam in the Modern World (ISIM) and occupies the ISIM Chair for the Comparative Study of Contemporary Muslim Societies at Utrecht University. His other region of specialization, besides Kurdistan, is Indonesia.

Hosham Dawod is an anthropologist at the Centre National de la Recherche Scientifique (CNRS) and a member of the Centre d'Etudes Interdisciplinaires des Faits Religieux (CEIFR). He has conducted fieldwork in the Middle East, specifically in Iraq and Saudi Arabia. He is the author of *La Crise irakienne: lectures anthropologiques* (Paris: Armand Colin, 2005), *Tribus et pouvoirs en terre d'Islam* (Paris: Armand Colin, 2004), co-editor of *La Société irakienne:*

communautés, pouvoirs et violences (Paris: Karthala, 2003) and co-editor with Faleh A. Jabar of *Tribes and States: Nationalism and Ethnicity in the Middle East* (London: Saqi Books, 2003).

Saad Eskandar was born an Iraqi Kurd in Baghdad and educated in the UK. His PhD thesis from the London School of Economics was on the Kurdish question under British-mandated Iraq. He has published several essays on Kurds and Kurdish nationalism, on federalism and other relevant issues. At present he is the general director of the National Archive in Baghdad.

Michael Gunter is a professor of political science at Tennessee Technological University in Cookeville, Tennessee, USA. He is the author of five critically praised scholarly books on the Kurdish question, the most recent being *Kurdish Historical Dictionary* (2004), *The Kurdish Predicament in Iraq: A Political Analysis* (London: Palgrave Macmillan, 1999) and *The Kurds and the Future of Turkey* (London: Palgrave Macmillan, 1997). He has also published numerous scholarly articles on the Kurds in such leading periodicals as the Middle East Journal, Middle East Quarterly and World Affairs and is (with Mohammed M. A. Ahmed) co-editor of *The Kurdish Question and the 2003 Iraqi War* (California: Mazda Publishers, 2005). During the summer he teaches at the International University, Vienna, Austria.

Gareth Stansfield is lecturer in Middle East Politics at the Institute of Arab and Islamic Studies at the University of Exeter and Associate Fellow of the Middle East Programme at the Royal Institute of International Affairs, Chatham House, London. His research focus is particularly upon the applicability of federal structures to Iraq and comparative analyses of consociational systems of governance. His publications include *Iraqi Kurdistan: Political development and emergent democracy* (London: Routledge Curzon, 2003), (with L. Anderson) *The Future of Iraq: Dictatorship, Democracy or Division?* (New York: Palgrave, 2004) and 'Governing Kurdistan: The strength of division', in B. O'Leary, J. McGarry and K. Saleh (eds), *The Future of Kurdistan in Iraq* (Philadelphia: University of Pennsylvania Press, 2004).

Fred Halliday was born in the Republic of Ireland in 1946 and has, since 1983, taught International Relations at the London School of Economics, specialising in international relations theory, especially in regard to social movements, and the Middle East. His books include *Iran: Dictatorship and Development* (London: Penguin Books, 1978), *Islam and the Myth of Confrontation* (London: I. B. Tauris, 1994), *Nation and Religion in the Middle East* (London: Saqi Books, 2000), *Two Hours that Shook the World:*

September 11, 2001 (London: Saqi Books, 2001), *The Middle East in International Relations* (Cambridge: Cambridge University Press, 2005) and *100 Myths about the Middle East* (London: Saqi Books, 2005).

Faleh A. Jabar is director of the newly established Iraq Institute for Strategic Studies (IIST) and research fellow at the School of Politics and Sociology, Birkbeck College, University of London. His work is focused on religion, Shi'ism, Islamism, nationalism, tribes, state and state formation, nation-building and political discourses in the Middle East. His recent publications include *The Shi'ite Movement in Iraq* (London, Saqi Books 2003), *Ayatollahs, Sufis and Ideologues* (London: Saqi Books, 2002) and (with Hosham Dawod as co-editor) *Tribes and Power in the Middle East* (London, Saqi Books, 2003). His forthcoming work is *The Authoritarian, the Totalitarian and the Democratic: The Ba'ath State and Post-Conflict Iraq in Perspective*, written during a year-long scholarship at the Institute of Peace in Washington DC.

Michiel Leezenberg teaches in the Department of Philosophy and in the MA programme 'Islam in the Modern World' in the Faculty of Humanities of the University of Amsterdam. In the 1980s and 1990s, he carried out extensive field research among the Kurds in Iraq and elsewhere in the Middle East. He has published numerous articles on the culture, society and politics of the Kurds, as well as a Dutch-language history of Islamic philosophy (English translation forthcoming from Cambridge University Press).

Maria O'Shea is a Research Fellow of the London Middle East Institute at the School of Oriental and African Studies (SOAS) and is now a guest lecturer at SOAS and King's College London. In her work, O'Shea examines changing perceptions of both Kurdistan and Kurdish identity over time and space. Among her prolific writings are *Kurdistan: Economic and political potential* (London: GIBRC, SOAS, 1992), 'Kurdistan: The mapping of a myth?', in M. O'Shea and R. Tapper (eds), *Some Minorities in the Middle East* (London: SOAS, 1993), published version of a commissioned report for the Foreign and Commonwealth Office, *Kurdistan and the Question of Iran's International Borders*, in K. McLachlan, ed, *The Boundaries of Modern Iran* (London: University College London, 1994), 'Kurdish Regional Costume', in Philip Kreyenbroek, ed., *Kurdish Cultural Identity* (London: Zed Press, 1994).

Abbas Vali teaches modern political theory and modern Middle Eastern politics in the Department of Politics and International Relations, University of Wales at Swansea. His publications include *Pre-Capitalist Iran:*

A Theoretical History (London: I. B. Tauris, 1993), *Essays on the Origins of Kurdish Nationalism* (Mazda Publishers, 2003) and *Modernity and the Stateless: Kurds and Power in Iran* (London: I. B. Tauris, 2005). He is currently working on issues of power, sovereignty and the limits of democratic reform in the Islamic Republic of Iran.

Sami Zubaida is Emeritus Professor of Politics and Sociology at Birkbeck College, University of London, and Research Associate of the London Middle East Institute at SOAS. His research and writings are on religion, culture and law in Middle Eastern society and politics, and on food and culture. Publications include *Law and Power in the Islamic World* (London: I. B. Tauris, 2003); *Islam, the People and the State* (London: I. B. Tauris, 1993) and (with Richard Tapper, co-editor), *A Taste of Thyme: Culinary cultures of the Middle East* (London: Tauris Parke, 2001).

Select Bibliography

'Abdu, Muhamad, *Collected Works* (*'Al-'Amal al-Kamila lil Imam Muhamad Abdu'*), 2nd edn, vol. 1, Beirut: 1979.

Aflaq, Michel, *Towards Renaissance* (*'Fi Sabil Al-Ba'th'*), 4th edn, Beirut: 1963.

al-Afghani, Jamaludin, *Political Writings* (*'Al-Kitabat al-Siyasiya'*), vol. 2, Beirut: 1981.

al-Azim, Sadiq Jala, *A Criticism of the Religious Thought* (*'Naqd al-Fikr al-Dini'*), 5th edn, Beirut: 1982. (See specially the chapter 'The Miracle of the Appearance of the Virgin and the Consequences of the Israeli Aggression' (*'Mu'jizet Dhohoor alAthra' wa Tasfiyet Athar al-Udwan'*), p. 97 and passim.)

al-Husri, Sati', *From Ottomanism to Arabism*, Arabic edn, Beirut: 1983.

—— *Ideas and Discourses in Arab Nationalism* (*'Ara'wa Ahadith fil Qawmiya al-Arabiya'*), Beirut: 1959.

—— *Selected Essays on Arab Nationalism* (*'Abhath Mukhtara fil Qawmiya Al-Arabiya'*), Beirut: 1974.

—— *What is Nationalism* (*'Ma Hiya al-Qamiya'*), Beirut: 1959.

—— *Lectures on the Formation of the National Idea* (*'Muhadharat fi Nusho' al-Fikra al-Qawmiya'*), Beirut: 1959.

al-Jazaiyiri, Prince Abdul Qadir, *Reminding the Sober and Enlightening the Distracted* (*'Tathkir al-'Aqil wa Tanbih al-Ghafil'*) Beirut.

al-Kawakibi, Abdul Rahman, *Collected Works* (*'Al-'Amal al-Kamila'*) ed. Muhamad 'Imara, Beirut: 1975.

al-Khatib, Ahmad, *The Society of Muslim Ulema in Algeria and its Reformist Role* (*'Jam'iyat al-Ulema' fil Jazaiyir wa Dauruha al-Islahi'*), Algeria: 1985.

al-Nafisi, Abdullah, *The Islamic Movement, Future Perspective* (*'Al-Haraka al-Islamiya, Ru'ya Mustaqbaliya'*), Cairo: 1989.

al-Sa'id, Rif'at, *Hassan al Banna: The Founder of Muslim Brothers Group* (*'Hassan al-Banna, Mu'asis Jam'at al-Ikhwan al-Muslimin'*), 5th edn, Cairo: 1984.

Anderson, Benedict, *Imagined Community*, London: Verso, 1985.

Arab Nationalism and Islam (*'Al-Qawmiya al-Arabiya wal Islam'*), seminar, The Centre of Arab Unity Studies, Beirut: 1982.

Avanayasyiv, *The History of Saudi Arabia* (*'Tarihk al-Arabiya al-Saudiya'*), Arabic edn, Moscow: 1985.

Awadh, Lewis, *The History of Modern Egyptian Thought* (*'Tarikh al-Fikr al-Masri al-Hadith'*), 4th edn, Cairo: 1987.

Bellman, Dieter, 'Bourgeois Arab Theories on the Cultural Function of Islam in Society', in *Islamic Studies in the GDR*, Berlin: Akademie Verlag, 1982.

Burgat, François, L'Islamisme au Maghreb (*'Al-Islam Al-Siyasi, Sawt al-Janoob'*),

Cairo: 1992.

Cleveland, William L., *The Making of An Arab Nationalist: Ottomanism and Arabism in the Life and Thought of Sati' al-Husri*, Princeton: Princeton University Press, 1971.

Enayat, Hamid, *Modern Islamic Political Thought*, London: Macmillan, 1988.

Gellner, E., *Nations and Nationalism*, London: Blackwell, 1992.

—— 'Nationalism', in *Theory and Society*, 1981, pp. 753–76.

Gibb, H. A. R and Bowen, Harold, *Islamic Society and the West*, vol. 1, Oxford:1950.

Hegel, W. F., *Lectures on the History of Philosophy*, 3rd Arabic edn, Beirut: 1983.

—— *Philosophy of Right*, trans. T. M. Knox, Oxford: Oxford University Press, 1967.

Hirmasi, M., *Society and State in the Maghrib ('Al-Dawla wal Mujtama' fil Maghrib al-Arabi')*, Beirut: 1987.

Hobsbawm, E.J., *Nations and Nationalism since 1978*, Cambridge: 1990.

Holt, P. M., *Egypt and the Fertile Crescent, 1516–1922: A Political History*, London: Longmans, 1966.

Hourani, Albert, *The History of Arab Peoples*, London: 1990.

—— *Arabic Thought in the Liberal Age*, Cambridge: 1983.

Ibrahim, Sa'ad Eddin, *The Islamic Awakening and the Concerns of the Arab Nation ('Al-Sahwa al-Islamiya wa Humoom al-Watan al-Arabi')*, Jordan: 1988.

Ibrahamian, Ervend, *Iran between Two Revolutions*, Princeton: Princeton University Press, 1982.

Ivanov, Nikolay, *The Ottoman Conquest of the Arab Countries 1561–1574 ('Al-Fath al-Othmani lil Aqtar al-Arabiya')*, Arabic edn, Beirut: 1988.

Jabar, Faleh A., 'The Gulf War and Ideology: The Double Edged Sword Of Islam', in *The Gulf War and the New World Order*, ed. Haim Bresheeth and Nira Yuval-Davis, London: Zed Books, 1991.

Keddie, Nekkie, *An Islamic Response to Imperialism*, Berkeley, 1983.

Kedourie, Elie (ed.), *Nationalism in Asia and Africa*, New York: 1970.

Khouri, Ilias (ed.), *Christian Arabs ('Al-Masihiyoon al-Arab')*, 2nd edn, Beirut: 1986.

Lewis, Bernard, *The Emergence of Modern Turkey*, Oxford: 1961.

Lutski, A., *The Modern History of Arab Countries ('Tarikh al-Aqtar al-Arabiya al-Hadith')*, Arabic edn, Beirut: 1980.

Madhoon, Rabi'a, 'The Islamic Movement in Palestine' ('Al-Haraka al-Islamiya fi Falastin'), *Dirasat Filistiniya Review*, No. 187, 1988.

Mortimer, Edward, *Islam, Power and Faith*, London: Faber and Faber, 1982.

Mudarisi, Muhamad, *Islamic Visions for Revolutionary Action ('Ru'a Islamiya Lil 'Amal al-Thawri')*, Islamic Cultural Centre n.d.

The National-Religious Dialogue ('Al-Hiwar al-Qawmi al-Dini'), Beirut: 1989.

Raziq, Ali Abil, *Islam and the Foundations of Governance ('Al-Islam wa Usul al-Hukm')*, Beirut: 1972.

Religion in Arab Society ('Al-Din fil Mujtama' al-Arabi'), essays offered at a seminar, Beirut, 1990.

Sara, Fayiz, 'The Islamic Movement in Palestine, Ideological Unity and Political Differences' ('*Al-Haraka al-Islamiya fi Falistin,Wahdat al-Idiolojia wa Inqisamat al-Siyasa*'), *Al-Mustaqbel al-Arabi Review*, 1990.

Shirazi, Ayatollah Muhamad, *Towards a One Thousand Million Muslim Government* ('*Nahwa Hukomat Alf Milion Muslim*'), Qum (Iran): (n.d).

—— Governance in Islam ('*Al-Hukum Fil Islam*'), Qum (Iran): (n.d).

Sivan, Emanuel, *Radical Islam*, New Haven and London: 1985.

Smith, A. D., *Theories of Nationalism*, Duckworth, 1971.

The Struggle of the BSP, National Command ('*Nidhal Hizb al-Ba'th al-Arabi al-Ishtiraqi,al-Qiyada al-Qawmiya*'), Damascus:1978.

Techonova, T. P., *Sati' al-Husri: The Pioneer of Secularism in Arab National Thought* ('*Sati'al-Husri,Rai'd al-Manha al-'Ilmani fil Fikr al-Qawmi al-Arabi*') Arabic edn, Moscow: 1987.

Toma, Emile, *The History of Modern Arab Peoples* ('*Tarikh Masiret al-Sho'ob Al-Arabiya Al-Hadith*'), Beirut: 1981.

Watt, M., *Islamic Political Thought*, Arabic edn, Beirut: 1981.

Yaziji, Halim, *et al.*, *Essays on Arab National Thought* ('*Buhooth fil Fikr al-Qawmi al-Arabi*'), vol. 1, Beirut: 1983.

Yasin, A., 'The Role of HAMAS in the Islamic Phenomenon in the West Bank and Gaza' ('Dawr Hamas fil Dhahira al-Islamiya fil Dhiffa wa Gaza'), *The New Jordan Review* ('Al-Urdun Al-Jadid'), no. 11, 1988, p. 45.

Ziyada, Khalid, *The Discovery of European Progress* ('*Iktishaf al-Taqadum al-Auropi*'), Beirut, 1981.

Zubaida, Sami, 'Theories of Nationalism', in G. Littlejohn (ed.), *Power and State*, Cromhelm, 1978.

—— *Islam the People and the State*, Routledge, 1989.

—— *The European State in the Muslim World*, unpublished paper, 1994.

Index